RELIGION, RACE, AND RECONSTRUCTION

SUNY Series, Religion and American Public Life
William D. Dean, Editor

RELIGION, RACE, AND RECONSTRUCTION

THE PUBLIC SCHOOL IN THE POLITICS OF THE 1870S

Ward M. McAfee

STATE UNIVERSITY OF NEW YORK PRESS

Cover: "Compulsory Education," *Harper's Weekly*, January 16, 1875.

Published by
State University of New York Press, Albany

For information, address State University of New York Press,
State University Plaza, Albany, NY 12246

Production by M. R. Mulholland
Marketing by Anne M. Valentine

Library of Congress Cataloging-in-Publication Data

McAfee, Ward.
    Religion, race, and Reconstruction : the public school in the
politics of the 1870s / Ward M. McAfee.
        p.   cm. — (SUNY series, religion and American public life)
    Includes bibliographical references and index.
    ISBN 0-7914-3847-3 (hardcover : alk. paper). — ISBN 0-7914-3848-1
(pbk. : alk. paper)
    1. Politics and education—United States—History—19th century.
2. Public schools—United States—History—19th Century.   3. Church
and education—United States—History—19th Century.   4. Afro-
Americans—Education—History—19th Century.   I. Title.
II. Series.
LC89.M33   1998
371.01'0973—dc21   97-37731
                                                                          CIP

10 9 8 7 6 5 4 3 2 1

Contents

ILLUSTRATIONS

Acknowledgments

My thanks are due to several student assistants—especially Sandra Schriver and Tony Becker—who helped me gather material for this study. I also relied heavily on the library staffs of both California State University, San Bernardino, and the Honnold and School of Theology libraries of the Claremont colleges complex. At the outset of this project, Candace Czerwinski of the Honnold library patiently guided me through innumerable "bibliotechnical" mysteries known only to reference librarians. At my home campus of CSU, San Bernardino, Edith Amrine was especially helpful in locating interlibrary loan materials. I found most of the primary materials for the project at the Huntington Library, in San Marino, California, where Frances Rouse, Kelli Ann Bronson, Jim Coy, Tom Canterbury, and Lida Bushloper were most gracious in their assistance. Special thanks are also due to the staff of the Special Collections at Hoskins Library at the University of Tennessee, at Knoxville. James B. Lloyd, Bobbie Painter, Bill Eigelsbach, and Nick Wyman made me feel very welcome during my sojourn there. Thanks are also in order to the staffs of the Bancroft Library and the Boalt Law Library, both on the campus of the University of California at Berkeley.

In researching and writing a book about the impact of public education on the national culture, I constantly recalled how my early teachers shaped not only my interest in the world at large but also the values that have guided me long after I have lost contact with them. Sidney Waller, my seventh-grade teacher at Central School in San Carlos, California, is especially held in fond memory. I have thanked him silently countless times over the years for sparking an intellectual curiosity in a twelve-year-old boy who then was without direction. His solid character remains in my mind the model of what a public-school teacher can be. Other teachers are to be thanked as well. My mother-in-law Evelyn Root, a high-school French teacher who taught her students far more than French, encouraged me to become better than I thought I could be. Finally, Don Fehrenbacher, my dissertation adviser of a generation ago and my later mentor, lives in my mind as a model historian.

A brief sabbatical leave, granted by the California State University, San Bernardino, for the Winter quarter of 1994, helped provide the focused time needed for writing a first draft. Kent Schofield, a colleague at CSU, San Bernardino, read and critiqued an early draft of this manuscript and provided appreciated encouragement and help. Finally, I thank my wife Lois, who patiently helped me edit the work and clarify my thinking and expression in the final draft.

INTRODUCTION

A generation ago, Eric Foner clearly demonstrated that the "free-labor" ideology defined the Republican Party of the 1850s.[1] That ideology contrasted the "backward" South with a positive portrait of the Northern free-market economy. It characterized slave labor as both degraded and inefficient, in contrast with entrepreneurial and productive free labor. The free-labor ideology celebrated the dynamic aspects of the emerging Northern industrial economy and equated the Declaration of Independence's "pursuit of happiness" with a capitalist promise that all can become rich. An enticing vision of worldly success conditioned Northerners to subscribe to the Republican program. The bourgeois values of Benjamin Franklin's "Poor Richard"—hard work, persistence, honesty, self-sacrifice—were the means of upward mobility in a free-labor economy. Only lazy and improvident persons, Republicans proclaimed, could possibly lose ground in the progressive economy of the North. Persons applying themselves in the workplace were bound to advance. This free-labor vision projected an image of a classless society that promised a free and abundant life for all who would simply apply themselves in their work. It constituted a happy mythology of what later was termed the American Dream.

Focusing on the hopes and fears of common white people faced with rising industrialization in the North, the free-labor ideology blurred the differences between capitalists and laborers in this new economy. It portrayed the individual workingman of the North as an entrepreneur turning his labor into expanding opportunities for earning wealth. The early Republican Party pledged that it would make America safe for this free workingman, threatened by the westward expansion of labor-degrading slave agriculture.

Foner notes that this idealized portrait of Northern working conditions then bore little resemblance to the emerging economic facts of life. The Republican ideology called up past images of equality and economic self-sufficiency at the very time when the independent mechanic or farmer was passing from the scene. In fact, the realities of industrialization then threatened the dignity of free labor. Development of the factory system magnified the social distance between employer and employee. Increasingly, imaginative businessmen viewed labor as just another commodity to be used in the quest for profits. Work tasks were simplified and routinized, and work settings became impersonal. With industrialization, skilled workmanship declined in economic importance. As craftsmen were needed less in the machine age, fewer young men were apprenticed to skilled workers. Pride in one's work declined, as it became impossible to determine where one's own work ended and that of someone else, or even a machine, began. Even as the Republican Party adopted its free-labor message, the ancient respectable identity of "workingman" was being undermined by industrialization. In the decades of Civil War and Reconstruction that immediately followed, the problem became far worse. Northern youth, being the most plastic of the human beings affected by these rapidly changing conditions, revealed a disturbing confusion of values. Increasingly, many young American males were perceived as directionless. By the 1870s, this problem had grown to crisis proportions. Crime rose. Young vagabonds roamed city streets looking for trouble and an easy dollar. Epithets, such as "hoodlums" and "street Arabs," were coined to describe the youthful denizens of a new ugly American urban environment. Growing prison populations concerned informed citizens. All of this directly challenged the Republican Party's free-labor ideology, which had been somewhat nostalgic even at the time of its original conception.

The mounting dissonance between the happy free-labor ideology and the new dynamic economic disorder challenged the Republican Party. What could explain the degradation of free labor at the very time that it had triumphed over the threat of the Southern economic system? Socialists blamed free-market capitalism itself. The Roman Catholic church blamed an unholy worship of worldly norms that accompanied the rapid rush of material progress. Republicans offered a rival explanation: Irish immigrants were the leading source of the growing urban criminal class. In Republican eyes, the essence of the Irish problem was their Roman Catholic superstition and their ignorance, both brought with them from across the sea. In short, the problem was foreign in origin. The Republican solution was to Americanize these degraded recent arrivals in the public school. As the decade of the seventies dawned, Republicans called for a radical expansion of public education to ensure that everyone in the United States could meet a single American cultural standard. Improvements in public education promised to expand equality of opportunity into the indefinite future. At the very time that industrialization was economically stratifying the population, Republicans continued to promote a vision of a classless America in which all diligent workingmen could become rich. The public school was center stage in the development of this corollary to the free labor ideology. Whereas in the 1850s the slogan of the Republican Party had been "free soil, free labor, free men," the revised ideology effectively replaced "free soil" with "free schools." With slavery vanquished, the ideology was remodeled in order to remain politically up-to-date.

In 1870, while poised to invade the Southern states, the public school was almost exclusively a Northern institution. In the South, the freedmen hungered for an education that had been denied them in slavery. Poor Southern whites had also been victimized by the defunct Southern slave economy. Poor whites in the South suffered illiteracy at rates that far exceeded Northern norms tolerable for white people. Free-labor ideologues had eliminated human slavery. Now they promised to remove the ignorance that remained as the unwanted residue of slavery's devastation. More was promised as well. The American public school would *morally* uplift the nation. The public school, informed by evangelical New England, would transform America, creating a middle-class society capable of performing well in a dynamic capitalist economy. By the revised Republican vision, mounting class alienation would be overcome by moral instruction in the public schools, where all would learn self-control and respect for private property. One nation, bound together by a "harmony of interests," would emerge from the crucible of the public school. In this way, the Union would be protected in the midst of the industrial revolution. In this vision, social stability and rapid economic change (i.e., "progress") peacefully coexisted.

While Republicans redesigned their message and planned to expand public education throughout the nation, the Roman Catholic church mounted its own educational offensive. With Catholic immigration on the rise, the church called for Catholic voters to exercise their growing political power. Specifically, the church asked Catholics to insist both on removing Protestant religious practices from the public schools and dividing the states' public school funds between Catholic and Protestant schools. For Catholic leaders in 1870, the issue of the day was historic Protestant domination of the American public school. Catholics were taxed to support these schools, which were characterized by daily Bible reading and the singing of Protestant hymns. To good Catholics, America's public schools were nothing more than Protestant institutions. Accordingly, they perceived themselves as being unjustly forced to develop their own private Catholic school system at great expense in order to preserve the faith of their fathers against a state-supported Protestant onslaught. Their goal was to get the state to take over the funding of their own parochial schools while not allowing the government to control either curriculum or school management. They wished to keep directing their own religiously segregated, publicly supported schools. To Catholics, this was a matter of simple justice. To Protestants, especially Republican Protestants, this challenge threatened to divide the Union into unacceptably divergent cultural camps.

Bible reading in the public schools, conducted under a format tolerable to all Protestant sects, had the support of American tradition. Most Americans then viewed maintenance of this tradition as essential for the moral health of the Republic. They regarded schooling without Bible reading as leading straight to the eventual eradication of all moral instruction from the curriculum. If Bible reading in the public schools were discontinued, they feared, an ethical confusion would grow in the populace. The Catholic push to remove Protestant practices from the public schools threatened traditional American norms of church/state relations. During Reconstruction, the Republican Party took up the defense of this religious civic tradition. In so doing, it cast itself in the role of preserving an old order that was inevitably passing away. In the 1850s, the Republican Party had glorified fading harmonious relations between capital and labor. In the 1870s, it continued this theme and added to it a glorification of anachronistic church/state practices. Popular acceptance of Protestant expectations in Bible reading and hymn singing in the public schools had worked well enough when the nation was overwhelmingly Protestant but could not be maintained easily in an increasingly religiously diverse society. The Republican Party capitalized on the shrinking Protestant American majority's desire to hold on to past practices. This constituted the unique twist of the Republican politics of nostalgia during the 1870s.

Ironically, this Republican defense of traditional civil-religious practices occurred in the midst of that party's efforts to revolutionize the American polity. Republican Reconstruction threatened to reshape American political life by centralizing in the federal government functions that historically had been left to the states. One benefit of the school controversy for Republicans was that it enabled them to portray themselves as traditionalists and defenders of unchanging American civil-religious norms at the very time that they were in fact constitutional revolutionaries. A tension between promoting radical political change and preserving the religious status quo defined the Republican Party during the last decade of Reconstruction.

Today, the word "Reconstruction" evokes popular memories of the nation's "first civil rights movement." It was that, but it was also different from the second civil rights movement of the 1950s and 1960s.

Reconstruction in the 1870s involved an ambitious effort to forge a national culture, heavy with evangelical overtones that demanded social conformity. During the 1870s, movement toward cultural homogeneity was idealized by the Republican Party as the nation's highest goal. By contrast, the civil rights movement of the 1960s promoted tolerating increasing cultural diversity and celebrating individual liberation from the constraints of social conformity. In this sense, the first civil rights movement's mood was alien to the spirit of the second one. In the 1960s, American public education was attacked by African Americans and other sufferers of ethnic discrimination. By that time, the African-American community was more aware of public education's historic objective of cementing white cultural homogeneity than it had been before.

In the 1870s, the Republican Party called for cultural unification through public education. The deep seated reasons for this push have already been mentioned but deserve reemphasis. In the 1870s, many Northerners hungered for assurances that both Protestant hegemony and the economic norms of dynamic entrepreneurial capitalism could be maintained. That majority wanted some sense of national coherence at a time of both rapid economic changes and dramatic changes in American religious allegiances. The Republican Party of the 1870s promised to bring into being one indivisible nation that never again could be disrupted by civil war. By means of public schools, Republicans promised to transform both African Americans and Catholic Irish along the cultural norms of Protestant New England.

In every way, the public education issue made good sense to Republicans of that decade. Following their destruction of slavery as an economic system, some Republican politicos feared for the future of their party. In fact, their complete success against slavery in the Civil War threatened to eliminate their party's reason for being. What could replace antislavery as the leading Republican idealistic issue? They needed an issue that could inspire the masses to continue to support the party. Protective tariffs and "sound" money might persuade former Whigs to remain Republicans. But the Whig Party had never been a dynamic majority party capable of swaying the masses beyond several isolated presidential campaigns headed by military heroes. Pro-business issues inspiring only a minority of voters lacked the potential to retain an electoral majority. A party with staying power needed a progressive vision for America's future. The public school issue had the capability of providing this vision and reenergizing the party's wellsprings of idealism. The Republican Party promoted the public school as the means to educate the recently freed blacks, elevating them to be worthy of the responsibilities of citizenship and suffrage. In addition, Republicans assigned the public school the task of Americanizing the children of Catholic immigrants, thereby keeping America safe from feared papal domination. Unlike Republican business-oriented concerns of the 1870s, the public school issue could not be cast by the Democratic Party as benefiting the rich at the expense of the common man. Indeed, on this one issue, Republicans could and did portray themselves as the true friends of all races and ethnic groups in all sections of the land.

Democrats sought to portray Reconstruction as an unwarranted, arbitrary, centralizing grab for power. Republicans took a radically different tack. They attempted to persuade the electorate that Reconstruction's goal instead was to remodel a nation divided and devastated by civil war and handicapped by the human degradation and ignorance spawned by slavery. The nation's need, Republicans proclaimed, was for social unity and expanding educational opportunity for the common person. Repeatedly the public school was turned to as the Republican mechanism to provide a progressive interpretation of Reconstruction. In many ways, the public school issue became the soul of the Republican program in the 1870s. It addressed the fears and hopes of the voters. The Northern electorate was concerned that the dynamic rise of industrial capitalism threatened to undermine America's traditionally middle-class ethos. During the Gilded Age, Americans perceived that the rich were becoming richer and the poor were slipping increasingly into vicious idleness and criminal activities. Northerners were concerned that both religiously and culturally America was dividing into separate and divergent ethnic enclaves within their section alone. Republican promotion of public education met these concerns. Up until 1870, the focus of Reconstruction had been on amending the Constitution. After that date, its central concern was in making these new constitutionally proclaimed abstractions real. One important aspect of this latter emphasis was promoting, expanding and protecting the public school.

The Republican Party failed in Reconstruction primarily in its public school agenda. Specifically, the Republican educational program ran aground on white racism. In the elections of 1874, the Republican loss of the House of Representatives was influenced by a widespread reaction against a Republican proposal to mandate racially integrated schools nationwide. This proved to be the turning point of Reconstruction. For the next several years, the Republican program was stalled due to the impossibility of passing legislation through both houses of Congress. During this time, Republicans resorted to a national campaign of anti-Catholic bigotry in hopes of flanking the forces of racial prejudice marshaled by their Democratic opponents. They claimed that this anti-Catholic campaign was designed to protect the traditional (Protestant) American public school from unwanted foreign influences. But this last attempt to revive Reconstruction also failed.

In the following pages, the story of the Republicans' public school crusade of the 1870s is told. This movement grappled with issues of race and religion and also with the very structure of the American polity. Indeed, this is a good example of how social history and political history often meet in what might be termed political culture. Spiritual concerns, child-rearing practices, public responsibility for maintaining common moral standards, the proper degree of allegiance that is due from a citizen to the nation, and whether or not the United States is a Christian nation—all swirled in a common political discussion on the ideal role of the public school in American life. Politicians—from school board members to presidents of the United States—entered the fray. Ministers, priests, rabbis, and pundits of every stripe offered their advice, much of it contradictory. A common concern for the children of America defined the debate—not as ends in themselves but as the malleable clay of a future national culture. Many of the arguments presented in this volume are still with us in the culture wars of the 1990s but in a completely different historical context. The historical narrative that follows is primarily intended to elucidate the meaning of American political culture in the 1870s. But it is also a tale that can give historical perspective to matters that concern us still as a national community.

1

Prologue to the Seventies

The American public school emerged in the early nineteenth century amid significant social and economic changes. In the beginning stages of industrialization in the United States, character traits associated with a Puritan-like self-discipline were demanded in work settings governed by the pace of machines. Whereas Puritan mores had been in decline for over a century, the necessities of industrial production demanded their partial resurrection. Punctuality, accuracy, diligence and perseverance were some of the traits that Puritans had held dear and which were at a premium once again in the emerging machine culture. A New England movement to found statewide public school systems promised to instill these old virtues in the upcoming generation. Simultaneously, many social habits suggesting lack of self-control came under increasing scrutiny. The American Temperance Society, founded in 1826 to combat drunkenness, was symbolic of this shift in American values away from the freedom-loving eighteenth century.[1]

Because of its focus upon shaping the values of children, the public school was the most important institution created to foster the renewed emphasis on self-discipline. The most important individual in founding this New England institution was Horace Mann, who served as secretary to the state board of education in Massachusetts from 1837 to 1848. Under his leadership, Massachusetts developed the first modern statewide public-school system in the United States. The development of internalized mechanisms of moral restraint was Mann's chief objective—even more important than disseminating academic knowledge. Mann harmonized the doctrines of the major Protestant sects to create a general catechism of moral teachings to be imparted in the public schools. Bible reading and hymn singing fleshed out his program of moral education.

The primary purpose of the public school was to create a common behavioral code for the entire society. Just as the new machines turned out standardized products, the public school was intended to standardize society itself. From the vantage point of Horace Mann, disparate elements in the population (especially increasing numbers of Irish Catholic immigrants) needed to be Americanized. Nonetheless, while the public school would supposedly promote social homogenization, African Americans were kept in different schools. Girls were also taught in separate schools at the outset of the public education movement. These exceptions to the emerging ideal of cultural standardization, apparent to observers in our own time, were glossed over then by most early public-school advocates.[2]

The new American public school systems were characterized by centralized state controls, state-based professional administrators removed from local community influences, and general taxes funding the enterprise. However, their primary characteristic was an agenda for standardizing American culture. Under the new educational order, the older practice of providing government funds to church-based schools to accomplish the job of educating the community was increasingly discouraged. For example, in 1825, public aid was cut off for New York City's Catholic schools. In the early 1840s, with Catholic immigration on the rise, Catholic Bishop John Hughes of New York City sparked a movement to reverse the trend favoring public education but failed. He only succeeded in getting permission to substitute the Catholic-preferred Douay Bible for the Protestant's King James version in the public schools of several Catholic wards in the city. Pressure for cultural homogeneity was not discouraged by this small compromise, and Catholic complaints continued. In the 1850s, Catholic Archbishop John Purcell of Cincinnati protested the Protestant flavor of the public schools, paid for in part by Catholic taxes. Purcell argued that Catholics should not have to pay these taxes and instead should educate their children in Catholic schools funded by themselves. This kind of proposition only steeled the public school reformers more against those whom they perceived as promoting socially divisive "sectarian" education.[3]

The coming of the Civil War pushed the public-school issue onto a national stage. The emancipation of millions of African Americans forced the nation and the victorious Republican Party to confront a multitude of new issues related to the freedmen's new status. Slavery had deposited most of its unfortunate victims at freedom's door without the ability to read and write or to cipher and conduct everyday business transactions. Many feared that if black Americans were left in ignorance the Republic itself might eventually crumble. This attitude placed an extraordinary societal imperative on public education to rectify the situation. Modern historians have debated the wisdom of that generation's emphasis on public education to the exclusion of all other African-American needs. Some have claimed that securing a healthy economic base was of far greater importance for the freedmen than learning to read and write. At the time, Radical Republican Congressman Thaddeus Stevens called for a land reform that would have granted to each freedman "forty acres and a mule." Historian Ronald E. Butchart and others have argued that Stevens's failure to win this essential economic reform doomed all other efforts, including the educational goal to eliminate black illiteracy. In Butchart's view, mass education for blacks, without the economic underpinnings of land reform, became simply a white mechanism to encourage pliant, docile black labor.[4] Other historians, such as William Gillette, have treated the failure to institute land reform as of little historic consequence. "Even if the blacks had become landowners," he has written, "they would not have escaped the poverty and indebtedness that plagued the cotton economy nor would they have avoided the decline and disappearance of the family farm in the South."[5] In any case, the Republican Party solution to African-American postwar poverty became mass education and not land reform.

Richard Henry Dana, Jr., had pressed for land reform. "We have got to choose between two results," he warned. "With these four millions of Negroes, either you must have four millions of dis-franchised, disarmed, untaught, landless, thriftless, non-producing, non-consuming, degraded men, or else you must have four millions of land-holding, industrious, arms-bearing, and voting population. Choose between these two! Which will you have?" Such sentiments expressed a desire in some quarters to force a redistribution of wealth amassed by slave labor. But, as Eric Foner has pointed out, the Republican Party in general was too wedded to the ideas of the sanctity of private property and self-help to consider seriously any meaningful distribution of planter wealth among the former slaves. Consequently, when Andrew Johnson summarily discontinued the hope of land reform by ordering confiscated lands be returned to their former owners, his presidential will was not overturned by successive Republican Congresses. Whether delivery on the promise of "forty acres and a mule" would have produced a dramatically different history than that which transpired can never be known. Suffice to say, its absence made a positive outcome for African Americans all the more tenuous. Encouraged by an active Southern resolve not to rent or sell land to blacks, an economic structure of black peonage and white control of the land ensured the continuance of a rigid racial/economic stratification, irrespective of any individual educational accomplishment.[6] Most

Republicans did not acknowledge the disjunction between this economic reality and their own free-labor ideology. A cognitive dissonance concerning the supposed empowerment accompanying mass education and a lack of meaningful economic opportunity continued until the end of Reconstruction and even beyond.

Almost as serious as the absence of land reform, traditional Southern indifference to public education blocked the progress of the African American. As *De Bow's Review* noted in 1868, the slave South had widely considered common agricultural labor as not needing any training in letters. This attitude continued into the era of post-emancipation. "No agricultural day laborers are ever highly educated," commented the Southern journal. "It does not pay in plowing and ditching as in the mechanical arts." Additionally, the education of blacks had traditionally been viewed in the South as endangering the public safety.[7] Throughout the South, the concept of public education had long been viewed as a New England idea, spawned by the very same people who had raised the Northern aggression against their region. Nevertheless, even before the war that New England idea had made some inroads in the Southern states. At the beginning of the war, North Carolina had been well along toward developing a meaningful public school system for whites. More than one author has speculated that if the Civil War had not completely disrupted prewar Southern beginnings in the area of public education full-blown public school systems on the New England model would have blossomed throughout the South in the 1860s.[8] Nonetheless, it is hard to conceive that a political culture generally dominated by a landed, planter aristocracy with no keen economic interest in mass education would have on its own developed statewide uniform systems of taxation for school support. Also, had the Civil War not occurred, blacks would not have been included in any native-grown public-school effort. Accordingly, the weight of historical judgment attributes the flowering of public education in the South to outside influences.

Those influences came South during the war in the wake of advancing Northern armies. Southern blacks recruited as Union soldiers were provided the rudiments of reading and writing both to raise their morale and make them more effective troops. Even before that, the military had engaged in some efforts to educate runaway slaves who fled to Union lines. Early seizure of the sea islands off the coast of South Carolina also inspired educational as well as temporary land-management experiments among Southern blacks.[9] The Freedmen's Bureau, created by Congress only weeks before Lee's surrender at Appomattox, further promoted black education in the South. The new agency cooperated with Northern philanthropic societies. The latter sent schoolteachers South, and the Freedmen's Bureau helped get them established in classrooms and provided a degree of protection against unreconstructed Southerners hostile to the very idea of educating blacks. By the end of 1865, there were 740 black schools in operation with 90,589 students enrolled.[10] The Northern teachers brought with them their values of intense nationalism and individual self-reliance. They exuded their cultural preferences for evangelical piety, self-control, and hard, steady work. They saw their mission to effect a moral reform among the former slaves, all in the process of helping to develop a true national culture founded on the Protestant work ethic. In line with the initial impulse that had driven reformers such as Horace Mann, they saw their purpose as creating cultural standardization. They were as ideologically opposed to true self-determination for African Americans as the former slave masters had been. They never questioned that their reform might not be appreciated by those about to be uplifted to the glorious New England standard. Indeed, they were oblivious as to how their takeover of many educational efforts begun by blacks themselves was viewed in the African-American community. In their view, the blacks could only benefit by their particular New England reconstruction of Southern culture. "New England can furnish teachers enough to make a New England out of the whole South," wrote one teacher, "and, God helping, we will not pause in our work until the free school system . . . has been established from Maryland to Florida and all along the shores of the Gulf."[11]

African-American reaction to this cultural invasion was mixed. The freedmen appreciated the teachers developing their educational skills but were annoyed at their intolerance of black cultural norms. For instance, the cultural value of group solidarity had been brought from Africa and was reinforced by the harsh realities of slavery. Northern teachers did not appreciate this value and instead viewed it as an obstacle to the development of modern, entrepreneurial individualism. Naively, these outsiders believed that hard work would always be rewarded with individual advancement in any environment. As true-believers in the free-labor ideology, the Northern teachers did not appreciate the enduring strength of the racial caste system of the South. As historian Jacqueline Jones has written, the encounter between these teachers and their black charges "amounted to a meeting between a rational, nineteenth-century middle-class culture and a traditional pre-modern one." Blacks did not appreciate the white teachers' moral lectures on matters regarding property rights and sexuality. African Americans commonly viewed the cultural standards of these New

England educational missionaries as too strict, inflexible, and unrealistic. Given this cultural distance, many blacks preferred African-American teachers to white ones, even when the former had less formal academic preparation than the latter. Essentially, blacks wanted to control their own institutions, including their schools, and white teachers were an obstacle to attaining this desire.[12]

While a cultural tension separated the Northern teachers from the black community, a more serious cultural gap divided these teachers from the Southern white community, which shared little of their free-labor and nationalistic assumptions. In the years immediately after the war, the white South tended to view these Northern educational missionaries as dangerous social revolutionaries. In July 1866, the *Norfolk Virginian* complained that the Northern teaching missions sent southward were motivated by spite and intended "to disorganize and demoralize still more our peasantry and laboring population." Accordingly, white Southerners burned black schools and ostracized and occasionally brutalized the teachers of African Americans.[13] This fact challenged the federal government to provide additional protection and encouragement of black education. Without such assistance, there could be no meaningful reconstruction of the South and no creation of a homogeneous, national culture.

The original act to create the Freedmen's Bureau had not explicitly provided for an educational role but had simply charged the agency to manage abandoned lands and in general deal with the transition from slavery to freedom. Under that vague mandate, the Freedmen's Bureau had begun its educational mission. On July 16, 1866, over President Johnson's veto, Congress passed a supplementary statute that specifically funded educational operations. Johnson charged that this new Freedmen's bill was unconstitutional. The constitutional justification for creating the Freedmen's Bureau in the first place had been the war power of Congress. With the war over, strict constructionists saw no valid reason for continuing what had been intended to be only a temporary agency. The presidential veto complained: "The Congress of the United States . . . has never founded schools for any class of our own people, not even for the orphans of those who have fallen in the defense of the Union." In making explicit provision for federally run schools, the Congress ventured onto new constitutional ground. In Republican minds, the war power argument remained valid years after war's end. As late as 1868, Republicans lectured their Democratic colleagues that the "war" continued as long as the spirit of slavery continued to obstruct the progress of African Americans. Using this logic, the Freedmen's Bureau won Congressional extensions until the end of the decade. In 1871, the bureau finally passed out of existence.[14]

On March 2, 1867, Congress officially took control of Reconstruction. With the exception of Tennessee, it dismissed the Presidentially reconstructed governments of every ex-Confederate state. It placed the ten remaining ex-rebel states under temporary military control and required them to write new state constitutions, with the proviso that black men could participate in the process and that former rebels could not. Tennessee was then the only ex-Confederate state with an elected Republican administration. Alone of the former Confederate states, it had ratified the proposed Fourteenth Amendment to the United States Constitution. On March 5, Tennessee validated the faith placed in it by creating a biracial (though segregated) statewide system of public education. General John Eaton, Jr., who during the war had organized a Mississippi Valley precedent to the Freedmen's Bureau, was appointed Tennessee's first superintendent of public instruction.[15]

During the war, several border slave states, under the influence of the federal military power, had written new state constitutions that had effectively reconstructed them. Maryland, Missouri, and West Virginia (summarily carved from rebellious Virginia in 1863) participated in this process. Their new constitutions had mandated public-school systems. Of these states, none but Missouri provided for the education of blacks, and that on a segregated basis. Nonetheless, the development of any public-education program was taken as a step in the right direction. It was common knowledge that the victorious North expected the former slave states to become more "Northern," and the development of public-school systems was primary evidence that this expectation was being met. In 1867, as the former Confederate states came under Congressional control, it was understood that the creation of public-education systems was expected of the Southern constitutional conventions.[16]

As the elections to these constitutional conventions were controlled by black votes, it was also understood that the new state constitutions would formally provide for African-American suffrage. Yet the mass of Southern blacks could not yet read or write their own names, and it was doubted that they had an ability to grasp the political issues of the day. Under these circumstances, they would be voted in herds as directed by their Republican managers. The idea of illiterates voting on a mass scale went against the grain of the common American understanding of essential prerequisites for good citizenship. Only the speedy establishment of public schools throughout the Southern states could possibly justify this hopefully temporary state of affairs.

Accordingly, all of the new Southern state constitutions provided for the establishment of state systems of public education, promising free education for all children. This is widely regarded as Reconstruction's most enduring reform. However, providing for public schools on paper did not necessarily mean that meaningful systems of public education would soon be established in the South.[17]

George Peabody, an American millionaire living in England, followed these developments closely. True to his New England roots, he wanted to encourage public education in the South and created a charitable fund worth several million dollars to do just that. Barnas Sears, who had succeeded Horace Mann as secretary of the Massachusetts board of education, was chosen to head the new Peabody Fund. Sears established his headquarters in Staunton, Virginia, to gain familiarity with Southern conditions. His purpose was to tease Southerners, with small seed grants, to push the development of public education themselves. As long as the public school remained a foreign, New England institution, public education could not long endure in the South. Its best chances relied on its being assimilated and internalized into the regional culture. That was the challenge facing Sears. A board of trustees, consisting of prominent Northerners and Southerners, was established to counsel Sears. Armed with the annual interest from the fund, Sears determined where and when to plant his "seeds" for the best effect. Over time, this work produced a revolution in educational attitudes in the South. Charles Sumner, the famous abolitionist senator from Massachusetts, commented at the outset that he could not recall any greater gift of national significance in American history.[18]

Earlier, others had tried to make public education palatable to Southern tastes. During the war, General Nathaniel Banks had worked to establish a public-school system in Louisiana. He attempted to win Southern sympathies by hiring only Southern white women as teachers. But his efforts failed to change white attitudes in any significant way. Barnas Sears knew of this record of failures and used the Peabody Fund's financial carrots only in ways to crack this phalanx of white racist sentiment, hostile to the very idea of public education. Slowly, through the efforts of Sears and public-school advocates emerging from the Southern states themselves, an enduring public-school culture took root in the South.[19]

While Sears worked to soften white opposition to the very idea of public education, African-American leaders fought to keep the racial caste mentality bred in slavery from being transferred to public education. They did not necessarily oppose racially segregated public schools, but they insisted that this not be mandated in their new state

constitutions. In 1867–1868, black delegates in the Southern state constitutional conventions succeeded in preventing such provisions from
being adopted. They hoped for a system in which individual public
schools, open to all, gravitated to the control of one race or the other on
the basis of parental choice. Early on, the goal of Southern blacks (such
as Rev. Francis L. Cardozo, who ran a well-respected black school in
Charleston) was not integrated education but rather fair treatment from
whites in the administration of public-school funds.[20] This could only be
ensured in a public-education system in which schools were open to all,
irrespective of race. South Carolina wrote such a provision into its new
state constitution, while in practice this system came to be operated on a
segregated basis. Most Southern states did not go even this far, preferring simply to defer to African-American wishes not to have segregated schooling mandated in the state constitutions themselves.[21]

The clear hostility of blacks to constitutionally mandated segregated schools was interpreted by most Southern whites as revealing a
black desire to associate with whites in "mixed schools." This was feared
as a first step toward racial amalgamation. Louisiana inaugurated the
only Southern school system that made any meaningful attempt toward
racially integrated schools, but this integration was approximated only
in New Orleans. Rural public schools in Louisiana were effectively
boycotted by whites. In other Southern states, no effort was made to
mix whites and blacks in public-school classrooms. Nonetheless, whites
throughout the South were convinced that African Americans harbored
a hidden intent to attend white schools in the not too distant future.

In South Carolina, where the new state constitution theoretically
allowed for mixed schools, a white protest railed against the evils of the
racial integration that it feared was sure to come. These white fears
served to reactivate latent white violence against educating blacks at all,
encouraging Ku Klux Klan burning of schools and terrorizing teachers.
In 1868, the Freedmen's Bureau's superintendent of schools noted that a
revived rebel spirit "thickened about" the schools.[22] Up until that time,
schools for blacks in many parts of the South existed only with the
support of military force, and it was problematic how long Northern
voters would be willing to support such an ongoing commitment. With
public school systems called for in the new Southern state constitutions,
the responsibility for educating the freedmen effectively passed from
the federal government to the Southern states themselves. By the end of
1868, all but three of the states undergoing Congressional Reconstruction had ratified their new constitutions mandating state-based
public-school systems. The three states remaining were Virginia,
Mississippi, and Texas. Of course, much remained to be done before any

meaningful public education would be established throughout the Southern states.

In designing their public-education strategy for creating a standardized national culture, Republican strategists kept one eye on the Roman Catholic church, which they regarded as their primary enemy in the North. In the South, white racism was the primary obstacle against public education. In the South, the enemies of the public school were presumably vanquished and under federal authority. In the North, they were growing in political power with each new wave of European immigration. Church pronouncements were squarely aligned against the American public school. In 1851, a papal encyclical had called on the church to provide for Catholic schools for Catholic youth. In 1864, another papal encyclical had damned non-Catholic public education as unacceptable. Increasingly, Catholic demands for dividing state school funds so that Catholic schools could be supported at public expense threatened the Republican push for cultural uniformity. Ironically as Republicans sought to expand the public school into the South, the institution's Northern base was in danger of being undermined by a growing enemy within. Accordingly, Republicans saw the need for a new federal agency to promote public education everywhere in the nation, North as well as South.[23]

Just as Northern teachers working under the protection of the Freedmen's Bureau felt a missionary commission to uplift the freedmen, public-school advocates in the North held similar attitudes toward Catholic immigrants, especially the Irish. In petitioning that Congress establish a federal agency to promote public education nationwide, the citizens of Medford, Massachusetts, revealed a paternalism that included both African Americans and the Irish in its sweep. In their words, the freedmen and the immigrating Catholic masses, "many of whom come here with ideas, tastes, and habits different from ours," required this effort. "The Anglo-Saxon blood on this side of the globe," their petition read, "must faithfully educate and peacefully lead the other races. It is our destiny, and *we must fulfill it.*" Republican Congressman Ignatius Donnelly agreed. Public education, he warned, should not be left to the states. He saw the nation in danger of cultural dissolution. With uneducated Irish immigrants and illiterate freedmen added to the electorate, the Republic was threatened with being directed by an "ignorant, bigoted, and brutalized population." He predicted that the nation itself might not last another fifty years if something were not done to keep ignorance from sinking the ship of state. Similar to the petition from Medford, Massachusetts, Donnelly's comments covered more than just conditions in the South. They were framed in terms of a need to reconstruct a nation threatened by a cancerous ignorance growing in all sections of the Union. The envisioned purpose of the new federal agency that would promote public education was to help reconstruct the nation in this broader sense.[24]

The Republican bill to create the new agency provided that its sole purpose would be to collect and disseminate data concerning public education nationwide. Democratic opponents to the measure were skeptical and viewed it as the proverbial camel's nose under the tent. Nonetheless, congressional Republicans had the votes and sent the measure creating a new Bureau of Education to President Johnson. Surprisingly, he signed it, believing the Republican sponsors of the measure who promised him that the new agency would not try to nationalize public education in the United States. Nevertheless, almost immediately it set out to do just this. The new federal Commissioner of Education, Henry Barnard, began a study of public education in the District of Columbia. Congress had begun a biracial but segregated system of public schools in the nation's capital during the war. By the end of the decade, some Republicans led by Senator Charles Sumner were interested in reforming this system to serve as a model for the nation. Throughout the antebellum period, the slavery issue had often focused on the District of Columbia, which as a territory was constitutionally under the direct control of Congress. With slavery destroyed, the District of Columbia remained in the spotlight as a potential proving ground for national public-school reforms.[25]

This ambitious agenda called for energetic leadership, but initially that was lacking. Commissioner Barnard's efforts were stalled by his own inability to focus his energies. He continued to serve as editor of the *American Journal of Education* even after his appointment as the first head of an important new federal agency. Overwhelmed by his combined duties, he blamed his problems on a small staff and insufficient office space; but even his friends knew better. One month after the submission of Barnard's first and only annual report, Congress put a revamped Bureau of Education under the Department of Interior. On October 27, 1870, John Eaton, Jr., officially replaced Barnard. Months earlier, even one of Barnard's close friends wrote to Eaton that Barnard's dismissal was necessary as the latter was "not in all respects adapted to the place he occupied." Under new leadership, the Bureau of Education came to fulfill the expectations originally placed in the agency by public-school reformers. Eaton's perspective was distinctly national on his arrival in his new job. Writing to Barnas Sears, Eaton offered as his own highest priority in public education "the relation of our free school systems to the vast and increasing vagabondism." This problem clearly transcended state lines.[26] Throughout the 1870s, Eaton's agency served as a nationalizing agency for public education. Republicans in Congress pushing public education as a national concern consistently relied on the expertise of Eaton and his small staff. From the time of Eaton's arrival in his new post until the end of Reconstruction, public education played an important role in the nation's political life.

On the eve of the 1870s, Horace Mann's public-school model had been replicated throughout the Northern states, and initial preparations had been made for spreading it throughout the South as well. The goal was clear. In the words of James P. Wickersham, principal of the Pennsylvania state normal school at Millersville, the intention of the postwar public-school reformers was "toward making homogeneous our social as well as our political institutions throughout the nation." In Wickersham's opinion, the "great lesson" that the Civil War had taught was "that the United States of America is a *nation,* and not a copartnership of states; and," he continued, "as a nation, our government ought not to release itself from all responsibility concerning education. . . . Without it, there may be reconstruction, but there can be no true union."[27] And the concern of reformers such as Wickersham was not merely toward remaking the South. They also hoped to shape the culture of the North in order to protect it from Roman Catholic inroads. They saw themselves as saving the Union from threatened forces of dissolution emanating from the lowest levels of society in all regions.

The adoption of the Fifteenth Amendment in 1870 especially signaled the need for a dynamic public-school crusade. In addition to the millions of illiterate black voters empowered by the amendment, growing legions of unlettered Irish commonly voted before they ever became citizens. Corruptible Irish voters, susceptible to demagogues, especially bothered Republicans such as James Garfield who also worried about blacks someday leaving the Republican party. Throughout the seventies, Garfield was fond of quoting Lord Thomas Macaulay who had predicted that American democracy would eventually self-destruct either as a result of the poor plundering the rich or the rich resorting to military dictatorship for self-protection. "Either some Caesar or Napoleon will seize the reins of government with a strong hand," Macaulay had written, "or your republic will be as fearfully plundered and laid waste by barbarians in the twentieth century as the Roman empire was in the fifth." That Garfield repeatedly referred to this gloomy prediction until his death in 1881 says much about not only his frame of mind but that of his audiences as well.[28] Republicans such as Garfield had supported the Fifteenth Amendment in order to continue their party's temporary hold on national power, but they greatly dreaded its possible long-term consequences in allowing the ignorant and dispossessed potentially to guide the destinies of the nation. Few white people identified their own racial attitudes as threatening the future of the Republic, but United States Commissioner of Education John Eaton, Jr., highlighted this factor. In fact, he saw it as perhaps the most important ingredient in the recipe threatening to poison the nation. "In its eagerness to wound others," wrote Eaton, "the white race of our country has injured itself." Whites who could easily be persuaded to educate white children often could not see an identical need to educate others. As a result, minority races were left trapped by an ignorance that ultimately threatened even whites themselves. By thus perpetuating the internal enemy of illiteracy, white racism weakened the Union.[29]

To observers foreign and domestic, American life appeared on the edge of anarchy. "Judge Lynch" and the vigilantism executed by both Klansmen in the South and Danites in Utah seemed to characterize a violent people easily resorting to firearms to resolve social problems. American children in urban slums roamed as packs of wild animals preying on the weak. While Reconstruction's focus was on the problems of the freedmen, a bare majority of America's illiterates was white. Commissioner Eaton noted that nationwide there were 2,879,543 white illiterates and 2,763,991 illiterate blacks. A significant number of illiterate whites, especially in the South, were the children of native-born parents. One author described them as a growing "army of white barbarians." While most Americans of that time spoke of uplifting the illiterate children of America through education, they were quite aware of an alternate vision that showed ignorance taking over the body-national as a contagion or cancerous growth. Even Massachusetts, the home of the New England based public-education crusade, was threatened. "Power lies with the majority," observed one English visitor, "and the majority in Massachusetts is going over to the Irish poor, to the Fenian Circles and the Molly Maguires."[30]

For some reflective Americans, the Paris Commune in the Spring of 1871 provided a glimpse into the American future. The *Chicago Tribune*, in describing the Paris mob as "an enemy that knows no law but that of grape and canister," knew of its readers' fears that similar mass underclass violence was brewing in their own country and not solely because of the poverty forced by economic hard times. Traditional mores were disintegrating before the public eye, and many were concerned.

Republicans compared the chaos of the French capital to the anarchic Irish mobs of America's cities. "Our own condition is at bottom so nearly analogous to theirs," reported the *New York Times*, "that save in a spirit of gloomy forecast, we have little reason to institute a contrast." Southern conservatives saw the Paris communists as the fruit of a contagion shared by Radical Republicans. Roman Catholics saw the Parisians as rebelling against Christian tradition, thus carrying on the degenerating consequences of the Protestant Reformation. Father Isaac Hecker, speaking for the Catholic perspective, noted that the cultural disease evidenced in Paris was in fact rife throughout all of western civilization. "We who live in Protestant countries," noted Hecker, "see society daily dissolving before our eyes." That Catholics, Republicans, and former Confederates could unite in common horror over the events in Paris was significant. All parties felt keenly a disintegrating America in need of unification, but they differed sharply on their prescription for curing the malady.[31]

Representing most of the country's wealth, Northern Republicans had the most to lose if the Paris Commune were ever acted out on American shores. More than any other group, Republicans obsessed about the underside of the industrial revolution. Currently, ignorant poverty-stricken African Americans were their political allies, but they worried about this fragile alliance. Especially, they worried about the large numbers of Irish poor entering the country. Neither the blacks nor the Irish seemed to be attuned to the free-labor ideology. *The Republic*, a political journal of the day, gave open voice to these fears in projecting a future time in which ignorant blacks and ignorant whites, both North and South, might coalesce for purposes of spoliation: "Suppose these ignorant voters should in any way find their interest one, or that their unguided passions should be turned in a single direction, and they should combine on any issue." The thought was not pleasant and revealed that confidence was often lacking in this supposedly optimistic age.[32]

These fears bred within the Republican Party a craving for middle-class uniformity and a cultural standardization that could protect the Republic against the specter of the Paris Commune. As a new decade dawned, the first in American history in which all men (whether rich or poor, or black or white, or educated or illiterate) could determine election results and thus steer the course of the nation, Republicans resolved to reconstruct the nation by means of the public school. The Reconstruction of the 1860s ended with the adoption of the Fifteenth Amendment in 1870. Yet few Republicans were willing to concede that the work of Reconstruction was over. The Union was still threatened by illiteracy, ignorance, and lack of moral training. This, Republicans widely agreed, could only be overcome by public education on a massive scale. Some sought to work this reform on a state by state basis, given that historically that institution had been a creation of state and local government. Others saw the emergency of impending national disintegration as warranting unprecedented centralized promotion of public education by the federal government.

At the outset of the seventies, the Republican Party faced the challenge of a Democratic Party that claimed allegiance to Republican norms. Democrats claimed themselves as loyal as Republicans to the Union, and supportive of the Reconstruction amendments and the new rights of freedmen. Democrats called this acceptance of past Republican accomplishments their "New Departure" strategy. They had concluded that the Republican Party could only benefit by Democratic reactionary resistance to the fruits of the Union victory on the battlefield. Senator Henry Wilson from Massachusetts was responsible for countering this Democratic Party "New Departure." As Chairman of the Republican National Committee, Wilson devised what he called the "New Departure of the Republican Party." In a widely read essay appearing in the *Atlantic Monthly* in January 1871, Wilson outlined the new Republican strategy which called on the public school to become the centerpiece of a new Reconstruction of all of American society, North as well as South.

In the article, Wilson confessed that the Republican Party apparently had achieved all of the objectives for which it had been created. Slavery had been destroyed, and the "slave power" had been dethroned. The freedmen had even been enfranchised to enable them to protect their own freedom by voting for the Republican Party. But, he warned, the heritage of slavery still lived in the form of illiteracy, ignorance, and undeveloped moral capacity. Concurrent with the miserable condition of the freedmen, he wrote, ignorant and illiterate immigrants from Europe were entering the country also to become voters. As never before, an unwanted cultural diversity characterized the voting class. Given this, the nation could not afford to drift and leave matters to chance. A genuine national unification through a national public school system was needed. Wilson recounted the early colonial days of his native Massachusetts when a heavy investment was made in the education of the common citizenry. General prosperity and individual self-control had been the result of this policy. The nation as a whole now needed a similar resolve. The Puritan economic values of "Poor Richard's Almanac" needed to be spread throughout the entire land and be adopted by all social classes. Only a national public-school program, he claimed, could protect property rights for the long term by creating a cultural unity on a proven New England standard.[33]

He realized that transferring public education from state to federal management would constitute a radical development. But he saw this as a natural progression of Reconstruction. "With the general rejection of the state rights heresy, state lines are becoming fainter," he wrote, "and state individuality is being more and more absorbed into national unity." He held up the model of Prussian public education, organized from the center. He pointed the Republican Party toward a new Germanic centralized political order. As Otto von Bismarck was centralizing a new German federation, the Republican Party was centralizing the American Union. As Prussia had invested heavily in primary education, the United States should do likewise. France had lagged behind in mass education, and it had suffered the ultimate consequence of its public-policy error on the battlefields of the Franco-Prussian War, just then concluding. The French people, he wrote, "ignorant, priest-ridden, and emasculated of their manhood, lies beaten on every field and helpless at the conqueror's feet. The lesson should not be lost on the American people." With a national school system, the United States could grow in prosperity, unity and military might. Without it, the disintegrating forces of illiteracy, ignorance, crime, labor upheaval, and cultural division would eventually tear apart the beloved Union. This was Wilson's warning and his prescription to avoid national catastrophe.[34]

The Democrats had claimed that they accepted Reconstruction. Could they accept Wilson's Republican "New Departure" for Reconstruction? Could they accept political centralization on the German model inherent in Wilson's national vision? He knew that they could not. He intended to reveal the strict states-rights limits of the Democrats' "New Departure." He intended to cast the Democrats as the opponents of a necessary reform in public education. He meant to expose them as real enemies of preserving the Union against ignorance, crime, and national disunity. He drew a new line of political demarcation for the next stage of Reconstruction, designed to create one nation unified by one set of cultural norms inculcated in national public schools directed from Washington, D.C. He knew who would oppose him. The South had already shown itself unwilling to surrender its distinct regional culture built around ancient racial prejudices. Talk of creating one nation in that quarter suggested to Southern ears the imagined terrors of racial amalgamation. And he knew of other opponents as well. The growing Roman Catholic church in America was not about to surrender to Protestant hegemony in the name of American nationalism. In 1870, the church made official the doctrine of papal infallibility, in part to shield Roman Catholic authority from the rising power of modern secular nationalism led by Bismarck's emerging German nation. In America, as in Europe, the Roman Catholic church stood firmly opposed to all dreams of cultural homogeneity that did not concede primacy to its own ancient spiritual authority. This fact pitted Wilson's New Departure against the political power of the Roman Catholic church. Up until 1870, Reconstruction had been about race. After that date, it was about religion as well.[35]

2

CHURCH, STATE, AND SCHOOL

The Cincinnati Bible War

In the 1870s, Cincinnati was the gateway to the great American West. The bustling metropolis was composed of many ethnic groups, holding a variety of religious preferences. Over twenty different Protestant denominations, representing almost 100 separate congregations, dotted the community. Among the Protestants, Methodists and Baptists predominated. Presbyterians were also plentiful but were divided between those holding Calvinist and Arminian theologies. Five synagogues gave Judaism a relatively strong representation. But Roman Catholicism provided the dominant force in Cincinnati. Its twenty-three churches constituted the largest single denomination. While still a minority, Catholics were far more unified than the Protestants, who were internally divided along racial, ethnic, and theological lines.

Roman Catholic Archbishop John Baptist Purcell towered over Cincinnati's religious landscape. Based in Cincinnati, his administrative territory included not only Ohio, but Kentucky, Indiana, and Michigan as well. By 1869, he had held this office for eighteen years. No Protestant cleric in the city had comparable influence. In fact, as of 1869, none of Cincinnati's Protestant ministers had served his congregation for more than three years.[1] Sixteen years before, Archbishop Purcell had established a separate Catholic school system in Cincinnati that by 1869 enrolled 12,000 children. By contrast, Cincinnati's public school enrollment was then 19,000. Given the facts of Catholic immigration, Cincinnati's school officials feared that in the next decade Catholic school enrollment might eclipse that in the public schools.

The city's school board began exploring possibilities of absorbing the Catholic schools into the public system. Purcell's own brother represented the Catholic interests in these talks. His price was not cheap. If a merger occurred, the public schools would be required to cease all Protestant practices, such as commencing each day with Bible readings and hymn singing. Rumors of these negotiations leaked to an anti-Catholic newspaper editor in the city. In September 1869, his headlines screamed of a Romish conspiracy to remove the Bible from Cincinnati's public schools. The Cincinnati Bible War was underway.

Before this exposé, negotiators had arrived at a tentative settlement: The Bible would be removed from the schools. The Catholic teachers of the formerly parochial schools would be retained in a new role as public school instructors, as long as they possessed teaching certificates from the state board of examiners. Physical control of the formerly parochial schools would remain in Catholic hands on the weekends, when religious instruction could be given to Catholic students.[2] This arrangement might have worked, but the vitriolic newspaper accounts of the talks stiffened the Archbishop's back. His instincts told him to kill the school pact in its cradle. He proclaimed his complete satisfaction with continuing separate private Catholic schools entirely at church expense. There would be no deal. The competition of Catholic schools and public schools would remain.

Deeply disappointed, school board negotiators vainly tried to reassemble the destroyed diplomatic edifice that painstakingly they had constructed. A subsequent peace meeting between board representatives and the Archbishop only served to exacerbate the division. Purcell railed at his guests, instructing them that no reasonable person could object to dividing public school funds between Protestants and Catholics, a practice traditionally followed in both Europe and Canada. All he had wanted was simple justice, but Protestant bigotry had killed the deal. However, he held out a slim hope. He planned to see the Pope within the year at the upcoming Vatican Council. He was willing to ask the holy pontiff's opinion on the matter at that time. He would do no more.

Given that Pope Pius IX for years had been calling for meaningful Catholic education for all Catholic youth, it was highly unlikely that he would approve of restricting religious education to weekends only. Dejected school board members then did something completely unpredictable. Angered over the Protestant reaction that had killed their negotiations, they voted to bar the Bible and hymn singing from Cincinnati's public schools independent of any deal with Purcell. Non-Protestants (Catholics, Jews, and Free Thinkers) constituted a majority of the board. The board made its decision at midnight on November 1, 1869, creating not only a local explosion but a national upheaval as well. The Rev. Amory Dwight Mayo, the most traditional of Cincinnati's three Unitarian ministers, drew national attention to the act of the board: "No state, to my knowledge," he proclaimed, "has ever forbidden religious instruction of an unsectarian character in its common schools, and the authors of the resolutions that propose to expel God Almighty from the schools of Cincinnati will certainly achieve the distinction of being pioneers in this radical reform."[3]

National journals, especially the popular *Harper's Weekly*, highlighted the Cincinnati controversy. The anti-Catholic cartoons of Thomas Nast stimulated the public imagination. Nast, who is known for having first typified the Republican Party as an elephant, the Democratic Party as a donkey, and Tammany Hall as a tiger, portrayed Roman Catholic bishops as crocodiles threatening the innocent children of the American public school. Inspired by the anti-Catholic media frenzy, innumerable Protestant sermons simultaneously thundered against the Cincinnati school board. The logic of the anti-Catholic crusade portrayed the school board action as part of an international Jesuit conspiracy being played out not only in the United States but also in Germany, England, Italy, and Spain. According to this campaign, the Catholic church was trying to force the modern secular state to accept its medieval, antiprogressive notions. At issue, anti-Catholic propagandists stressed, was the supremacy of the secular state over an antinational medieval spiritual hierarchy. This kind of interpretation might have fit concurrent events in Europe, but the facts of the Cincinnati affair had to be stretched considerably to match this mold. In fact, the school board had sought to establish its secular supremacy over traditional Protestant religious norms.[4]

The anti-Catholic movement that effectively began with the Cincinnati Bible War was of greater intensity than any similar outburst since the Know-Nothing crusade of the 1850s. The latter had helped shape antislavery politics before the Civil War. During the 1860s, anti-Catholicism had continued to simmer in the North because of the Roman Catholic church's open sympathy for the Confederate cause. Then came the Cincinnati affair. This new anti-Catholic movement would help mold the political culture of Reconstruction during its last decade. It would not create a new party, as had been the case in the 1850s. Instead, it readily found a home within the party of Reconstruction. Republicans thoroughly welcomed the reassertion of this long-standing religious prejudice. The dynamics of Reconstruction revealed why. White racism served as a brake on the centralizing trends of Reconstruction. But anti-Catholicism revealed itself as a potential facilitator of a homogenous union that alone could be capable of defending the nation against the supposed international Jesuitical conspiracy. The Protestant North was ripe to follow the lead of Cincinnati's defenders of American cultural traditions in the management of the public schools.

Local Cincinnati Protestants quickly took the offensive, winning a temporary injunction against the Bible ban from the city's superior court. Their case rested on a claim that Ohio's state constitution officially recognized and supported the Christian religion. As an agent of the state, the Cincinnati school board had supposedly violated the state's fundamental law in its anti-Bible decision. The Protestant plaintiffs also contended that Bible reading in Cincinnati's public schools historically had been handled with great sensitivity toward dissenting religious minorities. Since 1842, they claimed, no students whose parents had registered a protest had been forced to participate in the daily exercise of Bible reading and hymn singing. At issue, the plaintiffs emphasized, were the many children who received no moral instruction in their homes. The public schools were charged with the task of producing good citizens for the state. This could not be fulfilled, they warned, if the Holy Bible were removed from the classroom. All meaningful moral education was founded on that one spiritual source. The McGuffey readers used in Cincinnati's schools were filled with Christian references. If the Bible were banned, logically all of these texts would have to be morally neutered, and in the end only societal degradation would be encouraged.

Attorneys for the school board retorted that the plaintiff's claims were untrue. Over the years, many teachers had forced unwilling students to participate in religious exercises disapproved of by their parents. In addition, they argued that it was wrong in a religiously diverse society to have moral education be dominated by Protestants. They protested that the American tradition of separation of church and state should be extended to the American public school. If the McGuffey readers had to be rewritten in the process, it did not necessarily follow that all moral homilies would be removed. The McGuffey readers had many moral precepts based on the writings of ancient pagan authors. Even in a secularizing public school environment, they claimed, students could still be taught right from wrong. The school-board lawyers also attacked the idea that the Ohio state constitution supported either Christianity or a Protestant interpretation of it. The literal language of that document, they noted, only supported "religion," a vague term left undefined by subsequent legislative enactments. As such, the state constitution only favored kindly feelings toward all persons and a general reverence toward the mystery of existence. The argument of the board attorneys ultimately rested on the constitutional concept of "state police powers," the traditional powers of elected representatives to pass legislation deemed desirable by the majority for the health, safety, and morals of the citizenry as a whole.

The Cincinnati school board, representing the majority of the community, had determined that Protestant moral education in the state schools was no longer appropriate. In the absence of state legislation, making this jugment was a police-powers decision of Cincinnati's duly elected school board.[5]

Judge Alphonso Taft was the only member of the three-man superior court who liked the school board's decision. He found the police-powers argument adequate to support the board's decision, but he was unwilling to end there. In his opinion, the historic practice of Bible reading in the public schools violated the spirit, if not the letter, of Ohio's bill of rights. He was especially sensitive to Jews who throughout history had been forced to endure the religious preferences of Christian majorities. He even conceded that the widely hated Mormons had a fundamental right not to have their religious beliefs violated by the state and its agents. For him, even Buddhists and atheists shared this same basic human right: "The idea that a man has less conscience because he is a rationalist, or a spiritualist, or even an atheist, than the believer in any one of the accepted forms of faith," Taft wrote, "may be current, but it is not a constitutional idea in the state of Ohio." He concluded his official opinion by fondly recollecting Roger Williams and the long history of American religious liberty.[6]

Taft was a Republican of some political ability and ambition, yet he held liberal views on religious toleration. His party at that time tended strongly in the opposite direction. Popular Republicans in the early 1870s adhered to the anti-Catholic preferences of the Protestant majority. Taft's views in this case hurt him politically. In fact, they effectively barred him from elective office for the rest of his life. President Ulysses S. Grant would later appoint him to his cabinet, and subsequent Republican presidents would appoint him to diplomatic posts in Vienna and St. Petersburg. But no Republican holding such religious views could ever expect to be nominated for high elective office, let alone win at the polls. Taft belonged to the most liberal Unitarian congregation in Cincinnati. His minister was one of the very few Protestant voices supporting the school board decision. Whereas Democrats with these associations might thrive politically, a Republican could not. Branded by many fellow Republicans as a "Unitarian atheist," Taft would later be considered for governor of Ohio, but he could not be nominated.[7]

Stanley Matthews, one of the attorneys for the Cincinnati school board, somewhat shared Taft's fate. Like Taft, he too was an up-and-coming Republican. Unlike Taft, he was firmly entrenched in a thoroughly respectable, traditional Protestant theology. A staunch Calvinist,

Matthews was a Presbyterian elder. Nonetheless, he held firmly that the school board had taken the only position appropriate in a diverse society. Matthews was a close personal friend of Rutherford B. Hayes, then the Republican governor of Ohio. He would later be one of the close handful of associates that would engineer Hayes' successful run at the presidency of the United States. Hayes later rewarded him with a Supreme Court nomination, but it was rejected by a Republican Senate. Subsequently, a nomination to the Court by President Garfield was approved; and Matthews ended his career on the nation's highest court. Matthews' career evidenced only slightly more success in electoral politics than did Taft's. In 1877, the Ohio state legislature elected him to fill the remainder of John Sherman's term in the United States Senate, as the latter became President Hayes' Secretary of the Treasury. Matthews was not renominated in 1878, when the term expired.

The political career of Rutherford B. Hayes was more reflective of a successful Republican in an era of anti-Catholic reaction. A month before the superior court issued its final ruling on the Cincinnati Bible case, Hayes wrote to a Cincinnati resident who advocated keeping the Bible in the public schools. "We must not let them push religion out of the schools," wrote Hayes, "but we must avoid forcing it on anybody. You may ask, how are the two things to be accomplished? Well, it is easier to do the thing than to tell how to do it."[8] In the Republican Party at that time, especially on this particular issue, such blather was practical politics. Over the next several years, Hayes warmed to the controversy as he sensed its potential for winning votes. He easily participated in the rising anti-Catholicism and more and more frequently called forth the American public school as the crucible for a culturally unified nation. While at the outset being a rather inarticulate spokesperson, Hayes eventually emerged as the primary political beneficiary of the culture struggle that focused on the changing nature of the American public school. Both President Grant and James G. Blaine would fail in a similar quest. Ironically, Stanley Matthews would be at Hayes's side every step of the way, despite his early hometown stand on principle in 1869–1870.[9]

On February 18, 1870, the Cincinnati superior court rendered its verdict. Two judges ruled against the school board. Taft registered a lone dissent. The majority held that the true intent of the Ohio constitution favored Christianity (i.e., Protestantism). One of their arguments recalled John Wesley's dream of visiting hell and there finding representatives of every religious view. Then, the recounting of the dream revealed, Wesley went to heaven and found only Christians. Accordingly, by the internal logic of this recollected dream, the word "religion" in the state constitution meant "Christianity." The court majority noted that in attempting to remove the Bible from the city's public schools, the board promoted "infidelity" and thereby violated the Ohio constitution. The two judges professed not to understand the Roman Catholic position regarding the Bible in the schools, as the Catholics seemingly illogically opposed both "Godless" schools and Bible reading. Likewise, the majority found Jewish opposition to Bible reading in the schools incomprehensible, given that Jewish scriptures made up most of the Christian Holy Bible. In their majoritarian view, "Free Thinkers" and atheists had no position worthy of consideration. Consequently, they ruled that the temporary injunction against the board decision be made permanent. The defeated school board immediately appealed. While the public awaited the review and decision of the Ohio Supreme Court (a process that would take two years), the nation continued to debate the issue. "Nothing is more evident," one Protestant newspaper reported a week after the verdict, "than that the school question is now fully launched upon the public mind. Its consideration in all the principles involved, and all the practical bearings of the same, has become a living necessity of the times."[10]

Johann B. Stallo, representing Cincinnati's "Free Thinkers," ardently backed the school board. He was widely regarded as the articulate mouthpiece of saloon and dance-house patrons who opposed any kind of moral education while advocating easy divorce and free love. Stallo ridiculed the Bible as a basis for moral education, pointing to the story of Cain and Abel as teaching the virtues of fratricide, the tale of the Great Flood as authorizing genocide and Moses' slaying of the Egyptian as condoning everyday murders. The Bible, he said, promoted fraud and permissive sexuality, as shown in the stories of Jacob and Isaac and "the infamous acts of immorality and sensuality attributed to patriarchal and saintly personages." The Christian religion, he said, was "the faithful handmaid of despotism" in teaching passivity in the face of political tyranny. He saw Franklin, Paine, and Jefferson, "Free Thinkers" all, as true sources of American liberty. Removal of the Bible from the public schools, he somewhat flippantly suggested, would actually improve moral education in the Republic, and make better citizens by its very absence.[11]

Damon Y. Kilgore, another "Free Thinker," continued Stallo's attack on the Bible. Jesus, he said, had advocated sloth and desertion of family obligations. Did not the Nazarene instruct his followers to "take no thought for tomorrow?" As such, he had glorified poverty, denigrated material progress, and violated the progressive spirit of the nineteenth century. Did not Jesus teach his disciples to abandon their parents and brothers and sisters? Kilgore saw this latter teaching as particularly abhorrent. Little children, he said, were innocent and good. Yet Jesus taught them to hate those deserving of their fondest affections. Surely this doctrine, he said, should be banned from the public schools. Stallo and Kilgore's voices were joined by Robert Green Ingersoll, the most famous American atheist of his generation. The Bible, wrote Ingersoll, was a book that glorified mass murders and hideous atrocities as the will of God. Such teachings, he noted, could never "make our children loving, kind and gentle!" The public school, Ingersoll argued, was created to disseminate knowledge. Yet the Bible opposed knowledge. Indeed, he wrote, the Adam and Eve story denigrated knowledge as dangerous. Ingersoll saw the serpent as the true hero of the Bible tale as "he was the first schoolmaster, the first advocate of learning, the first enemy of ignorance, the first to whisper in human ears the sacred word *liberty*, the creator of ambition, the author of modesty, of inquiry, of doubt, of investigation, of progress and of civilization."[12]

While he stood with the "Free Thinkers" in opposing the superior court decision, Stanley Matthews sharply disagreed with them concerning the validity of the Bible as a textbook of good morals. He shared with his fellow Protestants the perception of the growing societal need to reach those American children not receiving a proper Christian education in the home. But he did not see the public school as the appropriate place for this religiously based moral education to be conducted. The church, he wrote, not the public school, was the proper agency to supply the remedy:

Cannot the church send out its ministers? Or are they too busy, day after day, in their studies, preparing to dole out dogmatic theology Sunday after Sunday, to the tired ears of their wearied congregations? Cannot they send out their Sunday-school teachers? Cannot they send out their missionaries? . . . Must we say that the church has grown idle and lazy, and can only hobble on its crutches, and therefore that our school directors must set themselves up as teachers of religious truth? No! Let the church cease to depend upon any adventitious or external aids. Let her rely solely upon the omnipotent strength of the spirit of the Lord that is in it. . . . Here is our work to evangelize, to save the lost and perishing crowd.[13]

A minority of other Protestants also urged that Christian moral instruction be removed from the public schools and that the churches fill the void. None other than Rev. Henry Ward Beecher took this position. While based in New York City, that generation's most outspoken preacher felt a close affinity to conditions in Cincinnati, where he had lived during his young manhood. While Beecher would frequently lend his prestigious voice on behalf of other aspects of the anti-Catholic movement during the course of the 1870s, he sided with Matthews in supporting the action of the Cincinnati school board. He said that he always opposed the Roman Catholic church for its authoritarian and controlling ways. Likewise, he was opposed to Protestants taking authoritarian positions. Forcing Protestant norms on Catholics, Jews, and atheists in the public schools was not right. True Christianity, he wrote, never seeks to remove the element of free choice. He saw forcing public school children to read the Bible each day as contrary to God's will. Beecher agreed with Rev. Samuel T. Spear, another liberal Protestant intellectual, who suggested that moral education could be conducted best in a Bible-free public school. Spear emphasized that true moral education is promoted by a teacher's living example rather than by written scriptural precepts. According to Beecher and Spear, the habits of patience, diligence, industry, steadiness of applications, submission to lawful authority, respect of others, cleanliness and good manners, self-control, truthfulness, and honesty were present naturally in humankind. They merely needed to be positively reinforced by a good teacher's moral example. By this logic, the Bible was not essential in a meaningful program of moral education; natural human goodness nurtured in a loving classroom environment, not the Bible itself, was the most important determinant of sound moral education. Most American Protestants, especially conservative Evangelicals, held a far less sanguine view of human nature.[14]

Typically, Beecher saw the removal of the Bible from the public schools as being guided by the Holy Spirit. For him this movement toward secularization was preparing the churches for a renewed crusade to reform America in Christ's image. Religious instruction in the public schools, he said, had long been woefully inadequate. Creeping materialism and secularization had been the fruits of Horace Mann's inadequate religious catechism in the public schools. Yet even if a better system of moral education had been devised a generation before, wrote Beecher, the march toward materialism would still have proceeded. In Prussia, thoroughgoing religious instruction had long been an established part of public education. Nonetheless, the Prussians had a well deserved reputation as the most irreligious people in Europe. Nineteenth-century progress and secularism seemed to march hand in hand. The family, Beecher wrote, was the critical institution so far as moral education was concerned. If a family was intent on providing a moral education based on religious teachings, the lessons would likely take root and flourish. If not, he wrote, no other institution, including the public school, could provide an adequate substitute. In Beecher's view, the problem was one beyond the scope of governmental solution. In any case, according to him, Divine Providence was directing the matter. Ultimately, he prophesied, there would be a good outcome.[15]

For liberal Protestants such as Beecher, human nature was basically good and the march of modern history was inevitably moving toward good results. Beecher was then developing a comfortable, platitudinous theology for America's rising middle and upper classes. This theology lacked traditional fears of eternal punishment for wrong-doing and abounded in a vague and Pollyanna-like reliance on Providence, which he also termed "the all-inspiring Love-power." Simultaneously, he acknowledged that the growing worship of wealth and worldly success (key characteristics of the so-called Gilded Age) was undermining the traditional religious values of the American family. "Home life," Beecher warned the readers of his weekly religious newspaper, "is the life of the nation." In the 1870s, that life was under increasing strains. He noted that the modern American family, enjoying a newfound material prosperity, doted on its children in all the wrong ways. It showered them with relative luxuries and starved them in any meaningful religious training. He looked to the present and immediate future of the nation with a sense of foreboding. "What missionaries shall assault this paganism," he cried, "for its temples are the hearth-stones of Christian homes."[16] Despite his reading of the danger signals of his place and time, Beecher himself advocated a theology of happy resignation and drift. The major thrust of his post-Civil War ministry was to rely passively on God's love to transform all of the chaotic changes wrought by rapid industrialization into a better world. His unquestioning, optimistic faith in the workings of free-market capital-ism made him enormously popular with his countrymen, equally mes-merized by the rapidly developing prospects of material power. The true tragedy of Henry Ward Beecher is that ultimately he theologically collaborated with that which he perceived to be the enemy. The evil that Beecher saw was the popular tendency to worship worldly success with an accompanying willingness to sacrifice anything and everything on its altars. Yet, while it was taking shape before his eyes, Beecher soothingly reassured his national following that all was ultimately well. In the end, he helped to further what he himself had identified as the new American paganism.

The old abolitionist Gerrit Smith agreed with Beecher that even before the Cincinnati challenge had alerted the nation, the superficial religious instruction common in the public schools had miserably failed. He recalled that in the early days of the crusade against slavery, he had called on public-school students to join the cause with little result. Thereupon, he had concluded that "there had been more head-work than heart-work in their schools." Now, with the Cincinnati Bible War, he saw an opportunity to suggest a necessary national reform: Destroy the public school! It had never been more than a bundle of compromises anyway. A properly constituted education, he argued, was one firmly established on a meaningful and thorough program of moral education. This could not happen in a public school any more than meaningful worship could occur in a government church. He rejected the argument that the public school was necessary to create a common American nationality from disparate elements. That popular notion, he said, served to make social conformity into the highest American value. Such a degraded ideal was no adequate basis on which to build a vibrant culturally diverse nation. Love of freedom, not conformity, had brought different peoples to America; and it was what kept them there. Dividing the task of educating the nation's youth among schools teaching different creeds and ideologies posed no threat in his mind to the health of the republic. Love of liberty would continue to bind all Americans. He warned that a forced homogeneity in the public schools ultimately would fail. "Whilst a coerced union engenders restless longings for disunion, a union in which there is the conscious freedom to separate is likely to be a contented and happy one." As the American people could not be brought together successfully by force, Smith called for abandoning the public school. "In our country," he wrote, "a government school should, like a government church, be reckoned to be a thing of the past." Smith's thinking, while interesting, represented only a very small libertarian segment of the American population.[17]

Despite these dissident Protestant voices, most American Protestants wanted to maintain the habit of Bible reading in the public schools. With the rise in Irish Catholic immigration, they felt under siege. In their eyes, the Roman Catholics were newcomers short on respect for legitimate, long-standing American traditions. Jews and others were small minorities that most Protestants expected to conform to local custom. Many Protestants insisted that mere Bible reading without comment, the normal practice in the public schools, in no way constituted sectarian education. "The reading of the Bible is not an act of worship," proclaimed one anonymous but typical opinion appearing in the public prints of the day. "The lessons chosen are naturally those tending to elevate the mind and soul and heart. Its object is to calm the mind and give wholesome lessons in moral rectitude." Other

Protestants quietly conceded that funding Protestant practices at public expense was unwarranted, but they feared making this admission lest Catholics be encouraged to attack the public school further. They worried that any concession to the Catholics might encourage other groups, such as Mormons and Chinese, to demand a rewriting of textbooks to remove all references that the latter found offensive. They feared that once other special interest groups began to join the Catholic complainers, public education would become vacuous in official efforts to maintain a facade of uniformity while accommodating disparate elements. Such a process could only define "education" as the art of learning nothing controversial.[18]

Horace Greeley urged no concessions to the Catholic position. The Catholic call for removal of the Bible from the public schools, he argued, was just a ploy. He charged that the Roman Catholic church would continue to oppose public schools under any and all conditions short of winning state support for their own religious schools. Indeed, Greeley reasoned, removing the Bible would only weaken the public schools by alienating "many of its oldest and firmest supporters." Others warned that removing the Bible from the schools would anger the Almighty, and divine retribution against the nation would follow. Many Protestants felt on the horns of a dilemma. Any course taken was seen as an unneutral act. Retaining the Bible was an unneutral act in favor of traditional Protestant practices. Removing the Bible was likewise perceived as an unneutral act, for it would suggest to children that religion was somehow dangerous or deserving of public approbation. Given these two extremes, they reluctantly supported the former, for they feared that it would "be much more difficult for Christian parents to raise their own children to respect the Bible if the state bans it from their schools." Many worried that any change from the status quo could only undermine moral education in the public schools. They feared that with the Bible removed from the schools, a new standard that "the common moralities of life have no deeper root than the varying custom of the hour" would come to govern public education. If this transpired, they predicted that teachers with religious sensibilities would abandon the public schools and be replaced "by men who scorn the imputation of a spiritual nature" and by women "cut adrift from the eternal verities of life." Under such conditions, children in the public schools would be regarded as "only thinking animals."[19]

Because of the Protestant mobilization over the Cincinnati case, few American communities directly banned the Bible from the public schools. Nonetheless, over the course of the decade, there was a marked drift away from religious education in the public schools. By 1880, use of the Bible was "all but extinct" in California's public schools due to unrelenting Catholic pressure. Bible reading also ceased in several major urban districts with significant Roman Catholic populations in the midwest and northeast. In 1881, several years after the Bible had been removed from Chicago's city schools, a correspondent of United States Commissioner of Education John Eaton, Jr., wrote him complaining of the city's "Godless schools." Elsewhere, the erosion of religious education in the public schools was far more subtle. More and more, curriculum planners sought systems of moral education based on "some simple form of scientific ethics" rather than on the Holy Bible. In some districts, readings from the New Testament were eliminated so as not to offend Jews. While few communities actually banned the Bible from the schools, the dechristianization of public education nonetheless made great strides during the 1870s. For all of the sound and fury of Protestant political rhetoric, the slow drift of educational change favored secularization.[20]

John H. Westerhoff III has studied the changing editions of the McGuffey readers throughout the nineteenth century and concludes that of the three principal editions of the textbooks (1836–1837, 1857, and 1879), the most radical changes were made in 1879. While still having some Christian content by twentieth-century standards, the 1879 version had significantly fewer Biblical materials than earlier editions. By 1879, none of the first edition's emphasis on salvation and piety remained. Moral precepts were still included, but only those applicable to the growing popular worship of success and accumulation of material goods. The gospel of the earlier editions taught that human beings were made for eternal life, to be found through Christian salvation. The gospel of the 1879 edition was different. While not denying God as the foundation of a moral life, it portrayed Christianity more as a means necessary for social stability and national prosperity than as an end in itself.[21]

School songbooks also changed at the end of the seventies. At the beginning of the decade, public-school music books commonly contained popular Protestant hymns. Songbooks produced in the 1880s were much more secular, emphasizing new songs designed to teach values needed to achieve success in the marketplace. Some references to God remained in the books of the eighties; but Christ, who had been in the foreground of public education in 1870, was all but gone by 1880. A pamphlet produced by the United States Bureau of Education in 1882 exhibited the transformation. It urged the teaching of "universal morality" in the public schools based on "a generous patriotism" and "inspired by justice." Nowhere in this pamphlet was any reference made to Christ or Christianity, the Bible, or even God.[22] Ironically, the dynamics of the contest over the Bible in the public schools inexorably led to an increasing secularization despite the fact that most of the contestants in the struggle were driven in their zeal by a strong religious faith. Only by deemphasizing the traditional Protestant use of the Bible in the schools could some semblance of peace return to public education in an increasingly religiously diverse society.

Some witnessed this change with a gloomy disposition. One citizen from Middletown, New York, projected existing trends in moral education into the American future. In his own time, he saw Christian moral education under attack. A modification of traditional public-school practices sought to accommodate complaints of Protestant favoritism. Ultimately, he predicted, society would opt to allow no moral education in the public schools for fear of offending some group. After several generations of public-school instruction devoid of moral values, externally applied force would gradually replace internal self-restraint as the principal bulwark of the social order. Without moral education, he reasoned, self-restraint would lose its motive power. Human beings would then do whatever they felt like doing at the moment. He prophesied that after a few generations of anarchic chaos, the New World experiment in individual liberty would end; and American democracy would be judged a failure despite its once glorious history.[23]

Horace Mann's public-school movement had promised that state schools would serve as surrogate parents for those children not receiving proper family guidance and support at home. Up until the 1870s, the public schools served in this capacity armed with Protestant-inspired moral education. After that decade, this resource grew more faint. Nonetheless, the societal expectation remained that public education would somehow "raise" those children not receiving proper moral direction at home. The task of the public school to meet the purpose for which it had originally been created became more difficult. Well into the future during eras of rising crime, the American public school would be widely blamed for failing to produce good citizens.[24]

Supporters of the public school divided on the issue of Bible reading in the schools. But in general, those wanting to retain the Bible in the schools implied that their position was synonymous with support for public education itself, which in turn was synonymous with patriotism and support of the Union. They suggested that those that disagreed with them, especially their Roman Catholic opponents, were of doubtful loyalty to the United States. In public commentary, these self-ordained super-champions of public education recalled the Roman Catholic lackluster commitment to the Union during the Civil War.

Even more frequently, they noted that Roman Catholics owed their ultimate allegiance not to the United States of America, but to a "foreign prince." Public school advocates charged that support of their movement was the best litmus-paper test of true American nationalism. In the South, Ku Klux Klan terrorists were then burning public schools. Accordingly, these midnight criminals demonstrated their disloyalty to American nationalism. In the North, Roman Catholics sought to remove the Bible from the public schools. Therefore, these dissenters also revealed their contempt for the nation. News from Germany, where Bismarck was fighting to free public education from the influences of an antinational Roman Catholic church, gave many of these concerned Americans a sense that there was indeed an international Jesuit conspiracy against everything that they held dear. Religious feelings, as well as racial attitudes, were heightened in the 1870s. The powerful emotions of religion and patriotism mixed in the cauldron of Reconstruction politics around the symbol of the public school.[25]

Visions of a Perfected Union

In the 1870s, promoting one national culture flourished as never before or since, with the possible exception of the World War I era. Nation worship in the 1870s even surpassed patriotic feelings that had been called forth during the Civil War. American nationalism during the Civil War had been tempered by a heightened sense of the worth of the individual human being, a result of the antislavery crusade. During the 1870s, individual liberty retreated as the primary American value. Instead, cultural conformity was pushed to center stage. The Republican Party adopted the public school as a nationalist homogenizing symbol. Unlike the Radical Republicanism of the early years of Reconstruction, this new nationalism derived its wellspring from both conservative evangelical Protestantism and Hegelianism from Bismarck's Germany. Its distinctive American roots were Hamiltonianism and Puritanism. As racism served to temper public enthusiasm for Reconstruction, the religious reaction sparked by the Cincinnati Bible War kept alive Republican hopes for continuing the party's nationalistic program.[26]

As evangelical Protestants saw an international Jesuit conspiracy seeking to undermine America in a focused attack on the public school, the Roman Catholic leadership in the United States succumbed to its own form of paranoia. When Henry Wilson's article promoting the public school as an instrument of national reconstruction was published in the January 1871 issue of the *Atlantic Monthly*, Catholic intellectual

Orestes Brownson wrote a revealing letter to Father Isaac Hecker blasting Wilson as a "tool of the fanatics." Brownson saw Wilson's idea as a first step in an evangelical plot toward outlawing the Roman Catholic church by federal law. "The plan of proceeding," Brownson wrote, "is to absorb all legislation touching the rights of persons and conscience in Congress, to make education national and compulsory and it is hoped by the aid of female suffrage, an essential part of the plan to succeed."[27] Brownson's worries, while extreme, were not wholly unwarranted. As he feared, the Republican program was then develop-ing strong tendencies toward a national majoritarianism that directly challenged the Roman Catholic church. As in Germany in the United States the church was entering a period of protracted siege by an emerging transatlantic nationalist political culture that glorified material power over any and all rival considerations.

Traditionally, Americans had prided themselves on their political individualism and their revolutionary antipathy to tyrannical central governmental power. Traditionally, the Roman Catholic church had often aligned itself with tyrannical central governmental power. But as Republican public-school advocates began idealizing the notion of using central governmental power to educate, remodel, and uplift American culture, the Roman Catholic press moved to fill the ideological positions apparently being abandoned by their opponents. The Catholic church sought to portray itself as the last best hope for preserving Lockean freedom and individualism against the centralizing evangelical Republicans. In an unsigned article most probably written by Orestes Brownson, *The Catholic World* portrayed Catholicism as a force for maintaining traditional Lockean rights of individual con-science. The essay identified a Republican-inspired tyranny of the majority as violating the theory undergirding the American Declaration of Independence. In Germany, the article continued, Otto von Bismarck was then seeking to crush individual liberty. In the United States, the Republican Party pursued a faddish but dangerous Bismarckianism. The essay defined Bismarckianism as "the pagan principle of the state, that all rights, even the rights of the church, and society emanate from the state, and are revocable at its will." The article warned America not to succumb to this siren call of modernism and nationalism, but instead continue to rely on the supremacy of individual conscience. In turn, it hoped that this free individual conscience would defer to the teachings of the Roman Catholic church.[28]

Some supporters of Bible reading in the public school argued that there was a historic national religious consciousness. Evangelical Protes-tantism, this logic proposed, had deep roots in American civic life that revealed a collective will. For example, Bibles were in every court of law and were used in ceremonies pertaining to assuming public office. The chaplaincy in both the armed forces and the national Congress witnessed to a historic connection of church and state. Open references to God abounded in American state constitutions. Protestantism, they claimed, had long defined the national identity. Protestantism, their argument went, did not need secular government; but the secular government needed Protestantism to feed the collective national spirit. "The most intimate union of the state with the saving and conservative forces of Christianity," proclaimed one proponent of this view, "is one of the oldest customs of the country, and has always ranked as a vital article of our political faith." These Americans regarded the Bible as "our national book" and opposed its imagined Jesuitical enemies.[29]

Evidence of this civil-religious consciousness could be seen in Massachusetts' centuries-old tradition of providing an annual spiritual state-of-the-state address. Once a year, a noted Protestant divine delivered a sermon to a joint meeting of the state governor and both houses of the state legislature. The origins of this practice lay in the earliest years of Massachusetts Bay Colony. In the 1870s, it still continued. As the intellectual elite of Massachusetts then regarded itself as instrumental in shaping the new national culture being forged in Reconstruction, the civil-religious practices then celebrated in that state are most relevant to discerning the new national order that Republicans actively fostered. In 1870, Rev. Julius H. Seelye, a professor at Amherst College, was given the honor of delivering this prestigious annual spiritual message. His remarks were inspired by the emotion raised by the Cincinnati Bible War and focused on the government's need of religion. Without religion, he said, the government lacked the authority required to secure social order; without religion, government lacked legitimacy. Without a government strengthened by true religion, he warned, the community would degenerate into a savagery founded alone on individual self-interest. He mocked those who saw removing the Bible from Cincinnati's public schools as separating church from state. Any thoroughgoing attempt to separate church and state, he proclaimed, "would be like trying to separate the heart from the body."[30]

Other participants in this annual Massachusetts civil-religious sermon in the 1870s addressed the same theme. All were highly supportive of connections linking church and state. In the 1874 message, Rev. Richard Gleason Greene emphasized that every government is characterized by a de facto state religion. In the United States of America, he said, that religion was Christianity. Throughout the Union, laws against "blaspheming the name of God and His son Jesus Christ" threatened to send transgressors to prison. But, he noted, no such laws had been enacted "against profaning the names of Jupiter, Vishnu, [or] Buddha." With the Catholic-inspired movement to remove the Bible from the public schools, he warned, the nation was at a crossroads. Would it retain Christianity [i.e., Protestantism] as the de facto state religion, or would it come to worship another god? If Christianity were rejected, he predicted, another religion would soon take its place. He himself saw materialism and atheism waiting in the wings in hopes of informing a new national faith suited for the Gilded Age. "The great governmental problem with man," he proclaimed, "never has been and never will be—religion or not?—but always—what religion? This, then," he emphasized, "is the form of the question now before the American people." "Government cannot exist in organic perpetuity," he concluded, "without some civil administration of some religion." Rev. Greene advised that citizens not holding a Protestant view be tolerated, but he urged that they not be allowed to destroy the traditional American civil religion. Nothing required them to stay in America if they did not like the religious customs of the people. If they could not abide what they found here, he suggested, they should move to a more congenial country.[31]

The political psychology of "love it or leave it" was most pro-nounced during the 1870s and was directed especially at Roman Catholics. Very few evangelicals supported teachers forcing non-believing students to partake in the daily religious exercises traditional in the American public school. To that degree, they respected individual rights. But they overwhelmingly agreed that a minority of dissenters should not be able to deny to the majority practices that the latter wished to retain. One Protestant minister referred to an opponent of keeping the Bible in the schools as "a conscience that takes everything and gives nothing." Many believed that those not able to tolerate majority preferences "had better leave the country, or, still better, never enter it." Roman Catholics, they thought, had been treated well in America. They were provided a free education by the Protestant majority who paid the overwhelming majority of the taxes raised to support the common schools. Evangelicals claimed that despite the fact that little Catholic money went to fund the public schools, Catholics demanded that these same schools be transformed to meet their complaints. Anti-Catholics held that Catholic energies could be better spent on attending the public schools and catching the spirit of American enterprise. Then, they reasoned, Catholics would begin to rise from their degrading poverty and begin to do what their fathers could not do—pay taxes to support public education.[32]

With all the talk that opponents of Bible reading in the public schools should leave the country, Max Lilienthal felt uncomfortable. As Cincinnati's leading rabbi, he had not taken the lead against the Bible in the public schools; but he had backed the school board decision once it was made. Catholics and "Free Thinkers" had been far more vociferous than Jews on the issue. As historic pariahs in western civilization, many nineteenth-century Jews in both Europe and America desperately wanted to be accepted by their country of residence. They often stretched to accommodate their growing assimilationist yearnings. The Dreyfus Affair in France at the end of the century would challenge this compromising mentality, but in the 1870s American Jews were primarily characterized by a desire to be respected as Americans first and foremost. Indeed, Lilienthal flatly said that he regarded himself as an American first and a Jew second. With religious bigotry rising, he felt a tug in opposite directions. On the one hand, he understood the Catholic complaint of Protestant practices dominating the American public school. On the other, he wanted a good reputation with his more numerous Protestant countrymen. To gain the latter, he openly expressed his dislike of Archbishop Purcell's attitude against compromise and what he saw as the unreasoning opposition of the Roman Catholic church to public education. Likewise, he swore his unconditional loyalty to the nation over any rival authority. In Germany, Jews also generally accommodated Bismarck's *Kulturkampf*, or culture struggle against the Roman Catholic church.[33]

By contrast, some evangelicals were unwilling to exalt a love of nation that was so much a part of the spirit of the times. While a leading anti-Catholic, Professor Tayler Lewis differentiated himself from Bismarck's super-nationalist battle with the Catholic church. Lewis and those Protestants sharing his views were unwilling to pledge their loyalty to the nation over any rival authority. They wanted the nation's leaders to recognize openly and publicly the national reliance on the Christian God. During the Civil War, Lewis wrote, many Christian backsliders had temporarily realized their dependency on the Almighty. "In the dark days of Chancellorsville and Chickamauga," he emphasized, "no one dared to whisper the impious dogma that the nation as such knows no God, no religion." He pointed to Lincoln's constant reference to right and wrong as eternal principles and the martyred president's open acknowledgment of God's direction of history in his second inaugural address. "How," Professor Lewis raged, "can there be a national conscience if there is no national religion, no 'higher law,' no connection between national acts and an acknowledged divine rule of eternal righteousness?" Lewis wanted a frank acknowledgment of the state's dependence on Christianity for its very existence.[34] Ironically, on an abstract ideological level, Lewis's view was identical with the Roman Catholic position that held that true religion should guide the state. The American anti-Catholic movement of the 1870s included adherents that placed church above state and others that placed state above church. But they were all united in their opposition to what Protestants popularly regarded as an international Jesuitical conspiracy.

Elisha Mulford, a thirty-seven-year-old Episcopal clergyman from Pennsylvania, attempted to harmonize the German and American perspectives on building a powerful, homogeneous nation. He was uniquely qualified for the task, as he had studied in Germany where he had imbibed Hegelian state worship. At the same time, his Protestant clerical credentials kept him rooted to the American variant of the anti-Catholic struggle. His thesis began with the typically American notion of the United States as "the work of God in history," "the perfected nation," and "the goal of history." This meshed perfectly with the Hegelian glorification of the state as the ethical ideal. The decay of nations, he noted, occurred not because of depletion of national resources, but rather due to "the dissolution of the moral order," which could only result in "the most awful crime and corruption of a people." For this Episcopalian Hegelian, the salvation of the nation, as of the individual, was to embrace Christianity, an act that would enable the nation to reach its final "destination." In his view, the Catholic church had corrupted Christianity. Protestantism alone could bring about the process of national perfection that constituted the centerpiece of Hegel's philosophy of history. Then Mulford turned to a concept that was foreign to American traditions but was nonetheless an integral part of the anti-Catholic movement of the 1870s. The perfected nation, he wrote, was "a moral organism." In his opinion, the collective life of the nation dwarfed any Lockean conception of individual rights. Wrong individual choices and the permissive libertinism of the Gilded Age, in his opinion, were threatening the progression of the United States toward national perfection. More centralized control was needed to restore the American march toward perfectibility. In this perspective, maintaining the Bible in the public school was only one small facet of a much larger drama.[35]

Today, this ideology cannot be found in modern mainstream publications. Modern politicians, even those who argue that American culture should celebrate pluralism less and unity more, are not informed by a Hegelian philosophy glorifying a tightly united culture and a powerful nation-state as its desired fruit. That style was more or less disgraced within western civilization by the later terrible witness of super-nationalist fascism. But its germs were present in Reconstruction, as they were in Bismarckian Germany. The sermons, speeches and writings of leading divines, philosophers and pundits strongly supported a cultural emphasis away from the decentralized polity that had characterized the United States up to that point. And these clerics invariably did not identify the future of American progressive thought with the Democratic party. Rather, the Republican party, the party of Reconstruction and the party of national progress, was the instrument of their desire.

Rev. Rufus W. Clark, pastor of the First Reformed Church of Albany, New York, urged that no concessions be given to Roman Catholics attempting to remove the Bible from the public schools. Just as Lincoln had refused to compromise over the issue of secession during the interregnum period of 1860–1861, Republicans in the seventies needed (in his view) to stand fast on the Cincinnati Bible War. "For one," he declared, "I think we had better wait until they take it [the Bible] from us, rather than stand trembling, and give it to them, while in population we are thirty-three millions to their six or seven millions." While not advocating the creation of any new official linkages between church and state, he ardently defended all existing connections between the two, especially regarding the presence of the Bible in the public schools. Public education unassisted by the Bible, he warned, would ultimately produce a national disaster. In his opinion, generations taught without the Bible in the public schools would "infer that if it is expedient and safe to have a school without a God, it is equally expedient and safe to have the family and society without a God."[36]

Roman Catholicism represented a convenient conspiratorial specter for those Republicans concerned with the vast social changes then undermining traditional American mores. The centrifugal forces of industrialization were threatening to tear apart the traditional spiritual fabric of the nation. Before the Civil War, the slave power had been used by Republican Party rhetoricians to explain all that was perceived to be wrong in the industrializing American Eden. With that demonic force defeated, the papal power (highlighted by the Roman Catholic proclamation of papal infallibility in 1870) provided the Republican Party with a new wellspring of identifiable trouble. Before the war, the American (Know-Nothing) Party had planted political seeds that came to full flower in the 1870s. Many Northern Know-Nothings had become Republicans after the collapse of the American Party in the 1850s. During Reconstruction, their old fears enjoyed a new respectability and merged with the mainstream Republican agenda to produce a homogeneous society under the direction of a strengthening federal government. Inspired by Bismarck's model in Germany, they dreamed of creating a new American nation.

Rev. Julius H. Seelye, already reviewed as an official religious pundit to Massachusetts' state government in 1870, was an intellectual molder of the theological underpinnings of this envisioned new order. As a philosophy professor at Amherst College, he promoted an argument partially reminiscent of John C. Calhoun's political theory. Calhoun had defended slavery by emphasizing that society is a natural entity and not a creation of rational human choice or social compact. He had portrayed slavery as a natural outgrowth of the inequality of man and not representing any violation of presumed inalienable human rights. Calhoun's reasoning had led him to reject John Locke and the philosophy underlying the American Declaration of Independence. That fact has made Calhoun somewhat of an oddity among American political theorists, yet Professor Seelye was no less an exception to the mainstream of American political thought. He too rejected the Lockian

FIGURE 2.1
"The American River Ganges." This famous Thomas Nast cartoon exemplified the Republican tendency in the 1870s to replace the defunct slave-power conspiracy with a papal conspiracy threatening to undermine American public education.

Harper's Weekly, September 30, 1871.

notion of the social compact as an agreement among individuals to preserve individual inalienable rights while promoting greater efficiency in political organization. "The state," proclaimed Seelye, "is not the result of any agreement or compact among individuals, as though it. would not exist were the compact wanting." Similar to Calhoun, he argued that the Lockian notion of a state of nature in which no government existed was ahistorical and ridiculous on its face. Having proved to his own satisfaction that the concept of inalienable individual rights was grounded on faulty logic, Seelye then proceeded to identify the numerical majority as the only legitimate sovereign in any polity. Unlike Calhoun, he identified the Union as the ultimate American political unit. But that was his only major divergence from the great South Carolinian and the other organic political theorists of the antebellum South. In Seelye's view, "true religion" provided the necessary guidance to the sovereign majority. Thus informed, the polity could never allow misguided individual conscience to interfere with the public good. And, as Bible reading in the view of the sovereign majority was necessary for the maintenance of good social order, it was beyond legitimate criticism from any minority dissidents.[37]

Lockean thought had encouraged Reconstruction's early insistence on racial political fairness, but the latter was not necessarily dependent on the former. The nationalist notions of Professor Seelye could also support egalitarian reforms. Indeed, Seelye's primary purpose was to defend the traditional American public school, which had historically proven itself to be a driving force of egalitarian uniformity. Seelye's thought directly contradicted the concept of inalienable individual rights, but that Lockean concept was not immediately essential for reconstructing one nation, guided by one cultural standard and controlled by one party. As the years of Reconstruction progressed, a vision of cultural homogeneity, not of individual freedom, increasingly shaped the Republican program.

As early as the 1830s, Alexis de Tocqueville had warned of a majoritarian tyranny arising within American culture. The famous French commentator on American mores had noticed that an American majority potentially could become more powerful than any European monarch, because it could claim a far greater moral authority. American majoritarianism, he warned, carried within itself a potential spirit of conformity to repress all controversy. Bismarck might try to achieve something similar in Europe, but Tocqueville had predicted the likelihood of this outcome occurring first and most thoroughly on American shores. The Frenchman had mourned the increasing passing of variety and diversity in human thoughts and opinions within western civilization. He foresaw the emergence of a new American mass culture that presaged Europe's own future.[38] During the 1870s, anti-Catholic nationalists on both sides of the Atlantic sought to give this prophecy specific content and form.

Republican promoters of a dominant Protestant nationalism hoped that the overwhelmingly Protestant South might open its collective heart to the spirit of this emerging transatlantic national fervor. Yet Southerners generally remained aloof from the Northern anti-Catholic revival emanating from the Cincinnati Bible War. To Southerners, the essence of the Republican program was racial political equality. Northern Catholic Democrats were their political allies in obstructing a national Republican majority. Instead of being tempted by the new religious Republican nationalist argument, the South continued to rely on state's rights. Nevertheless, Southern Protestants found their own unique ways of combating Roman Catholicism. The Southern Baptists verbally attacked the Roman church as "a mummy," a "dead thing . . . bedecked with pagan tinsel." Nonetheless, they did nothing to fight the papist enemy in the Northern states, where it was rapidly growing in power. Instead, they engaged in a somewhat ludicrous missionary effort to convert the city of Rome itself to the Southern Baptist faith. "In a life and death encounter, the policy of the warrior is not to strike at the members, but at the head and the heart," proclaimed Alabama's Rev. Edwin T. Winkler before a Southern Baptist convention. In this struggle, one Southern Baptist missionary was dispatched to Rome to convert the citizenry there.[39]

In contrast to Southern whites, African Americans eagerly joined the anti-Catholic crusade. Their motives were complex. First, they were by and large Protestants. Second, they had not forgotten the Catholic church's pro-Confederate tendencies during the Civil War. Third, they believed that Roman Catholic hostility toward public education could only hurt them, a people desperately in need of government-funded educational opportunity. Immediately after the war, the Catholic church had made a concerted effort to convert the freedmen, but lack of success led it to back off. Explaining this change, one Protestant commentator wrote: "The colored people at the South just now want what Rome does not love to give—education. They want schools and teachers, and not priests and the baby-shows of the altar."

The African-American vote in Cincinnati worked as a block to punish Catholic school board members who had voted to ban the Bible from the public schools. In the eyes of white Republicans, new black voters were seen as partially offsetting new Irish Catholic voters that invariably backed the Democratic Party. Rev. William Aikman, a

Protestant cleric, viewed African Americans as "the bulwark of this American people against the rush of Romanism toward political power." In his view, assisting black civil rights furthered the more important Protestant cause against a growing Catholic international conspiracy. "In helping them," he wrote, "we do a work for the church in all the land." Some racially prejudiced Northern Protestant Republicans muted their antiblack attitudes because of their greater, more immediate fears of a Roman Catholic political takeover in the North. Similarly, religiously prejudiced Southern Protestant Democrats restricted their religious bigotry because of their more pressing fears of black political dominance. In short, Reconstruction politics gravitated between rival antipathies—racial and religious.[40]

Some anti-Catholic extremists advocated amending the United States Constitution to empower the federal government to maintain the traditional Protestant hegemony. William Strong, who President Grant appointed to the Supreme Court in 1870, led the movement to amend the Constitution to strengthen the Protestant position. His father had been a Congregational minister, and he himself was a Presbyterian elder. Stridently anti-Catholic, Strong fervently opposed the removal of the Bible from the public schools and all other efforts to remove references to God from civic life. His movement had first arisen during the Civil War, almost as a desperate effort to gain divine favor when the nation was threatened with extinction. At that time, the national plight was reminiscent of the trials of Israel and Judah in ancient times before the hosts of Assyria and Babylon. Hopeful of avoiding the fate of these vanished Hebrew nations, the National Association for the Amendment of the Constitution had been formed in 1864, later to be renamed the National Reform Association. Strong was a leader in the movement from the start and was elected the association's president in 1867. The movement languished at the end of the decade but suddenly revived with the Cincinnati Bible War. Strong's membership on the nation's highest court did not dampen his zealotry in this cause. If anything, it lent a greater aura of respectability to the movement. The symbolism of Strong's appointment by a Republican president at the height of the Cincinnati Bible War was not lost on a religiously sensitive nation.[41]

Strong hoped to amend the Constitution's Preamble so as to acknowledge "Almighty God as the source of all authority and power in civil government" and "the Lord Jesus Christ as the ruler of all nations and his revealed will as the supreme law of the land, in order to constitute a Christian government, in order to form a more perfect Union." He also wanted to strengthen the powers of Congress to suppress all non-Christian religions and to modify the First Amendment so as to tolerate only variants of Christianity. The suggested amendments were advanced to empower a Protestant majority to interpret them as it chose. Everyone at the time, including Protestants and Catholics, understood the anti-Catholic intent of this movement. The societal propensity to amend the Constitution during Reconstruction encouraged Strong and his followers, who included a United States Senator, two state governors, three federal judges and numerous state and territorial supreme court justices, three state school superintendents, eleven Methodist and Episcopal bishops and twenty-five college and university presidents. Strong's organization held regular national conventions and published its own journal during the early 1870s. Nonetheless, Strong's proposals were too extreme to receive serious consideration by Congress. In 1876, a weaker proposed amendment designed to preserve the Protestant status quo against Catholic inroads won unanimous Republican support in the United States Senate. It too would fail. Indeed, it would serve as a last Republican effort to revive the then-dying embers of Reconstruction and the centralized religious nationalism that Reconstruction required to endure. Until the end, Justice Strong's movement to amend the Constitution gave witness to the religious roots of the Republican impulse to reconstruct a fractured, regionalized nation.[42]

Strong's movement did not typify the anti-Catholic upsurge of the 1870s. Even a majority of those Americans holding anti-Catholic views viewed it as too extreme. Nevertheless, even persons opposed to Strong's specific suggestions sympathized to a degree with his cause. Liberal Protestant leaders such as Henry Ward Beecher never confessed to such feelings, but his sister did. And the attitudes of Harriet Beecher Stowe were more typical in this regard than those of her brother. Typically, her novels were permeated by the Protestant religiosity in which she had been raised. In *My Wife and I; Or, Harry Henderson's History*, a novel first published in the early 1870s, she bewailed the increasingly secular drift in public education and American life in general: "The Brahmins educate their sons so that they shall infallibly become Brahmins," she wrote; "the Jews so that they shall infallibly be Jews; the Mohammedans so that they shall be Mohammedans, but the Christians educate their sons so that nearly half of them turn out unbelievers—professors of no religion at all."[43] Justice Strong had intended to halt this educational drift and ensure that Protestant Americans educate their sons and daughters so that they would infallibly become Protestants. And many Republicans wished him well even though they stopped short of supporting his specific proposals. They sensed that something was terribly wrong with the drift of

American society and were glad that fanatics such as Strong were at least forcing a discussion of the problem.

In 1873, Joseph P. Thompson published his *Church and State in the United States*. Designed for both American and German audiences, it serves as a veritable window into an ideology increasingly informing Reconstruction. Thompson consciously distinguished what he perceived to be his own moderate position from that of fanatics such as Strong. In his own terms, Thompson sought to strike a balance between what he called the "centralizing" and "disintegrating" forces inherent in the American political tradition. In his opinion, the Fourteenth Amendment provided a means to achieve an ideal balance. Under the second section of that constitutional amendment, he saw each state as empowered to disfranchise its Catholic voters, with the only penalty being a proportional reduction in that state's representation in both the House of Representatives and the Electoral College. In this way, he wrote, the amendment enabled states rights, or the primary "disintegrating" force in American political life, to serve the noble national purpose of maintaining Protestant cultural hegemony. Thompson worried that loss of political representation might deter states from selecting this available constitutional mechanism to curb growing Catholic political power. And so he suggested an alternate course that could achieve the same objective without the unwanted penalty. The Constitution, he said, empowered Congress and the states to bar Catholics from holding office. Thompson's constitutional logic justifying this course was tortured. He argued that as Catholics owe their primary allegiance to a foreign prince, they could not honestly swear to uphold the Constitution of the United States, something constitutionally required of all office holders under Article VI, paragraph 3. Hence, in his opinion, they could be barred from holding office. Apparently Thompson saw no problem with a rather specific caveat closing that same constitutional paragraph: "No religious test shall ever be required as a qualification to any office or public trust under the United States." In Thompson's mind, his suggestion did not involve any religious test but rather an issue of fundamental loyalty to the nation state. "The United States," he wrote, "cannot permit a double sovereignty upon its soil." He refused to allow Roman Catholics to hide behind the constitutional shield of religious liberty. In language inspired by the German *Kulturkampf*, Thompson wrote: "Government, no less than religion, is from God. Conscience shall not harbor conspiracy; religion shall not foster revolution."[44]

Thompson was embarrassed by his own country's apparent inability to deal with the supposed mounting Catholic conspiracy. He confessed that he knew that Germans popularly regarded the United States as politically disorganized and incapable of dealing with the conspiratorial Ultramontane threat. Indeed, this perception had motivated him to write his book describing the various constitutional tools that he thought could be used to enable the *Kulturkampf* to succeed on American shores. The true problem, he said, was not lack of American constitutional authorization to wage a meaningful anti-Catholic campaign. The problem was that too many Americans lacked the will to act and were too preoccupied with their own selfish business affairs. But, he noted, this traditional American habit of inattentiveness to national needs had been overcome before. The nation had eventually awakened to the slave power conspiracy. American patriots confronted and defeated this threat to the national existence. "Thus slavery was demolished," he wrote, "and thus, too, will political Romanism be trampled out."[45]

Justice Strong's crusade to amend the Constitution, as well as the writing of Thompson's book, had occurred in the context of the Cincinnati Bible War. In 1873, with the ruling by the Ohio Supreme Court on the Cincinnati Superior Court injunction, that struggle finally came to an end. The Ohio Supreme Court overturned the Superior Court decision. Ironically, a five-man Republican court decided in favor of the Cincinnati School Board. The Republican judges in this case virtually had no choice to decide otherwise. At the time of the Superior Court decision, it was expected that the Ohio state legislature would enact specific laws fleshing out the state constitution's vague statements in favor of religion. In 1870, John Eaton, Jr., had confidently reported that soon the Ohio legislature would bar local school boards from discontinuing Bible reading in the public schools. Three years later, thanks to Democratic Party vigilance in Ohio, nothing had happened. In the absence of that kind of legislation, the Ohio Supreme Court determined that the legitimate legislative authority in this matter rested with the local school board.[46]

The Cincinnati School Board case was not decided on a matter of individual right. The opinion of the court did not involve a question of Lockean religious liberty. Typically for that time, the concept of majority rule governed the matter. In the absence of a statement of majority preference by the Ohio legislature, the majority will of the Cincinnati School Board determined the issue. In upholding majoritarianism as the highest political and judicial value, the Ohio court did not offend the guiding spirit of the age, no matter how the decision may have seemed on the surface.[47] In this way, the Cincinnati Bible War ended abruptly and without dramatic flourish.

Brought to life by the Cincinnati controversy, the national religious culture struggle found a new nesting place even before the Ohio matter was finally decided. A new issue, one with greater prospects of political success, attracted the disparate opponents of Roman Catholicism. Roman Catholics were demanding public money to fund their parochial schools. Virtually all Republicans were united in opposing any division of the school funds to allow Catholic schools to be conducted at public expense. Republicans had openly differed over the best course to follow in the Cincinnati Bible case. While most had opposed removing the Bible from the public schools, others were willing to concede the issue in order to bring peace to the public schools. A small vocal minority of Republicans even backed the Cincinnati School Board on the grounds of religious liberty. By contrast, the new issue regarding Catholic access to the school fund worked to unite Republicans. As such, it was a far better vehicle for anti-Catholic nationalism than the Cincinnati Bible case. The defeat in that controversy was largely disregarded as Republican anti-Catholicism coalesced around a more promising issue.

In the early 1870s, the anti-Catholic political movement was carried on primarily at local levels. It was there that debates over the presence of the Bible in local public schools and control of school funds obviously predominated. A few advocates, such as Justice Strong, proposed federal constitutional amendments, but the struggle remained localized. Slowly, however, the issue began to percolate up into national forums. By 1875, it finally emerged to dominate the Republican party's nationalizing agenda, involving President Grant and several leading Republican aspirants to succeed him.

Living in times when anti-Catholicism is far less apparent in American life, we are easily tempted to overlook the anti-Catholic movement that arose with the Cincinnati Bible War. With modern racial tensions at fever pitch, we easily focus on the 1870s' movement for racial justice, which certainly was then the centerpiece of Reconstruction. By emphasizing religious affairs, this account does not seek to diminish the meaningful struggle for civil rights that occurred then. What it does attempt to achieve is a memory of other events that contributed to the political culture of Reconstruction. Given the obvious decentralizing force of white racism that then existed both North and South, it is easy to understand why most modern historians have come to view the supposed centralizing impetus of Reconstruction as weak, especially after the ratification in 1870 of the last of the racially oriented Reconstruction amendments to the Constitution. Nonetheless, a centrifugal ideological force toward a unified culture then did exist. And it was especially strong among the Northern evangelical Protestants that made up the bulk of Reconstruction Republicans. This phenomenon can be seen most readily in the anti-Catholic crusade that began with the Cincinnati Bible War and continued with local battles over dividing the school funds.

3

Dividing the School Funds

William Marcy Tweed, the most notorious political boss in nineteenth-century America, inaugurated the 1870s' struggle over the school funds. From his power base in New York City's Tammany Hall, Boss Tweed controlled the state's Democratic Party as the 1870s began. Irish Catholic immigrant votes provided the core of his constituency, making Tweed most sensitive to Roman Catholic desires regarding educational matters. In 1869, the New York legislature enacted a bill introduced by Tweed himself to grant state funding to private schools of two hundred students or more. The measure promised to relieve the Roman Catholic church of part of the burden of maintaining its own school system throughout the state. Few Protestant or Jewish sectarian schools enrolled two hundred or more students, so the bill's purpose was transparent. Reportedly, one influential Catholic politico exulted after the passage of the act: "This is the little finger, and we must persevere 'til we get the whole hand."[1]

The idea of the state underwriting formerly impoverished Roman Catholic schools thoroughly outraged New York's Protestant Republican taxpayers. The Catholic schools were reportedly staffed by European-born priests, "educated in the principles of French or Italian despotism." In the language of public-school advocates, these teachers imparted to their students "the coarsest superstitions of the Middle Ages." Republicans charged that Tweed's school legislation constituted "a direct attack upon the essential theory of our public school system." In the act's first year of operation, New York's sectarian schools (the overwhelming majority of them Roman Catholic) received $200,000. New York's Republicans mobilized to end this practice.[2]

In the battle over Bible reading in the public schools, a minority of Republicans had broken ranks, arguing that they wished to deny Roman Catholics their only legitimate reason for opposing public education. In contrast, Republicans united in opposing the long-standing desire of the Catholic church to tap state school moneys. Ironically, this shift in focus subtly encouraged the slow drift of traditional Bible-based moral education out of the public-school curriculum. While most Republicans openly acknowledged that the decline in moral education would eventually result in "national suicide," their fear of a divided Protestant majority weakened their resolve on that front. Their highest priority was keeping liberal and conservative Protestants together in an effective anti-Catholic political movement. "At the beginning of our late war," wrote one Republican, "the greatest fear we had was a divided North. With a united North we were sure to conquer. In the conflict that is now opening, our greatest source of fear is a divided Protestant community." Maintaining the all-important Republican majority was the highest value, and religious unity served this end better than division.[3] The Republican public-education program centered its attention on the school-fund issue.

In 1872, Illinois and Iowa Republicans amended their state constitutions to prevent any state aid to sectarian institutions. A similar proposal was offered in New York's state senate, but it failed despite united Republican support. Every Democrat voted against it. In the 1870s American political parties north of the Mason-Dixon line were closely identified with religious affinities. Republicans accused the Northern Democratic Party, a majority of whose constituents were Protestants, of "pandering to a foreign church as it formerly crouched before domestic slavery."[4] Republican association with the anti-Catholicism popular with virtually all Protestant sects of that time was clear and obvious. With the subdued resolution of the Cincinnati Bible War, Republican attentions noisily focused on the supposed Roman Catholic takeover of New York. Republicans warned that this insidious Jesuit conspiracy would soon expand elsewhere unless actively confronted by a united Protestant community. Between 1869 and 1873, Republican propagandists pointed out, $1,395,388.51 in New York state funds went to Roman Catholic schools, orphanages, and hospitals. By contrast, only $56,956.74 and $25,851.56 went to Episcopalian and Jewish institutions, which came in second and third respectively among sectarian charities receiving state funds. No less than J. Pierpont Morgan, already on his way to becoming America's most famous financier, joined the crusade of alerting the public to these figures. His name was on the executive committee of the New York City Council of Political Reform, the primary local organization seeking to end the practice of state and local aid to religious institutions, especially schools.[5]

As the Tweed Ring came under attack and Tweed himself was tried and imprisoned for his many documentable crimes, the practice of overtly subsidizing Roman Catholic schools in New York ended. Nevertheless, the contest between Republicans and the Catholic church continued in educational affairs. In 1873, one New York state senator proposed a compulsory education law that would send vagrant children to either Protestant or Catholic "protectoraries" in order to receive a moral and academic education. (The bill did not indicate how Jewish vagrant children would be processed.) The measure proposed that the state give children religious identities that the children themselves might not necessarily recognize. It was defeated, but was cited by Republicans as evidence of the general Roman Catholic effort to take control of part of the state's public education funds. The Gray Nuns Act, passed by the New York Legislature in 1871, served as more evidence. The Gray Nuns were a Roman Catholic teaching order. The act, which was strengthened by the New York legislature in 1875, allowed these nuns to teach in the New York public schools without taking any of the certification tests normally required of public-school

FIGURE 3.1

"The Public School Question:
What Sectarian Appropriations of the School Fund Is Doing and What It May Lead To." These two cartoons portrayed the division of the school fund as leading to diverse and undesirable public schools.

Harper's Weekly, August 30, 1873.

teachers. Republicans loudly proclaimed that the Gray Nuns Act was only a surreptitious ploy to allow Roman Catholics to take over public education in school districts with Catholic minorities. As the decade wore on, the Republican press increasingly encouraged vigilance against Gray Nuns inundating New York's public schools.[6]

For its part, the Roman Catholic church kept up a steady barrage against public education throughout the 1870s. Church officials questioned the salvation of parishioners who allowed their children to attend public schools. One extreme faction at a St. Louis Catholic convention in 1873 denounced the public schools as "curses to the country, floodgates of atheism and sensuality, and of civil, social and national corruption." One Catholic layman named Zachary Montgomery made agitation against public education his own personal crusade. Publishing his tracts in the San Francisco Bay Area, he blasted public education as "a poisonous fountain, fraught with the seeds of human misery and death." Through public education, he warned, the state attempted to control the consciences of its citizens. Rather than seeing American public education as representing a societal tendency to separate church and state, he portrayed it as an invasion of the secular state into the religious lives of the citizenry.[7]

A national economic depression which began in 1873 served to stiffen the long-standing Catholic resolve to destroy traditional American public education. Before the economic downturn, enrollments in Catholic schools had steadily grown with immigration into the country. But hard times reversed the trend in parochial-school enrollments. As overall population figures continued to increase, Catholic enrollments began to decline. Catholic parents could no longer afford even the small sums required to send their children to Catholic schools. Increasingly, their choice was either one of no education for their children or the public schools.[8] In this souring economic environment, church propagandists became ever more strident against the public schools. It was unjust, they charged, to tax Catholics for the support of public schools to which in good conscience they could not send their children. Traditionally, in Europe and Canada, school funds had been divided between Catholic and Protestant institutions. Why, in the name of justice, Catholic officials asked, could not a similar arrangement be made in American states? Local concessions to Roman Catholics concerning Bible reading in the public schools did not stop their complaints about being barred from the school funds. If the Bible was read in the public schools, Catholic writers blasted them as "Protestant publics." If it was not, they described them as "Godless schools." By their lights, only a division of the school fund along religious lines could end the controversy.

Despite church opposition, Catholic parents sent their children to the public schools. Before these errant parents, Bishop Richard Gilmour of Cleveland waved the possibilities of excommunication and eternal damnation. "We authorize confessors to refuse the sacraments to such parents as thus despise the laws of the church and disobey the commands of both priest and bishop," Gilmour's pastoral letter of 1873 announced.[9]

While simple economics served to exacerbate the Catholic problem, more was at work driving matters toward religious warfare. In Europe and America, a cultural struggle deepened over fundamental loyalties. In Europe and America, citizens were increasingly forced to confess their ultimate allegiance to either church or state, Christ or Caesar. Neither side in this struggle was in a compromising mood. The forces of rising nationalism, industrial progress and material power were arraigned on one side, the traditional authority of the Roman Catholic church on the other. Whatever their complaints against the secular and materialist tendencies of the age, Protestants tended to support them nonetheless. "Progress" was the only choice imaginable for them in a contest with ignorant, backward medieval retrogression. For its part, Catholic officialdom viewed these struggles over the education of Catholic children as the foretold time of tribulations when the faithful would be tempted by evil subtly masquerading as improvement.

One might think that the Constitution's First Amendment, applied to the states through the Fourteenth Amendment, could quickly have ended this controversy. By 1870, both amendments were already part of the Constitution, but the modern interpretation of them was not then developed. The overwhelming majority of Americans then believed that the Constitution only prevented the federal government from supporting a religious establishment. State and local governments were then free to do whatever they wished on this score. They could support Protestant practices in the public schools. They could fund Catholic schools, or they could demand that public education be completely secular. In short, in the 1870s this issue was not framed as one involving constitutionally protected individual religious rights. Rev. Samuel T. Spear, a liberal Protestant who had broken ranks in supporting the removal of the Bible from Cincinnati's public schools, openly lamented the lack of any constitutional defense to prevent Catholics from taking over public education in those communities where they constituted a majority. He acknowledged as fact that the First Amendment only restricted the federal government and did not apply to the states, calling this condition "a defect in the Constitution itself." Accordingly, Spear ardently backed a proposed constitutional amendment offered by Elisha P. Hurlbut, a former New York state supreme court justice, to apply the First Amendment to the states and empower Congress to attack directly any Roman Catholic efforts to marry church and state at the local level.[10] Hurlbut's suggested amendment read as follows:

> Neither Congress nor any state shall make any law respecting an establishment of religion, or prohibiting the free exercise thereof; or abridging the freedom of speech, or of the press; or the right of the people peacefully to assemble and to petition the government for a redress of grievances. But Congress may enact such laws as it shall deem necessary to control or prevent the establishment or continuance of any foreign hierarchical power in this country founded on principles or dogmas antagonistic to republican institutions.[11]

In Hurlbut's view, up until 1870 the primary constitutional contest in Reconstruction had been between freedom and slavery. But with the Cincinnati Bible War and the declaration of papal infallibility in 1870, he saw the national political commitment to restructure the Union entering a new stage. In his view, the new primary contest pitted democracy against a foreign theocratic challenge. The old Reconstruction concerned a domestic challenge to democracy. The new focus concerned an international challenge to American national government. Hurlbut claimed that several states were on the verge of Roman Catholic domination. In his view Congress needed explicit, constitutional authority to reconstruct any Northern state succumbing to the Catholic menace. Hurlbut advocated that the national government remove papal authority to appoint Catholic bishops, an action that Bismarck later instituted in Germany. Similar to the Prussian leader, Hurlbut favored a frank acknowledgment of the supremacy of state over church authority. Although he openly professed his Christian faith, Hurlbut was willing to render effective supremacy unto Caesar.[12]

Hurlbut's proposal, and the general cause of keeping Catholics from dividing the school funds, united not only conservative and liberal Protestants but lured even atheists and free thinkers to the Republican cause to preserve the American public school. Even those unconcerned with religious issues feared a Balkanization of public education, a result that they saw inevitably stemming from the Catholic position. If the latter were adopted, they saw no rationale which could prevent Chinese Buddhists or Mormons or "free lovers and communists" demanding their own separate schools, funded at public expense. Roman Catholics weakly replied to this concern by proclaiming that only Roman Catholics, Protestants and Jews had opinions worthy of official respect, and that the division of school funds should be limited to these few groups. Anti-Catholics ridiculed this logic. Two or three divisions of the school fund might have worked in Europe, wrote Henry Ward Beecher, but in the United States "we should be required to make twenty or thirty."[13]

At that time, Catholic schools in the United States were commonly light on academics and high on imparting church dogma. Why, non-Catholics asked, should the state ever allow public moneys to be spent to support inferior education? To emphasize this point, the Protestant press revived an essay written by Catholic polemicist Orestes Brownson in 1862. In this piece, Brownson himself admitted the low academic quality of Catholic schools in the United States. This temporary independence of mind embarrassed Brownson for the rest of his life, as Protestants used it against his church over and over again. By 1870 however, Brownson was very much back in the Catholic ideological harness arguing vehemently for dividing the school funds and against Judge Hurlbut's proposed amendment. During Reconstruction, he and other Catholic writers focused not on the academic deficiencies of Catholic schools but rather on their moral excellence. Only Catholic schools, they argued, could adequately prepare souls for eternal life.[14]

Catholics searched for chinks in their enemy's armor. Certainly, they thought, the emerging anti-Catholic alliance of conservative and liberal Protestants, atheists and free thinkers could not hold together. Catholic writers appealed to conservative Protestants to break with the coalition and instead join with Catholics against a common atheistic enemy. As the public schools became ever more secular, they warned, only atheists were served. "The infidel schools may indeed serve the interests of a few infidel parents," wrote one Jesuit commentator, "but will they *equally* serve the interests of those who have a faith?" This direct appeal to conservative Protestants produced minimal results. At that time, anti-Catholicism was stronger than fear of atheism among American Protestants. Indeed, the Republican Party welcomed outspoken atheists. The popularity of Robert G. Ingersoll as a Republican orator demonstrated this, whereas fervent Catholic Republicans were an exceedingly rare and quiet commodity.[15]

In the Republican mind, the principal problem with Roman Catholicism was its lack of ultimate commitment to the United States. Not only did Catholics hold primary obedience to a foreign head, they refused to accept the Republican dream of a culturally unified nation. Their desire to establish their own separate schools demonstrated that.

In their separateness and their suspected disloyalty, Catholics and defeated rebels were lodged in the same Republican pigeon hole. In 1875, Republican reaction to an unsuccessful proposal to divide Missouri's school fund amply revealed this mental association. *The Chicago Tribune*, a Republican newspaper, blasted the Catholic attempt in Missouri as a "Bourbon" plot. At that time, the term "Bourbon" was regularly associated with unreconstructed Southerners. Yet it also fit the Catholic church. The new age demanded cultural standardization, and the Roman Catholic church refused to submit. As such, it constituted a "Bourbon," reactionary and anti-national force.[16]

In the South, the Ku Klux Klan and other terrorists waged war against the public school. In the North, the Roman church and its priestly enforcers did likewise. The Republican and Protestant press carried stories of specific incidents of local priests urging observance of minor midweek religious festivals to disrupt the public schools. Yet Republicans knew that public funding for parochial schools, rather than simply harassment of public schools, was the principal Catholic goal. In 1873, the local public school board in Poughkeepsie, New York, officially took over the local Catholic schools, retaining all of the Catholic teachers and leaving day-to-day operations much as before. In effect, this arrangement gave public funding to Catholic schools; but on a theoretical level, the schools were now public schools governed by the local (pro-Catholic) school board. This mode of takeover was practiced wherever local Catholic majorities could gain control of school boards. Catholics called it "The Poughkeepsie Plan," and this manner of effectively dividing the school fund was actively urged within the American Catholic community.

Protestants believed that Roman Catholics, similar to Southern "Bourbons," resorted to violence to achieve their educational objectives. In the Spring of 1872, a public school in a Catholic neighborhood in St. Louis burned to the ground, eliminating all public competition with a nearby Jesuit school. Arson was charged in the Protestant press.[17] From the Protestant perspective, Catholic hostility to American public education was completely unwarranted. Protestants felt that they made valiant attempts to accommodate Roman Catholics, all to no avail. The old Protestant practices of moral education were being continuously modified so as not to offend Catholic sensibilities. Yet, whatever compromises Protestants made, these were never enough to satisfy the Catholic complainers. As the public schools became more secular and less Protestant, they were labeled "Godless" by Catholic critics. Catholics also kept up a constant attack against public-school textbooks, which taught that the Protestant Reformation was a positive advance in the history of western civilization. They also opposed public-school textbooks for not providing appropriate moral training. By contrast, textbooks prepared for Catholic schools provided students with a tight rein on any tendency to exercise independent judgment regarding moral matters. One such book, written by Cleveland's bishop Richard Gilmour, emphasized the virtue of obeying church authorities. It told the story of King Ozias (Uzziah or Azariah) of Judah. Ozias had usurped priestly authority and subsequently had been "covered with a leprosy that never left him." "Until the day of his death," Gilmour's text continued, "Ozias remained a public example of how God punishes the presumption of a layman who assumes the duties of a priest." Catholics feared "the loose and irreligious independence of the age" and sought to quarantine their children in their own schools.[18]

For Roman Catholicism, priestly authority resting on papal infallibility was the only safe foundation in the turbulent modern world. In Protestant eyes, this attitude was far too restrictive. The latter saw Catholic education as "calculated to produce dependent men and women, who never go beyond the limits marked out for them, and never walk without the leading string." In the words of Henry Ward Beecher, Catholic education encouraged stupidity—"the mere not resisting or not discussing—the condition of inactivity, or torpid swallowing and deglutition." Catholic education, he charged, was designed to produce passive "clams." By contrast, he proclaimed, "Protestants are not clams. They are winged and legged. They wander wide, and fly far." Consciously or unconsciously, Beecher's biological metaphors suggested that Protestants were higher than Catholics on some imagined educational evolutionary scale.

As for himself, Beecher was apparently winged. In 1874, he was accused by Theodore Tilton, a long-time associate, of wandering wide and flying far. The specific charge was that Beecher had an adulterous affair with Mrs. Tilton, a largely substantiated claim that ultimately all but ruined Beecher's reputation.[19] Catholic critics charged that Beecher's fall was an inevitable result of a loose, ever-changing Protestant theology that lured the winged Beecher to fly too close to the dazzling sun of American freedom. Catholics held up the example of this modern Icarus as a symbol of what was wrong with the drift of western civilization in general and with American liberal Protestantism in particular. The pace of modern industrial life had outstripped human ability to determine moral choices in any grounded, deliberate and meaningful way. Beecher and others like him had naively assumed that expanding personal freedom automatically produced good results. Catholics took advantage of Beecher's plight to instruct the Protestant majority on what they saw to be obvious flaws in the dominant American worldview.

Orestes Brownson stated the matter most directly: Henry Ward Beecher, and most Americans for that matter, had no higher value than "the spirit of the age." Current public opinion, or any behavior that might gain a temporary public acceptability, molded Beecher's fluid theology. Brownson labeled this ethic as a "revived paganism." Shortly before being publicly accused by Tilton, Beecher himself had provided corroborating evidence for Brownson's analysis. Writing in his *Christian Union*, Beecher had noted that fear of hell was no longer regarded with much seriousness in his own progressive Protestant circles. He described his age as a period when "old restraints" were dissolving and as "a time when all is adrift." "Set free from ecclesiastical bondage," wrote Beecher in 1871, "men are experimenting with their liberty in all directions. . . . There is a kind of chaos." Typical of Beecher, he urged his readers not to be concerned about the moral dangers of living at such a time, for a loving God would surely see both the nation and its citizens through safely to a better place. Regarding any possible violations of "the great law of responsibility" that might occur in this new experimental age, he assured his followers that God would "act in accordance with the most profound humanity."[20]

Brownson dreaded that God should ever mimic humanity, profound or otherwise. In his view, humankind was thoroughly depraved and in need of the church's moral guidance. Brownson rejected the idea that a democratic majority or shifting public opinion could ever be trusted in moral matters. He was unalterably opposed to the Republican vision of a majority-driven cultural standardization, characterized by an inclination to "overpower and trample on all minorities." He interpreted his own generation as especially corrupt. The Gilded Age, he reported, had "materialized the mind" and had created a passion "for sensible goods, or material wealth and well-being." In his opinion, American culture had come to worship only mammon, even in the form of income encrusted with gutter values. Anyone who did not attain affluence in such a culture was branded as worthless. He saw this Protestant-inspired American cultural assumption as a breeding ground of corruption and criminality. The mounting numbers in America's prisons attested to a society in grave trouble. Materialism, in Brownson's view, was the world of Caesar that Christ had commanded his followers to reject. Yet it was the essence of industrializing, postwar America.[21]

Brownson held to the dream of his New England youth of a perfected America, but his version of this religious tradition had a

Catholic twist. Unless America converted to the Roman Catholic church with its unchanging, bedrock traditions, he predicted, it would ultimately destroy itself in moral chaos. Brownson was sensitive to the fact that enunciation of the doctrine of papal infallibility had brought his church under heavy criticism. In contrast, he emphasized that Protestant Americans suffered under the democratic delusion "that the people are infallible." Adamantly, he warned against placing any trust in public opinion. "We are a mass of rottenness," he grieved. He saw his contemporary society pervaded by a dishonesty that served "to enrich a few sharpers by impoverishing the many." Broken families and increasing numbers of illegal abortions signaled for him a deep-seated moral decay that had its roots in the Protestant Reformation. Even Catholic households were infected by what he saw as a corrupt American ethos. He mourned that the United States of America was beyond any realistic possibility of redemption.[22]

In his last essay published before his death, Brownson held out a small hope that division of the school funds to enable Catholic schools to thrive at public expense might yet reverse the societal descent. He urged his fellow Catholics to push this issue in politics with even greater vigilance. "The great question for us Catholics and the great question even for our country," Brownson wrote in this final piece, "is the school question." Privately, he remained pessimistic that American democracy could be saved from what he saw as its self-destructive dynamic. He wrote to Father Isaac Hecker that he feared that the church's historic battle with sin could not be maintained on American soil. Catholics immigrating to the United States imbibed American "freedom from all restraint, unbounded license." Very quickly, he noted, they rejected their traditional faith and obedience to the church. He saw Catholics born in America as even worse than the culturally transformed immigrants. "How many Catholics can you find born and brought up in the country," he asked Hecker, "that do in reality hold the church to be higher than the people?" Forgetting the damage to the Catholic cause wrought by his own essay of 1862, he recalled all that he had done to promote Catholic education. But he confessed that he really lacked faith that Catholic schooling could make any meaningful difference in changing the historical pull toward American democratic materialism. Sadly, he noted that no reconciliation of Roman Catholicism with American values was possible "except by sacrificing the Catholic ideal to the national."[23]

Nagged by physical infirmities in his last years, Brownson sank into a deep depression. His disillusionment was atypical of American Catholic leaders. Most of them agreed with Father Hecker that the future of the international Catholic church was indeed in America. Under attack by rising nationalisms on both sides of the Atlantic, the church was most likely to succeed in America due to Catholic immigration. Hecker was in no mood to surrender, for he viewed demographic trends favoring Catholicism in the United States. In Europe, Catholics believed that they would be very fortunate to hold their historic defenses. But in America, many were then confident of ultimate victory. Brownson was a rare pessimistic exception. Most Catholic leaders dreamt of a future Catholic America. Similar to their Protestant opponents, the American Catholic hierarchy yearned for cultural standardization, albeit a Catholic one. They believed that Catholicism would eventually triumph in this culture struggle due to the shallow nature of Republican nationalism, which they noted did "not touch the internal play of the passions." By contrast, they emphasized that Roman Catholicism potentially linked all of mankind in one baptism and one churchly authority uniting "everything connected with the inner and higher world, . . . homogeneous and harmonious." Similar to conservative Protestants, they hoped for ultimately amending the American political tradition to allow for greater church-state ties. One American Catholic essay described the state divorced from the church as "like the body separated from the soul, dead, a putrid or putrefying corpse." Logically, a church-state marriage in the Catholic mold allowed that a papal directing hand from Rome would play a prominent role in the American future.[24]

Both camps in this religious war could see that their enmity only served to encourage the growing secularization of American life as the easiest way of maintaining social peace. However, each side anticipated victory, and neither side felt itself to blame for the negative results of the struggle. Protestants blamed Irish Catholic immigrants whom they saw as arrogantly refusing to accept American norms. Catholics blamed Protestants for originating the schism in the Reformation and further argued that Republican nationalists were preparing the way for the antichrist. Protestant polemicists retorted that the antichrist had already arrived in the form of an infallible pope. They urged that Catholics become Americanized in the public school. The official Catholic position held that American public education was maintained by "the arrogance of the state and the jealousy which human power always manifests of the divine authority." Father Hecker noted that the American public school succeeded only in fostering disrespect for parental and any other authority. According to Hecker, young Americans of the 1870s, educated in the public schools, were a threat to the future of the republic. A typical product of American public education, he noted, was "impatient of restraint, regards father and mother as old-fogies, narrow-minded, behind the age, and disdains filial submission or obedience to them, has no respect for dignities, acknowledges no superior, mocks at law if he can escape the police, is conceited, proud, self-sufficient, indocile, heedless of the rights and interests of others—will be his own master, and follow his own instincts or headstrong will."[25]

Hecker and other Catholic leaders preferred no education to traditional American public education and claimed that only the intelligent minority really required academic instruction. For the rest, they held, learning only served to disrupt the social order. Hecker held that the masses were best given a moral education only under the authority of the church. Protestants could find no common ground with this extreme official Catholic stance and consequently felt thoroughly justified in labeling the Roman church "the bulwark of ignorance and prejudice." They commonly portrayed Catholics as hostile to public libraries as well as public schools and accused Catholic-dominated public school boards of wanting to lower the wages of teachers to the starvation levels acceptable for instructors within parochial schools. If the Catholic war against public education succeeded, Protestants warned, all Americans would become as bestial as the Irish, who were seen as the degraded results of the Catholic educational idea.[26]

A bloody riot in New York City on July 12, 1871, reinforced the Protestant resolve that the masses needed to be uplifted through public education. This affair was widely blamed on Irish-Catholic lack of both self-control and respect for the rights and opinions of others. Occurring several months after the infamous Paris Commune, the July 12 riot was popularly seen (at least in Protestant circles) as an indication of what America was fast becoming and the social consequences of mass ignorance. These were the facts of the affair: Irish Catholics had rioted against Scotch-Irish Orangemen exercising their "free speech" in celebrating the historic Battle of the Boyne, King William's conquest of Ireland almost two centuries before. Ninety Scotch-Irish Protestants, flanked by state troops sent to protect them from possible violence on their festival day, had been assaulted as they marched through the Catholic wards of the city. The troopers quickly put down the disturbance but at the expense of fifty-six lives and eighty maimed and wounded. Henry Ward Beecher's organ characteristically saw the bright side of this tragedy: "Comparatively few innocent persons were among the sufferers," *The Christian Union* reported. Beecher's editorial on the subject one week later remained steadfast in support of Protestant civil liberties: "The Orange societies should parade next year, without a banner less or one inscription rubbed out." The incendiary nature of the Orange Irish practice of annually goading Roman Catholic Irish on July 12 was lost on anti-Catholic Republicans.[27]

Before the riot, Roman-Catholic church officials had pleaded with New York City's Irish-Catholic community not to disturb the peace, whatever the provocation from arrogant Protestants. But this fact did not save the church from harsh Protestant criticism. Anti-Catholic propagandists charged the church with failing to educate the Irish to respect the rights of others. The only thing that the church was credited with having accomplished with these immigrants was in training them to observe certain medieval ceremonies and to give monetary contributions to the church itself. Henry Ward Beecher noted that the riots were a direct result of the Catholic philosophy of leaving the masses in ignorance. This policy, he emphasized, did not make men obedient. Rather, in a democratic environment, it left them susceptible to demagogues of the worst sort. In his opinion, this event proved that the Roman Catholic schools were "utterly unsafe educators for our future citizens." "The state," he concluded, "cannot safely segregate the children of its most bigoted nationality in schools by themselves."[28]

In stark contrast to their portrayal of the Irish, anti-Catholics romanticized German immigrants and, in fact, all things German. The German propensity to authoritarianism was idealized as "the obedience without which there is no true freedom of nation or of man." While Germans exhibited a strong proclivity toward atheism, anti-Catholic Protestants tended to excuse it away as less offensive than Roman Catholicism. "Superstition on the one hand, and infidelity upon the other; this is our fearful dilemma," wrote Henry Ward Beecher in comparing Irish and non-Catholic German immigrants. Nonetheless, Beecher left no doubt that he preferred the German shortcoming to that of the Irish. Following a massive German parade in New York City celebrating the fatherland's victory over France, Beecher exulted that it was larger than even the St. Patrick's Day parade of several weeks before. "Let the Germans balance the Irish," Beecher concluded. "Providence has provided for us a compensation." Republicans overwhelmingly agreed, and set the recruitment of Germans into the Republican fold as a high party priority.[29]

In some areas of the North, anti-Catholicism seemed even stronger than white racism. This was young W. E. B. DuBois' impression, growing up black in Great Barrington, Massachusetts in the 1870s. He later recorded that in his youth he felt relatively accepted in the largely white social environment of his origins. "The racial angle," he wrote, "was more clearly defined against the Irish than against me."[30] But, in reality, conditions were far worse for African Americans than for Irish Americans. Both the Fourteenth and Fifteenth Amendments had left loopholes for states to disfranchise ignorant and illiterate voters, Irish or black. In the North, anti-Catholic spokesmen had put the Irish on warning: Become literate, or eventually suffer the political conse-quences.[31] In the North, this threat would never be executed. When the constitutional loopholes were ultimately exploited to disfranchise ignorant and illiterate voters, Southern blacks were the ones to suffer— not the Northern Irish Catholics. Despite all of the anti-Catholic rhetoric in the Northern states in the 1870s, the Irish Catholics were better situated than African Americans.

The Irish immigrants were concentrated in a region where the public school was a relatively well-established institution. Likewise, they benefited from a powerful international church serving as their advocate and providing alternate educational facilities to challenge the cultural hegemony of the public school. The dynamics of the environ-ment in which the Irish Catholics found themselves offered them expanding opportunities. Even the original inclination of their own church to stunt the academic preparation of most Catholics was modified in the cauldron of cultural competition. The challenge for Catholic schools was increasingly to be just as good academically as the public schools in the North. Generations of Irish-Americans benefited from this competition. In the South, where the overwhelming majority of American blacks then resided, public education was resisted as a foreign New England concept. When southern states eventually created public-school systems, they were created primarily for the benefit of whites. Despite DuBois' provincial childhood impressions, "the racial angle" was primarily against African Americans in the United States.

Nonetheless, in the 1870s, African Americans and white Repub-licans were allied against a common Irish-Catholic foe that supposedly threatened to undermine American progress. In the North, compulsory education increasingly became the Republican panacea to solve "the Irish problem." If the Roman Catholic church would not encourage academic education for the masses, and Irish parents would not require their children be sent to the free public schools, the state could mandate that all children reach a certain cultural standard. Henry Ward Beecher compared the state to Jesus Christ in calling the little children unto Him. Indeed, Beecher granted that in the progressive modern world, the state was "the great master" that could do virtually anything for the common good. A Bismarckian government, using Prussian means of compelling the education of all, promised unending progress for an uplifted people. "The state has the right to legislate for the public good and determine

FIGURE 3.2

"Reading the latest News from New York." Infallible Pope: "That's a bad look-out. If they put a stop to Ignorance what is to become of Me?"

Harper's Weekly, January 9, 1875.

what you can do and what you can't," Beecher proclaimed in justifying compulsory education. While some educational leaders in the North argued that the idea could not work effectively in practice, by 1874, twelve states had enacted compulsory education laws. In the end, these laws proved to be largely unenforceable. However, they did provide part of the political sword play of the educational contest of the 1870s.[32]

The argument in favor of compulsory education warned that compelling children to go to school was preferable to compelling them as adults to go to prison. The apparent link between ignorance and criminality persuaded many to the justice of this cause. The Catholic church challenged this assumption. In its view, academic ignorance was not the problem; declining faith was. The public school, Catholic spokesmen claimed, was weaning otherwise good Catholics from the faith of their fathers. "The children of Catholics must be trained up in the Catholic faith, in the Catholic church, to be good exemplary Catholics," wrote The Catholic World, "or they will grow up bad citizens, the pests of society." In the dynamic environment of the United States, cut loose from any permanent spiritual moorings, children from decent old-world Catholic families grew into criminals. This, said the Catholic press, was not the fault of the Catholic faith; and it could not be prevented by secular public schools. It was the fault of a chaotic American social environment and could be only resolved by dividing the school fund to encourage meaningful moral education. Catholic apologists added that the really big crimes in American life were not the doings of nominal Roman Catholics, who were commonly involved in only petty theft. "A gigantic swindle, a scientific burglary, a nicely planned larceny, an adroit forgery, a diabolical seduction, or a deliberate and long-contemplated murder by poison or the knife" were, in the words of The Catholic World, normally the fruits of Protestant upbringings.[33]

The 1870s educational-religious turmoil had begun over the issue of Bible reading in the public schools. It had then shifted to the debate over dividing the school fund. Ohio had generated the first conflict; New York, the second. Both of these states were important politically for control of both the North and the nation. In 1873, the geographic focus of the struggle again became Ohio. In the 1872 elections, the Republicans had scored impressive gains nationwide. After those elections (both congressional and presidential), Reconstruction appeared invincible as the national Democratic Party experienced a low point in its historic existence. Then, in 1873, state election results in Ohio gave the Democrats new hope. Economic downturn and national Republican scandals seemingly gave the Democrats a new advantage. Ohio Republicans looked for issues to recapture their old momentum. They linked themselves to a women's temperance crusade, a noneconomic issue that had anti-Irish overtones, given the common association of Irish and whisky. Unfortunately, crusades against liquor and saloons alienated the beer-loving Germans, whom Republicans needed for victory. Ohio's Republicans readjusted their strategy. A Bismarckian attack against the Catholic desire to divide the school fund rather than shrewishly whining about the Irish fondness for whisky promised to win Germans back to the Republican fold.

Rutherford B. Hayes, who had chosen not to seek reelection for governor in 1873, challenged his Democratic successor in 1875. Hayes's campaign was directly anti-Catholic and pro-public education. *Harper's Weekly*, the most popular anti-Catholic Republican organ, pushed Hayes's cause: "We have among us," commented the journal, "a large foreign population who call themselves Democrats, yet who are laboring to destroy that system of education that can alone make democracy successful." The "'Democratic-Catholic alliance'" was blasted by Hayes's supporters, who warned the electorate to be ever vigilant against the Roman Catholic church's foreign desire to divide the school fund. The Democratic Ohio legislature had passed the Geghan bill giving the Catholic clergy access to the chaplaincy in Ohio's prisons and asylums. This, Hayes's supporters warned, was merely the opening wedge for a Catholic takeover of all public functions in the state of Ohio, including its public schools. During the campaign, Hayes attended numerous rallies at which printed signs abounded giving witness to the rising political power of the anti-Catholic movement: "Hayes and Free Schools," "The Book Before the Priest," and "No Geghan Bill for Us" were typical banners in this campaign.[34]

On October 12, 1875, Hayes won at a time when national Republican scandals continued to mount and Ohio and the nation were wracked with economic depression. In this one election, the Republicans had proven the political potential of anti-Catholicism. Through Hayes' subsequent successful campaign for the presidency, the issue of blocking the Catholic attempt to divide the school funds grew in national importance. Beginning in Cincinnati in 1870, the anti-Catholic public-education crusade had shown potential as a Republican issue. Six years later, it came into full flower. Entering the presidential race of 1876, Hayes became its primary beneficiary.[35]

Throughout the early 1870s, anti-Catholicism was a cultural and political phenomenon. Evidence of it was shown in many publications, as well as in many events of the day. However, a hefty pamphlet illustrated by Thomas Nast entitled "Miss Columbia's Public School," best revealed its characteristics and style. Distributed as popular anti-Catholic literature, this piece in parable form demonstrated the Republican psychology in the Northern states. The setting of this cartoon-illustrated fantasy is an American public school, made up of an ethnically diverse group of children. Their teacher is Miss Columbia, a feminine counterpart to "Uncle Sam" and a stock symbol of the American Union for political cartoonists of that time. All of the children in this school are reasonably well-behaved, except for one apelike Irish child with angry beady eyes, a small nose, flaring nostrils, and a wide thin-lipped mouth (usually open haranguing his fellow students). The quarreling provoked by this opinionated youth especially bothers a student simply called "the Northern boy." The Northern boy dreams at night of an evil personage named "the Infallible One," who steals his family Bible "bequeathed to him by his Puritan father." This nightmare puts the Northern boy on his guard. The next day in school, Miss Columbia notes that a student has left his dirty fingerprints all over her beautiful Bible. She tells the class that she knows who committed the act. She assumes that it is public knowledge that the Irish boy besmudged her Bible. She urges the other boys to stop their "selfish pursuits for a short time to bring him to a sense of his duties" and warns the class that if the transgressor remains unpunished, she will have to thrash the Irish boy herself.

At recess, the Northern boy shares his nightmare with Miss Columbia, who interrupts to alert him to "a black figure" darting through the yard and down a back alley. Suspicious, she leads the Northern boy to examine the foundation of the school and finds it partially undermined. She shares her belief that the "black figure" is a Jesuit who periodically rips bricks and mortar away from the foundation, hoping apparently to topple the entire structure. Returning to the classroom, they both come on the apelike Irish boy "in the very act of seizing the Bible and throwing it out of the window." The Northern boy grabs the transgressor and forces him to put the Bible where it belongs. Sulkily, the Irish boy vows revenge: "I'll be even with you yet," he spits; "my time is soon coming." At his departure, Miss Columbia shares with the Northern boy the uselessness of trying to compromise with Irish Catholics in educational matters and shows him an inferior textbook authored by "Father O'Bigotry." The Northern boy promises Miss Columbia that he will organize the other boys and "decide on some plan to get us out of these ugly snarls." Encouraged by his resolve, Miss Columbia urges the Northern boy to forget his past troubles with his Southern brother: "Do you not see that while you two, the original pupils of my school, are contending with each other, those who have only come among us lately will usurp all your rights, and, in fact, it will only be the story of the camel over again?"[36]

The next day, the Northern boy confronts the Irish boy and demands that he apologize to Miss Columbia. The Irish boy refuses and replies: "Let her go to blazes. . . . This is our promised land, and we're bound to have it. . . . The Pope himself is going to sit in Miss Columbia's chair, and she can be afther [sic] looking for another place." Later that same day, an Orange Scotch-Irish boy assures the Northern boy that the latter can count on his support. An even more robust German boy likewise pledges his assistance as long as the Northern boy lets him enjoy his beer. That night, the Northern boy dreams again, but this time it is not a nightmare but a vision of a school yard united against the Irish boy. In his dream, "even the heathen Chinee" joins the alliance. Boys of all racial and ethnic backgrounds combine in driving the Irish boy and all his relatives from America. The dream concludes with all of the Irish destroying themselves with whisky consumption back in Ireland. The parable ends with an acknowledgment of the worth and patriotism of "liberal Catholics," as opposed to those under the sway of the Jesuits. Those who follow the latter, the author reports, can "go back where they came from."[37]

Northern voters resonated to the nationalist message that an organic union, replete with Protestant religious overtones, possibly was needed to prevent a Roman Catholic conspiracy from taking undue advantage of a American decentralized federation. From the Protestant perspective, mounting Roman Catholic immigration brought ignorance and criminality in its wake that threatened the course of American progress. Republicans then were considering increasing federal controls over public education, in large measure to further the cause of educating the freedmen. But this push had implications for transforming Roman Catholic children in the North as well. Republicans hoped that a national culture would emerge eventually from the crucible of federally promoted and protected public schools. During the 1870s, the nation stood at a crossroads. At stake was the nature of the Union itself. Similar to Bismarck, Republicans suggested cultural unity as a national ideal.[38]

But did the American people really want cultural unity? Democrats sensed that they definitely did not. The Republicans, Democrats conceded, indeed intended to remake America in the public school. They warned that Republicans planned to educate all Americans in the same classroom to make one, homogeneous American people. Republican opposition to religiously segregated Roman Catholic public schools, Democrats hinted, possibly revealed a subterranean Republican antipathy toward racially segregated public schools as well. Increasingly Democrats asked directly: Did Republican plans toward building a unified national culture include ultimately forcing blacks and whites into the same public-school classroom? In the

FIGURE 3.3

"The Irishman and the Black Boy."
"I say, you young Naygur, is that a Thavern?"
"No, it's a school. Can't you read?"
"Rade, is it? Hivin save his Riv'rince, do you want to
bring me down on a level wid yourself, you young Haythen?"

Harper's Weekly, May 15, 1875.

early 1870s, Democrats shot this question at a party that had step by-
step advanced the cause of African-American equality without ever
relinquishing its Northern white power base. Democrats quickly found
popular fears of racial integration as a most effective antidote to their
own defensiveness in issues involving the Roman Catholic church.

Reconstruction stalled as this Democratic ploy proved its worth in electoral politics. In the end, white racism proved even more powerful than rising anti-Catholicism.

4

EDUCATING THE FREEDMEN

The African Factor

While evangelical zeal encouraged the creation of a homogeneous nation, white racism worked in the opposite direction. And the latter influence proved to be stronger and more deeply seated than any other considerations. Its persistence in western civilization has been long and enduring. Millennia ago, Aryan conquerors swept into western Europe, the Middle East, and India, carrying their racial prejudices with them. In India, they segregated the population on the basis of skin color. The historiographic debate over whether American slavery created, or was created by, racial prejudice is overshadowed by this ancient pedigree of white racial preference. Unfortunately, as Carl Degler has so clearly demonstrated, all Caucasian countries reflect this inheritance in varying degrees.[1] Reconstruction briefly confronted this long history. Republican reformers sought to achieve a modicum of racial equity among people carrying heavy cultural baggage. In the end, the challenge proved too great and the experiment ended.

Albion W. Tourgee, one Northerner who spent much of the 1870s in North Carolina courageously encountering this unique historical opportunity, later commented that white racial feeling is like "the spots of the leopard" that remain through generations and generations. For the remainder of his life, Tourgee fought the good fight against tremendous odds, never wearying despite his realization that the best that could be reasonably hoped for was slow, incremental change. "It may not be possible to avert all evil," he wrote, "but no effort should be spared to lessen it as much as we may." Looking back in the 1880s over the lost opportunity to transform America by increased spending in public education, Tourgee saw the African factor as the difference between success and failure. If only one race resided in the United States, he sadly concluded, there would be no doubt that "the spelling book" would become "the scepter of national power." White racism undermined any movement for meaningful national unification through mass education.[2]

In both the North and the South in the 1870s, white people generally viewed black people as culturally debased. Their language referred to the "darker side" of human nature that led straight to moral ruin. In the minds of white people, African Americans represented a forbidden world of being. In their imagination, Africa was the fountainhead of decadence and evil. In 1875, Democrat John S. Hager elaborated upon this view in a speech before the House of Representatives. Blacks, he said, had not progressed over the entire course of recorded history. "Degeneracy and decay" accompanied them wherever they were found on the globe, especially in Africa. Southerners uncritically accepted this negative interpretation of African history. A low regard for the African past worked to excuse the sins that Northerners had identified with the holding of slaves. Usually Northerners preferred to stress that slavery had brutalized African Americans.³ Consequently, they tended to be more sanguine that blacks could be improved by a positive educational experience. Nonetheless, whites both North and South in the 1870s generally concluded that as matters then stood, blacks were a culturally diseased portion of the population. Only their interpretations of the source of the malady differed.

In the antebellum years, slavery had quarantined blacks into a separate world of existence. Leon Litwack has shown that even in the free states before the Civil War social intercourse between blacks and whites was tightly segregated along racial lines.⁴ The separation continued after general emancipation. In the 1870s, few public schools North or South were racially integrated. While experiments might readily occur in "mixing" boys and girls in the same classroom, racial "mixing" in schools was strongly resisted. While white Protestants might urge the mixing of Protestants and Catholics in the same classroom in hopes of promoting one American culture, their desire to integrate dissolved in the presence of the African factor. The typical white American in the 1870s regarded racially "mixed" schools with as much grace as mixing healthy children with another group infected with smallpox.

Whites feared that racial integration in the public schools would surrender their children to a culture more immediately appealing than their own. For all of their talk of white superiority, Caucasians readily appreciated the relative fragility of their own culture. They believed that black students would "infect" white children with a tendency to choose the easy ways of enjoying life, in contrast to the more difficult patterns of self-sacrifice that they regarded as having built white civilization and "progress." Congressman Hager was quite direct in conceding this point. "While we cannot raise them up to our level," Hager told the

House, "they may drag us down." He did not think that the supposed
innate superiority of whites was enough to protect white children in
racially "mixed" educational surroundings. Thomas Francis Bayard, a
Delaware Democrat, agreed. In a speech before the United States
Senate, he noted that mixed schools "would be most injurious to the
moral tone of the community, subjecting these little children at their
tenderest age, when most impressionable, to all moral influences, to
contacts which cannot but be harmful."[5] The white mentality revealed a
seeming contradiction. On the one hand, some whites had speculated
that inferior blacks would die out in free and open competition with
stronger whites following emancipation. On the other hand, whites
openly feared that their own culture would be overcome in a free and
open competition with black culture in integrated public schools.
Joseph H. Rainey, the first black elected to the House of Representatives,
directly addressed this point to his white colleagues: "Why this fear of
competition with a Negro?" he asked.[6]

In many whites' perception, blacks equated freedom with irre-
sponsibility. Once emancipated, some freedmen had taken to the road
and lived off the land, understandably reveling in their time of
"jubilee."[7] In the eyes of many whites, as the novelty of freedom
evolved into a more routinized existence required for survival, blacks
continued to exhibit irresponsible behavior. In the public schools of
Washington, D.C., where many blacks continued to immigrate in their
quest to escape the memory of slavery, black students were
characterized as unruly. Two of the black trustees of the African-
American schools of Washington and Georgetown, while advocating
mixed schools for their race, sadly remarked that black students
suffered from "the hereditary effects of the deprivations and wrongs of
centuries." Another black trustee commented that "the moral faculties"
of black students were "not sufficiently awakened to feel the force of
higher motives."[8] Slave culture had been characterized by numerous
external controls. Living in a new world of freedom, African Americans
often appeared to white observers as lacking in self-restraint. That some
black officials themselves held such opinions demonstrates how per-
vasive this assessment was at that time.

Many whites feared where the African-American search for
freedom might end. To them, African-American culture appeared to
advocate "license" and "permissiveness," pejorative terms for freedom.
Interestingly, their attitude toward blacks was somewhat comparable to
the Roman Catholic attitude toward Protestants. The official Roman
Catholic position held that "license" and "permissiveness" had been
unleashed by the Protestant Reformation. Catholic intellectuals saw

Henry Ward Beecher's scandal as contemporary evidence of the disintegrative, self-destructive tendencies inherent within freedom-loving Protestantism. White Americans—even Protestants, even Henry Ward Beecher himself as revealed in the columns of his weekly newspaper—were fearful where the American experiment with maximizing individual liberty might eventually end. In the face of all of the dynamic social and economic changes characterizing the Gilded Age, the black variant of American freedom was especially fearsome. Whites associated it with a potential for societal degeneration that they sensed in their midst.

Whites in the 1870s had a seemingly insatiable curiosity concerning the perimeters of African-American freedom. Numerous books were published to meet this interest. One was authored by Charles Stearns, a Yankee teacher who moved south and became a planter. Similar to other Northerners, he was struck by the devaluation of work that seemed to characterize the entire South, whites and blacks alike. For his Northern audience, he detailed the irresponsibilities of African-American freedom as he perceived them. Charles Nordhoff, a well-respected Northern commentator on numerous subjects, described the inclination of blacks to engage in petty theft. "He learned it as a slave," Nordhoff emphasized, "and has not yet unlearned it." Stearns's book described blacks as having an exaggerated sense of their own abilities that bore no relationship to reality. He praised them for their relatively good-natured outlook and lack of vindictiveness, but castigated their seeming lack of ambition. By Stearns's account, blacks had little urge to excel as individuals, and instead felt a strong need to conform to black community expectations. He described them as born procrastinators and lacking the gift of perseverance.[9]

Sexual promiscuity in the black community particularly interested Stearns. Marriage in African-American society, he wrote, lacked the elements of individual commitment and fidelity. Accordingly he said, black family arrangements were a "complicated snarl." Many whites, not just Stearns, were fascinated by black sexual habits. Southern white males had long participated in the pleasures of black sexuality that had been readily available in slavery, but that was not a subject for respectable conversation in Victorian America. For public display, Southern whites raised what appeared to Charles Nordhoff as a "frantic and desperate" crusade against the sexual danger represented by the black male. Southerners, wrote Nordhoff, were "fearful, to a degree that seems to a Northern man absurd, of combinations and conspiracies among the blacks to murder the whites and outrage their women."[10] White sexual fantasies were definitely involved in the white resolve to keep schooling racially segregated, as whites regularly projected that the evils of miscegenation and "racial amalgamation" would certainly result from "mixed schools."

Edward King, a British visitor to the Southern states during 1873–1874, was careful not to lump all African Americans into one common pool of behavioral characteristics. He saw about one-third of Southern blacks "in a very hopeful condition." Another third he perceived as "absolutely good for nothing" and preferring "theft to honest labor" and making "no steady progress in morality, refinement, or education of any kind." The remaining third he saw as blending the characteristics of the two extremes. As a newcomer to America, he quickly sensed his hosts' aversion to racially integrated schooling. He himself confessed to holding similar racial attitudes. But then he saw Southern white and black children playing together in the streets of Natchez, something that was far beyond his own experiences as a boy. Why, he asked himself, did white Southerners hold such strong views about mixed schools when throughout their lives they regularly associated with blacks in social intercourse? The matter remained a mystery to him. He could provide no explanation.[11] The answer lay in American expectations surrounding the common school. The public school was designed to be the crucible of one common culture. It was structured to create a common respect for all of its members. The boys in the streets of Natchez in 1873 came together briefly from different worlds to which they readily returned. That experience posed no threat to the maintenance of historic white racial separateness. Mixed schools did.

Stearns's book discussed the relative educational abilities of African Americans. In his opinion, while black students excelled in oratory they had no aptitude for mathematics. On the positive side, blacks were described as having a shrewd sense of insight into human nature and having excellent survival skills in living by their wits, a talent that their extreme poverty demanded. Steams advocated mixed schools and a national system of public education.[12] If an advanced reformer calling for national integrated schools could hold such definite and unflattering racial views, it takes little imagination to project the attitudes of those opposing racial integration in the classroom. Some of those against mixed schools believed education wasted on African Americans. Mark Twain and Charles Dudley Warner poked fun at this latter attitude in their novel of the period, *The Gilded Age*. Colonel Sellers, a character in the novel, offers that education would only give the "niggro [*sic*] . . . a wider scope to injure himself." The fictional colonel recommended that blacks only be given education to elevate their souls but not to "disturb the niggro as he is."[13]

Sir George Campbell, a member both of England's Parliament and the British imperial government in India, offered his opinions on the American race problem to a transatlantic white readership. Known for his interest in ethnology, Campbell focused on dysfunctional family systems among African Americans. In Africa, he wrote, traditional polygamous marriages had worked well. But in the African-American experience, the white monogamous family model had only been loosely applied due to the economics of slavery. He described the African-American family as it had developed in slavery:

> The relation between parent and child was especially weakened, or rather not created. The parents were not really responsible for the children; on the contrary, the women were sent to work, and the children were carefully tended by persons appointed by the masters for the purpose, like calves or lambs or any other valuable stock. Parents had little affection for children thus reared, and children owed no respect and obedience to parents. The family as we know it is, in fact, a novelty to the Negro since emancipation, and such institutions are not perfected in a day.[14]

This kind of analysis had been part of the standard abolitionist complaint against slavery. While earlier helpful in proving the evil of slavery and furthering the cause of black liberation, by the 1870s this portrayal provided ample excuses for quarantining what was widely regarded in the white world as a culturally diseased segment of American life.

In the 1870s, both blacks and Irish were seen as having many of the same faults. Both were perceived as living only for the moment with no thought for the morrow, as lacking an enterprising spirit necessary for capital accumulation, as dissipating their lives in sensual pleasures, and as living lives dominated by ignorance and gross superstition. But Protestants expected that Irish-Catholic cultural flaws would be erased by a common-school education. They eagerly sought to integrate the Irish in their public schools, which they hoped would liberate these Catholics from their perceived medieval superstitions. White Protestants actively fought all Catholic attempts to segregate Irish newcomers into separate state-supported schools for themselves alone, which they branded as anti-American in both practice and theory. When having the Irish in mind, Northern public school advocates could wax eloquently on how schools mixing Protestants and Catholics were ideal for the health and well-being of American democracy. Protestants had no fear of the outcome of free cultural competition with what they regarded as "unprogressive," medieval, backward beliefs in a public school setting. By contrast, Roman Catholic officials feared this mixing as a threat to their hold on the minds and hearts of Catholic youth. Catholic spokesmen regarded the Protestant drift toward nineteenth-century worldliness as the "easy way" that would corrupt their children.[15]

In the religious struggle over education, Catholic ideology was the delicate, fragile set of cultural norms in danger of being dragged down and corrupted in a mixed common school environment. On the racial front, white cultural norms occupied a comparable place and needed isolation, protection and encouragement in order to survive, as they were too delicate to endure in free and open competition with free-spirited African-American cultural habits. In both situations. the white Protestant majority prevailed. Roman Catholics were denied separate state-supported schools. Blacks were promised (but often denied) separate state-supported schools.

In the Gilded Age, white Protestants were especially sensitive to losing self-control. Increasing numbers of white Americans were then engaging in excesses that would have shocked their parents. Even the great Henry Ward Beecher was among the accused. Although they regularly swore their allegiance to traditional biblical precepts, their real daily behavior revealed them worshiping at the shrines of industrial mammon. Emotionally and spiritually, white Americans were not ready for racially mixed schools and the excessive personal freedom that they associated with that possibility. Consequently. the African factor revealed the hypocrisy of the Republican Party's exaltation of one common school for all Americans.

Among white Americans, Charles Sumner stood out as a great exception. Throughout all of his adult life, the Senator from Massachusetts had taken a stand in favor of racially mixed public education. In 1849, he had taken the case of one Sarah C. Roberts, a black girl in Boston seeking to be admitted in one of the city's white public schools. He had then argued that racial segregation "is in the nature of *Caste*, and, on this account, a violation of Equality." He had sought to persuade the court that racial segregation hurt both blacks and whites—the blacks in being informed by the state that they are regarded as inferior beings, the whites in training them out of "that grand revelation of Christianity, the brotherhood of man." He lost that case, but his position was enacted into law in 1855 when racially integrated schools were mandated statewide by the Massachusetts legislature. Thereafter, Massachusetts' public schools were theoretically "mixed," an accomplishment that Sumner hoped to make national before his death.[16] His strategy to bring about this end was simple. First, he sought to make the

Washington, D.C., public schools a showcase for the nation by bringing into being integrated schooling in the nation's capital. From there, he would press to make public schools racially integrated in all of the states. If a national system of public education came into being along the way, he would insist that it mandate "mixed schools."

Black Americans of that generation widely regarded Sumner as their best friend in Congress and generally deferred to his leadership. While Sumner's widely perceived attitude of moral superiority easily offended whites, blacks tolerated this trait, for it was usually employed in their behalf. He was one of the very few white Americans of his generation who did not regard blacks with a condemning spirit. For his time, his racial views were certainly unorthodox within the majority community. One of John Eaton's brothers, working to build the Republican party in Memphis, Tennessee, wrote that among African Americans Sumner was held in almost god-like reverence. He wrote that while whites generally regarded the Massachusetts Senator as "pigheaded," Sumner widely enjoyed a reputation as "the granite and formative foundation of the Republican Party" among "the emerging element of the party." Because of this, he was a force to be reckoned with in the public school battles of the 1870s.[17]

In the first days of the decade, Sumner staked out his place in the emerging school movement. His chosen battle ground was Virginia. All except three of the former Confederate states had been readmitted by Congress by January 1, 1870. These three were Virginia, Mississippi, and Texas. Of this group, Virginia was especially symbolic, given its status during the war as the most populous Confederate state. Early in 1870, Virginia petitioned Congress to accept its new constitution, the approval of which would restore normal state government to the Old Dominion. Sumner balked. What especially aroused Sumner, and the Republican Congress in general, was a growing suspicion that the state might not enact the public school system that was promised in its new constitution once Congress restored Virginia's powers of state sovereignty. Evidence for this belief had accumulated during the ratification campaign the previous summer.[18]

In the contest for governor of Virginia, a conservative candidate had defeated a Radical. The governor-elect was Gilbert C. Walker, originally a carpetbag Republican who had bolted from the party and ran as the candidate of the Conservatives (an alliance of conservative Republicans and Democrats). He supposedly had indicated that in office he would never institute a public school system.[19] Orchestrated by Sumner, the Republican strategy called for readmitting Virginia under certain conditions that compromised the state's sovereignty. Specifically,

Virginia was barred from ever disfranchising blacks on grounds such as illiteracy and was required to fulfill its constitutional pledges to inaugurate a meaningful system of public education. These stipulations went above and beyond the mandates of Congressional Reconstruction that had been determined in 1867. Opponents to the Republican bill charged that Congress could not constitutionally dictate the future course of a sovereign state. In retort, Republicans simply resorted to the authority of Article IV, Section 4, popularly known as the "Guarantee Clause" of the Constitution. This provision states that "the United States shall guarantee to every state in this union a republican form of government." The Congressional majority reserved the power to determine exactly what that vague provision meant in application.[20]

Sumner's proposal for Virginia required that that state never amend its state constitution to strip blacks either of the right to vote or the opportunity to receive a public education. In the earlier battle over the language of the Fifteenth Amendment, Radicals had failed to muster the two-thirds majorities needed to ban disfranchisement of blacks on nonracial grounds. But in the Virginia bill, which required only simple majorities to pass, the Radicals had the votes to accomplish the same end. They constitutionally underwrote this mandate with the vague Guarantee Clause. Democrats and a few Republicans argued that this was unfair. Democratic Senator Allen G. Thurman of Ohio said, "Have you not gone far enough without now assuming that you can do by a mere act of Congress what in the very nature of our system can only be done by amending the Constitution itself?" Supporters of the measure dismissed all talk of unconstitutionality. They regarded Congress as the final voice on that issue. Throughout American history, the United States Supreme Court had generally deferred to Congress. In the rare important instances that it had not, the Court had gotten into political trouble. For Republican Senator James Harlan of Iowa, the Dred Scott decision was of recent enough memory to continue "to shake the confidence of the American people in the integrity of that high tribunal." Congress absorbed the latent power of the Court and in 1870 did not fear the judiciary. Completely frustrated, Senator Thurman whined: "Have we got that far that the states are reduced to the condition of counties and that Congress can mold even their fundamental law according to its mere will?"[21]

The specter of Tennessee's recent history hovered over the deliberations concerning Virginia. In 1867, Congress had exempted Tennessee from the conditions of the First Reconstruction Act, a reward for that state's voluntary ratification of the Fourteenth Amendment. Thereupon, Tennessee had been restored to its normal place in the Union. Its senators and representatives had been seated in Congress. Its Republican government had created a state system of public education with no apparent dictation from Congress. John Eaton, Jr., a Superintendent of Schools in Toledo, Ohio, had been appointed to head the new Tennessee public school system. Then, seemingly overnight, conditions changed. The Ku Klux Klan arose and blossomed. Conservatives captured control of the state legislature in 1869 and rapidly dismantled what Eaton had built. With Tennessee public education a lost cause, Eaton moved to Washington, D.C., where he became United States Commissioner of Education in 1870.[22]

As Congress discussed what to do with Virginia, conservative state constitutional delegates in Tennessee met to rewrite Tennessee's fundamental law. They specifically outlawed racially mixed schools, a prohibition that congressionally reconstructed states were then afraid to write explicitly into their constitutions. Before 1869, Tennessee had been an example of what could be accomplished in Reconstruction by a friendly reliance on state voluntarism. In January 1870, it provided a strong argument for Congress to reduce states to the status of counties. "We have imposed conditions upon all rebel states heretofore restored save one, the state of Tennessee," intoned Ohio Republican Job E. Stevenson before the House of Representatives. "And what loyal man does not regret that we did not lay conditions upon her?" Virginia, Mississippi, and Texas paid the centralizing price for Tennessee's fall from grace.[23]

Conditions in Georgia also spurred Republicans to use the Guarantee Clause in the cases of Virginia, Mississippi, and Texas. Georgia had seemingly finished the Reconstruction process. Then, suddenly, the Georgia legislature expelled black Republicans elected to that body for no other reason than their race. Congress could not let this pass without notice. Immediately before taking up the issue of Virginia, Congress discussed remanding Georgia to a provisional status. In such an environment, many Republicans were wondering aloud whether white Southerners could ever be trusted to conform voluntarily to the new constitutional principles of racial political equity. If not, the Guarantee Clause existed to force them to change. Virginia was the first of the last three unreconstructed Southern states to bear the brunt of this temporarily heightened feeling. Charles Sumner sensed the time was ripe to redefine states rights to the point of extinction. Debating the merits of the Virginia bill, he proclaimed that "the states have no power except to do justice." "Any power beyond this," he added, "is contrary to the harmonies of the universe." Democrats and a few Republicans complained, but they lacked the votes to thwart the majoritarian will.[24]

In his argument to force special conditions on Virginia, Sumner demonized the state's governor-elect. He focused on a campaign document prepared by the Walker forces that implied that the governor would not enforce the public education provisions in the new state constitution. "This person chosen governor by Virginia pledges himself in advance to break down the proposed system of public schools," railed Sumner. "What greater atrocity at this moment can be proposed? How can you organize Reconstruction except on the everlasting foundation of education?" After some retorts that the Walker broadside represented little more than meaningless campaign hyperbole, Sumner pulled from his pocket a letter from an anonymous Virginia public-school advocate reaffirming Walker's hostility to mass education at taxpayer expense. "The election was carried by an immense, gigantic, immoral fraud," concluded Sumner. "It was carried by an appeal to the rebel people throughout the state that they should take the control of the state and in that way nullify the constitution and trample out the system of common schools. That is the great fact which dominates over this question."[25]

Indiana's Oliver P. Morton agreed with Sumner. He noted that earlier Republicans had conceded that once a former rebel state was readmitted by Congress it would be free to go its own way. But, he added, "experience has now shown that we cannot stand upon that doctrine. We must follow the doctrine of Reconstruction to its consequences, and if necessary we must deal with these states after they have been readmitted." This revision of understanding necessitated reducing the states to the level of provinces whenever Congress should determine the need. On January 21, the Senate version passed, imposing special suffrage and educational restrictions upon Virginia's state sovereignty. Four days later, the House concurred. In the process, a precedent was established that the Guarantee Clause remained alive even after state readmission.[26]

Mississippi was next to feel the centralizing arm of Congress. The Virginia precedent was blood in the water for those intent on creating a unitary nation-state. In the debate over the Mississippi bill, a states-rights advocate asked Republican Senator John J. Howard of Michigan if he would like Congress to regulate the public school system of Michigan. Howard quickly shot back. If his state, he said, ever did something as reactionary as discontinuing public education, he would be the first "to appeal to the Congress of the United States to apply the corrective and to exercise this great power of guarantying a republican form of government, whether my state should will or nill." Were these first steps in creating national educational standards constitutional?

Senator Morton reaffirmed that Congress was the only legitimate judge of the question. In his opinion, neither the United States Supreme Court nor the states had any role in the matter. Republican Senator Richard Yates of Illinois agreed. In the dynamic constitutional environment in which his generation found itself, Yates felt no loyalty to the idea that public education was a matter solely for the states to shape. He felt no tie to constitutional tradition or to even the concept of judicial precedent. Slavery, he said, had been a precedent; the Dred Scott Decision had been a precedent. For himself, Yates proclaimed, all that mattered was "the light of the nineteenth century," not the dead and putrefying hand of precedent![27]

In the debate on Mississippi, the home of Jefferson Davis, the centralizers gloried in their uncheckable power. Senator Howard reaffirmed that the Guarantee Clause was "without limitation." For those concerned with questions of constitutionality, Senator Yates expressed his utter contempt for the Supreme Court and everything associated with the legal profession. He confessed that he himself had once been a practicing attorney and knew all the games played in courts of law. For himself, he trusted the voice of the democratic national numerical majority more than deceitful, elitist jurisprudence. "Do not be afraid of decisions of the Supreme Court," he encouraged his fellow Senators. "Whether the Supreme Court stands in the way or not, there is a spirit and a power in this enlightened age which will compel conformity to truth, right, justice, and liberty." And, he emphasized that the Guarantee Clause should be used not only in reference to the Southern states. Some Northern states were fast becoming worthy candidates for Congress's disciplining power. In his opinion, Northern communities such as Cincinnati that outlawed Bible reading in the public schools were overdue for Congressional discipline. He saw the aristocratic power of the Roman Catholic church behind the actions of the Cincinnati school board as no different from the aristocratic power of the old Southern slavocracy. In his opinion, the times demanded Congress impose one national standard in public education. Popular anti-Catholicism fed the Republican urge to centralize American government, which was a necessary first step toward systematically assaulting historic white racism.[28]

Southern Public Education During Reconstruction

Early in 1870, Congress imposed Virginia's special conditions on Mississippi and Texas as well.[29] In these three related instances, the Guarantee Clause was used to restrict the independence of supposedly sovereign states. Virginia was quick to conform to the will of Congress.[30] On March 2, 1870, Virginia's state legislature elected William Henry Ruffner superintendent of its new public school system. Ruffner had worked with Robert E. Lee in the administration of Washington College after the war and was highly regarded by the South's premier folk hero. Lee himself was an advocate of public education for all of Virginia's children, an attitude somewhat uncommon among that state's white population in 1870. Six months after Ruffner's appointment, Lee was dead. But Ruffner's past association with the great man strengthened him in his new post.

Ruffner worked closely with Barnas Sears in shaping Virginia's new public school system. As head of the Peabody Fund, Sears had chosen Staughton, Virginia, as his headquarters, where he was readily available to Ruffner. News of the close collaboration between Ruffner and Sears pleased Congress that Virginia was moving as expected. Ruffner had more difficulty with his fellow white Virginians. Many Virginians resented being forced to create a public school system by congressional mandate. Accordingly, Ruffner unleashed a propaganda campaign designed to prove that Virginia's public education was not a "Yankee invention," but rather the fruit of George Washington and Thomas Jefferson's thoughts on schooling. Additionally, he urged that public schools would improve the behavior of African Americans and that racially segregated schools would "gradually overcome [their] contemptible ambition to associate with white people." Ruffner even attempted to tap anti-Catholic feeling to build local support for public education. He reminded his Protestant constituents that the Roman Catholic church strongly opposed public schools and that Virginians could demonstrate their distance from Roman Catholicism by supporting public education.[31]

A master of public relations, Ruffner founded an educational journal and used its first issue in October 1870 to trumpet the support of Governor Walker's regime for the new school system. In an open letter from Walker, public education in general and even schooling for blacks was warmly endorsed. Walker's letter was immediately followed by one from Ruffner to all of Virginia's county superintendents of schools. He urged them to employ black teachers for black schools and to nominate blacks as well as whites to serve on local school boards. Such public expressions eliminated all congressional doubts as to whether or not Virginia was conforming to its dictates.[32] In November, Ruffner's schools opened their doors to the children of the state. By the close of that first academic year, Virginia could boast 2,900 schools, 3,000 teachers, and an average daily attendance of 75,722 pupils. Educational progress continued in Virginia until 1872, when the state entered a long financial crisis that negatively affected public education there. The Peabody Fund contributed generously to Virginia to keep the state's system operational during hard times. The problem centered on the state's large debt. Conservatives argued that the state's first obligation was to pay interest on the debt, even if that meant that public education would not have adequate funds. Some public school advocates openly pushed for the state to repudiate its debt. They argued that most Virginians had suffered heavy financial loses because of the war and that investors in state bonds should not be exempt from sharing in the general hardship. Money diverted from schools to pay interest on the state debt, they argued, doubly hurt an already beleaguered people. Conservatives retorted that if the poor people (who had enough money to waste from twenty-five to fifty cents a day on liquor) wanted public education they should demand that their school taxes be raised. All through this imbroglio, the conservatives were secretly aided by a state treasurer who hated public education. He diverted money earmarked for the schools to other purposes even beyond paying interest on the state debt. By the end of the decade, when his methods were exposed, it was estimated that over a half million dollars had been lost to Virginia's public schools through his deceit. During these years of penury, black schools suffered disproportionately. What was the attitude of Congress, given this turn of events? Republican congressmen remembered Virginia's initial obedience and the excellent public relations work of Ruffner. The back room dealings of the state treasurer only became known after Reconstruction was over. So far as meeting obligations on the state debt serving as Virginia's highest priority, Republicans were generally opposed to repudiation of contractual financial obligations. As a result, Congress never did follow through on its threat of 1870 to intervene in Virginia in order to preserve a meaningful public-school system.[33]

Initially, Mississippi also readily complied with the congressional mandate to create a public school system. Unlike Virginia, Mississippi had a Republican administration led by Governor James L. Alcorn, a native white Mississippian of some social standing. Mississippi's counterpart to Ruffner was Henry R. Pease, a New Englander who had worked with General Banks in creating Louisiana's public schools during the war. Pease subsequently directed the Freedmen's Bureau schools in Mississippi and had a good reputation as a public school reformer. But there was an underside to Pease's school administration. Paid county school boards served as Republican Party patronage centers. Their existence and their accompanying costs fed the arguments of

Mississippi public school opponents who said with some justification that the entire system was a mass of corruption and waste. One Mississippi school teacher wrote U.S. Commissioner of Education Eaton directly of the problems that he encountered on the job. He complained that he had been recruited with the understanding that his remuneration would be one-hundred dollars per month, but once on the job he received less than half that amount. And that lesser sum was not paid in United States currency, but rather in state script, worth only five cents on the dollar. He described a Republican politician on his county school board as excusing the teacher's treatment by noting that education was not all that valuable because "the more a man knows, the more sorrow he will have and the more to answer for." "I told him," the teacher emphasized to Eaton, "that if what he thought was true, . . . that he should, as soon as he got to Jackson, bring in a bill to abolish schools." Despite his lack of official support, the teacher noted that he fulfilled his calling by teaching fifty local black children during the day and thirty African-American adults at night. He ended the letter by declaring that he would head to the Pacific coast as soon as the school term was over.

Superintendent Pease was motivated by idealism, not by the dreams of graft that inspired many of Mississippi's Republicans. Large sums were raised to support public education; but as the example of the disgruntled correspondent of Commissioner Eaton displayed, sometimes little of that money actually supported education. As a scalawag landowner, Governor Alcorn quickly cooled to the Republican educational agenda which called for heavy taxation on real estate. Corruption doubly soured his attitude. These factors lost the Republican Party support among former Whigs, such as Alcorn. Had Pease been able to control the system that he nominally headed, perhaps these losses might have been justifiable. Unfortunately, prospects for improvement soon evaporated altogether as Pease was replaced by Thomas W. Cardozo, someone more attuned to the pecuniary needs of party hacks. From the local white perspective, Mississippi's public school system became a mechanism for income redistribution to both corrupt politicians and the impoverished black community that had been denied the promise of "forty acres and a mule." Black Mississippians did not press for racially mixed schools but rather for their "fair share" of the school fund. As blacks constituted a majority of Mississippi's population, considerable amounts of money were involved. Many white Mississippians proposed that taxes gathered from whites should be reserved for white schools alone and that blacks should have only those taxes arising from their own community. But whites were not in the majority and could not translate this desire into statute. Nonetheless, in 1871, white anger exploded in the eastern counties of the state. Schools were burned and teachers whipped in this Ku Klux Klan uprising. One of those beaten was A. P. Huggins, Winston County's Superintendent of Schools. In Congress, Ben Butler waved Huggins' bloody nightshirt in demanding a national crackdown on Klan terrorism, and a classic term in American political history was born.[34]

Thomas W. Cardozo, who replaced Pease in 1873, is acknowledged in accounts of every interpretive slant as the worst example of a corrupt African-American Republican leader in the Reconstruction era. Under his tenure as Mississippi's school chief, the state debt mounted. High taxes resulted in nonpayment in many cases and a consequent forfeiture of lands to the state. By 1875, one-fifth of the state's area had been seized for this reason. Manufacturing enterprises and railroads, businesses favored by Republicans, generally escaped the tax burden that fell disproportionately on real estate. This example reveals one reason why public education contributed to the hard feelings generated by Reconstruction in the Southern states.[35] Congress had not demanded that Mississippi have a corruption-free system of public education, and so it had no cause to consider federal intervention in that state.

The situation was different in Texas. There, a relatively honest, tightly centralized public school system was created under the control of Jacob C. de Gress, a young United States Army officer who had emigrated from Prussia at the age of ten. De Gress, who had no prior experience in education, ran a military-style operation that won few local friends to his system. The Texas school law of 1871 demanded compulsory education for all persons between six and eighteen years of age. As there were no school buildings, they had to be constructed all at once, causing high taxes to be imposed on a people whose economy lay in a post-war shambles. De Gress tried to ease the immediate pain by getting the legislature to approve bond issues to build the schools, but his request was denied. Unlike Mississippi, political corruption did not accompany the high school taxes; but these taxes were unpopular nonetheless. The compulsory component in the law especially grated individualistic Texans. Few American communities at that time actually required school attendance on the Prussian model. Many Texans felt that they were being singled out for extraordinary punishment. For married teenagers the law created special hardship. In 1871, one seventeen-year-old wife pleaded for some common sense: "I have a husband to care for, a child to nurse, clothes to wash, meals to cook, and a house to clean. If they make me attend school another year, everything will go to ruin." Texans regarded their public school teachers and administrators as outsiders with foreign ideas. Democrats played on this local mistrust and falsely blamed the rising school taxes on corruption, as was indeed the case elsewhere. Catholic voters in Texas organized against the system. Even Germans were appealed to on the grounds that despite its Prussian origins, the tightly centralized Texas school system would never accommodate their contribution to cultural diversity. The Democrats' antipublic school campaign succeeded; and in the fall of 1872, Democrats won control of the state legislature. The following spring, they radically decentralized the Texas school system over the Republican governor's veto. The following year, private schools, including those operated by the Roman Catholic church, were allowed to share in the school fund. In 1875, Texas adopted a new constitution that abolished the office of state superintendent of public instruction and eliminated the requirement for compulsory attendance, which by then had become a dead letter anyway.[36]

For differing reasons, Virginia and Mississippi had not offered Congress a clear-cut cause for following through on its threat of post-admission intervention. Texas did. The dismantling of public education in that state was obvious for all to see. William Alexander, Texas' Republican Attorney General, composed an official position paper in September 1873, emphasizing that the Texas legislature's repeal of public education deliberately violated the clear and specific limitations on Texas's sovereignty that Congress had imposed in 1870. Barnas Sears also made sure that Congress could not ignore the issue. In May 1873, he publicly discontinued the disbursement of all Peabody money in Texas due to the anti-public-education spirit there.[37] Given the publicity surrounding Texas' blatant challenge to Congress, a failure to respond threatened to weaken the public perception of the Guarantee Clause. In the end, Congress did nothing to punish Texas, but that is different from saying that it ignored the matter. The problem did not become acute until 1873, at which time Congress was debating the creation of even greater federal involvement in public education. If federal control over education had been instituted, the Texas problem would have been absorbed into a general reform. By 1873, the spotty record of public education in the Southern states had led many Republicans to lose faith that Southerners could ever create meaningful public school systems on their own without outside financial assistance. Once a federal education system came into being, the Texas problem would be solved.

Georgia had helped generate the congressional emotion that had rained down on Virginia, Mississippi, and Texas. There too, public education was struggling. After receiving a hand-slapping by Congress, Georgia politicos initially behaved correctly by congressional lights, and in 1870 passed legislation to create a public school system in the state.

The new law mandated racially segregated schooling but promised that both sets of public schools would be treated equally in the disbursements of state funds. Unfortunately, the system was never established. The following year, the Democrats won control of the state legislature and proclaimed that the Republicans had left state finances in such disarray that the installation of a new, expensive state public service was impossible. Georgia Democrats charged that the state's Republicans had made off with half a million dollars intended for public schools. These stories seemingly justified doing nothing to promote mass education. Nevertheless, white Georgians openly expressed their contempt for educating blacks at state expense. "It is well known," Charles Stearns wrote about conditions in Georgia, "that the sight of a Negro school house stirs up the rabid feelings of a Ku-Klux gang, as the sight of water is said to disturb a mad dog."

While Klan attitudes dominated in rural districts, in Georgia's larger towns and cities demands frequently arose for public education.[38] In 1873, Georgia finally reinaugurated a statewide system of public education. The new system barely limped along. But Superintendent of Schools Gustavus J. Orr, in the tradition of Virginia's Ruffner, mounted an active public relations campaign to build support for public education in the state. The emergence of the likes of Ruffner and Orr was significant. As more and more Southerners became spokesmen for public education, the idea had a better chance of being implemented than when regarded as a New England concept. Barnas Sears's strategy of using the Peabody Fund to win Southerners to the public school idea was gradually succeeding. Meanwhile, black public education made little progress. Even in Republican Southern states, very little meaningful education occurred for blacks. In the latter states, political corruption and gross incompetence by and large conspired to produce a dismal result.[39]

Republican writer Charles Nordhoff described Arkansas Republicans as having wasted and stolen most of the school fund of that state, forcing the closure of many schools. The Republican governor appointed party hacks as county clerks and collectors of taxes. Normally these appointees were not from the counties they served, a fact that made the prostitution of their offices all the easier. School taxes disappeared under such circumstances. An honest Arkansas Republican reported to John Eaton in disgust: "It would be impossible to convey to you any adequate idea of the fearful condition of the State Administration in the estimation of the people. . . . The course of the villains who have stolen into power is such that some of value to the party, such as would give credit to it, cannot be induced to advocate the party in such hands."

Typical of many other Southern Republican governments, honest men in Arkansas tended to serve in the visible role of state superintendent of public instruction. In 1873–1874, J. C. Corbin, an African American educated at Oberlin College and Ohio University, held that office. He did his best given the limits of his authority and the realities of how the governor used public education to build his own political machine. A corrupt system was headed by an honest front man, providing future historians with contradictory elements to be used in support of a variety of interpretations. In any case, the schoolchildren of Arkansas were not well served.[40] One Arkansas school official blamed the state's dismal performance on the requirement of maintaining costly duplication of schools to ensure racial segregation in thinly populated areas.[41] The point was valid but in no way excused using the schools as part of a systematic pattern of political patronage and corruption.

Nordhoff provided detailed descriptions of how Republican regimes in Louisiana exploited that state's theoretically integrated system of public education. Members of the legislature were appointed to local school boards, which they used for purposes of distributing political patronage. Public school teachers became their political tools or did not continue in their jobs. Describing Louisiana's teachers, Nordhoff wrote: "Their work is not to teach school but to talk up the man who appoints them." He compared this operation to the "Tammany thieves in New York." Given the fact that rural whites generally boycotted the mixed public schools of Louisiana, this political corruption was conducted in virtually an all-black school system. While a politically privileged minority of blacks temporarily benefited from these illicit practices, African-American parents frequently complained of mismanagement in their children's public schools.[42]

Natchitoches Parish in the early 1870s annually received from $15,000 to $20,000 in school funds. The parish then had one all-black school with three teachers. One of the teachers was Raford Blunt, an African-American Louisiana state senator who could neither read nor write. He had been appointed to the school board and then had participated in his own appointment as teacher, in absentia in every sense but his claim to a teacher's salary. Black children in New Orleans' mixed schools fared better, as those institutions were showcases largely free from the gross political corruption conducted more easily in the state's isolated, rural, black-belt districts. Even Republican state superintendents did not deny the political exploitation of public education in Louisiana. In 1874, one of these reported: "An appeal is made to the general assembly to give this subject a rigid investigation and adopt suitable measures for the protection of the school funds from further alienation." Some modern historians have acknowledged the corruption of public education in Louisiana during this time. In his review of Reconstruction in Louisiana, Joe Gray Taylor has provided this assessment: "Without question there was much stealing of school funds in Louisiana during Radical Reconstruction."[43]

White hostility to black education hampered public education in the South, but often the supposed friends of African Americans were as bad as their enemies. Short-sighted blacks participated in this corruption to the detriment of their people's educational yearnings. Evidence of this exploitation heightened white opposition to public education that would have been there even had corruption not been present. In Florida, school-related positions were used to fund political operatives working to get out the black vote for Republicans. Illiterates were commonly appointed teachers if they were known to be effective political organizers. Education was not effectively valued in this system, no matter what some have claimed, both then and since. The Republican Florida constitution stated that after 1880 voters registering for the first time would be required to be literate. But in the early 1870s, 1880 seemed far away; and winning the next election was more important than attacking illiteracy.[44]

Florida's Republican superintendents of public instruction were by and large able men who believed in their mission. However, none of them remained long on the job. First came Rev. Charles Beecher, brother of Henry Ward Beecher and Harriet Beecher Stowe. In 1873, he was replaced by Rev. Jonathan C. Gibbs, an African-American graduate of Dartmouth. Even historians of the racist Dunning school credit him as "an able man and . . . respected for doing his work as well as the circumstances would allow." He died in office after about a year of service and was replaced by Samuel B. McLin. He too served only briefly, and in leaving complained of corruption at the county level. McLin was followed by a succession of superintendents who continually complained of local school officials who had little interest in educating children. In Florida, as elsewhere in the Republican South, superintendents of public instruction served as the honest face on a corrupt body. And honest men could not long serve in such a capacity.[45] Republican William Watkin Hicks, one of these latter-day Florida superintendents of public instruction, bluntly described conditions in his official report to Commissioner Eaton in 1874:

While a few of our county superintendents are in every way worthy, qualified, and efficient officers, a large majority are notoriously unfit for the position and utterly incapable of performing their duties. The literary qualifications of some of them, if judged from the letters and annual reports sent to this office, are of a very primitive type, and some are so indolent, incompetent, or uninterested, as to omit the making of an annual report at all. The truth is that this and all other offices in any way connected with the educational interests of the state must be entirely and forever divorced from party politics. Too frequently has the county superintendency fallen into the hands of men who have prostituted it to their political advancement or made use of it for the pecuniary gain it brought. This should not be.[46]

The corruption associated with Southern public education in the Republican-controlled states was also found in Alabama. Robert Somers, an English aristocrat visiting that state in 1870–1871, described public education there: "The system of administration seems . . . very faulty, if not corrupt. The late state superintendent of education embezzled or misappropriated the funds; and a county superintendent in north Alabama, following so good an example, ran away with several thousand dollars entrusted to him for the payment of teachers." Somers also commented that the employment of partially illiterate teachers in Alabama's black schools opened the whole system to public ridicule. "Common sense itself," he wrote, "is struck completely dumb" by such practices. In 1873, most of Alabama's public schools ceased operations due to an inability of the state to pay the teachers. Only in Alabama's cities were schools kept open.[47]

Before the Civil War, North Carolina had developed the closest model that the South then had of a meaningful public school system. But after the war, the urge to revive it was dead. Fear that emancipation would inevitably lead to mixed schools in any public school system was the cause of the change. In North Carolina's state constitutional convention of 1868, a new public-school system was drafted on parchment. But after the state's readmission in that year, conservatives successfully kept the system from adequately functioning. A state supreme court decision, interpreting a single clause in the new state constitution, played a decisive role. The clause required each county to pass by majority votes all tax levies that were not otherwise "necessary." The question of whether public school expenses were "necessary" was then appealed to the state supreme court that ruled that they were not—this despite the fact that the state constitution required that public schools be maintained for four months a year. This court decision left the issue of public education in North Carolina to the determination of local majorities. In counties with white majorities, fear of mixed schools effectively killed proposals to raise school taxes. In the divided government that characterized North Carolina during Reconstruction, the superintendent of public instruction was Republican Alexander McIver. But he could do little to build an effective system due to this judicial ruling and the Democratic legislature's unwillingness to act. As a result, public education languished in the state even beyond the end of Reconstruction.[48]

South Carolina presented an entirely different picture. During the winter of 1869–1870, the South Carolina legislature had enacted a system of effectively racially segregated public schools. Most then agreed that a segregated system had the best chance of enduring in a state with high racial feeling. By June 1870, about 60,000 pupils evenly divided between blacks and whites were enrolled in the state's new public schools. Almost immediately, a serious problem arose for the new system's teaching staff. County treasurers delayed paying them their salaries. Certificates, promising them real money at a later date, were dispensed to teachers, who were forced to sell them to speculators at significant discounts in order to survive. Quickly, it became apparent to all that political corruption was undermining public education in South Carolina.[49]

In 1871, a taxpayers' convention held at Columbia protested the massive waste of precious revenues supposedly raised for public education and other good purposes. The dynamics of this corruption had racial overtones. Early in the Republican administration of South Carolina, most important political jobs went to whites despite the African American majority in the state. For one year, blacks were in the majority of the lower house of the legislature, but this was not typical. By and large, blacks were forced into political posts of lesser importance, such as local positions serving the new school system. Unfortunately, many of these ambitious men succumbed to skimming off funds intended for public education.[50] Comparisons with the operations of the Tweed Ring in New York were frequently made.[51]

In the late summer of 1872, James L. Orr raised a howl against the drift of events in his native state. As South Carolina's last governor under Presidential Reconstruction, Orr had initially opposed Congressional Reconstruction but subsequently joined the Republican Party in hopes of shaping public policy under the new order. But by the end of 1872, he was openly expressing his disillusionment. As the most prominent "scalawag" in South Carolina's Republican government, he blasted the system of heavy taxation that had not resulted in demonstrable services to the people of the state.[52] Justus K. Jillson, South Carolina's Republican superintendent of public instruction, agreed with Orr on the extent of the mismanagement. In 1872, he noted, $300,000 had been appropriated for public education, yet not one dollar was dispersed to meet actual school expenses. His use of language to describe this situation was not moderate: "Public confidence has been betrayed and destroyed; school teachers and school officers have been forced to labor without receiving their salaries. The whole system is, in its present condition, a reproach to those who claim to be its friends and advocates." Rather than claim political corruption, Jillson gave more the impression of massive incompetence in accounting for funds at the county level. The following year, he cited "ignorance, incompetency, and inexcusable neglect of duty on the part of many school-officers." In 1874, he added that South Carolina's teaching force was largely "incompetent, inefficient, and worthless." "Too many teachers," he wrote, "are found in the schools without the proper spirit for their work." Jillson's disparagement of South Carolina's teachers was grossly unfair. What could he reasonably expect in a state where teachers were not paid for services rendered?[53]

In 1873, the growing negative national image of Republican South Carolina reached a critical stage when James S. Pike published a widely read critique of Republican corruption in what he termed "the prostrate state." Pike's credentials as a Republican, former abolitionist and a member of the Lincoln administration made his assessment all the more damning. Similar to others, he compared this "'huge system of brigandage'" to Boss Tweed's regime in New York City. The difference between the two, he noted, was that in New York publicity of wrongdoing led to reform. In South Carolina, he wrote, the African-American majority was seemingly immune to any revelations of political corruption, despite the fact that blacks themselves suffered the most from a fraudulent system of public education. In reviewing this important book, Henry Ward Beecher did not dispute Pike's allegations of runaway corruption, but he did regret the author's categorical portrayal of the black community as impervious to the need for reform.[54]

In 1874, another taxpayers' convention held in Columbia adopted a novel approach to the subject, claiming that the failure of the public school system in that state left South Carolina without "a republican form of government."[55] South Carolina's Republican state central committee rushed to counter the taxpayers' protest to Congress. In a white paper, the committee did not completely deny the rampant corruption in the state, but claimed that it was endemic throughout all of South Carolina history. In prewar days, the statement claimed, corruption "was carried on . . . with the artistic skill of more experienced operators, and not easily seen." Brazenly, the report credited the Republican party for bringing public education to South Carolina, but it completely avoided any mention of unpaid teachers and disappearing school funds. South Carolina's troubles, the committee continued, were due to pampered landholders not used to having their property taxed. Before the war, taxes to run the government had been raised from individuals, the trades and the professions; real estate had largely been exempt. But under the new Republican order, real estate bore the brunt of the increased tax burden. This angered antisocial land barons, who had conspired not to sell their uncultivated excess holdings to freedmen in order to keep the latter in a condition of peonage. Given these realities, the white paper argued, little pity was due the taxpayers. Then the piece concluded with an argument appealing to anti-Catholic sentiment: The landed Bourbons of South Carolina were equivalent to the privileged Catholic aristocracy of Europe that Bismarck was then so admirably battling. In short, the committee suggested, racial Reconstruction was part and parcel of a world-wide struggle against reaction and privilege.[56] While the state central committee argument revealed how religion and race were both involved in Reconstruction rhetoric, it more importantly sought to mask the obvious failures in South Carolina's public-education experiment.

If the record was dismal in Southern Republican states, at least in those locations there was some activity in the area of educating blacks. This was not necessarily the case in those former slave states that never joined the Confederacy and therefore had not been forced to undergo Congressional Reconstruction. Kentucky, which refused to educate blacks at white expense, belonged to this camp.[57] In Maryland also, nothing was done by the state government to assist black education which was conducted solely by private charities such as the "Baltimore Association." Delaware also made no provision for the education of African-American children. In 1872, a bill to create a black public-school system passed the lower house of the Delaware legislature but died in the Senate. Delaware's all-white public school system had been created in 1829, and it remained unchanged well into Reconstruction. "The Delaware Association for the Moral Improvement and Education of the Colored People" played the role in Delaware that the "Baltimore Association" played in Maryland. But in both instances, this charitable work reached only a small fraction of the states' black children. Finally, in 1873, the Maryland legislature passed a law providing in theory for a black public school system supported solely by black taxes. Congress was then debating whether to grant federal educational aid to the states. States such as Kentucky and Maryland were motivated to provide at least on paper for black schools in hopes of qualifying for this anticipated aid. Delaware was confident that nothing would come from Congress, and so it did not even theoretically approve of black public schools. After years of congressional debate and inaction, Kentucky finally moved to flesh out its theoretical system of black public schools. In 1874, it approved of an educational expenditure of fifty cents per black child per year. The symbolism of this ridiculous act speaks across the decades. White racism, here termed "the African factor," encouraged the making of educational bricks without straw.[58]

5

FEDERAL AID TO EDUCATION

The nationalizing thrust of Reconstruction and the resistance to public schools in the South convinced some Republicans of the need to centralize public education.[1] Days after Congress commanded that Virginia immediately flesh out its system of public education, William F. Prosser delivered a major address to the House that proposed to inaugurate a national educational system along the centralized Prussian model. The scheduled end of the Freedmen's Bureau, together with his own state's dismantling of public education, spurred this Tennessee carpetbagger to action. Rumor held that John Eaton himself had written the Tennessee representative's speech. The impending adoption of the Fifteenth Amendment gave Prosser's remarks before the House great poignancy. His argument was powerful. Millions of new, illiterate voters were about to be empowered by the Republican Party. Accordingly, that party had a moral obligation to eradicate illiteracy as soon as possible. Prosser suggested that Congress provide an initial two million dollars to fund a new national system. He publicly wished that the seven and a half millions that had been "wasted" in purchasing "the snows of Alaska" were still available for what he considered this better purpose. He also noted millions sent for engines of war. In his opinion, federal money was more urgently needed for public education; for what good could be accomplished in defending the country's borders if the nation was rotting from the inside out due to ignorance?

Albion Tourgee joined Prosser's cause, lobbying President Grant concerning the need for an expanded federal role in public education. In addition, a New York publisher sent John Eaton sufficient funds to reproduce the speech "to aid in its circulation." Office seekers also wrote Eaton, asking for positions in the new federal bureaucracy needed to flesh out Prosser's dream. One was even so forward as to suggest his favorite locations for an appointment, designating "Texas back from the Gulf Coast" or "East Tennessee." With interest mounting, Eaton was invited to deliver an address to the National Teachers' Association on the topic. However, not all of the attention was favorable.

Barnas Sears wrote Eaton of his fears that the very idea of a national public-school system was guaranteed to squelch the development of the pro-public education sentiment he was trying to encourage among Southern whites. Sears cautioned discretion, and was skittish of Eaton even circulating information of national education systems as they existed in Europe. "People will say," he advised Eaton, "that all those countries are under monarchical governments and that such centralized systems of education are not adapted to a republican form of government like ours. . . . Avoid exciting State jealousies and reviving the old question of State rights." Others were even more negative. Given Prosser's increased notoriety, the Ku Klux Klan focused on his district and "persuaded" enough voters to stay at home on election day to bring about the crusader's defeat in November.

With Prosser gone, Representative George Frisbie Hoar of Massachusetts introduced a first bill "To Establish a National System of Education." Recognizing the significance of this action, Democrats mobilized to kill this new centralizing creature in its crib. Aided by state-centered Republicans, they argued that the Fifteenth Amendment by itself would solve the problem of national illiteracy. Their argument was seductive: Armed with the ballot, black men could tax the property of whites in their home states and erect meaningful systems of public education there. In short, national schools were not needed.[2] They spread fear of the federal bureaucracy that would accompany a national school system. Political patronage and corruption were sure to characterize this new army of federal office holders. In addition, they argued, the federal government would do a poor job of educating, as shown in the dismal performance of Washington, D.C.'s schools. Direction of education, they emphasized, was best left as close to the local level as possible.[3] The few Republicans who spoke against Hoar's proposal were primarily concerned with not doing for the South that which it should do for itself. "Let us not," warned William Lawrence, a Republican Congressman from Ohio, "commit the fatal error of inducing the states of the South to make no provision for the education of their people." Lawrence was quite ready to use the Guarantee Clause to force the South to fulfill its educational duties, but he regarded Southern illiteracy as a Southern problem resulting from the sin of slavery. It was their sin, he emphasized, not his; and they should pay for its elimination.[4]

George Hoar was frustrated by this bipartisan barrage. The arguments of his opponents spanned the ideological gambit, from states-rights Democrats to Guarantee-Clause Republicans. But he discerned one common thread uniting them. Both Democrats and Republicans opposing a national school system saw illiteracy in the South as the problem of some other place, of some other people, of some other community. The nation, he warned his colleagues, was at a crossroads. It could acknowledge itself as one people and one community or it could retreat. The dream of one unified nation, born in the fires of civil war, could die. The "new birth of freedom," anticipated by Lincoln in the Gettysburg Address, could be aborted. Americans could slink back into their state boundaries and define themselves again as citizens of Massachusetts, Ohio, or Illinois; or they could claim their common nationality and fully and finally become Americans, one people, indivisible.[5]

Here at the outset was the core of the problem. In 1870, Americans might romanticize Bismarckian nationalism, but they did not think of themselves truly as one people. They did not behave as one people. They were a diverse and disunited people. Blacks and whites did not constitute one community. In the eyes of many whites, black illiteracy and ignorance was not a white problem. And when they were forced to pay for African-American schools, as they were compelled to do in those Southern states with Republican majorities, whites constantly complained of having to do for others what those others should be doing for themselves. Similarly Northerners tended to view illiteracy as predominately a Southern problem. Representative Hoar pleaded with his countrymen to see it as a national problem that ultimately would affect even those groups and regions seeking to quarantine themselves against it. His bill, he said, was the best hope for an enduring democracy in the United States.[6]

Hoar received a degree of support from an unexpected quarter. Congress had just finished disciplining Virginia on the issue of public education. Nonetheless, early support for federal educational reform came from this denigrated state. Democrat William Henry Ruffner, who had just been appointed as Virginia's superintendent of public instruction, came out publicly for greater federal involvement in public education. Although he emphasized that he was not in favor of a national system of public schools, he urged that some form of federal aid to state-based education be inaugurated. Ruffner's gesture was excellent public relations. One of Ruffner's close friends privately admonished him: "Congress does not mean justice! It means humiliation first, and a precedent for intolerable aggression afterward." Nevertheless, for the next two decades, Ruffner continued to call for federal aid. His explanation to his fellow conservative Southern Democrats was designed to be persuasive for that limited constituency: Congress, he emphasized, owed federal educational assistance to the blacks. By contrast, he argued, the white South owed the blacks nothing; the white South had helped partially civilize blacks through the institution of slavery. The white North, on the other hand, had freed illiterate blacks to compete economically and politically with whites. Without education, blacks were bound to lose this contest. The short sighted action of the white North was cruel in the extreme. In addition to injuring the blacks, Ruffner's argument continued, the white North had wronged the white South by expecting the latter to pay for the precipitous mistake of the former. Accordingly, federal aid to education was simple justice to the South, black and white alike.[7]

Hoar's focus was national, not regional. If the United States wanted to compete in world markets, the nation as a whole had to become educated. England had grown overconfident and had found its products outclassed by Prussia and other continental countries at the Paris Exposition of 1867. This realization had stirred England to undertake a significant reform in its system of public education. Hoar warned: "Let not America incur the disgrace of lagging behind all civilized nations in that popular education of which she set the first example." If America did nothing, he continued, eventually there would be a price to pay. His measure required all states to make adequate provisions for public instruction by July 1, 1871, or suffer the consequences of having the federal government take over public education in the states that were remiss. According to his bill, the federal schools were required to be "open alike to all children of suitable age, without distinction of color or race." Here was a red flag before the bull of white racism. Hoar's choice of language strongly suggested that racially mixed schools would be forced on those states requiring federal schools.[8] The Hoar bill had powerful friends. Hoar's brother was then Grant's Attorney General. In addition, Senator Henry Wilson of Massachusetts adopted Hoar's idea and wrote a widely read position paper on national education which was published in January 1871 in the *Atlantic Monthly*. At the same time, the bill had powerful enemies, even in the Republican Party. Henry Ward Beecher came out against it in December 1870. At the heart of his opposition was his fear that the enormous federal bureaucracy that the measure would entail would encourage "unlimited jobbery and corruption." Many Republicans then were becoming disgusted with political corruption and saw danger signs of still more opportunities for it in the bill. Their feeling was coalescing into the Liberal Republican movement. The proposal of a massive, new federal bureaucracy at a time when the Republican Party was splitting internally over the issue of corrupt political patronage was not auspicious.[9]

Republicans cool to Hoar's idea let Democrats lead the opposition. John T. Bird, a New Jersey Democrat, warned the House that the bill represented Bismarckianism at its worst. He portrayed the German chancellor as building a political machine both in public education and government through the power of patronage. A centralized system of governmental patronage was emerging in Germany which Bird warned could easily be duplicated in the United States by the Hoar bill. "Will not fifty thousand New England school-teachers scattered throughout the South be able to control the vote?" he rhetorically asked. While acknowledging the popularity of Prussia's defeat of France in the American press, Bird cautioned that the German people were the "most interfered with" of all the populations of Europe. They had the least political freedom. The American model of states rights, not the German model of centralized government, was the ideal. He warned of the Republican Party tendency to romanticize German centralized efficiency and order.[10]

In the early 1870s, Americans wrestled with two social models, one encouraged by Bismarck's Germany and one solely from the American past that had been partially discredited in the war to save the Union. The issue was whether locally controlled public institutions were better than those controlled from the national center. Slavery had been one such local institution. The widespread mayhem and destruction associated with its demise made centralization an emotionally attractive alternative. Religious prejudice pushed many Americans to consider a thorough remaking of the American polity in the image of the new Germany. But racial prejudice led them back to the traditional American preference for local control. A disgust of "Grantism" (as political corruption was then coming to be called by some) undermined the Hoar bill, but race was even a larger factor. Under the provisions of the bill, the president of the United States (presumably informed by his Commissioner of Education) would determine when a state did not have a school system in place serving "all" of the school-aged children of a state. At that time, even Northern states such as Illinois did not provide public schools that were open to blacks. By the provisions of the Hoar bill, even Northern states could be taken over by federal bureaucrats insistent on racial mixing in the public schools.[11]

In the Roman Catholic press, Father Isaac T. Hecker led his church's opposition against the Hoar bill. The Republican program for national schools, he wrote, planned to eliminate all diversity and bring about a perfect "social and religious unification . . . molding the population of European and of African origin, Indians and Asiatics, Protestants and Catholics, Jews and pagans, into one homogeneous

people, after what may be called the New England Evangelical type."
This, he wrote, was not the "Union" that so many Americans had died
to save. The Republicans, he charged, were confusing "unity" with
"union." "Union implies plurality or diversity," wrote Hecker. "Unity
excludes both." White racism gave force to Hecker's argument.[12]

At the same time that the House was debating the Hoar bill with
its implications for mixed schools, the Senate was discussing a proposal
of Senator Sumner that would bring mixed schools to Washington, D.C.
Sumner's long-time Republican associates had urged him to shelve the
measure, arguing that the races were then too far apart in their real-
world conditions to be melded together in any practicable way. Sumner
bristled at the charge that his bill was impractical. "Whatever is correct
in principle must be correct in practice," he told his fellow Republicans.
"I stand on this rule . . . I insist that whatever is correct in principle is
practical. Anything else would make this world a failure and obedience
to the laws of God impossible." He warned that a continuation of
segregated schooling could not uplift African Americans, because it
would brand them as the unique outcasts of American society. Slavery
had performed this segregating task up until 1865. Race-specific public
schools continued the separation after that date. The Republican Party
he admonished, could not afford to be either negligent or neutral on this
issue. Either it would continue to attack the stigma of caste, a cause
which Sumner saw as the very soul of the party, or it would subtly
"encourage and foster" racial stigma.

This was the kind of debate that Republicans dreaded. Talk of
mixed schools had barely surfaced in the debate over the Hoar bill. In
the House, Republicans had worked mightily to keep the serpent
largely hidden from view. But Sumner forced the issue into the open in
his debate on the future of the public schools in the nation's capital.
And everyone in both houses knew the intimate connection between
the Hoar and Sumner proposals. Rules adopted for Washington. D.C.,
could later be grafted onto a national school system.

Democrat Allen G. Thurman, Senator from Ohio, delighted in
countering Sumner's advanced racial position. Confidently, he boldly
advanced to attack even the strongest point in his enemy's forces. He
pointed to the fact that Roman Catholics were taxed to support the
public schools although in good conscience they could not send their
children to them. Soon, he predicted, white parents, even white parents
from the North, would know their Catholic neighbors' dilemma, when
they would be taxed to support racially integrated schools that they
would never let their children attend. He described Sumner as the
radical champion of despotism, advocating the smothering of traditional

American liberty in the name of centralization and uniformity. By contrast, Thurman posed himself as an old-fashioned advocate of decentralized government and local self-determination.

In the 1850s, Republicans had faced a much easier challenge. Concerning the issue of slavery in the territories, the Republican goal had been to keep the West reserved for the common white man seeking economic opportunity. In the 1850s, white racism and the ideology of equality of opportunity had meshed perfectly in the party's "free labor" rhetoric. Conditions in the 1870s were different. In this new era, equality of opportunity and white racism collided in the ideal vision of the American common school. Mixed schools were the logical extension both of the common school idea and the Republican civil rights movement. But the overwhelming majority of whites at that time refused to consider sending their children to schools with significant numbers of black children. During and immediately after the war, this Republican handicap had not been apparent. In the days immediately following emancipation, Republicans righteously could push for even segregated education for blacks. With the passage of time, foot dragging concerning public schools for African Americans in both the North and the South convinced some Republicans that equality of opportunity for black children could only be guaranteed in schools with white children in attendance. But white racists, constituting the overwhelming majority of the electorate, could not abide this result. With the rising specter of racial integration in the schools, Henry Wilson's Republican "New Departure" agenda for education became a house divided against itself. This became all too apparent in the debate over the Sumner bill in early 1871, held only weeks after the publication of Wilson's stirring article.

Listening to the debate over Sumner's bill, frustrated Republican Senators squirmed in their chairs. Senator Frederick A. Sawyer, a Massachusetts-bred Republican representing South Carolina, confessed that he wished that the issue had never come up. But now that it had he saw no course but to back Sumner, all the while expressing great fear regarding what the mixed schools issue might do to the Republican Party. Republican Senator Thomas W. Tipton of Nebraska noted that relatively few blacks resided in either Sumner's Massachusetts or his own state. For the record, both states had racially integrated public schools. But he had no doubt that if blacks moved in large numbers to either state the whites there would demand segregated public schools. With very few exceptions, Tipton said, white people everywhere, North and South, Republicans and Democrats, felt the same way. He feared this issue could only spell utter disaster for his party, and for that reason he promised to vote against the Sumner proposal.

Hiram Revels then rose and spoke. The moment was pregnant with historic meaning. Mississippi's Revels was the nation's first African-American senator. Since being seated in 1870, he had kept relatively silent, playing a back-bencher role. But this discussion demanded his inclusion. Black people, he said, had not pushed for mixed schools. They preferred the company of members of their own race over associating with white people. But, he said, mandated racial segregation by the white majority was an intolerable insult to his race. If "mixed schools" became the law of the land, he prophesied that blacks would still choose to go to school with members of their own race. Unreasoning white fear was the cause of the problem. He predicted that if people were freely allowed to send their children to any public school, blacks would still choose to go to black schools, leaving the whites to themselves.[13]

That which had started as a debate over a minor bill with little chance of passage blossomed into a full-blown debate on both the nature of the national community being formed in the process of Reconstruction and the uniform standards necessary for such a community. The existence of the Hoar bill over in the House magnified the Senate debate's importance. Joshua Hill, a white Republican from Georgia, was next to speak. He validated Revels's claim that blacks had little urge to integrate with whites and in fact preferred their own institutions, including their own schools and churches. But he refused to support Sumner's proposal, viewing it as an annoying ideological bit of legislative grandstanding. Henry Wilson then rose and supported Sumner. This was a highly symbolic gesture, as Wilson's name was closely associated with the national schools proposal in the House. For those still waiting for clues if national schools meant mixed schools, Wilson's entry into the fray was prime evidence.[14]

John Sherman, Republican senator from Ohio, witnessed the mixed-schools debate with disgust. Determining to end the matter quickly, he proposed that the Senate immediately go into executive session, to which a majority of his embarrassed colleagues readily assented. After thirteen minutes of meeting in private, the doors of the chamber were reopened; and the Senate quickly and quietly adjourned. The issue did not arise again in that session. But from then on, mixed schools and federal involvement in public education were inseparably linked.

Hoar's bill was discussed for the last time nine days later. His proposal was not allowed to come to a vote by the House leadership. Congress was then enmeshed in the discussion of a second Ku Klux Klan bill. A first KKK bill had been passed the year before. The second bill slightly broadened its language. Supposedly designed to crush the Ku Klux Klan, which had often targeted black school houses, these measures were seen in part as first steps in creating an environment in a which public education could endure. By taking race-related cases out of local courts and putting them into United States District Courts for trial, the likelihood of conviction of klansmen accused of burning schools and terrorizing teachers increased significantly. This legislation set the stage for the next session of Congress and a more serious consideration of increasing the federal government's role in public education.[15]

Hoar and other Republicans of like mind decided to alter their strategy for the next session. Initially, they had backed the creation of a national school system, and it had generated paranoia over the possibilities of mixed schools being forced on the nation. For their second round, they decided to try a more moderate approach. Southerners such as Ruffner of Virginia had encouraged the idea of federal aid for Southern public education. Accordingly, Republican educational planners decided to propose that the proceeds from public land sales be put in a federal fund to assist state-based public education systems wherever they existed nationwide. By this method, Southern states such as Virginia that had inaugurated public school systems would be rewarded; and states such as Kentucky, Maryland, Delaware, and Tennessee that had failed to invest in public education would be left without any federal aid. The plan seemed well-conceived at the outset, but white paranoia weighted it down and eventually sunk it. The bogey man of mixed schools, which was nowhere alluded to in the legislation, nonetheless frightened away much potential support.

Gordon Lee, the principal historian of federal aid for education, has noted that by inaugurating their crusade with a frank and open appeal for a national school system, Republican reformers burdened their cause in the years following as opponents charged that subsequent moderate proposals were but stalking horses for the reformers' real desire, which was to centralize public education in the United States. Lee concluded his review of the Hoar bill in 1871 by noting: "It is not unlikely that, had there been advanced in 1870–1871 a more moderate, less controversial program, much of subsequent educational development would have been markedly different." But Lee did not take Charles Sumner into account. Sumner was incapable of approaching this issue in a "moderate" way. He intended from the outset to force the issue of mixed schools, whether the white majority wished to consider it or not. Even had a more moderate proposal been offered by Hoar at the outset, Sumner's irrepressible stridency would most probably have activated a mixed-schools hysteria in any case.[16]

On January 15, 1872, the moderate successor to the Hoar bill was introduced in the House. Tactfully, Hoar played only a supporting role in this legislation. Ostensibly, Mississippi's Legrand Winfield Perce was the author of the bill. Perce was a trained lawyer who had been raised in New York and went South with his regiment during the Civil War. Discharged with the rank of colonel, he settled in Mississippi and entered politics. Elected to Congress, he was appointed to the House Education and Labor Committee and became a close ally of George Frisbie Hoar. In 1871, Perce was appointed chair of the committee, and in this role came to sponsor the proposal to apply the proceeds "arising from the sale of public lands" to public education. The idea came from John Eaton, Jr., the United States Commissioner of Education. Perce's bill called for one-half of the proceeds to be placed in a perpetual fund known as the National Educational Fund. The other half of the income, together with the annual interest accruing from the National Educational Fund, was to be apportioned each year to the states having meaningful public school systems. State officials were required to submit reports of how the funds were spent in order to qualify for continued federal aid. John Eaton, Jr. was designated by the bill to determine whether each state was in compliance with the terms of the bill. Eaton had long desired greater centralization of American public education along the Prussian model. If the bill passed, he would have his opportunity. The bill made misappropriation of funds a felony, with exclusive jurisdiction in such cases resting in the federal circuit courts.[17]

For years Democrats had blasted Republicans for wasting federal land holdings on privileged railroad corporations. In 1872, Republican public-school reformers co-opted this argument and turned it to their benefit. A Republican campaign pamphlet portrayed the Perce bill as potentially protecting the public domain from ravenous railroad corporations: "Every educator will hereafter insist, that if appropriations for railways and other projects shall be made, they must not be aided by robbing the school fund." Not only did the Perce bill enable the party to redefine itself as against grasping corporations but as pro-Southern as well. Early in the debates over the measure, Perce accepted a friendly amendment to make the proposal especially pro-Southern. The amendment called for the funds to be dispersed on the basis of each state's population of school-aged children (four to twenty-one years of age). As the South had more school-aged children in proportion to its overall population than any other section, this was a significant gesture toward the former slave states. Originally, the Perce bill had proposed to dispense funds simply on the basis of overall population statistics.[18]

The Perce bill was designed similar to twentieth-century federal grants-in-aid measures. As such, it invaded traditional state police powers and sought to manipulate them through federal controls. The innovation did not escape the discernment of states-rights Democrats, who charged that the bill was foreign to the American constitutional tradition. Archibald T. McIntyre, a Georgia Democrat in the House, was especially outspoken. Republicans retorted that the design of the Perce bill was really nothing new. The Morrill land-grant college act of 1862, they noted, had contained mechanisms for punishing states that did not fulfill the conditions of that bill's federal aid to higher education.[19] Nonetheless, McIntyre continued to pursue the bill with determined ferocity. Ultimately he got to the heart of his concern: "I say to gentlemen representing Southern states that this bill is a Trojan horse. In its interior are concealed the lurking foe—mixed schools." The Republican agenda, he warned, envisioned transforming the United States Commissioner of Education into "The Minister of Public Instruction, the term used in Prussia." He announced that the Republicans would continue centralizing until they had "a uniform system of textbooks." McIntyre predicted: "Those books will have to be 'loyal,' and to be loyal must be published near Cambridge or Boston, with the Puritan Confession of Faith attached to the multiplication table." In closing, he warned that if the Republicans succeeded in passing this bill, nothing could thwart their centralizing designs.[20]

The fears of Southern Democrats opposing the Perce bill projected this scenario: First, federal aid to education would bribe the Southern states into providing thoroughgoing state-based systems of public education. Next, Congress would mandate mixed schools nationwide. States would be forced to swallow mixed schools or lose their federal aid. First dependency on the federal government would be created. Then Congress would dictate racial integration. Some were suspicious that the very language of the Perce bill could be used to mandate mixed schools without additional legislation. The bill required that public schools in states receiving federal aid must "be free for the admission of all children." Clearly, white public schools were not "free for the admission of all children." The United States Commissioner of Education, in administering the act, could use this language to force mixed schools on the nation. In the words of John M. Bright, a Democratic representative from Tennessee, the whole system was designed to prepare the children of the states to become "victims to be offered upon the altar of an imperialized government." William S. Herndon, Democrat from Texas, warned that race mixing in public schools "would gradually warp and imperceptibly change the youthful mind from all its former teachings, and thus array the son against the father, and the daughter against the mother." Not only Southerners were concerned about mixed schools. Democrat Michael C. Kerr of Indiana was equally exercised over the prospects of what he called "mongrel schools" and "forced association." The bill threatened to change American racial cultural norms, and Republicans were on the unpopular side of the issue. Before the Civil War, Republicans had enjoyed the strategic advantage. Then they had appealed to Northern racial fears with the "slave-power conspiracy" thesis. In the 1870s, Democratic Party rhetoric used much of the same style in what might be termed a "mixed-schools conspiracy" thesis of centralizing Republicans intent on amalgamating the races. This political message had the potential to win converts to the Democrats North as well as South.[21]

Representative Hoar then spoke. He blasted the states-rights argument, terming it a phony excuse not to correct social injustices plaguing America. "When measures are proposed in Congress," Hoar said, "[the] Democracy clamors that they should be left to the states; when proposed to the states, it clamors that they should be left to counties or localities. In the county or locality, they are left by that party to the Ku Klux Klan, who burn the school house and murder or whip the teacher." The Perce bill, he said, was no more threatening than the Peabody Fund, which had won universal praise from members of all parties and sections. That private fund distributed only $100,000 annually, but its affect was tenfold in encouraging states and locales to support public education. He estimated that the Perce bill would distribute many times that amount and would do untold good in the war against illiteracy. Barnas Sears, the agent of the Peabody Fund, agreed and lent his considerable influence in supporting the measure.[22]

The year before, Hiram Revels had risen to speak in a Congressional debate heavy with racial overtones. Now it was Joseph H. Rainey's turn. The first African American elected to the House of Representatives pointed to obvious facts. Illiteracy, especially among his own people, swamped the Southern states. Even in those Southern states with public education systems, only a fraction of those in need were being served. Then his speech took an interesting twist. In the North also, he said, many children were effectively denied schooling. He pointed to statistics gathered by Eaton's staff that showed that 126,000 children in Illinois were outside that state's public school system. Some of these were blacks, denied access to Illinois' all-white public schools. "This mental midnight [illiteracy]," he said, "is a national calamity, and not necessarily sectional." With federal land devoted to public education, he hoped that all American children might finally come to experience educational opportunity. The South Carolinian left the obvious unsaid. Rainey most certainly also hoped that United States Commissioner of Education Eaton would use his powers under the Perce bill to discipline states North as well as South for systematically denying educational opportunity to children of his race.[23]

Rainey's allusion to conditions in the North was telling. Illinois was then in the process of changing its practices to allow blacks to share theoretically in public education for the first time. But the process was exceedingly slow, and blacks in Illinois had yet to receive any meaningful educational opportunity in that state's public schools. In 1872, Thomas W. Harvey, Ohio's State Commissioner of Common Schools, bluntly reported that blacks in his state remained outside the public school system despite a state law requiring otherwise: "The statute providing for the education of the colored children in the state is, in its practical operation, a failure." On the district level, whites in Ohio regularly blocked access of African Americans to educational opportunity despite what was written in state legislation. In the Far West, conditions were especially bad. There, all ethnic minorities were effectively barred from the public schools. Nevada's supreme court ruled in 1872 that districts could not block black children from the public schools. But making this ruling real on the local level was more difficult than announcing it from the bench.

In his first report to Congress, made one and a half years before the Perce bill, Commissioner John Eaton, Jr., had highlighted Indiana's discriminatory treatment toward blacks. In practice, he noted, blacks in Indiana were "denied all use of the school fund." That same report highlighted Illinois' banning black children from its public schools while taxing black parents for the support of all-white public schools. Blacks were barred from educational opportunity North as well as South. Congress knew this as the debate over the Perce bill proceeded. Northern states, as well as Southern, were ripe for federal discipline in their management of public education. Congressman Rainey's speech gently reminded his white colleagues of this fact.[24]

The Perce bill raised additional concerns completely unrelated to matters of race. Specifically, the bill subtly threatened to undermine the Homestead Act of 1862. Some feared that the federal government might begin to encourage land sales to speculators to raise money for education, leaving less free land for impoverished homesteaders. Congressmen interested in special internal improvements projects also worried that public education could hog all federal largess under the Perce bill. Roman Catholics also spoke out against the bill. Democratic Representative William R. Roberts, an Irish-Catholic immigrant representing

New York, opposed the bill because parochial schools could not share in the federal aid.[25]

Constitutional issues were also raised. Those fearful of mixed schools relied on states rights. In countering such logic, one Perce-bill supporter was especially inventive, arguing that under the Constitution's territories clause Congress had unlimited authority to make rules and regulations concerning federal lands, even if it amounted to a new, massive federal involvement in public education. Perce himself relied on the Guarantee Clause: "I do not believe there is a gentleman on the floor of this House," commented Perce, "who will assert that a republican form of government could be maintained by a people entirely ignorant." On February 8, 1872, the Perce bill passed the House with several crucial amendments. The most important of these sought to calm the fears of mixed schools. Those states that maintained racially segregated public schools were approved as passing muster under the terms of the bill. Another amendment altered the basis of aid, providing that it go primarily to those states with the highest illiteracy rates for the first ten years, the basis of apportionment reverting to the numbers of school-aged children after that time. This amendment clearly favored the South.[26]

The bill then went to the Senate. With the mixed schools possibility removed from the bill, Senator Charles Sumner viewed it with disdain. He often had said that he preferred no public education to racially segregated public schools. For a whole year, the bill languished in committee. In the meantime, the Republican Party sought to exploit the bill in the presidential campaign of 1872. Commissioner Eaton enlisted William Prosser's assistance in writing essays in favor of the measure. In a Republican campaign document addressed to the poor whites of the South, two principal points were emphasized. First, this literature stressed that the vote in the House on the Perce bill had been 117 to 98. Of those voting "aye," 103 were Republicans. Of those voting "nay," 78 were Democrats. In short, the pamphlet crowed, the Republican Party was the true friend of poor white Southern families wanting educational opportunity for their children. Second, the tract emphasized that four-fifths of the federal aid dispensed under the bill would be spent in the South during the first ten years. This annually would have the effect of twenty-five Peabody Funds. With the possibility of mixed schools removed from the bill, the Republican Party was able to make an old-fashioned appeal to white voters in a heretofore hostile section of the country. Just as "free labor" rhetoric had helped capture Northern white voters to the party before the Civil War, Republicans now hoped that "free schools" rhetoric might bring Southern whites into the fold:

Laboring men of every Southern state, this is the supreme question for you. The nation offers you aid in the education of your children too long kept in ignorance. By this aid your schools can be made efficient, and your children can be prepared for usefulness and honor. The Republican Party offers you this boon, and the Democratic Party opposes it. Shall your party prejudices stand in the way of the interests of your children? Does not this action of the Republicans demonstrate to you that they are zealous to elevate and inform the people, and are willing that the resources of the North should be devoted to the advancement of the people of the South? Let every man who has a son or a daughter to educate ask the candidate for his suffrage, how he has voted and how he will vote upon this question, and be guided by his answer in his vote.[27]

As early as 1871, the party faithful had sensed that the Republican identification with the public-school movement had potential to attract votes among Southern poor whites. Southern Republicans fully exploited this phenomenon in the Presidential election of 1872. As long as the party could keep the mixed-schools genie from unleashing its terrible, destructive power on the party's fortunes, this tack had definite potential. But Charles Sumner was determined to free the genie, considering disaster in the pursuit of a noble ideal as preferable to success that compromised principle.[28]

In the North, Republican propagandists presented the Perce bill differently. There it was portrayed as a measure designed to bring urban hooliganism and juvenile crime under control. A pro-Republican article in *Scribner's Monthly* followed this formula. What both the North and the South ultimately needed in the 1870s, the article proposed, was a national system of education that hopefully would grow out of an initial program of federal aid to the states. The article presented the notion of traditional parental rights over children as outmoded in the advanced nineteenth century. The article stated: "What right has Paddy O'Flinn, just over from the bogs of Ireland, to bring up his family of ten in utter ignorance?" National controls were needed to save the Union from degeneracy growing from illiteracy in the North as well as in the South. "Has the Republic no right to live?" asked the anonymous author. "Shall she continue to nurse in her bosom the viper which will one day sting her to death?"[29]

"Does the land-education act go through?" wrote a Northern correspondent of Commissioner Eaton. "I am anxious to see it do so." Waiting for the Perce bill to emerge from the Senate committee, George

Hoar waged his own campaign in the press. Privately he feared secret, Republican opposition to the measure more than open attacks from Democrats. He especially worried about the role that Senator Justin Morrill might play in the upper house to undermine the bill. As the Republican father of federal aid to agricultural and industrial colleges, Morrill did not like the bill's diversion of federal land proceeds to primary and elementary education. In a piece written for *Old and New,* Hoar compared the lavish federal expenditures on agriculture with the meager resources allocated to elementary education. Clearly, he wrote, some Republicans who had no constitutional scruples when it came to aiding agriculture could forget their nationalism when the education of children appeared as a rival cause for federal funds. Morrill and his supporters were indeed hostile to the bill. The President of Illinois Industrial University, a beneficiary of the Morrill Act, complained to Eaton that while aid to elementary schools was a nice thought, the need for federal assistance was far greater in higher education. "My long observation tells me that with intelligent leading citizens the Common Schools will be thoroughly sustained, with or without [federal] public funds. Their support can be gained easily by direct [state] taxation. But institutions of higher education must be fostered by [federal] public aid." He wrote Eaton of the many long generations of contributions that had painfully built the endowments of Harvard and Yale. If the West and South were to have comparable institutions, additional federal assistance was needed. Congress had created the land-grant colleges under the Morrill Act. In his mind, this fact morally bound Congress to make sure that they enjoyed better than "a dwindling and puny growth."[30]

Advocates for elementary education were also at work. Virginia's William Henry Ruffner kept up his own provincial campaign for federal aid. His argument was couched in terms to be persuasive to those with states-rights sensibilities. He portrayed the federal government as unjustly foisting millions of illiterate voters [African-American males] on the states. As the states, especially in the South, lacked the resources to correct the federal government's mistake, the nation itself needed to provide the remedy through federal aid to education. Numerous black Virginians agreed with Ruffner. One of these, a teenaged boy working his way through Virginia's Hampton's Institute, recalled in his old age his feelings from the early 1870s: "Even as a youth," Booker T. Washington remembered, "I had the feeling that it was cruelly wrong in the central government, at the beginning of our freedom, to fail to make some provision for the general education of our people in addition to what the states might do, so that the people would be the better prepared for the duties of citizenship."[31]

As Hoar and Ruffner continued the good fight, Legrand Perce went home to Mississippi to seek reelection. Certainly the leadership role that he had played thus far in an issue of growing importance in the Republican Party called for him to be returned to his Congressional post. But back in Mississippi, he ran into a growing African-American desire to occupy more of the important political positions available to the state's majority party. As black voters supplied the majority of this majority, they enjoyed the numbers to carry the day in local party caucuses. Accordingly, John Roy Lynch, a twenty-four-year-old former slave, defeated Perce for the Republican nomination. Lynch acknowledged that Perce had been a "strong and able man." He had no complaint that Perce had not adequately represented the interests of all of Mississippi's Republicans. Lynch merely wanted his House seat. As a result, Lynch was sent to Congress as its youngest member; and the Republican Party lost a leader in the cause of public education.[32]

Despite the loss of Perce, the measure went forward. Important party leaders, including President Grant and Vice President-Elect Henry Wilson, were open advocates of federal aid to public education. But crucial Republicans in the Senate were either indifferent or plotting to ambush the bill. Senator Frederick A. Sawyer, a carpetbag Republican from South Carolina, was chair of the committee responsible for the bill. While he should have been grooming the bill for Senate acceptance, he was preparing to leave the Senate to become Grant's new Assistant Secretary of the Treasury. Virginia's Ruffner made the short trip to Washington and lobbied the Senate corridors, but his efforts were for naught. Sawyer was absent on the day that the bill came before the Senate for action. Senator Morrill moved that as the bill lacked appropriate sponsorship from Sawyer, it should be passed over. The suggestion was taken, and the bill never came to a vote.[33]

The next year, Hoar tried anew with a bill bearing close resemblance to the defunct Perce measure. Again he appealed to the common nationality of all Americans and the need for one national community to attack the national disease of illiteracy. In 1872, the idea had received the backing of the overwhelming majority of House Republicans, but in the session of 1873–1874, there was a new mood in the House. The onslaught of economic depression in the Fall of 1873 cooled Republican support considerably. Many Republicans recoiled from devoting much of the public domain to public education. Instead, they said, it should be reserved for the poor seeking free homesteads in the West. Economic depression drove representatives inward, away from patriotic consideration of national long-term needs. Their local constituents were hurting and focused on simple economic survival, and the Republican tradition of free homesteads again became an important political symbol. Suffering from depression, people in the northwest cared less about other people's problems. What did the new Hoar bill offer them? What did it do for their children? Under the Hoar bill most of the federal aid would go to the South, which was increasingly far away in their concerns.[34]

Republican Henry Laurens Dawes of Massachusetts provided the killing blow. He had been an avid supporter of the Perce bill and even supported the idea of forcing mixed schools on the nation. But the winter of 1873-1874 changed his perspective. Economic depression, he said, was not the right environment in which to begin a new expensive federal program. In that era, imbalanced federal budgets were excusable only in wartime conditions. With economic downturn, less revenues were entering the federal treasury. If federal aid to education were inaugurated, new taxes would have to be levied on an already suffering people. In that environment, depression encouraged governmental cost-cutting. Mere survival was the order of the day.[35]

The depression eliminated an important economic dynamic that had been pushing the nationalizing public-school agenda forward. Between 1861 (when the Republicans first came to control the federal government) and 1869, the federal protective tariff had been revised steadily upward. As the income from this source came to be greater than governmental expenses, annual budgetary surpluses suggested a lowering of tariff walls, leading pro-tariff Republicans to search for any worthwhile federal project that might eat up revenues and thereby maintain a justification for high tariffs. The idea of massive federal aid to public education had been conceived in this protectionist crucible. But the depression of 1873 changed the political equation. With economic downturn, the era of budgetary surpluses was over. Early in 1874, analysts predicted that in that year, for the first time since the end of the Civil War, the federal government would post an annual deficit. "Retrenchment" was on everyone's lips, even those of public school reformers.[36]

The depression awakened a specter of dwindling opportunity for the common man. Good free land was disappearing fast. The great American giveaway to impoverished Europeans and Americans, a historical phenomenon that began with Christopher Columbus, was apparently winding down. Historian Frederick Jackson Turner would articulate this gut fear in poetic academic language two decades later in the midst of the nation's next depression. In the 1870s, San Francisco newspaperman Henry George anticipated his thesis. George, an amateur economic philosopher who would become world famous later in the decade, wrote prophetically in the early 1870s: "It [free land] will be all gone some time before the year 1890, and no child born this year or last year, or even three years before then, can possibly get himself a home stead out of Uncle Sam's farm, unless he is willing to take a mountain top or alkali patch, or emigrate to Alaska." George opposed using any of the public domain for education, railroads or any purpose other than actual homesteading.[37] The depression of 1873 made his position a catechism for most politicians.

Together with the changing political dynamics of the depression of 1873, the mixed schools phobia killed the Hoar measure. Despite the fact that the new bill explicitly let each state arrange its own public schools as it thought best, the measure was suspect nonetheless. Charles Sumner was then pressing for the adoption of his Supplementary Civil Rights Bill, of which the cornerstone was a mandate for mixed schools throughout the nation. Democrats argued that Hoar's concession to segregated schooling was meaningless; for if the Sumner bill passed, mixed schools would be required everywhere. They charged that the Hoar bill was cleverly designed as a federal bribe to keep Southern states from destroying their public school systems once the Sumner bill passed. The mixed schools conspiracy they said, was designed for two stages. First, federal money would be showered upon the states to encourage a firm commitment to public education. Second, racially integrated education would be required to meet the expectations of New England's self-appointed social engineers. Hoar and Sumner were both from Massachusetts. More important, they were intimate friends. Democrats said that the true purposes of the Hoar bill could only be appreciated by examining Sumner's Supplementary Civil Rights Bill.

As arguments against the Hoar bill mounted, scandals from the Grant administration diminished hope that any major federal project could avoid political corruption. The Credit Mobilier scandal, which involved both Henry Wilson and James Garfield (two Republicans identified with the idealistic public-education crusade), hurt Hoar's cause. Reluctantly, Hoar concluded that the time was not right to press the issue. Colleagues advised that maybe after the congressional elections of 1874, conditions might be more auspicious. They were wrong. The depression continued, and federal aid to education was dead for the remainder of the decade.[38]

Through good times and bad, white racism prevented any meaningful national education reform movement. The Republican Party's elite could wax eloquently about the beauties of Bismarckian centralism for public education in the United States. However, each specific educational reform proposal dredged up the imagined horrors of racially mixed schools. For many, states rights provided a convenient historic shield against racial integration. In the North, centralization rhetoric was encouraged by anti-Catholic hysteria. But in the nation at large, nationalistic talk of one people and a uniform culture emerging from one common-school experience for the children of all races spawned a different popular reaction. As the Hoar bill died early in 1874, the country remained extremely nervous over the prospect of mixed schools. Senator Charles Sumner refused to drop the topic, despite a clear lack of support from his life-long Republican colleagues. The African factor remained on high heat. In 1874, it would explode, and the resultant political damage would change the course of Reconstruction.

6

RECONSTRUCTION'S RACIAL DISSOLUTION

A Foolish Consistency

David Donald, the principal modern biographer of Charles Sumner, does not flatter his subject. Donald's Sumner has the personality of a posturing schoolmaster, cocksure of his own correctness, oblivious to the judicious advice of friends. Sumner, wrote Donald, was addicted to "that illogical logic that carries a premise to its utmost conclusion." This trait was glaringly apparent in the Massachusetts Senator's lonely crusade for mixed schools. Racially integrated public education alone, he urged, would fulfill the inner logic of the nation's highest ideals as expressed in the Declaration of Independence. He scorned protests from contemporaries that a national mandate to integrate the public schools would result in an abandonment of public education throughout the South. His logic was flawless. Segregated schools were in the spirit of slavery and perpetuated racial-caste consciousness. But then he went beyond simple rationality into "that illogical logic" noted by Professor Donald. In Sumner's view, it was better that the public schools be destroyed altogether than to flourish in a context of racial segregation. Compromise with evil would only deepen the wrong done to blacks by the sin of slavery. Best irradiate the evil all at once, root and branch, than to collaborate with it in any way. Yet, when women's advocates pleaded with him to fulfill his professed belief in the equality of the sexes by pushing immediately for the inclusion of women's voting rights in the Fifteenth Amendment, they were told that the time was not right. Sumner could be wholly political on the issue of women's suffrage, which was not a practical cause for the 1870s. Unfortunately, neither was racially integrated public schooling. Other civil-rights strategists tried to counsel him that educating the masses of freedmen by any means necessary was a higher immediate priority They warned that fighting his preferred battle at that time was guaranteed to end in disaster. Sumner was deaf to such talk. In his mind, the battle for mixed schools had to be fought and casualties had to be suffered, even though defeat was certain from the outset.[1]

During the Civil War, Sumner had held Abraham Lincoln in a degree of contempt. Though he socialized with the President and his wife frequently, Sumner thought that Lincoln delayed and compromised when he should have acted decisively. Yet, several months after the great man's death, Sumner conceded that "history dwells on results rather than the means employed." Three years later, he elaborated on this sentiment:

> Every man must have certain theories, principles by which governments should be conducted. But where we undertake to apply them to practical problems, there are many difficulties to be overcome, many concessions which must be made in order to accomplish the desired result. The old proverb has it "the shortest way across is often the longest way round," and nowhere is this truer than in legislation. It is not every Gordian knot that can be cut: some must be patiently untied.[2]

Some historians still criticize Abraham Lincoln for not having made the destruction of slavery a war aim from the outset. He is still criticized for only freeing slaves behind enemy lines in his Emancipation Proclamation, while leaving those in Union-held territory temporarily enslaved. He is still criticized for slowly coming to the position that some *educated* African-American men might be made voters. Nonetheless, the fact remains that Lincoln both saved the Union and moved it ever closer toward fulfilling the ideals of the Declaration of Independence. Lincoln was a master at patiently untying Gordian knots so as to leave lasting reforms for posterity. He was an idealist with an impeccable sense of timing. This latter quality was lacking in Charles Sumner. Instead of working a transformation in American attitudes, Sumner's mixed-schools crusade terminated the racial progress of Reconstruction and instead inaugurated the long period of reaction that followed. We cannot know if a more patient, cautious, Lincoln-like approach might have borne better fruit. All we have is the historical record that Sumner's uncompromising strategy helped produce.

Historians rarely criticize Sumner for the course he pursued regarding public education in the early 1870s. Commonly, he is regarded as an early prophet of a better day to come. Prophets are expected to take uncompromising positions. But Sumner was more than a prophet. He was also a legislative leader and one of the very few white men in that decade who were fully trusted in the African-American community.

His influence was tremendous for either good or evil. Albion Tourgee was then a lesser-known worker in the cause for racial justice. In later decades, he assumed the Sumnerian mantel as the white man most deserving of African-American respect. Tourgee's career as a consistent, ardent champion of civil rights ultimately matched Sumner's own. But in the 1870s, he was a little-known carpetbagger trying to bring about better race relations in North Carolina. Tourgee lived and worked at the grass roots of the civil-rights struggle. Sumner could lose himself in abstract ideals in the Senate's chambers for the rhetorically elite. Tourgee's world was more immediate and real.

In 1874, after observing the local damage produced by Sumner's well-meaning public-school ideals, an enraged Tourgee wrote of the Massachusetts senator's arrogant and destructive misjudgment in timing. He claimed that Sumner knew nothing of the actual condition of African Americans living in the Southern states. He suggested that Sumner's Supplementary Civil Rights Bill, mandating mixed schools for the nation, was "just like a blister-plaster put on a dozing man whom it is desirable to soothe to sleep." In his opinion, what blacks then needed was opportunity to improve themselves separately from whites. They could not progress by enflaming white fear and hatred against them. Just emerging from the degradation of slavery, blacks needed to stabilize themselves in their new condition of freedom. Tourgee's highest priority was to get as many blacks educated as fast as possible. Forced integration could only serve to derail this most basic reform. After blacks had become "used to freedom, self dependence and proper self-assertion" and after the tremendous gap between themselves and the white masses had been narrowed, schools could be integrated. In utter disgust, Tourgee wrote of Sumner: "I have no use for those who prescribe for diseases without knowing their nature." In his opinion, Sumner was a "visionary quack" who had put back the "rehabilitation of the South ten or twenty years."[3]

Sumner viewed himself as the only true mentor of the black race. He instructed African Americans on their rights and impatiently and imperiously urged them forward. He loved the Declaration's ideals with all of his being. To him, they transcended the petty realities of his time and place. He meant well, but his advice was guaranteed to end in disaster. Such was the judgment of most of Sumner's contemporaries and even some of his closest friends. Today, of course, Sumner's views are orthodox and well in tune with modern sympathies. But in other times, racially integrated schools have not been regarded as the indispensable touchstone of public education. W. E. B. DuBois, only a boy in the 1870s, later examined Sumner's idea that mixed schools alone could generate self-respect in black children. DuBois noted that in a social environment of bigotry, racially integrated schools were guaranteed to crucify young African Americans. "There is no magic," DuBois wrote, "either in mixed schools or in segregated schools." In his opinion, a loving and safe environment that encourages learning, irrespective of the racial composition of the classroom, alone was essential for meaningful education. Carter Godwin Woodson, the well-known African-American social critic and historian of the early twentieth century, agreed with DuBois. His desire was for "common-sense schools," taught by "teachers who understand and continue in sympathy with those whom they instruct." Integrated schools taught by teachers secretly or openly harboring racial contempt for blacks clearly failed as "common-sense schools."[4] Such nuances were alien to the steel-trap mind of Charles Sumner.

Barnas Sears was Sumner's most respected opponent on the subject of mixed schools. Scars reasoned that the South's whites needed to be won to the cause of public education before any enduring reform could be worked for African-American education. Sumner's bill seriously alienated that essential white support. Sumner placed a higher priority on integration than education. Sears placed a higher priority on education than integration.[5] Historian William P. Vaughn has severely judged Sears for opposing Sumner. He credits Sears with aiding and abetting the delay of the South's "coming to terms with social reality." In Sears's own perspective, he was protecting the struggling seedlings of public education in the South at a time when it was not clear that they would ever take firm root and flourish. "Coming to terms with social reality," in the way intended by Professor Vaughn, would have necessarily scuttled Sears's mission. Historian John Hope Franklin acknowledged this social reality of the 1870s when he wrote: "Even the friends of Negro education and many of those who frowned on separation were forced to the unpleasant but inescapable conclusion that the only real chance for success in the education of Negroes lay in the establishment and maintenance of separate schools." Nonetheless, most modern historians (Franklin included) find Sears distasteful for his dance with the devil. By contrast, they exalt Sumner who consorted only with angels, whatever the results.

United States Commissioner of Education John Eaton, Jr., had to choose which of his two long-time political allies to support—Sumner or Sears. Eaton was aware of what he called "a most blind prejudice against any and all efforts to improve the condition of the colored people by education." He was also mindful of the beginnings of a public-school-advocacy element beginning to bloom the South. To kill this support, he realized, would be lunacy. The key question in his mind was whether the Sumner measure would help or hinder the cause of African-American education. He met with both Sears and the President. Grant, already at odds with Sumner over the latter's opposition to the president's Santo Domingo Treaty, told both men that he would veto any bill mandating mixed schools. Eaton too concluded that he must oppose the measure. Sumner's bill, Eaton subsequently wrote, "was the expression of a theory of equality right in itself," but he rejected it for its predictable destructive consequences.[6]

More than commingling with whites, African Americans wanted equal funding for their own schools. In some states, North as well as South, black schooling was practically nonexistent. They hoped that Sumner's strategy of pushing for mixed schools might at least frighten whites into creating meaningful, separate black schools. Many blacks confessed this hope to Barnas Sears, who warned them that their strategy might backfire. If Sumner succeeded, black teachers would certainly suffer loss of employment. In that age, black teachers were invariably reserved for black schools alone. Once installed, mixed schools would teach the lesson to African-American children that only white people could be teachers, that only white people could be authorities. These were the ugly "social realities" of mixed schools in the 1870s.[7] Nevertheless, some blacks vociferously joined Sumner in his demand for mixed schools. Two of these were William Syphax and William H. A. Wormley, both trustees of the District of Columbia's black schools and close friends of Sumner. They quoted scripture: "Train up a child in the way he should go, and when he is old he will not depart from it." Children taught in segregated schools, they noted, were trained to accept a separate and inherently unequal status in later life. Integrated schools alone could break down the caste consciousness inherited from the institution of slavery. Syphax and Wormley also knew that racially separate schools, which theoretically might be equal, were rarely funded at truly equal levels. This had been their experience in the nation's capital. Mixed schools alone could ensure that black schoolchildren would be given adequate educational support. Mixed schools would also end the midnight targeting of black schools by arsonists. If schoolhouses continued to burn after integration, white children would suffer equally with blacks. Classroom competition with whites, they added, would also stimulate African-American ambition and self-respect and "add dignity to their character."[8]

Other arguments supported the Sumner measure. Former abolitionist leader Wendell Phillips said that black schools inevitably failed because poor black parents had neither "'the education to see defects'"' nor the organizational experience to raise complaints to bring about educational improvements. He hoped that mixed schools, by mixing children of both the poor and well-to-do, would remedy the problem, as well-to-do white parents would not tolerate inferior schools. Frederick Douglass saw matters differently. He assumed that wealthy whites would never send their children to mixed public schools and instead would transfer them to private schools. For Douglass, the virtue of racial public-school integration lay in his anticipation that it would mix the poor of both races in one educational setting. In Douglass's view, America's best hope for eliminating racism lay in replacing race consciousness with class consciousness. In mixed schools, the poor of both races could discover their shared oppression at the hands of wealthy whites.

Other arguments for mixed schools included the injustice of black children having to walk by white schools for long distances before reaching the one designated for their race. Segregated schools were also not cost-effective in small rural districts, where the population did not warrant the establishment of two schools. Invariably in such situations, both North and South, only one white school was created and black children were denied any educational opportunity. Anti-Catholics also worried that the precedent of racially segregated public schools served to encourage the Roman Catholic attempt to create religiously segregated public schools.[9] Senator Sumner was intimately familiar with all of these arguments. He had used them for years, without effect.

Historians have generally treated the Sumner measure as a threat to the white South. Yet, much of the early focus in the debates on the Supplementary Civil Rights Bill regarded the school situation in Ohio. More than any other state, North or South, Sumner highlighted Ohio's failure to provide educational opportunity for black children. Rural blacks in Ohio were regularly turned away from all-white schools and provided no separate schools of their own.[10] Ohio's elected politicians were not activists in changing the school situation in their state.[11] Likewise, Ohio's Supreme Court refused to address the injustice done to Ohio's rural black children, left without any educational opportunity. The court ruled that the Fourteenth Amendment, by itself, did not require black public education and claimed that the courts could do nothing in the absence of enabling legislation. Sumner held a different opinion, which was supported by Thomas M. Cooley, one of the most influential legal minds of that generation and a leading expert on constitutional affairs.[12] In any case, Sumner intended that his Supplementary Civil Rights Bill would enact the intent of the Fourteenth Amendment for public education. Existing school practices in Ohio and other Northern states, not simply the Southern states, were directly threatened by his measure.[13]

In the early 1870s, the United States Supreme Court had not as yet attempted to define the Fourteenth Amendment, which was the basis of the Sumner bill. In this judicial vacuum, legislators discussed the bill's constitutionality. Some saw the proposal as justified by the privileges and immunities clause of the Fourteenth Amendment. Indiana's Oliver P. Morton and others argued that it was up to Congress to define the extent of the privileges and immunities of American citizens. They saw no role for the Supreme Court in the matter. In their view, a meaningful public education was one of those privileges owed to citizens of the United States, especially after the Fifteenth Amendment allowed for universal manhood suffrage.[14] Other senators saw justification for the Sumner bill in another part of the Fourteenth amendment, namely the equal protection clause. Sumner himself preferred the more expansive possibilities of the Thirteenth Amendment as the constitutional foundation of his measure. Similar to his bill, that amendment, he said, had been intended to destroy slavery "root and branch."[15]

Of course, Democrats present in these debates held far more restrictive views of the Constitution and charged that Sumner's bill was blatantly unconstitutional. Republican Zachariah Chandler reminded Democrats that as the Republican Party had saved the Constitution, any Democratic-Party interpretations were irrelevant. "Every shred of it that is left you owe us," he lectured the opposition, "and you ought to get down on your knees and thank us for saving what we did." Republicans, he said, not Democrats would define what the Constitution meant and what it did not mean.[16] In 1873, the Republican United States Supreme Court handed down the *Slaughterhouse Cases*, which thereafter Republican centralizers had to confront. In that decision, the Court narrowly defined "the privileges and immunities of citizens of the United States." Public education was not included in its minimalist construction. Thereafter, Democrats regularly threw the *Slaughterhouse* decision into every debate about mixed schools.

North and South, public-education opportunities remained minimal for African Americans. Delaware continued to do nothing. Texas proceeded to destroy its public school system, largely in order to jettison tax-supported black education. In several Illinois school districts, school officials barred black children from new graded schools or forced them to attend racially segregated ungraded classrooms within the physical plants of the graded schools. In those situations in which the number of black children did not warrant the hiring of a separate teacher to oversee a segregated ungraded classroom, the few children affected were simply barred from attending school at all. A recent change in the Illinois state constitution supposedly guaranteeing educational equity was simply ignored. Kentucky and Maryland continued to stall the implementation of any meaningful black public education.[17]

In Ohio's urban areas, whites received graded schools long before blacks. The numbers of black students were often too few to warrant a modern graded school. For this reason, black parents often pushed for the admission of their children into all-white graded schools, but to no avail except in Toledo and the town of Delaware, Ohio. Those two Ohio communities integrated their schools in 1871. In Delaware, Ohio, African Americans quickly learned of the psychological disabilities accompanying attendance at white schools with white teachers, encompassed in a general atmosphere of white racism. Some black parents insisted on maintaining Delaware's black school as a safety valve for those students who could not adapt to the indignities accompanying racially integrated education.[18] This situation was unique. In most of Ohio, a rigid segregation was the foe to be confronted.

One can understand the frustration of black parents daily encountering a negative educational environment for their children. Whether schools were segregated or integrated, they were the losers. Understandably, they were angry. It was the responsibility of their political leaders to channel their anger in a way best to bring about positive change. Many black leaders looked to Charles Sumner for guidance at this crucial moment as they had in the past. The Massachusetts Senator advised that they show no caution and charge headlong toward federally mandated mixed schools. In his mind, there was only one correct solution to this problem. He urged African Americans to make "mixed schools" their battle cry, no matter what the cost. Of course, they would suffer that cost, not Charles Sumner. A few blacks ignored his advice. Similar to blacks living in Delaware, Ohio, African Americans in Galesburg, Illinois, fought to maintain a separate black school in the face of local white insistence that the white schools be integrated to reduce the costs of maintaining separate black schools. In 1873, at a time when other Illinois communities were stubbornly refusing to integrate their schools, Galesburg's board of education voted for mixed schools. Black parents demanded that at least one of Galesburg's two black schools be kept open, a request that was honored until that school was burned to the ground on February 27, 1874. The African-American parents then insisted that the other black school be maintained in its stead, which was honored until it too was destroyed by fire five weeks later. Only then did these holdouts concede defeat and send their children to the predominantly white schools. In Brooklyn, New York, a similar drama occurred, as one set of black parents drafted a petition demanding that the city's schools be integrated and another insisted that their black schools be maintained as in the past. Not all African Americans viewed the issue of mixed schools in the same way.[19] Sumner himself could not understand why all African Americans could not accept what he himself saw as a self-evident truth—that separate schools violated the spirit of equality. He was especially concerned with black representatives in Congress who did not share his zeal on the subject. "I regret much to see," he wrote, "how little pluck there is among colored representatives." He saw them as afraid of alienating President Grant, who was known to be against the mixed-schools idea.[20] He could not fathom a legitimate reason why any African American might actually prefer segregated schools. He kept these feelings hidden from view, as in public he sought to create the impression of an overwhelming African-American ground swell for mixed schools. To the casual observer, blacks indeed seemed to be urging mixed schools as African-American petitions inundated Congress. However, a careful reading of them reveals important differences from Sumner's own views.[21]

The same black congressmen whom Sumner chastised in private for their lack of support made speeches in favor of the measure.[22] Their motives for backing the bill were complex. Events in Missouri had suggested that a threat of mixed schools could push white authorities to improve separate black schools as a compromise acceptable to both sides.[23] Historian Michael Perman has shown that black politicians learned to appreciate how the mixed-schools bill could be exploited to drive white office-seekers from effective electoral competition. For years, black politicians had not been allowed to compete for the best state positions. A black Republican in South Carolina had complained: "We colored people vote the Republican ticket. When they get in, by colored votes, they give us nothing. We have a white governor, a white secretary of the commonwealth, a white chief justice." The rise of Sumner's mixed-schools crusade suggested a remedy. White Republican candidates who could not accept the concept of mixed schools were deemed unworthy of African-American support. This tactic, valued by black office seekers primarily for its practical results, pleased Senator Sumner who interpreted it in more idealistic terms. In general, the issue drove scalawags (native white Southern Republicans) out of contention for offices, leaving the field to sympathetic carpetbaggers and African Americans. In the short run, the maneuver was effective in getting more African Americans in office. In the long run, it was disastrous, as with the disappearance of scalawags the Republican party lost its majority status in a growing number of Southern states.[24]

Early on, blacks had been told that Republican candidates had to be white in order to attract white votes. African Americans, they were told, had to vote Republican, whereas whites had a choice of which party to support. Blacks begrudgingly tolerated this for several years, but eventually demanded their share of power created in the main by black votes. They channeled their new assertiveness by blasting the Republican Party's refusal to pass Sumner's Supplementary Civil Rights Bill. As the Democrats' "New Departure" had claimed to be in favor of equal rights for blacks, African Americans threatened to leave the Republican Party if Sumner's bill failed in the Republican Congress.[25] Blacks in the North applied the same pressure to squeeze more patronage out of a stingy Republican establishment. In the summer of 1873, Peter H. Clark, an African-American teacher in one of Cincinnati's black public schools, organized Ohio's black Republicans to meet at Chillicothe on August 22. His purpose was to present a list of demands to the state's Republican power brokers. Historically, only one token Republican office had been reserved for Ohio's African Americans. Clark meant to change this pattern by waving aloft Sumner's bill, the African-American equivalent of the bloody shirt within the Republican party.

The Chillicothe convention discussed the virtues of the Sumner measure at length. Its delegates genuinely cared about the bill's promise of equal public accommodations in railroads and hotels. Clark codified their discussion into a petition to be sent to white Republican leaders. "When Clark drew up his list of particulars," Historian Leonard Ernest Erickson has written of the event, "the bulk of the complaint was about patronage and the lack of civil rights; the attention given to inadequate school facilities was confined to a mere 'whereas.' And he proposed no prescription as a remedy." While many black children in Ohio were then effectively denied public-education opportunities, Clark knew that if Congress mandated mixed schools, he would lose his teaching position. Additionally, most blacks had no ideological preference for racially integrated education. While they hoped that Sumner's leadership would somehow improve educational opportunities for their race, their primary attraction to his Supplementary Civil Rights Bill concerned public accommodations.[26]

The wording of another petition passed by the National Convention of Colored Persons is revealing. It protested directly against racial discriminations in railroad cars, hotels, and restaurants but made no similar protest against all-black schools. Instead, it merely claimed the constitutional authority to outlaw segregated education. It also called for public schools to be open to all, which is subtly but significantly different from insisting on integrated schools. A petition sent to Congress by the South Carolina legislature was similarly worded. Segregated public accommodations were forthrightly condemned. Regarding the public-school section of Sumner's bill, the petition claimed that South Carolina already enjoyed its benefits by virtue of the state constitution. In fact, this was not the case. The South Carolina petition claimed that it desired the passage of Sumner's mixed-schools provision only for less fortunate states. South Carolina's state constitution provided that the public schools were open to persons of all races. But, in practice, South Carolina then had a segregated public-school system. The only attempt at integrating the state's school facilities had occurred at the college level, an act which resulted in whites boycotting the state university. At lower levels of public education, South Carolina's black children theoretically "chose" to go to all-black schools. This was not Sumner's own understanding as to how his Supplementary Civil Rights Bill would affect public education. Alonzo J. Ransier, a black Republican congressman from South Carolina, carefully selected his language in speaking in favor of Sumner's bill. He defined "mixed schools" as "non-proscriptive schools." This was his own state's interpretation that in fact allowed rigidly segregated public schools.[27]

Apparently, Sumner fully understood such nuances as he himself privately regarded black leaders as not sufficiently committed to racially integrated education. By way of comparison, a petition by Sumner's closest African-American followers was written to fit the exact specifications of the Massachusetts senator. "Our tender children," this petition read, "are taught by separate schools that they are not as good as other children. White children are taught by white schools that colored children are inferior, and are to be despised. Such are the debasing results of the separate-school system." This language clearly endorsed racially integrated education as the only acceptable mode of teaching American children of any race.[28]

The mixed-schools issue in Mississippi state politics illuminates the political dynamics of that time and place. Mississippi's black Republicans supported carpetbagger Adelbert Ames for the party's gubernatorial nomination, thereby defeating the candidate supported by most of the state's scalawags. Ames had tongue-lashed his opponent on the latter's opposition to racial integration in public education. Yet following his election and inauguration, Ames did nothing to bring about mixed schools. Mississippi's schools remained segregated. Instead, Ames focused on trimming state expenditures in a declining economy. Even here, Ames passed by an opportunity to move toward mixed schools. By merging small, inefficient, racially separate schools in certain areas into cost-efficient mixed schools, the state clearly could have saved money. Apparently he was not *that interested* in financial retrenchment. Why did this idealistic crusader not act? Because he knew that it would foment a race war that could quickly get out of control. Then why had he waxed so eloquently on the subject during the campaign? To get elected, and that was all. The issue was little more than an abstraction used to foil those white Republican candidates who expressed the concerns of their white constituents. Meanwhile, scalawags streamed out of the Republican party, thereby sharpening the racial identities of the two major parties and heightening the racial tensions in the state. Talk of mixed schools helped create racially unmixed political parties. In 1875, both the Ames regime and future Republican hopes were toppled by brazen white Mississippians, daily growing ever more confident in their racial solidarity. Talk of mixed schools (never intended to be translated into action) thereby destroyed Mississippi's only realistic vehicle of black power.[29]

The Mississippi example shows just how irresponsibly the mixed-schools idea was thrown about in 1873–1874. Leading this parade toward disaster was Charles Sumner. Historian Richard H. Abbott has summed up the matter well:

Sumner's proposal put his Republican colleagues in a bind. If they rejected his bill they would risk alienating black voters in the Deep South, where they provided almost all of the party's votes. But if they passed it, whites would be offended, not only in the South but in the North as well. It provided a classic illustration of the problems the Republicans faced in trying to organize a biracial party.[30]

While African Americans tended to have a stronger emotional attachment toward the public-accommodations provisions of Sumner's bill, whites focused most intently on the mixed-schools clauses. While most whites were by no means eager for integrated hotels and rail cars, they were enraged by even the abstract idea of mixed schools. For example, a protest petition from Virginia's Democratic legislature made no direct mention of public accommodations, focusing almost solely on mixed schools. William Ruffner, Virginia's superintendent of public instruction, saw mass support for his school system begin to erode under the mixed-schools' storm clouds. All of Virginia's enemies of public education came to the fore. They even attacked the very concept of the public school, integrated or segregated. Professor Bennett Puryear of Richmond College led the opposition. Free schools, he argued, not only would eventually promote race mixing but also result in "free books, free lunches, and free clothes." Rev. Robert Lewis Dabney of the Union Theological Seminary of Virginia argued that public education usurped parenting rights and thereby weakened families. In the end, he predicted, racial amalgamation and social anarchy would be the proven fruits of the public school. Ruffner was at a clear disadvantage in Virginia's racist environment, but he fought back using arguments that he thought might prove effective. He reaffirmed his loyalty to racially segregated public schools. Separate schools for blacks, he wrote, worked to build a healthy race pride among blacks and thereby diminish any inclinations toward racial integration. From his base in Staughton, Virginia, Barnas Sears observed the white backlash over Sumner's bill firsthand, in all of its fury. He sensed that his educational mission in both Virginia and the rest of the South was in jeopardy.[31]

In Missouri, small doses of mixed-school rhetoric had proven beneficial in gaining better financed all-black schools.[32] But as the agitation stretched into 1874, Democrats won the state outright; and the mixed-schools factor suddenly turned against black educational progress. The state had been partially restored to Democratic control in 1870, when Liberal Republicans joined with Democrats in a coalition of sorts. No longer moderated by any Republican influence, a new Democratic legislature in 1874 moved against public education by decentralizing its administration down to the local level. There, subtly denying blacks their educational rights became a studied art form. Missouri's public-school system languished until 1885, another casualty of the Sumner bill.

The mixed-schools backlash was North and South. New Yorkers compared the Sumner proposal to the Fugitive Slave Act of 1850 and vowed that if passed the measure would be observed more in its public rejection than in its lawful application. Samuel Sullivan Cox, a Democratic congressman from New York City, predicted that massive civil disobedience would follow in the wake of an enacted Sumner bill.[33]

Sumner's Bequest

Given the push and pull of black demands and white threats, Congress remained stalemated on the issue. Then, suddenly, Sumner died; and the shock of his death accomplished something that he had been unable to do in life. Instantaneously, his bill was revived and for the first time enjoyed real chances of passing. On March 10, Sumner had attended to his duties in the Senate. He complained to one colleague of

pains on his left side, but these soon passed. That evening, he enter-
tained guests. After their departure, he experienced severe chest pains
and sent for his doctor who gave him a palliative. The next morning,
Sumner himself sensed that the end was near. Visited by E. Rockwood
Hoar (brother of George Frisbie Hoar), Sumner pleaded that his friends
not let his civil rights bill fail. In his final hours, that wish alone consumed his failing heart. His death stunned the nation. His friends had
gotten so used to his chronic ill health that they expected him always to
survive. When the end came, they were genuinely surprised and deeply
moved. Sumner had always been there. He was one of the founding
fathers of the Republican party. Even during his long absence from the
Senate following his beating at the hands of Preston "Bully" Brooks,
Sumner's empty seat had silently testified to the brutality of the slave
culture. Later, upon returning to the Senate, he had prodded a cautious
Lincoln toward advanced moral positions and had been with the
assassinated president during the latter's final hours. He had been a
guiding spirit throughout Reconstruction. His strident voice was so
familiar. And then, he was gone. Once again, his empty chair bore silent
testimony—this time to the horrible lingering hold of the slave culture
on the nation in the form of racially segregated public schooling.[34]

The symbolism of Sumner's funeral arrangements riveted the
attention of the nation. His body was sent home to Boston, arriving on
Saturday evening, March 14. On noon of that day, old friends and
admirers massed at Faneuil Hall to remember his tremendous influence
over their lives. One speaker confessed that with Sumner gone it felt as
if they were all lost "little children." A poem by John Greenleaf Whittier,
written especially for the occasion, described Sumner as a "tall, strong
light-house." With that light extinguished, many Republicans felt a
profound sense of disorientation. For years, his moral beacon had given
them comfort, even when they themselves had strayed from its path.
That evening, Sumner's body was taken to Boston's Doric Hall. Over
the Sabbath, it lay in state, protected around the clock by an African-
American honor guard. During daylight hours, from forty to fifty
thousand mourners streamed by the coffin to pay their last respects.[35]
Samuel Johnson delivered a eulogy at the city's Parker Memorial
Meeting House. No death since Lincoln's, entoned Johnson, had so
affected the nation. And Sumner, emphasized Johnson, was greater than
Lincoln, for Lincoln had been willing to save the Union with slavery
intact, whereas Sumner remained uncompromising. Sumner's death
placed a new premium on idealism over practicality and on moving
ahead to complete the legal structure of civil rights on a foundation of
sand if need be.

Johnson reminded his hearers of just how degraded the nation had become in its worship of practicality during the Gilded Age. Money worship and political corruption tempted even the best of men. But Sumner had remained unstained by his times. He had remained true to his calling as a prophet and statesman and had spent his last breath encouraging others to do likewise. In Brooklyn, Rev. Henry Ward Beecher delivered a similar eulogy. Speaking as one tarnished by his times, Beecher described Sumner as a rare man of pure principle, standing out starkly amid a decadent generation. He had made them feel clean by his presence. In Whittier's words, Sumner had been "white souled, clean-handed, pure of heart." His passing only emphasized the gradual degradation of American civilization. His moral energy no longer was there to redeem a lost generation. "No son bears his name," wept Beecher that Sunday morning. Yet, Beecher prophesied, "his virtues will live after him." It was for the living to pick up his fallen standard and claim it as their own. In that gesture, they might yet be redeemed. The inscription on the floral wreath at the foot of Sumner's casket prodded the consciences of the thousands shuffling by in their grief: "Don't let the Civil Rights Bill fail!"[36]

Several days after Sumner's death, Vice-President Henry Wilson wrote that he had urged Sumner a year before to rest in order to preserve his failing health. The great man had replied that he could never rest until his Supplementary Civil Rights Bill became law. "The failure to complete that allotted task was his regret in his last moments," wrote Wilson. "Loving hands will complete that unfinished work. As we bear him to his burial, may we not hope that his last injunction will be heeded?" It was the least that a sinful generation could do. An outpouring of praise from his congressional colleagues, both Republicans and Democrats, both Reconstructionists and their opponents, followed. William Kelley described Sumner as the last of a small group of "moral heroes" who transformed the republic by their pressing vision. He compared Sumner to St. Simeon, who on lifting the infant Jesus was willing to die as he had lived to see his redeemer. In this metaphor, the unpassed civil rights bill was the infant Jesus. The year before, a practical George Hoar had tried to distance mixed schools from federal aid to education, but now he called for the enactment of Sumner's last wish. Passage of "that great and crowning measure of justice" alone could lay Sumner's soul to rest. Other congressmen confessed that they had not appreciated the depth of Sumner's commitment to mixed schools. They had misread his repeated urgings before a disinterested Congress as a "mere passion for notoriety." But the finality of his deathbed bequest convinced them of the necessity to act. One of the most eloquent congressional eulogies came from Lucius Q. C. Lamar, a Mississippi Democratic congressman hostile to both Reconstruction and Sumnerian ideals. Nonetheless, at that moment, he praised Sumner's passionate pursuit of social justice. "In him," Lamar noted, "this creed seems to have been something more than a doctrine imbibed from teachers, or a result of education. To him, it was a grand intuitive truth inscribed in blazing letters upon the tablet of his inner consciousness, to deny which would have been for him to deny that he himself existed."[37]

Following the congressional eulogies, Carl Schurz spoke at a memorial service for Sumner held at Boston's Music Hall. Contrary to the gush of uncritical praise that had characterized almost every Sumnerian eulogy up to that moment, Schurz attempted to be more real. He described a man who often "appeared distant, self-satisfied, and cold" and a mind that "loved to move and operate in the realm of ideas, not of things." Schurz also compared Lincoln with Sumner: "No two men could be more alike as to their moral impulses and ultimate aims; no two men more unlike in their methods of reasoning and their judgment of means." While conceding that Sumner had been "the very embodiment of the moral idea," Schurz noted that Sumner had never been an effective politician. He had seemed incapable, the German-American leader emphasized, of applying the art of compromise to achieve real progress. In life, he said, Sumner had been a "prophet" and a moral counselor. Then the tenor of his eulogy abruptly shifted. In death, Schurz continued, Sumner's uncompromising spirit was ultimately triumphant in shaping the practical political agenda. Even the practical Schurz confessed that Sumner's death had reawakened in him the beauty of uncompromising action striving for a seemingly impossible dream. In this same vein, James Freeman Clarke described Sumner as "an old knight-errant dropped into our time." The Massachusetts senator's entire life-witness shown brightly in the spring of 1874. In death, Charles Sumner led his party in the way of Don Quixote. The unfortunate result of this heady but temporary quest would be the practical undoing of Reconstruction.[38]

Harper's Weekly, the leading Republican journal of that time, repeatedly recounted Sumner's last hours. "The last thoughts and the last words of Mr. Sumner were for his civil rights bill," reported the magazine. "He was right in believing its passage to be a duty which the country could not honorably neglect." Then the journal made an especially revealing editorial remark. It noted that it did not oppose *de facto* segregation. If black people preferred to go to separate schools, "there is no complaint from any quarter." On the other hand, *de jure* segregation, or racially separate schools mandated by state law, could no longer be tolerated. As debates in the Congress were to reveal, most supporters of Sumner's bill held this same interpretation. It was not one that Sumner himself had condoned. The very essence of his argument for mixed schools demanded real racial integration, whatever the preferences of the victims of caste consciousness might be in fact.[39]

New Jersey's Frederlck T. Frelinghusen led the struggle to get Sumner's bill approved in the Senate. Similar to *Harper's Weekly*, Frelinghusen saw the bill as allowing *de facto* segregation in the public schools. As South Carolina and Mississippi had *de facto* segregated school systems, ostensibly maintained by parental choice, so could Ohio and other Northern states. Only current laws segregating the races into separate schools would be obliterated by the passage of the bill. Nevertheless, even this modest idea upset Allen G. Thurman, Ohio's Democratic senator, who unsuccessfully moved to strike the provision concerning public education. Daniel D. Pratt, an Indiana Republican, tried to calm his colleague from Ohio. "Where the colored people are numerous enough to have separate schools of their own," claimed Pratt, "they would probably prefer their children should be educated by themselves, and there is nothing in this bill which prohibits this." In sparsely populated rural areas of the North, the bill would allow a few African Americans to attend white schools. This, he said, would enable them to acquire educational opportunity for the first time. This, he said, was only elementary justice. But he did not envision that the bill would ever work any social revolution.[40]

In the months following Sumner's death, Republican George S. Boutwell alone spoke for the Commonwealth of Massachusetts in the United States Senate. Representing the fountainhead of New England's social conscience, Boutwell morally challenged his fellow Republicans. Almost alone among them, he stood foursquare against segregated education, whether of a *de jure* or a *de facto* nature. "If it were possible, as in the large cities it is possible, to establish separate schools for black children and for white children," he said, "it is in the highest degree inexpedient to either establish or tolerate such schools." "The doctrine of human equality," he emphasized, could only be taught in schools that were integrated not just in theory but in reality. Boutwell's understanding was true to Sumner's spirit. Likewise, so was the understanding of Edward Shaw, an African American who had organized a black convention in Nashville advocating mixed schools a month and a half after Sumner's death. A long-standing maverick in Tennessee's Republican party, Shaw had been urged by Sumner's associates in Washington, D.C., to call the meeting to contradict the claims of William G. ("Parson") Brownlow, Tennessee's scalawag senator. Brownlow fought the Sumner bill, claiming that the majority of blacks had no real desire to attend racially integrated schools. Shaw effectively organized a convention of black voices damning Brownlow and calling for *de facto* integration.[41]

The language of the Sumner bill encouraged this intraparty quarrel over its true meaning. The bill stipulated that all persons in the nation were "entitled to the full and equal enjoyment of the common schools."[42] Under the bill, enforcement could only be triggered by individual suits in federal courts. Each suit would have to claim that access to a particular common school had been denied. Under these conditions, if both races voluntarily accepted segregated public schools, caste consciousness could continue indefinitely. From a purely legal standpoint, those Republicans who claimed that the bill would not likely result in any social revolution were on solid ground. However, other factors challenged this minimalist interpretation. First and foremost were the well-known attitudes of Senator Sumner himself. Could any measure so dedicated to his memory long be kept in a caste harness? Second and even more important, white racial paranoia refused to allow any ambiguities on this most sensitive subject. The debates over federal aid to education, so recently concluded, clearly demonstrated this. The raw nerve endings of historic white racism became enflamed at the barest hint of meaningful acceptance of blacks into the common American family. Third and last, the very ethos of the American public school suggested meaningful integration. The public school "mixed" both Catholics and Protestants, as well as the native and foreign born. When mixed gender schools were discussed, all assumed that they encompassed schools in which boys and girls actually went to school together, not merely schools in which boys and girls might theoretically go to school with one another. The same assumptions shaped the popular understanding of the Sumner bill. Indeed, the popular reaction to the measure indicated that more than theory was at stake. Had Sumner lived, he never would have allowed the aforementioned ambiguity to develop. He would have insisted upon truly mixed schools or none at all. Predictably, his stridency would have eliminated moderate Republican support. Had he lived, his attitudes would have killed his own bill in its legislative cradle, and it would never have gone on to do its historic damage. Ironically, his very purity as an ideological prophet would have ultimately rescued African Americans from the backlash that was bound to ensue once his Supplementary Civil Rights Bill passed the Republican Senate.

The white public response to the measure was not moderate. A Memphis newspaper recoiled in outrage over the thought of "lovely children with pure Caucasian blood throbbing through their pure white veins" intermixing "with dirty, lousy pickaninnies." On the other side of Memphis' racial divide, Edward Shaw added fuel to the fire. Speaking before an African-American audience of various colors and hues, Shaw noted that white people said that they dreaded mixed schools because such institutions would inevitably lead to racial amalgamation. "I don't want you Negroes to come into our parlors," he said, imitating the typical white reaction. Then, looking out on his audience of black, tan, and nearly white faces, he added: "From the looks of this congregation, it seems that white people have been in our parlors oftener than we have been in their parlors." "They say," continued Shaw, "Oh! You want to marry our daughters." "From the looks of this congregation," he repeated for emphasis, "it seems that one could hardly marry any other than their daughters!" Shaw accurately identified both the sexual fears involved in the Sumner bill and the forced racial amalgamation that had occurred in slavery.

Sumner, wrapped in ideology, had kept himself aloof from anything so vulgar as the sexual fires burning in the furnaces of historic white racism. Parson Brownlow knew better. Reflecting on these passions, he predicted that the bill once passed would destroy any movement in his state toward public education. In addition, the bill did not even have to be enacted to decimate the Republican party in his state. Merely the popular perception that the bill was a party measure achieved that. "I adhere to principles of practical utility, instead of running wild after abstractions," Brownlow wrote justifying his own opposition to the bill. "It is not a question as to whether we will have mixed schools," Brownlow emphasized, "but whether we shall have any system of public instruction at all." Brownlow knew his fellow whites well. Democratic Senator Lewis V. Bogy of Missouri spoke for the perspective of the latter. Mixed schools, Bogy claimed, would lead directly to "moral debauch" and "saturnalian revel" and "pander to all the baser passions of our nature." Blacks, he said, had "course animal natures." Close and intimate contact with them, he fretted, could not but degrade whites. This was the manner in which whites expressed their sexual fears.[43]

Harper's Weekly argued earlier that the bill did not necessarily require racial integration. Once emotional temperatures began to mount on the issue, the Republican journal joined the fray as Sumner himself would have done. Only genuinely integrated public schools, it now conceded, would ever eliminate the ugly habit of caste consciousness. On the other side, Democratic Senator Thomas M. Norwood of Georgia challenged the integrationists' most basic assumption. White racism, he confidently predicted, would long survive mixed schools. "This prejudice," he trumpeted, "is universal. Education does not subdue it. Christianity does not abate it. Civilization but intensifies it." White racism, he prophesied, would "perish only with the last expiring [white] man."[44] But he and those of like mind never intended to allow this proposition to be tested. Before that, they would destroy the public schools and rely solely upon private education. Many African Americans scorned this threat, but not Rev. W. B. Derrick, a black Methodist preacher from Richmond, Virginia. He noted that as soon as the Sumner bill became law, public education would die in his region because of lack of white support. "Then who will be the losers," he asked, "the blacks or the whites? I need not tell you."[45]

During the course of his lifetime, Senator Sumner had established that the principle of equality embodied in the bill was far more important than whether black children were actually educated or not. This stance made him appear at times as one who placed purity of principle over real people. However, to his credit, he always pushed for an active federal role in education, which if implemented would have had the indirect effect of denying the states a check on his mixed schools idea. In 1870, in the readmission of Virginia, Mississippi, and Texas, he had shown how the Guarantee Clause of the Constitution could be used to require states to offer public education. But by 1874, even some of Sumner's old Radical colleagues preferred to forget those precedents. Oliver Morton allowed that states could discontinue public education, if that was their desire. But he refused to countenance the continuing national toleration of *de jure* racially separate schools. Wisconsin Republican Senator Timothy Howe agreed: "Let justice be done," he righteously proclaimed, "though the common schools and the very heavens fall." Republicans who cared more about the immediate needs of real people than the requirements of pure ideology opposed the bill. "We see a great and beneficent system imperiled by an attempt to reduce an abstraction to immediate practice," grieved the Republican editor of the Richmond *Evening State Journal*. Alexander McIver, the Republican superintendent of public instruction in North Carolina, opposed the measure for the same reason.[46]

Oregon Democrat James K. Kelly warned that the Sumner bill was merely a first step toward the Republican dream of nationalizing public education that had been in evidence in the federal-aid-to-education bills of the previous several years. Events were building, he predicted, for a great national referendum on "Caesarism" in the upcoming congressional elections. "Caesarism" was a term with multiple meanings at that time, but Kelly meant it to denote the Republican Party's tendency to move ever closer towards a centralized national government. Kelly hoped that the Republicans might then discover that they had "been digging their political graves" in the mixed-schools matter. Noting the Republican affinity toward Otto von Bismarck, Senator Bogy concurred that soon American voters would have an opportunity to choose whether or not they preferred moving toward a German-inspired imperial government. "The individual German," he said, "is fast drifting into the condition of an educated slave." In the Sumner bill debate, Bogy portrayed his Republican opponents as exchanging the American tradition of local self-determination for a mess of "centralism, political Caesarism, or imperialism."[47]

In one way, Bismarck's nation-building task was easier than that of his Republican counterparts. While religious differences annoyed the German chancellor, he did not have to confront racial hostilities in building his centralized empire. The situation in America was different. In the United States, the aroused power of white racial emotions threatened to topple the party that dared to promote true national homogeneity in the public schools. Delaware Democrat Eli Saulsbury declared that the ultimate Republican design was "the amalgamation of the races." Georgia's Thomas M. Norwood made even more insidious remarks. He described the Sumner bill as "bringing about the happy consummation . . . when the white man and the black, the mulatto and quadroon, the coolie and digger Indian, shall be gathered together, a united family, in one unbroken circle around one common soup bowl and using the same spoon, while shielded by the stars and stripes and regaled by the martial measure and inspiring strain of 'John Brown's soul is marching on.'" New Jersey Democrat John P. Stockton was less sarcastic and more direct. "You have at last," he said addressing the majority party, "put your hand on the holy of holies. . . . I do not believe that any party so reckless as this can come before the people of the United States and maintain its position." Within the Republican party, Tennessee's Senator Brownlow had been spreading the same warning to no avail. Even strong supporters of Tennessee's public schools could not abide mixed schools. One of these wrote Brownlow that he regarded the Sumner bill "with horror." "It is the meanest proposition I ever saw," this correspondent concluded. "I would leave any party, or act with any party to defeat it."[48]

During that spring, many speculated on Republican motives for suddenly pushing the Sumner measure that had been ignored for so long. Democrats suggested that Republicans were pandering to their African-American constituency. They frequently quoted the hyperbole that had characterized Edward Shaw's Nashville convention. That convention's resolutions had labeled any Republican not supporting the Sumner bill as a Judas, "'with whom we will never, never join hands nor support, but will regard, as our public and private enemy, more terrible to meet than a savage beast." Republicans, said Democrats, had caved in to this "African ultimatum." Ohio's Senator Thurman claimed that with Republicans the Nashville demands had "more power . . . than the Constitution."[49] Almost as an aside, Democrats noted that Chinese in the Western states would also benefit from the Sumner bill. No Chinese were allowed into the public schools of the states of the Far West. All that would have to change, the Democrats reminded their California and Oregon colleagues, if the bill passed Congress.[50]

Republicans attempted to deny that black demands were shaping their legislative agenda. Senator Boutwell claimed that the bill was simply the fulfillment of his party's commitment to human equality, which had characterized Republican principles from the beginning. Scalawag James L. Alcorn of Mississippi chose a different response. His own faction had recently lost out to carpetbagger Adelbert Ames in an intraparty power struggle. Ames had ridden the mixed-schools issue to victory, only to prove once in office that the issue was the stuff of rhetoric more than substance. This recent history grated on Alcorn's spirit. Sarcastically announcing for the Sumner bill, he bluntly stated that never again would he allow himself to be on the wrong side of the mixed-schools banner. "The colored people of my state demand the passage of this bill," he said. "I yield to that demand. My refusal would excite them to anger; they would keenly feel the injustice and wrong. I bend gracefully to their will." More than anything else, this performance proved the Democratic allegation.[51]

In supporting his charge that Republicans cared more for black demands than the Constitution, Senator Thurman emphasized a recent case decided by the United States Supreme Court. That spring, Democrats enjoyed reminding Republicans that a Republican Court had ruled in the *Slaughterhouse Cases* of the year before that the privileges and immunities of United States citizens did not include public education. Senator Norwood castigated his Republican opponents for having so little respect for the Constitution as to proceed with the Sumner bill, which he said did not meet the Supreme Court's description of the Fourteenth Amendment's limitations. In the debate over the bill, Democrats promoted the concept that the Supreme Court is the final arbiter of constitutional issues. In the context of that time, this notion suited their political purposes. A generation before, the founder of the modern Democratic party had been quite blunt in his famous Bank veto that the Court should never be given such an exalted status in a government based on the will of the people. Andrew Jackson was not beyond ignoring the Supreme Court when it differed with him. But in 1874, Democrats were eager to swear allegiance to judicial supremacy. "I thank God," said North Carolina's Augustus S. Merrimon, "we have such a Court at such a time."[52]

Republicans were embarrassed by their own Court's definition of the Fourteenth Amendment. *Harper's Weekly* noted that the amendment had been created to protect African Americans from unfriendly state governments and that the Court was violating the intent of the framers in its narrow interpretation of the privileges and immunities clause. But then it suggested that the Slaughterhouse ruling could be avoided by basing the Sumner bill on the Fourteenth Amendment's equal protection clause.[53] Senate Republicans were less conciliatory than the magazine and were of a mind to confront the Court directly and base the legislation on the privileges and immunities clause, irrespective of the *Slaughterhouse Cases*. As Democrats moved away from the constitutional views of Andrew Jackson, Republicans apparently adopted them. In fact, Republicans had articulated the view of judicial subservience to Congress throughout Reconstruction. In the view of Republicans, final authority to interpret the Reconstruction amendments rested with the Congress alone. Senator Morton quoted the last section of the Fourteenth Amendment: "The Congress shall have the power to enforce, by appropriate legislation, the provisions of this article." "Who shall be the judge of what is the appropriate legislation?" Morton asked rhetorically. "Congress only. It is not for the courts to judge and determine whether the legislation is appropriate." Wisconsin's Timothy Howe added that the final constitutional ruling on the Sumner bill would be made by the people's elected representatives sitting in their legislative capacity and not by the Supreme Court. "When the legislative tribunal has spoken," claimed Howe, "its discretion guides the judgment of every other tribunal and the judgment of the whole people of the United States. The tribunal of last resort has spoken, and from its decision there is no appeal upon this question but to the people." New Jersey's Senator Frelinghusen claimed that the intent of the privileges and immunities clause had been to make United States citizenship primary and state citizenship derivative. In his view, each citizen of the United States came under the protection of the national government for the most fundamental rights, the *Slaughterhouse Cases* notwithstanding.[54] Yet, for all of their anticourt bravado, Republicans feared a higher authority than Congress—that of the people. In the autumn, when the midterm elections were held, Democrats were confident that the people themselves would reject the Sumner bill.

Democratic Senator James Kelly warned the Republicans that the people would not accept their brazen attempt to move toward drawing criminal jurisdiction from the several states into the federal jurisdiction. Ironically, historians have discovered that at that very moment President Grant's Attorney General was in fact relaxing enforcement of the legislation passed in 1870–1871 for the protection of the voting rights of African Americans. Not only were the federal courts not equipped to handle the increased caseload, the will was lacking in a Grant administration that sensed that the voting public was tired of protecting African-American civil rights. Nevertheless, the radical fires were still burning brightly in a Senate inspired both by Charles Sumner's deathbed wish and African-American threats supplying impressive political muscle behind the favorite bill of the late Massachusetts senator. The behind-the-scenes maneuverings of officials in the justice department were not widely known at the time. The debates and activities of the Senate were well publicized and known to all concerned citizens. In the public mind, the Republicans were not retreating from Reconstruction but were moving it into its most radical stage to date. Only in hindsight can historians interpret the force of Reconstruction as already spent by the Spring of 1874.[55] The autumn elections loomed ahead to determine the issue.

At 7 A.M. on May 23, after an all-night session, the Senate passed Sumner's bill by a healthy margin. The bill passed the Republican Senate with the party stamp of approval. The public response was quick. Henry Ward Beecher's paper noted that Sumner had proven a more effective legislator in death than he had in life. A Cincinnati newspaper predicted disaster for the Republican party. A New York Republican paper called the mixed-schools portion of the measure "legislative insanity" and worried both for the future of the party and the public schools. While Democratic organs found it hard to restrain their glee, Southern newspapers uniformly damned the measure. One Democratic editorial gloated that this action was "the last nail in the coffin of the late Republican party."[56]

Apparently, Republican Senator William M. Stewart of Nevada did not sense the need for caution. Concerned that some states might begin dismantling their systems of public education, he proposed that a new constitutional amendment require all states to maintain systems of public education. "This proposition of the Nevada senator is most remarkable," stormed the *Savannah Morning News*, "not only as a demonstration of the bitter malignity of its author, but as illustrating the views which he and the insatiable fanatics who act with him entertain of the functions of the federal government and of the rights of the states." Stewart's proposal coming immediately on the heels of the Senate's passage of the Sumner bill raised the specter of Republican "Caesarism" even higher. United States Commissioner of Education John Eaton, Jr., broke under the weight of what public education was being asked to carry. Believing in the ideals of the Declaration of Independence yet opposed to the mixed-schools provision of the Sumner bill, Eaton suffered what later generations would call a nervous breakdown. He escaped to the mountains of his native New Hampshire for a long recuperation.[57]

Two-thirds of Senate was insulated from the upcoming elections, but all House seats were on the line. The Republican House hoped to postpone the measure until after November, and by clever parliamentary maneuvering managed to do so. The *Savannah Morning News* accurately foresaw that this made little difference: "By staving off the vote for the remainder of the session the question will be remitted to the people to be decided at the fall Congressional elections, when . . . a Congress will be returned from the North, South, East and West that will consign this civil rights bill to rest with its author."[58]

At that time, the Congress was also debating whether to complete construction on the Washington monument. Just as the mixed-schools issue was designed to complete the ideals of the Declaration of Independence, plans were afoot to construct the last half of the obelisk dedicated to Washington's memory. Concerned representatives doubted whether a structure of the height planned could withstand the heavy storms occasionally experienced in the capital city. Others were more sanguine and accused those admonishing caution of not holding the father of their country in high esteem.[59] Similarly, those accepting the challenge of Sumner's bequest saw themselves as fulfilling the nation's highest ideals. Those who warned that their extended edifice would come crashing to the ground were brushed aside as not holding the Declaration's ideals in high regard. In the case of the Washington monument, the laws of physics would determine the outcome. Popular feeling and racial prejudice, as revealed in the congressional elections of 1874, alone dictated the ultimate result of the mixed-schools controversy.

7

BACKLASH: 1874

At the outset of 1874, North Carolina had been partially restored to Democratic party control. The governor was still a Republican, as was the state superintendent of schools. The mixed-schools question made the defeat of the latter officer a certainty, even though he publicly opposed the Sumner bill. His party's association with mixed schools could not be forgiven. Scalawag Republicans in North Carolina, tending to be poor and unable to send their children to private schools, felt the mixed-schools issue most keenly and deserted the party in droves. Before the U.S. Senate's passage of the Sumner bill, North Carolina's Democrats had planned to court the African-American vote. But with the mixed-schools paranoia decimating white Republican ranks, North Carolina Democrats seized the opportunity and preached white solidarity against the supposed African threat. The Sumner bill succeeded in completely changing North Carolina's political climate, thereby explaining Albion Tourgee's outrage against Sumner's political naïveté. A year later, essayist Charles Nordhoff toured the state and wrote: "The Republicans admit that the Civil Rights Bill has nearly broken up their party in the state. It was the predominant issue in the canvass of 1874."[1]

In that election, Alexander McIver was defeated for state superintendent of North Carolina's public schools. He had served in that role since 1871 and had done the best job possible with the meager resources at his disposal. Stephen D. Pool, McIver's redeemer opponent, won by a landslide. Once in office, Pool corruptly squandered Peabody Fund money, using it to purchase a house for himself. Resigning in 1876 because of this scandal, he was replaced by his cousin who was equally dishonest. Public education in North Carolina, which had been struggling while McIver was in office, entered a steep decline after the election of 1874.[2] Albion Tourgee had foreseen this result. Anyone with any knowledge of the factions making up the North Carolina Republican party saw in advance that the Sumner bill inevitably led to educational retrogression. Despite their frustrations in always having to accommodate white racism for "practical" reasons, some black leaders in the state also had opposed the mixed-schools idea as foolhardy, for they knew that their children would pay a price for this political mistake. Before 1874, North Carolina's constitution was silent on racial segregation in public education, although racially separate schools mandated by state legislation had characterized North Carolina before 1874. The following year, the constitution was changed to write school segregation into the state's fundamental law itself. Rather than eliminating the stain of caste, Sumner's mixed-schools provision worked to make it virtually indelible.[3]

Democrats in Alabama also gorged on the mixed-schools issue. In 1872, few Alabama Democrats had been able to stomach Horace Greeley, their party's nominee for the presidency. Because of this, many had stayed away from the polls. That had been a low point for the Alabama Democracy. Two years later, Sumner's bill lifted them out of their demoralization. Mixed schools enabled Alabama's Democrats to come roaring back with full confidence and belligerent strength. In 1874, the state's Democrats portrayed the electoral campaign in black-and-white terms. Either voters were white-supremacist Democrats or pro-black Radicals. Mixed schools eliminated any middle ground. Many of the Alabama's white Republicans temporarily considered founding a new Citizens' Union Party devoted to maintaining racially segregated schools while supporting the rest of the Republican program. Ultimately, Alabama's white Republicans did nothing, shamed into silence by their party's association with mixed schools. In 1874, Alabama scalawags either abstained from voting or went over to the Democrats. For African-American candidates in Alabama that year, the short term results were excellent. More black candidates were elected in 1874 than ever before. Thirty-three blacks were elected to salaried offices. The mixed-schools issue had helped them to drive white rivals from the field in African-American districts. Yet from a more significant perspective, 1874 was disastrous for Alabama's blacks. Consisting of less than half of the electorate, blacks needed white allies to build an ongoing political coalition. Mixed schools alienated those allies, leaving the African-American minority position exposed and vulnerable, thereby encouraging increasing acts of white cruelty and terrorism. In victory Alabama's redeemers made at least some attempts to be fair to blacks in the allocation of public-school funds. Some historians note that Alabama's redeemers scored somewhat higher marks in public education than had their Republican predecessors. To that small degree, Alabama's blacks fared better than their counterparts in North Carolina.[4]

FIGURE 7.1

"The Target."
In 1874, violence against black schools and their teachers increased in the
Southern states. Note the burned schoolhouse on the left side of this cartoon.

Harper's Weekly, February 6, 1875.

Unlike North Carolina and Alabama, Tennessee had already been
completely "redeemed" before 1874. Nonetheless, the mixed-schools
backlash in Tennessee increased acts of terrorism against black public
schools and their teachers. One of the latter was Julia Hayden, a
seventeen-year-old African-American graduate of Nashville's Central
College. Throughout her short life, she had eagerly sought self-
improvement and desired to pass on what she had learned to others of
her race. On completing her studies, she moved to western Tennessee

and began teaching in a black school. Within three days after her arrival, two armed white men came to her boardinghouse and loudly demanded to see the teacher. Overhearing the commotion, Miss Hayden fled to an inner room of the house, where she bolted the door. The gunmen followed, and when she refused to come out, they fired at the locked door, killing the young teacher cowering behind it. "Against the colored schools and teachers," concluded a *Harper's Weekly* story on Miss Hayden's assassination, "the rage of the Southern Democracy has risen to the height of a real insanity." "The agitation of the so-called Supplemental Civil-Rights Bill," concluded Tennessee's Democratic state superintendent of schools, "was hurtful to a degree that cannot well be estimated." United States Commissioner of Education John Eaton had already concluded as much on his own. Old friends had written him of the ugly mood in the state since the Senate's passage of the Sumner bill.[5]

In the words of Tennessee's Parson Brownlow, Sumner's bill was regarded by poor whites in Tennessee as an "oppressive and abominable usurpation." "The mere threat to pass it," he wrote in a letter written several weeks after the Senate approved of the measure, "is the greatest insult and outrage which has ever been attempted upon the honest, hardworking people of small property, or no property at all." He called the measure "'a bill for the encouragement of riot and chaos in the Southern states.'" When the state elections finally came in early August, Democrats experienced an even bigger landslide than they had expected. Analysts credited the outcome to mixed schools. Hearing the electoral results, poor whites from the countryside poured into Knoxville and other urban centers to celebrate. As for Brownlow, he interpreted the result as a requiem for his party in all of the Southern and border states.[6]

The campaign of 1874 provided the Democrats with their own version of the "bloody shirt." A political observer in Kentucky that year perceptively noted that "the chap who talks loudest and with the best common sense about the probability of our daughters marrying niggers always comes in about four lengths ahead." With the specter of sexual intimacy between the races being fostered in the dreaded mixed schools of the future, poor whites felt a bravado that is born of desperation. Speaking for this element, Henry Watterson's Louisville *Courier-Journal* commented: "The Civil Rights Bill may be passed, and signed by the President. If it does, there will be a war of races, a revolution, the overthrow of universal suffrage, and a military government in Washington. If the North is ready for this, so is the South: We have touched bottom and can go no further. We have reached the point where gravitation stops and turns back." John D. White was the only Republican to be elected to Congress from Kentucky in 1874. He was elected from a white district, and he won by lambasting his own party for allowing itself to become identified with the Sumner bill, which he termed "the root of all evil."[7]

The mixed-schools issue was similar to a poison which in small doses helps fight a disease but in massive amounts proves fatal. In small doses, it had pushed Kentucky to enact black schools, a long overdue reform. Then came the crusade to enact the fallen Massachusetts' senator's bequest, and Kentucky's supporters of expanding educational opportunity for African-American children ran for cover. John Marshall Harlan was one of these. Later winning immortality for his lonely dissents in favor of civil rights on the United States Supreme Court, Harlan was then a politically ambitious Republican in Kentucky. He purposefully kept himself aloof from politics that year because of the mixed-schools firestorm. The following year, he ran for governor advocating "separate-but-equal" schools for Kentucky's blacks. Kentucky had been tardy in providing any public education for blacks, and when it came in 1874 it was funded at levels grossly unequal to that provided for whites. In his electoral contest of 1875, Harlan's call for equal funding was courageous. Nevertheless, in the minds of some modern historians he should have been a forthright advocate of mixed schools on the model of Charles Sumner. Later on, when removed from the rough and tumble world of public opinion, sitting on the Supreme Court, Harlan would sound like Sumner. But as long as he practiced the political art of striving for politically attainable goals in the electoral arena, he was more practical. Even so, he lost his bid to be governor of Kentucky in 1875. His call for equal funding was one of the factors leading to his defeat. Nevertheless, in challenging Kentucky's white majority to treat blacks fairly, he provided a model of how an idealist in politics should behave—ever pushing the limits of what is possible within reason. Unlike Sumner, Harlan knew that the journey of a thousand miles begins with single steps. Unlike Sumner, he was willing to sacrifice pure ideology for real educational gains. Even in taking that stance, he was "ahead of his time."[8]

In Virginia, results were similar to those in Kentucky. Early in 1874, Republicans held almost half of Virginia's congressional delegation— one senator and four representatives. The election of 1874 reduced this count to one lone representative. The tactics used by Virginia's Democrats in this campaign were revealed by William Terry, who was running for a House seat. Terry had served in the House between 1871 and 1873. His campaign literature proudly recalled his votes against federal aid to education. It boasted of his consistent opposition to the educational reforms of "the New England men—the Radicals of the Radicals—the advocates of centralization, the whining, Puritanical oppressors of the South." Hoar's federal aid bills, Terry's propaganda proclaimed, had been "nothing less than the Civil Rights Bill in disguise." "The hideous mixed-schools feature of the Civil Rights Bill" had been hidden away deep in the Trojan horse of federal aid, but Terry boasted of having recognized this threat immediately. By contrast, his literature continued, his Republican opponent (Fayette McMullin) supported federal aid to education as late as 1874, despite the fact that the Senate's passage of the Sumner bill clearly revealed the Republican master plan of racial amalgamation.[9] Needless to say, Terry defeated McMullin.

Missouri also had earlier included five Republicans in its congressional delegation. The election of 1874 left no Missouri Republicans standing. After the landslide, Thomas P. Akers (a leading St. Louis Democrat) identified the Civil Rights Bill, and especially its mixed-schools provision, as the determining factor. "No Civil Rights Bill," said Akers, "can rend the web which Nature has woven in Her powerful loom." The election, he said, proved that the "natural instincts" of racial preference, presumably created by God, were stronger than any human effort to overcome them.[10] In 1874, only sixteen Republicans were elected from all of the former slave states to the House of Representatives. And some of these only got there by loudly denouncing Sumner's handiwork.[11]

Many of the Northern states exhibited a similar pattern but on a lesser scale. For example, Illinois' and Indiana's Republicans lost three House seats each. In addition, Indiana's Republicans surrendered a Senate seat. Ohio's Republicans lost five House seats. Pennsylvania's Republicans lost a whopping ten House seats and one in the Senate. New York Republicans lost one Senate seat and five in the House. Similar results were recorded throughout many other Northern states. While on the whole this constituted less of a dramatic drop than experienced in the Southern states, cumulatively the effect was a major shock to Northern Republicans. Sumner himself had realized that his bill was deeply resented throughout much of the North. Northern whites had long "quarantined" their African-American neighbors.[12] The war and the Reconstruction spirit had ameliorated this segregation somewhat, but Northern resistance against racially integrated public schooling remained very strong. A variety of Reconstruction-era Northern-state laws promising racial equity and fairness in public education were simply ignored in implementation.

Graded schools exacerbated the problem. Introduction of the graded school was then an educational reform sweeping the nation, especially the Northern states. Greater specialization, resulting from age and skill classifications, defined the new graded schools. As white students were apportioned into graded classrooms, Northern African-American children typically were shunted to all-black ungraded classrooms, often located in the physical plants of otherwise graded schools. In only a most superficial way were such schools racially integrated. Had graded schools never come about, and had both white and black children continued to receive ungraded instruction in segregated one-room schoolhouses, the injustice of segregated schooling would have been more tolerable for black parents. But this new form of close-quarters segregation was extraordinarily humiliating and demeaning. Any black parent with any sense of pride had to be outraged by such conditions and more than willing to join the cause for mixed schools. Newton Bateman, Illinois's state superintendent of schools, admitted that he could morally accept *de facto* segregated schools. But he found the new Northern practice of all-black classes within otherwise white graded schools morally repugnant. Illinois's legislation designed to ensure racial equity in the common schools made no difference when it came time to arrange the details of public education on the local level. Apparently whites in Illinois intended to send a message by these locally determined practices that blacks were not welcome in their region. Bateman railed against this unfair treatment but confessed his powerlessness to effect any meaningful change.[13]

Indiana's whites were just as mean-spirited, perhaps even more so. Since 1869, Indiana had provided for racially separate black schools. Then, as the Senate was passing the Sumner bill, the superior court of Marion County in Indiana declared that local black schools were demonstrably inferior, a conclusion that led the court to mandate racial integration locally. It based its ruling on the equal protection clause of the Fourteenth Amendment and a provision in the state constitution that required racial equity in public education. The decision was quickly reversed by the state's supreme court, which ruled that the funding of local black schools was appropriately in the realm of state police powers and beyond the scope of the Fourteenth Amendment. The mere fact that blacks were given any kind of public schools demonstrated to this court that the mandate of the state constitution had been fulfilled.[14]

In 1874, the public mood in Indiana was similar to that in Alabama. In fact, the Democratic party platforms in both states adopted identical public-school planks in that election year. Both platforms denounced the federal attempt to "take control of the schools." Impressed by this, *Harper's Weekly* commented: "Upon no other point is there more hearty Democratic accord." The South recognized this new intersectional commonality of racial feeling with gratitude and increasing confidence. After the subsequent national landslide buried the Republicans, the *New Orleans Times Picayune* commented on the hardening of Northern racial attitudes: "Any attempt to interfere with their school system is resisted at the North with far greater energy than can be brought to bear against the exercise of federal authority at the South." Continuing its commentary upon the political revolution wrought by Sumner's bill, the *Times Picayune* concluded: "The effects of the bill on the public schools of the North have been sufficient to arouse a large amount of popular resentment. Nowhere is the forced admission of Negroes to the schools resisted with more passionate earnestness than in Indiana and Illinois and other Western states."[15]

Throughout the Northern states in 1874, the Democratic party state platforms denounced the Supplementary Civil Rights Bill. The Republican party countered this noisy opposition with relative silence. Only in Michigan did the Republican party strongly endorse the measure. Even Sumner's own Massachusetts Republican party resisted speaking out on the issue. Popular opposition to mixed schools was fully exploited by Democrats overjoyed at the political gift left to them by Sumner's bequest. The Democratic harvest was especially rich in Pennsylvania. Since 1854, Pennsylvania law had mandated that districts with twenty or more black children had to provide for black schools. That same law had stipulated that in districts with less than twenty African-American children, the white schools had to accommodate them. In May 1874, at the same historic moment when the Senate passed the Sumner bill, the Pennsylvania senate passed a civil rights bill of its own, designed to repeal the law of 1854 and enforce mixed schools throughout the entire state. As in the federal Senate, the Pennsylvania senate divided along party lines concerning the measure. Because of this, the Republican party of Pennsylvania bore a double burden of both state and federal legislative behavior that white voters generally found repulsive. A Democratic newspaper in Harrisburg set the tone of the campaign by asking the electorate if they were "'quite ready to sleep in the same bed with their colored brethren, . . . or even to place their children in the same rooms at school with pickaninnies.'" A newspaper in Lancaster charged that mixed schools were "obnoxious" and that blacks "ought to be satisfied" with their separate schools. "This is the question to meet and decide at the coming election," warned York's

Democratic organ a month and a half before voting day. "There never
was a squarer political issue made, and, much as the Radical newspapers dislike the dose, they must swallow it." A week later, this same
newspaper outlined the issue facing the voters: "This Civil Rights Bill
was the last bequest of the brilliant but fanatical Sumner to his party
and the country, and it promises to destroy the one or degrade the
other." The outcome was never in doubt as Pennsylvania's Republicans
were buried at the polls.[16]

In Connecticut, Democrat William W. Eaton (no relation to John
Eaton, Jr.) was elected to the U.S. Senate on an anti-mixed-schools
platform. Eaton's success led Truman Smith, a former Republican
senator from Connecticut, to urge that his party immediately jettison
the mixed-schools provision in the Sumner bill. Reviewing Smith's
advice, *Harper's Weekly* cautioned that any retreat might sacrifice the
momentum of Reconstruction. What it failed to acknowledge was that
Reconstruction's momentum had already been lost by the Republican
mistake of having made mixed schools a party measure. By the late
summer, a Democratic takeover of the House of Representatives in the
elections of 1874 was a virtual certainty, irrespective of any last minute
change of course by the national Republican party. Sensing the impending disaster, one contemporary biographer of Charles Sumner wrongly
suggested that if the great man were still alive even he would see the
necessity of backing off .from mixed schools, an issue that was
destroying Republican chances in the upcoming elections. Sumner had
never left any doubt what he would do under such circumstances: He
would go down fighting for pure principle rather than ignobly retreat to
be able to fight another day.[17] Among a generation of Southerners that
had suffered defeat and devastation, the Republican dilemma was
wonderful to behold. The Mobile *Register* exulted:

The white people of the North have awakened from their nightmare. The Negro is no longer the fashion. . . . The North have
come to their senses. [*sic*] The Negro has disgraced and ruined the
party which pushed him forward, and the oscillating pendulum of
public opinion is now swinging over to the side of the Southern
white man. Fred [Douglass] might as well give it up. The North
have found that they could not make a silk purse out of a sow's
ear, and have cast Sambo overboard.[18]

As long as the Republican civil rights movement had not incon-
venienced Northern whites, it moved forward. But the mixed-schools
issue brought it to an insurmountable stone wall.

The pivotal state of Ohio was most vulnerable to the threat of a Sumnerian mixed-schools mandate. In 1874, only 5,950 of the state's 23,020 African-American children attended any kind of school. In rural areas, black children were commonly banned from white schools. In areas where separate black schools were possible, often the location of these schools made attendance a practical impossibility. In 1874, similar to action in Pennsylvania, the Ohio state legislature had come close to enacting a mixed-schools bill. The vote had divided predictably along party lines. The Democrats enjoyed being identified with what proved to be the popular course.[19] Former Republican governor Edward F. Noyes damned the Democrats for "appealing to the passions and prejudices of ignorant white men." Republican Senator John Sherman assured fellow whites that black children were bound to be no trouble in Ohio's public-school classrooms. The voters were unimpressed either with Republican accusations or assurances. Ohio too posted a Democratic victory.[20]

The Ohio state Democratic platform that year gave prominence to the mixed-schools issue. The document noted that Sumner's Supplementary Civil Rights Bill intended to mandate mixed schools, something that the Ohio Supreme Court had ruled was not required by the Reconstruction amendments to the U.S. Constitution. The platform went on to suggest that the *Slaughterhouse Cases* of the United States Supreme Court supported the state supreme court's specific decision on public education. It concluded that the Republican party measure intended "to compel mixed schools in Ohio, by the infliction of severe criminal punishment and civil penalties upon all who resist that unconstitutional attempt." By contrast, the Ohio Republican platform made no specific mention of the Sumner bill or its Ohio equivalent, referring only to the party's proud civil rights record of supporting "equal civil and political rights to all citizens." Republican reticence to discuss specifics reflected a weakness that Democrats eagerly exploited. As election day drew near, Democratic party orators in Ohio focused voter attention on the Sumner measure as "a bill of disorder, a bill of violence, a bill to stir up mutual hatred between the races." "When they punish men for refusing to have the whites and the blacks at the same table, or on the same benches at the theater, or in the schools," proclaimed General Thomas Ewing at a Democratic rally held in Cleveland, "they are invading a province that does not belong to government." Following the state elections, which occurred on October 13, the *Cleveland Daily Plain Dealer* sensed a landslide in the making. The initial results indicated to this Democratic party paper that "the attempted application, through political action, of wild social or moral ideas, which conflict with personal liberty in never so light a degree will surely end in the overthrow of the party making the attempt."[21] When the general election of November 3 reinforced this initial impression, the newspaper editorialized why the tremendous voter backlash had occurred:

> The Republican party has attempted to *legislate* the people up to an ideal standard of morality. . . . It has interfered with the private rights of the citizen, and sought to regulate social tastes, customs, and prejudices by legal enactment. . . . It is at variance with the very cornerstone of our democratic idea: the drift of the party is ever towards a despotic centralization of power at Washington, as opposed to the wise safeguards to republicanism contrived by the fathers.[22]

The Ohio election revealed that racial matters outweighed religious concerns when both were simultaneously before Northern voters. Among Ohio's electorate, Republicans enjoyed an advantage of being identified with a Protestant defense of the traditional American public school. In 1874, a state constitutional amendment barring any use of state funds for parochial education was on the Ohio ballot. Republicans had confidently predicted its adoption. Unfortunately for them, the anti-Republican racist mood that year swept away even proposals such as the school-funding amendment that in a more racially neutral political environment would have succeeded. But within this defeat was an opportunity for Republican resurrection, not only in Ohio but across the North. *The Independent*, a New York Protestant weekly, was the first to see it. It editorialized that the Republicans needed to cease taking advanced stands in racial matters and focus on its religious advantage alone. The newspaper suggested that the dangerous influence of a powerful Democratic/Catholic alliance seeking to undermine the public school was readily apparent in the Ohio contest. *The New York Times* agreed in suggesting that the national Republican party work mightily to shift the political focus from racial to religious concerns, for in the latter the party had a clear advantage that it needed to exploit.[23]

During Reconstruction and shortly after, Ohio was a Presidential breeding ground. Grant, Hayes, and Garfield all hailed from Ohio. This was no accident. Ohio was needed for Republican success in Presidential contests. Unlike some other Northern states, political outcomes in Ohio were rarely predictable. In the years following the Civil War, the margin for victory in Ohio was paper thin. This fact placed Ohio on the fulcrum of determining the political course of the nation itself. The elections of 1874 demonstrated to Republicans that in order to win Ohio (as well as most other states) the crusade for racial equity had be de-emphasized. At the same time, Republicans saw opportunity in making anti-Catholicism the party's highest priority. Ohio was the perfect testing ground in this strategic shift.

When race was uppermost, the Democrats benefited. The public school had been key in the contest over race. It remained center stage as the national Republican agenda shifted to religious matters. In 1874, the Republican party had mounted an offensive to bring about a unified nation by means of racially mixed schools. As that attempt failed, the party took up defensive positions to protect the public school's historic mission of making one people out of disparate religious elements. In this new Republican defensive strategy, the Democrats were portrayed as cat's-paws of a culturally divisive Roman Catholic church intent on splintering American public education into a variety of sectarian expressions. As long as the racial focus remained dominant, Democrats effectively attacked Republican centralization and "Caesarism" working to create an unwanted cultural homogeneity (described as "racial amal-gamation" by Democrats). With a shift to a religious focus, Republicans more safely continued their campaign for cultural unity, recast as preserving traditional Protestant norms. The adjustment was deter-mined by the electoral majority's prejudices, both racial and religious. The new Republican emphasis allowed the party to be recast as the defender of the traditional American way, in contrast to appearing as its destroyer, an image that damaged the party as long as racial con-siderations were dominant.

Shifting from a racial to a religious emphasis promised to show political centralization in a different light, one potentially more accept-able to the electorate. Regarding the Sumner bill, any national mixed-schools mandate eventually would have required an elaborate federal enforcement machinery. The centralizers' nationalist agenda was ap-parent on the face of that issue. Battling a Catholic threat to the states' school funds allowed a far more subtle approach toward political centralization. First, Republicans would have to persuade the electorate that the Catholic threat to the public schools was real. The ground work for this had already been laid in the years following the Cincinnati Bible War. Second, they would propose a constitutional amendment to enlist the federal government in fighting the political clout of the Roman Catholic church, which was very powerful in some key states, such as New York. Third, once adopted, this new Reconstruction amendment would allow the federal government to move into public education, all in the name of preserving the traditional American public school against foreign religious infiltration.

Immediately after the elections of 1874, most Republicans were still in shock over the massive defeat they had just suffered. *The Winchester Journal*, a Republican newspaper in Indiana's Randolph County, aptly captured the mood of the moment: "The Republicans are not on the ragged edge any longer but clean gone fell over and are now quietly sneezing at the foot of the precipice." Ohio Congressman James A. Garfield wrote a friend, "The Deluge has come and gone, and we see the face of the new political earth." John Eaton, Jr., was even more humbled. Refocused following his nervous breakdown which had occurred at the time of the Senate's passage of Sumner bill, Eaton made a heroic effort to disengage from any taint of Republican imperial "Caesarism." He emphasized that, rumors to the contrary, his office was no part of any conspiracy to centralize public education. His only role, he stressed, was to disseminate information to state-based public-school professionals. According to this obsequious confession, his only role was to empower local officials with more knowledge, thereby enhancing local control and states rights. His tone revealed the psychological extent of the political rout that had occurred.[24]

Predictably, President Grant blamed the Sumner bill for his party's electoral disaster. The Philadelphia *Evening Bulletin*, which had strongly supported the measure before the election, agreed with Grant once the election results were known. "As a measure of party policy it may have been inexpedient to agitate the question in Congress," the paper conceded after the fact, and then added weakly as a means of explanation, "but the bill, as originally introduced, was Mr. Sumner's, and he bequeathed it to his colleagues with a solemn injunction that it should be passed." The Democratic *York Gazette* (York, Pennsylvania) highlighted Sumner's bill and noted that all by itself it produced "a tendency to drive every decent Radical out of his party and into the Democratic ranks." The Republican *New York Times* also identified Sumner's bequest as a key reason for the defeat. Of New York City's 304 schools, 9 were "exclusively for colored pupils." New York's voters had no intention of changing the city's educational and racial habits.[25] Neighboring New Jersey was much the same. William W. Phelps, a New Jersey Republican congressman, blamed the mixed-schools issue for his own failed campaign for reelection. Other Northern sources concurred that mixed schools had helped damage Republicans in the North.[26]

Senator Allen G. Thurmon of Ohio credited voter backlash against Republican centralism for his own party's tremendous victory in all sections of the land. The *Sedalia* [Missouri) *Democrat* especially emphasized this theme: "The right of the people of the states to local self-government was involved, and it had to be met and settled, and it is settled." The *Richmond Daily Dispatch* gloated that the election effectively killed the Sumner bill. The *Cincinnati Daily Enquirer* taunted Republicans: "Come on with your Civil Rights Bill gentlemen."[27] Many newspapers and commentators failing to mention mixed schools as a cause of the backlash talked in more general terms of "Caesarism" as the source of voter anger. "Caesarism" was an imperious attitude that editorial writers rarely defined but with which that generation was very familiar. Caesarism could be found in President Grant ordering the army to shore up an unwanted Reconstructionist regime in Louisiana. Caesarism was reflected in the dying political program of the Radicals, designed to create racial equity through national mandates. Caesarism could even be found in the contemporary sermons of New England's Puritanical descendants. That fall, Henry Ward Beecher, the most famous of these Northern preachers, revealed the intellectual flavor of "Caesarism": "Liberty," he said, "does not mean opposing government; it means the most absolute submission to government, provided it is a right government."[28] In our own time, this attitude is often called "political correctness," the one right way determined by a "morally superior" intellectual elite. Then, this attitude was simply part of what the Democrats called "Caesarism," the American counterpart of Bismarckianism in Germany. Caesarism assumed that government should be centralized, with one standard applied to all.

Governor James Milton Smith of Georgia defied Caesarism at an Atlanta celebration over the midterm election results. No more, he told an excited post-election throng, would the South have to fear national mandates concerning African Americans. Henceforth, he told his audience, "we intend to control the poor creatures ourselves." Senator John B. Gordon recoiled at the governor's undiplomatic language. As an emerging architect of Southern redemption ideology and practice, Gordon knew that finesse was what was needed to dispatch the damaged legions of Caesarism. Talk of states rights and direct allusions to abusing African Americans, he feared, might reawaken the dying Northern Reconstruction spirit. Following Smith to the podium, Gordon demonstrated an alternative model designed to retain the Southern political momentum. He told the crowd that the election results made him feel like an American again. His rhetoric was cast in a slick veneer of nationalist celebration. He praised the national electorate's choice of "Constitutionalism" over "centralism." A week later, the *Atlanta Constitution* contrasted Smith's and Gordon's presentations and advised its readers to emulate the style of the latter. "At this time we must be as wise as serpents," the editorial admonished, "even if we are not as harmless as doves." Gordon's language was carefully designed to solidify and strengthen the new Democratic national majority[29]

The *New York Herald*, a Democratic party organ, confidently predicted that Caesarism would never rise again. Around the world, it reported, Caesarism was in decline. The year before, Louis Thiers had fallen from power in France. Gladstone's recent defeat in England was seen in the same light. Given this world-wide trend, the *Herald* saw even Bismarck's days numbered.[30] This lesson was not lost on the Republicans. Just as Senator Gordon had come to appreciate the need for sophistication in bringing about a successful strategy of redemption, Republicans concluded after 1874 that they too needed to be more artful in presenting their ideology of national reconstruction. In preparation for the 1876 presidential election, Republicans began to redefine the need for centralism in religious terms. Central federal controls, they argued, were needed to keep the Roman Catholic church from destroying "nonsectarian" public education at the local level. For the next several years, Republicans emphasized that a national political shield was needed against an international papal conspiracy to undermine the American public school. Contrary to the *Herald's* claim, Caesarism was not yet dead. It was down, but not out.

Postmortem analyses of the election results mentioned a variety of influences other than mixed schools and Caesarism. While conceding that the Civil Rights Bill was a matter of "questionable expediency," Thurlow Weed highlighted public ill will over the "Salary Grab" Act of 1873. Some Republicans credited the landslide to the simple fact that the party had been in power for a long time. It could not be expected to hold its national majority forever. Nonetheless, these commentators urged that the defeat be regarded as a helpful purifying experience and not dissuade the party faithful from supporting the Supplementary Civil Rights Bill. Others cautioned that the party back off from all moral causes appealing only to splinter factions, such "as prohibition, woman suffrage, and other humbugs of like character." In Massachusetts, a traditionally rock-ribbed Republican state, prohibition had damaged the party in 1874. A popular backlash against a prohibitionist Republican governor allowed a Democrat to win that office.[31] In Congressional races in Massachusetts, "Butlerism" (the bullying and corrupt politics practiced by Ben Butler) had encouraged voters to remove the Republican rascals. Butler himself lost his House seat. In explaining his own downfall, Butler did not credit public feeling against the patronage politics associated with his name. Instead, he identified his own caution in pushing the Sumner bill before the election. In his role as the bill's sponsor in the House, he had practiced delay rather than pushing the measure through. "The people turned from us because we were a do-nothing party," reflected Butler, "afraid of our shadows." In his own particular district, this unique explanation probably did account for the loss of some of his previous support.[32]

"Grantism" was also credited with helping to cause the landslide. That term connoted that aspect of "Caesarism" associated with the corruption of Grant's administrations. Some highlighted the ongoing economic depression; yet others countered with the suggestion that one year of suffering following the Panic of 1873 was insufficient to erase the popular reputation of the Democratic party as the party of depression. Andrew Jackson's war against the Bank of the United States had led to the Panic of 1837 and James Buchanan had been president at the time of the Panic of 1857. These memories were yet fresh. Nonetheless, the current depression was indeed a factor. Even though neither major party at that time promised an active governmental assault on the causes of the depression, voters then as now associated the economy with political campaigns and their results. While both parties had responded to the depression by cost-cutting promises designed to lighten federal tax burdens, the Democrats were more active in this regard. Democratic candidates also tended to be softer on the currency issue than Republicans, and voters wanting monetary inflation for relief from debts were more likely to vote for the Democracy.[33]

No one explanation suffices to explain the Democratic landslide. Just as contemporaries could not agree what caused the result, neither have historians of the event. Some very prominent historians have completely dismissed the mixed-schools issue as being an important factor. Although a close student of public education in the 1870s, James M. McPherson reports that the Democratic victories nationwide were "due mainly to economic depression, political corruption, and the turbulence of Southern politics." William P. Vaughn, another researcher of public education in the decade, also rejects the thesis that a backlash against the Sumner bill played a significant part in the midterm elections of 1874. He too cites "economic depression, charges of political corruption, and Reconstruction problems in the South." William B. Hesseltine's work identifies business-class yearnings for economic intersectional stability as determining the result.[34] Eric Foner too emphasizes economic factors and goes so far as to claim that by 1874 the depression had virtually killed off the free-labor Republican ideology. No doubt the depression was one important factor, but its overemphasis by modern historians is unwarranted. In the subsequent presidential campaign of 1876, the Republicans had two additional years to become associated with economic hard times, yet popular Republican stump orators such as Robert Ingersoll continued to use free-labor rhetoric with good effect, a fact that indicates that the traditional economic message of the Republican party was still alive and well at that later date. Additionally, if the 1874 elections had been an overwhelming economic protest, greenbacker inflation schemes would have played a much more predominant role than they did.[35]

The elections of 1874 broke the back of Reconstruction. In that election, Republicans lost control of the House of Representatives, and therefore were unable to enact additional Reconstruction legislation. The elections turned what had been a strong Republican House majority into a strong Democratic majority. As soon as the new House was seated in 1875, it had the potential of stymieing any enforcement of Reconstruction by depriving the army of funds needed to police the Southern states. Additionally, the new House had the potential to impeach a President enforcing past Reconstruction mandates and force him to withstand a humiliating trial, albeit before a still narrowly Republican Senate. Though not likely, these possibilities precluded an active enforcement of past Reconstruction legislation. After 1874, the Republican party was scrambling simply to regain lost ground.

Among modern historians, William Gillette has studied the electoral contest of 1874 most closely, as it is key to his story which he entitled, *Retreat from Reconstruction*. In his account, the backlash against mixed schools is emphasized over all other factors. He describes that issue as driving many Republican voters to reject for the first time the legitimacy of the federal government interfering in traditionally state and local matters, such as public education. He credits that issue with driving scalawags en masse from the party. He emphasizes the issue's impact in Northern states as well. While his account is in no way mono-causational, it does highlight the mixed-schools issue.[36]

The significance of this one issue in radically diminishing scalawag support for the party cannot be overemphasized. Historians have spent much energy in debating whether "Whiggish" or "Jacksonian" economic preferences attracted native-white Southerners to the Republican party. This controversy is far less significant than what motivated them to drop out of the party's ranks. There is little dispute on this latter question. By making mixed-schools rhetoric the litmus test of their support, African Americans by-and-large defeated scalawag candidates. The departure of scalawags from the party assisted the forces of Southern reaction that grew increasingly confident of ultimate success.

Not only did mixed schools seriously undermine the future of the Republican party in the South, the issue also forfeited the party's moral advantage, at least so far as popular perceptions were concerned. White Northerners identified with the "moral" outrage of Southerners over forcing racial intimacy in the public schools. Before 1874, white racism often appeared as the dying ideology of slavery. During and after 1874, it was recast as the bulwark of civilization itself. Southerners had long portrayed it as such but had not found a sympathetic ear in the North. Matt W. Ransom of North Carolina sensed this new "moral" advantage when he told the House early in 1875 that Southerners like himself were not opposed to racial integration due to any low prejudice. To the contrary, he emphasized, sustaining the "character" of the white race was "an honorable conviction." Hatred, he said, did not motivate Southern intentions. Rather love of the highest civilization alone informed their hearts.[37] The electoral campaign had tipped the rhetorical advantage away from the Republican party, as "civilization" and "character" concerns came to replace any emphasis on "rights."

Michael Perman has written that up until 1874, both political parties had battled to capture the political center. In 1872, the Democrats' "New Departure" had imitated Republican support for the Reconstruction amendments with an eye to capturing the moderate vote. In the Southern states, scalawags had generally constituted this essential political center. The mixed-schools controversy squandered this asset. "White men will not send their boys to school with Negro boys," commented a North Carolina newspaper. "As to sending their daughters to such schools, the land will run with blood before they will do it. They cannot be forced to do so even at the point of a bayonet."[38] Whereas Northerners had found it difficult to understand the old Southern rationale for the institution of slavery, they did sympathize with this related Southern sentiment concerning the public schools. This factor, more than any other, helped Democrats capture the political center in 1874, something that their earlier "New Departure" strategy had failed to do.

The new national mood was also reflected in changing constitutional fashions as evidenced in the evolving pronouncements of Thomas M. Cooley, that generation's most prestigious constitutional authority. In 1873, Cooley had supported Reconstruction activists who claimed that the equal protection clause of the Fourteenth Amendment could be used as a judicial weapon against *de jure* segregation. By 1875, he was developing a different course in attacking Reconstruction activists for having misused the Constitution's Guarantee Clause.[39] Of course, these two constitutional provisions were not related to each other, except as potential tools for Reconstruction. As the public mood began to cool concerning civil rights, leading constitutional voices both in and out of government increasingly began to favor the enemies of Reconstruction.

Southerners more than others sensed that the political momentum had shifted to their side. This was evident in New Orleans, where whites had barely tolerated a mixed-schools experiment forced on them by a Republican regime. The facts that the numbers of African Americans accepted into this experiment consciously had been kept small and had involved the mostly New Orleans' "black" elite of quadroons and octoroons helped maintain the public peace.[40] The national mixed-schools debate inevitably changed this local equation. Early in the debate, local African Americans left out of the experiment became emboldened to demand entry. As a national referendum against mixed schools loomed on the horizon, local whites resolutely called for an end to the small degree of racial integration that already had occurred in New Orleans. A confrontation became inevitable. George Washington Cable was then a reporter for the New Orleans *Times Picayune* that covered a weeks-long imbroglio over the racial composition of the city's schools, beginning in December 1874, just one month after the national election results were known. According to the newspaper accounts, the immediate confrontation began when two black women brought three African-American girls to enroll them in New Orleans' all-white girls high school, located in the city's upper school district. The principal told them that the girls could not be enrolled as he had not received authorization from the superintendent of schools to accept any black children. This white officiousness angered the women, and their demeanor in turn "insulted" the whites who observed the "tumult." White high school girls circulated a petition opposed to integrating their school and took it to the city's leading Republican newspaper, perhaps wishing to initiate a confrontation of their own.

Arthur E. Adams, an employee of the Republican paper, made the crucial mistake of making light of the girls' protest. What followed was a tragic comedy of errors. First, rumors circulated that Charles W. Boothby, the city's superintendent of schools, had ridiculed the girls' petition. Acting on this rumor, a gang of fifteen white men roughed up Boothby, only to discover later that they had vented their anger upon the wrong man. A disheveled Boothby repeatedly insisted on his non-involvement in the affair.[41] Second, as the truth emerged that Adams and not Boothby was the villain who had besmirched the dignity of the girls, a self-appointed enforcer of the honor of Southern womanhood tracked down Adams "and cowhided him until he was tired." All of this activity by whites encouraged African Americans to make the next move. Thirty young blacks then went to the all-white boys high school, also in the upper district. They articulately presented their qualifications for admission but were ultimately shouted down by white students who demanded that they leave the premises or suffer physical harm. Some of the blacks then drew pistols in defense, cautiously retreating from the school with nothing resolved.

A delegation of white male students then descended on Superintendent Boothby's office and demanded that their school not be integrated and threatened to enforce their decree by violence if necessary.[42] The next day, the *Times Picayune* reviewed the larger context of this local struggle. "This feeling, and this determination," the editorial emphasized, "are not confined to Louisiana, or to the states of the South. They exist in equal intensity wherever there is a public school established and supported by the energy and the means of the white people."[43] With the reassurance of a supportive North, as demonstrated in the recent elections, the white students remained inflexible. Superintendent Boothby pleaded with the black student group that was seeking admission to the high school to maintain the delicate status quo. The superintendent believed that he had persuaded them to settle for the right to take the entrance exam, just to prove that they were indeed qualified by academic performance. But half the group continued to press for both the right to be tested and, more important, to be admitted to the school. A second confrontation occurred at the boy's high school, again resulting in the white students forcing an African-American retreat on threat of violence. Flushed with victory, the white boys then marched to the girls high school and offered their manly assistance "in resisting the 'mixture' experiment."[44]

The following day, the white boys became more dangerous. About thirty of them invaded numerous elementary schools, driving African-American students out of mixed classrooms. In defense, sixty black men then organized to halt this abuse. Armed with stones and clubs, they went to meet the white boys. Fighting raged for several hours.[45] On December 20, the school board closed the city's public schools for the holidays and did not reopen them until early January, by which time tempers had subsided, and integrated public education resumed on the modest scale that had characterized the city's schools before the December confrontations began. After that time, blacks exercised more caution in asserting their rights to attend any public school. P. B. S. Pinchback, a black Louisiana Republican who several years earlier had served briefly as the state's governor, spoke for his race. "We have, in violation of our solemn obligation, refrained to a large extent from forcibly attempting to mix the schools, the result of which is that today a majority of the

schools are unmixed." Later that year, E. J. Edmunds, a light-skinned
African-American mathematics instructor, was hired to teach at the
white-boys high school. Eleven white boys resigned the school in
protest. But Edmunds's impressive credentials and his teaching skill
worked to overcome any further outbursts of white racism. New
Orleans' public school system continued racially integrated until 1877,
when Louisiana finally fell into the hands of the Democratic party.[46]
      While the December battles over New Orleans' mixed schools
raged, the House Republicans discussed the Sumner bill in light of the
electoral landslide. Some suggested that legislating a requirement for
equal funding among separate black and white schools made more
political sense than continuing a suicidal pursuit of mixed schools.[47]
True Sumnerians refused to countenance any such compromise with
evil. True to their fallen leader, they preferred nothing if they could not
have everything; and they were willing to combine with anti-black
legislators to defeat any "separate but equal" mandate. They were
willing only to tolerate a "mixed-schools" interpretation of "equality."
"If you cannot legislate free schools," said Republican Barbour Lewis, "I
prefer that the bill should be altogether silent upon the question until
other times and other men can do the subject justice." John Roy Lynch,
the young black Mississippi congressman who had replaced Legrand
Perce, noted that it was as wrong to segregate African Americans into
separate schools by law as it would be to allow Irish Catholics to have
legally mandated separate public schools. In his state, racially separate
schools did not exist in law but existed in fact, presumably by the
preference of blacks to go to their own schools. In his mind, all of the
white hysteria over racially mixed schools had been over an abstraction.
He belonged to that faction that believed that *de facto* segregation would
continue to be practiced after the bill made *de jure* segregation illegal.
Yet, for his own part, he was reluctant to give up that abstraction that
had caused so much damage to his party. Richard H. Cain, an African-
American congressman from South Carolina, was more mature, both in
years and in attitude. He emphasized that while he agreed with Lynch
both that only an abstraction was involved and that the white attitude
was unreasonable, the latter still had to be taken into account, as it
represented majority feeling in a democratic government. He was
willing to see mixed schools cut from the bill, in order to proceed with
the remainder, concerning equal access to public accommodations.[48] The
House passed the Civil Rights Bill without any reference to public
education. On February 27, 1875, the Senate concurred in the House
version. Several days later, President Grant signed the Civil Rights Act
of 1875, the last gasp of racial Reconstruction. On March 3, the Forty-

Third Congress adjourned, and Republican control of the federal government ended.

This chapter has heaped blame on Charles Sumner for this result. Other historians have interpreted these events much differently. William P. Vaughn castigated Barnas Sears for opposing mixed schools and noted that the "failure to provide for federally enforced school integration in the 1870s made acceptance of this social and legal necessity a far more difficult task ninety years later."[49] Professor Vaughn's judgment rests upon the mistaken assumption that achieving federally mandated mixed schools in the 1870s was a practical possibility. While few historians have made any such claim, most have tended to absolve Senator Sumner of any major responsibility for the political disaster that followed his deathbed imperative. Representative of these, Michael Perman has emphasized that the internal dynamics of Republican politics was far more significant than any power that Sumner's bequest may have had to shape human sentiment. Hunger for office tempted African-American and carpetbagger candidates to club scalawag rivals with the mixed-schools issue. Likewise, the desire of Northern Republicans to keep blacks loyal to the party drove them to support the untenable proposition of mixed schools. Yet, was not Sumner involved in shaping the factors highlighted by Professor Perman? Who had browbeaten African Americans during the last years of his life to prove their collective manhood by becoming more strident over a demand for mixed schools? Who had urged their leaders that an uncompromising pursuit of correct principle was always the best course? Certainly Sumner's ideological leadership helped exacerbate the conditions described by Professor Perman that forced the Republican party toward Reconstruction's fatal precipice.[50] Admittedly, making harsh statements regarding any historical figure risks skewing the narrative of history into a simplistic tale of "good" and "bad" people. Yet, the historian who never finds fault in historical characters risks implying that history had to turn out just as it did. Then one is left with only a tale of inevitable events leading to a predetermined result. Certainly, historians should not fall into the trap of hindsight in making their judgments.[51]

Following the debacle of the mixed schools issue, the national Republican party moved to change the political focus from racial integration to one more promising of electoral success. If white racism was the albatross of the Republicans, popular anti-Catholicism was the cross of the Democrats. In 1875, Republicans chose to use religious prejudice as a political counterpoise to racial prejudice. This tactic had been experimented with during the early 1870s primarily at the local level. After 1874, it became a primary Republican weapon at all levels of government. As the voters had rejected the Republicans in that year for following a centralizing education agenda that was perceived as threatening white civilization, the party came to emphasize centralized solutions to the presumed Roman Catholic problem relating to public education. The progress of western civilization, claimed Republican orators, lay in the balance in this struggle against the forces of medieval backwardness and a mass ignorance that undermined democratic government. Otto von Bismarck, the German "Caesar," had effectively blocked an Ultramontane threat to his nation's public schools only by centralizing political power in a fragmented Germany. Something similar was needed in the United States. As the infallible Pope had an international priestly army responding to every whim emanating from the Vatican, Americans needed a strong centralized government as a countervailing "American" power, directed by Republican anti-Catholics in Washington, D.C. An anti-Catholic crusade boded to make "Caesarism" respectable again.

In 1875–1876, racially mixed schools disappeared from political addresses—at least those given by Republicans. Henceforth, Republicans tolerated racially separate public schools. The threat of religiously separate public schools was another matter. Playing up the latter suited the religious and ethnic prejudices predominant in the Northern states. The Republican campaign on racial matters in 1874 had only served to enhance Roman Catholic political fortunes by diverting mounting popular hatred and distrust away from that church.[52] Correspondingly, the Democratic party resurgence in 1874 had served the political interests of the Roman Catholic Church. In 1875, this became the central theme of Republican propaganda as race gave way to religion. Only the political focus on the health and well-being of the American public school remained constant.

8

THE ANTI-CATHOLIC ANTIDOTE

By the time that the mixed-schools issue came to a head in 1874, Reconstruction was already in retreat. Beginning in 1873, economic depression steadily had forced the federal government into a retrenchment mode undermining the Republican program. Governmental tasks could not be centralized, federal services could not be expanded, without an increasing flow of revenue into the federal treasury. Hard economic times challenged the centralizers' dreams. But the retreat of Reconstruction did not mean that the urge to create a meaningful national administration was spent. In the midseventies, Reconstruction was similar to an army looking for favorable ground on which to make a defensive stand. Low on money, defeated on the mixed-schools issue, the centralizers sought a secure position from which to make at least one major effort to recapture the lost momentum.

Circumstances demanded a new political discourse. In the past, Republicans had relied primarily on a rhetoric of national loyalty and had emphasized that Democratic party successes risked throwing away the hard-won Union victory in the Civil War. "Every Democrat was not a traitor," Republicans had often repeated, "but every traitor was a Democrat." That familiar slogan failed to carry the elections of 1874. Accordingly, Southern Democrats, flush with the victories of 1874, chanted for "home rule" in the few formerly Confederate states still under Republican regimes. Implicit in this slogan was the understanding that home rule meant white rule. Loyalty to race, even in the North, had proven itself to be stronger than loyalty to Republican nationalism. An antidote was needed. Fortunately for Republican prospects, a remedy was at hand. Democratic victories, warned Republicans, led straight to "foreign rule" from Rome. "Every Democrat might not be an Ultramontane," Harper's Weekly proposed, but "every Ultramontane is a Democrat."[1] The old discourse of nationalism was thereby remodeled to fit new exigencies, for supposedly only a vigilant Republican national government could thwart Rome's growing influence on American shores.

At the same time, and without much fanfare, racial advances continued. In 1875, San Francisco integrated its ninety-seven African-American school children into the city's previously all-white schools. (Despite this step, Chinese remained barred from San Francisco's public schools.) In Delaware, blacks were offered their first public-school opportunities in 1875, albeit in separate schools supported only by taxes raised in the African-American community. In that same year, Georgia boasted of enrolling a total of 50,359 African-American children in its revived segregated public-school system. Key Southern leaders in the cause for public education—men such as Georgia's Gustavus J. Orr and Kentucky's H. A. M. Henderson—came out in favor of federal aid for education, a cause long identified with Republican "Caesarism."[2] Barnas Sears noted every advance on the racial front and predicted that with the destructive mixed-schools issue out of the way, public education in the Southern states would begin to acquire mass support as never before.[3]

Early in 1875, the New Orleans school board reached a modus vivendi. No more attempts would be made to integrate increasing numbers of African-American children; and, on the other side, no more attempts would be made to destroy the existing experiment in interracial schooling by means of white intimidation and violence. Thus, New Orleans' open wound was temporarily cauterized.[4] Yet the real news on the Southern front of public education was Gustavus Orr. As Georgia's school chief, he had taken his state from an anti-public-education attitude to one of willingness to educate black children at white expense, something that Delaware and Kentucky then refused to do.[5] Despite the national backlash against mixed schools, Republicans quietly relished the fact that racial educational progress continued to be made. Even though Orr was a Democrat, he and other Southern educational reformers like him were carrying the work forward in the region where the need was greatest. They were doing work that the Republicans wanted done.

As the seventies progressed, public education became a dominant issue nationally. In May of 1874, the *Atlantic Monthly* recognized this rising interest by inaugurating a new editorial section devoted solely to educational issues. For the next four years, this section constituted one of the principal parts of the journal. "The future of nations depends on the education they receive," pronounced one *Atlantic Monthly* editorial in 1875.[6] Republicans had also sensed the public's increasing interest in educational issues. In 1874, they had erred in allowing Sumner's mixed-schools proposal to define their party's position in public education. In the following year, they succeeded in reshaping the school issue to avoid almost completely the racial sensitivities of the white majority while at the same time exploiting that same majority's anti-Catholic biases. The first test of this new strategy was in Ohio.

In the 1874 canvass in Ohio, the Democratic tide had swept aside not only the matter of mixed schools but also a Republican-backed state constitutional amendment forbidding any state aid to religious schools. This fact encouraged Republicans to interpret the Ohio election as enabling a Roman-Catholic grab for state school funds.[7] The following spring, the state's Democratic legislature and governor enacted the Geghan Act, portrayed in the Republican press as a pro-Catholic measure. Roman Catholics countered that this legislation simply protected religious liberty. The Geghan Act required that local and state prisoners in Ohio be allowed "equal access to ministers and priests of all faiths." At that time, chaplains in Ohio's prisons and jails were all Protestants, while in fact a majority of the inmates were Roman Catholic. Once enforced, the Geghan Act would predictably lead to the dismissal of some Protestant clergy and the hiring of new Catholic chaplains. Many Protestants arrogantly viewed this as the termination of any hope of Roman-Catholic prisoners receiving a modicum of effective moral instruction while behind bars.[8] Demographics were changing in Ohio, where the state's cities were rapidly becoming Roman Catholic. Ohio's public schools had heretofore effectively been Protestant schools. But everyone could see that this would soon change. The Cincinnati experience of 1870 loomed as indicating future trends. Extending the logic of the Geghan act to education, Ohio's urban public schools might soon, for all intents and purposes, become Roman-Catholic schools. Hence, the Geghan bill subtly alerted Ohio's shrinking Protestant majority that a Catholic takeover of public-education funds might be imminent.

At the time when the Geghan bill was being debated, Ohio's Catholic press had openly threatened to end the political career of any Democrat who voted against the measure. Alertly, Republicans exploited this. *Harper's Weekly* displayed a political cartoon with a Catholic bishop, holding a whip, facing down a Democratic party hack. A fawning ape like Irish-Catholic voter, chained to the bishop's arm, completed the drawing. As Republicans geared up for the 1875 elections, the Geghan bill provided grist for their political mills.[9] When the state Republican convention met in Columbus in June to nominate a governor, both anti-Catholicism and pro-public-education attitudes were prominent.

In the early 1870s, Ohio's gubernatorial elections had been extremely close. In 1873, Democrat William Allen had won the governor's chair with a margin of only 817 votes. Given the fact that the national

Republicans were blamed for the economic downturn, Allen's reelection seemed assured. Ohio's Republicans were then identified with an unpopular deflationary monetary policy. Ohio's only Republican Senator, John Sherman, had ardently backed the Resumption Act of 1875, which was designed to remove inflationary paper money from circulation in favor of gold. Democrats were then divided on the money question, but Allen himself was a vocal champion of inflation to help average people with paying off their debts. The Republicans needed a noneconomic issue to overcome the Democrats' popular appeal on the money question. An anti-Catholic crusade met the Republicans' needs perfectly. Not only did the issue divert public attention away from racial matters but away from economic concerns as well.[10]

At the outset, Alphonso Taft had the inside track for the Republican gubernatorial nomination. From the Republican perspective, Taft was safe on the money issue, but Republicans lacked confidence that they could carry the gubernatorial election on a hard-money platform alone. Taft had the support of Rutherford B. Hayes, who had been Ohio's governor from 1868 to 1872. Yet on June 2, Hayes himself was nominated by the Republican convention for an unprecedented third term. Hayes explained this unexpected turn of events in his diary:

> I persisted in declining to the last. The leading other candidate before the convention, Judge Taft, of Cincinnati, is an able and good man. But he had such a record on the Bible question in the schools that his nomination was impossible. I did all I could to remove the prejudice against him and to aid in his nomination. . . . I was nominated notwithstanding, 396 for me, 151 for Taft.[11]

The memory lingered of Taft's lone Superior Court dissent against the Protestant effort to halt the removal of the Bible from Cincinnati's public schools. At a time when religion and public education were linked in the public mind, Taft was clearly the wrong candidate for the Republican party. Taft himself realized this and in subsequently campaigning for Hayes told a rally in Columbus that the election would turn on the public school issue. Privately, Hayes himself communicated the same message to former speaker of the House James G. Blaine, who hungered to be the party's presidential nominee in 1876.[12] On July 10, Hayes instructed another confidant to keep "'the Catholic question'" in the forefront of the campaign. "If they [the Democrats] do not speak of it, we must attack them for their silence. If they discuss it or refer to it, they can't help getting into trouble." James Garfield, helping Hayes in the campaign, recorded in his diary on July 23 that he was working on a speech "on the Catholic question as relating to our modern education." Several days later, Garfield identified the Ohio campaign as part of an international culture struggle occurring in both Europe and America. "Our fight in Ohio," he noted, "is only a small portion of the battle-field." On July 31, Hayes pressed the issue in a major address in Marion, Ohio: "Those who mean to destroy the school system," said Hayes in referring to Roman Catholics, "constitute a formidable part of the Democratic party, without whose support that party, as the legislature was told last spring, cannot carry the county, the city nor the state." He closed the address with these words: "So I would say to the friends of the public schools: 'How do the enemies of universal education vote?' If the enemies of the free schools give their 'unbroken, solid vote' to the Democratic ticket, the friends of the schools will make no mistake if they vote the Republican ticket."[13]

Democrats decried the Republican strategy of appealing to low prejudice, but then they themselves had been guilty of a similar sin the year before.[14] Only the focus of the prejudicial appeal had changed, from race to religion. Each party was willing to take advantage of the uglier side of human nature when it suited its purposes. Even Alphonso Taft, himself a victim of religious prejudice within his own party, joined the frenzy. Catholic clergy, he emphasized during the campaign, were guilty of giving ultimate allegiance not to their nation but to their church. Every true American, he suggested in point of contrast, was devoted to the nation itself and no higher authority. Unwittingly, Taft identified the most insidious aspect of the international anti-Catholic crusade of the 1870s. In Germany's simultaneous culture struggle against Roman Catholicism in the name of unbridled nationalism, encouragement was given to a new secular religion of statism that eventually devolved into a hideous Nazi mutation two generations later. In the United States, Taft's nation worship constituted the ugly underside of the triumphant nationalism that emerged from the American Civil War. Hegelian in its intellectual origins, it was then viewed especially within Republican ranks as thoroughly modern and harmonious with the nineteenth-century idea of "progress."[15]

During the gubernatorial campaign, Hayes promoted the public school as the great uniting agent in American culture, blending different cultures into one national mold. One nation and one people were held up again and again as the Republican cornerstones of Reconstruction's civil religion. Hayes warned that a dark sectarian, international conspiracy sought to divide the American nationality by gaining access to the distribution of public-school funds. Occasionally, Republican anti-Catholic orators were hooted down, as Garfield was at Delphos, Ohio, in early September. But these incidents did not dishearten the Republican faithful. In Hayes' words, Ohio's Republicans were "acting on the defensive" in this struggle.[16] The year before, the Republican party had clearly been on the offensive in pushing for racially integrated public schools. But in thwarting the Catholic desire to divide the school funds, Republicans could legitimately portray themselves as merely defending the "American" status quo. Earlier, in seeking to make racial differences irrelevant in a public-school crucible, the Republicans had experienced bitter defeat. In defending traditional Protestant religious practices in the same setting, they fully expected victory.

Ohio's Roman Catholics ineffectually responded to the Republican public-school crusade. Instead of remaining calm and countering Republican hyperbole with well-reasoned disclaimers, the Catholic press railed hysterically against what it termed the "Methodistico-Calvinistico-Beecheristico-Free-Love-Radical-Republicans." Such stridency only strengthened Hayes's cause and fortified Republican confidence. Ben Wade, the former Republican Speaker of the House who had almost become president during the impeachment trial of Andrew Johnson, confided to Hayes in September that the Ohio campaign might propel the gubernatorial candidate all the way to the White House itself. An excited Hayes shared this prophecy with his wife Lucy. Even earlier in the campaign, the Terra Haute *Express* had confidently asserted that "the man who is elected governor of Ohio this fall will be the next presidential nominee of his party." In October, Hayes defeated Allen by a margin of 5,544 votes, a very healthy victory by Ohio standards. His campaign carried both houses of the state legislature for the Republicans as well. This was achieved at a time of deepening economic depression in a state that was far from being safely in the Republican camp. Once in office, Hayes and his legislature quickly repealed the Geghan Act. Nationwide, Hayes was garnering a reputation as a champion of Protestant-American cultural norms. Step by step, Wade's prediction was coming true. In the words of one of Hayes's biographers, under the Ohio governor's orchestration "sectarian control of the public schools emerged from local, subterranean discussion into a major national issue."[17]

During the Ohio campaign, Cleveland's Bishop Richard Gilmour was quoted by the Republican press as putting church ahead of state. "We are Catholics first," Gilmour had said, "citizens next." Republicans used this remark to equate the Roman Catholic church with the Ku Klux Klan, which also resisted the moral authority of the nation. Both organizations were "separated from the community." Each was "an empire within an empire." The Klan had been outlawed by congressional statute, yet its spirit continued to thrive throughout the Southern states. The national struggle against white racism had obviously failed. Republicans were hopeful that the blossoming of anti-Catholic fervor could produce greater success toward a national centralization.

The first civil rights movement had begun at the national center and collapsed when it reached down to the local level for implementation. By contrast, the anti-Catholic culture struggle had begun locally, in such events as the Cincinnati Bible War. By the midseventies it was expanding to affect national politics. After Hayes's victory, the *North American Review* recounted past struggles on the issue of the Bible in the public schools and the Catholic proposal to divide school funds. Up until 1875, the journal reported, the issue had been fought primarily at the local level. But Republicans were pushing the issue onto more prominent stages. "Recently, and especially Ohio," the influential Boston journal noted, "this controversy has gone beyond the limit of the city and town, and has become an open and controlling element in a state election. It bids fair to become a national question."[18]

The Republican party needed to appear traditional and conservative in spurring the nation toward the imagined centralized new order. In the mixed-schools fiasco of the year before, the party had appeared bent on radical social change. That effort had failed, but Republicans learned from that experience. Voters viewed the public schools, in the words of Pennsylvania's James P. Wickersham, as "the center of our national life."[19] White Americans were willing to experiment with racial integration only around the periphery of the national life. But, Republicans sensed, integration of children from diverse religious backgrounds in the name of national unity might well be another matter. In manning their religious barricades, Republicans called for a renewing crusade for centralized government in order to defend the very essence of American culture—the traditional (Protestant) public school—from a foreign enemy. A year later, after Hayes had been nominated to the presidency, William Dean Howells recalled that the Ohio governor's meteoric rise to national prominence began with his anti-Catholic campaign of 1875. "The liberal Germans and the freedom-loving voters of all the churches made common cause against the priests," noted Howells, "and the triumph that ensued was owing to the abhorrence excited by the attempt upon the public schools."[20]

Coming into the presidential campaign of 1876, this theme was a certain vote-getter in the Northern states. Republicans hoped that the same theme might play well in the South as well. Certainly, the overwhelming mass of white Southerners were Protestants and viewed the new dogma of papal infallibility as did their Northern cousins. As

Southern states were "redeemed" [the Southern term for being restored to white supremacy], Southern state constitutional conventions typically rewrote their fundamental law to require racial segregation in the public schools. Nevertheless, these same conventions exhibited that Southerners were alive to anti-Catholicism as well as to issues of racial purity. Alabama and Missouri both banned state aid to parochial schools in their white supremacist constitutional conventions of 1875. The following year, North Carolina did likewise.[21]

Evidence existed for a potential North-South axis on religious matters. In many ways, religious intolerance was stronger in the South than in Ohio and other Northern states. In February 1875, North Carolina's Democratic legislature expelled one J. William Thorne for holding religious beliefs unacceptable to the mainline-Protestant majority. As a member of the "Progressive Friends" denomination, Thorne claimed to believe in a supreme being but held that there were many things in the Bible with which he did not concur. For this transgression, he was tried in the North Carolina house of representatives as an atheist. No one came to his defense. Embarrassed traditional Quakers even rejected him. In a last desperate effort to retain his seat, Thorne publicly swore allegiance to the following creed: "There is but one living and true God; everlasting, without body or parts or passions; of unfinished power, wisdom and goodness; the maker of all things visible and invisible." This concession was not enough to save him, and he was expelled on religious grounds.[22]

While not involving Roman Catholicism, the Thorne affair demonstrated that Southern Protestants were quite serious about defending their traditional faith against all enemies, foreign and domestic. Republicans hoped that a movement with elements of a conservative evangelical religious crusade might eventually succeed in reversing the erosion of white Republican voting strength in the Southern states. Apparently, some Southern blacks also appreciated the potential of this rhetorical shift away from race as good for their own people. One of the leading accusers in the Thorne case was an African-American North Carolina state legislator. Nineteen-year-old Booker T. Washington also was attuned to the new sensitivity regarding matters of religious faith. Delivering a commencement address at Virginia's Hampton Institute several months after the Thorne affair, Washington proposed that it would not be wise for the United States to seize Cuba from Spain, even though such an action would end slavery there. He urged that Cuba not be brought into the American empire, because the addition of so many Catholics into the country would further heighten an unwanted but growing cultural diversity. The Southern white audience in attendance applauded the young black orator with great enthusiasm. Anyone seeking public approval in the South knew that anti-Catholicism was one theme guaranteed to win favor, even across the racial divide. Consequently, Southern white Catholics with any political ambition generally sought to distance themselves from the educational stands taken by their church. For example, A. M. Keiley, the Catholic mayor of Richmond, publicly opposed his church's campaign against traditional American public education to the warm approval of his constituents.[23]

Nevertheless, any Republican hope that anti-Catholicism might prove stronger than white racism in the South was naive at best. *The Enterprise and Mountaineer*, the leading newspaper of Greenville, South Carolina, reflected typical Southern attitudes on matters of both race and religion. It reported stories of how the Roman Catholic church was involved in an international intrigue to take over the United States. It also claimed that Roman Catholics were bigger liars than black people. But then it revealed why racial prejudice could never be upstaged by religious bigotry south of the Mason-Dixon line. Given the right environmental conditions, the paper hypothesized, Roman Catholics could be converted to Protestant beliefs. White Roman Catholics could change, but blacks could never be anything else but blacks. "The leopard cannot change his spots," the paper concluded. Even in the heat of reporting the Thorne affair, the Wilmington (North Carolina) *Daily Journal* left no doubt that religious animus could never blind Southerners to the primacy of race. The essential fact, reported the *Daily Journal*, was that the national Democratic party was both the party of white supremacy and Roman Catholicism. For this reason, the South could never afford to indulge anti-Catholicism in any systematic way.[24]

Northern and Southern Protestants then both practiced what is called "civil religion"—the cultural habit of blending communal patriotic interests with the trappings of traditional religion. But in the two sections the specific contents of this civil religion differed significantly. The Southern version focused on the ever-remembered, glorious "lost cause." By contrast, the Northern version celebrated the desirability of a national unity that the spread of public education promised to bring into being. At the beginning of the 1870s, this nationalism was partially shaped by Protestant practices then dominant in the public schools. But as these practices were gradually removed from public education during the decade, a more secularized nation worship along the lines favored by the likes of Alphonso Taft came to fill the increasing spiritual void. This constituted the evolving civil religion of Reconstruction. The South did not respond well to the Republican anti-Catholic overture because its own civil religion remained tied to themes glorying in the "lost cause," not a reconstructed homogeneous nation.[25]

In some Southern areas, Roman Catholicism cooperated with Southern civil religion, which admittedly had strong Protestant undercurrents. An example of this occurred in Texas, where public education was undermined by a temporary alliance between white supremacists and Roman Catholics. In 1875, these two elements succeeded in abolishing the office of state superintendent of public instruction in that state. They also succeeded in eliminating the state requirement for compulsory education, an unenforceable provision from Texas's Reconstruction years. A new state constitution in 1875 decentralized public education, so that henceforth all important decisions were made at the local level, beyond the purview of national monitoring. The motives for these changes were both racial and religious. Many white Texans still did not approve of educating blacks at public expense and sought to strangle African-American schooling at the local level. For their part, Catholic Texans united against "Godless" public schools.[26]

While a new politics shaped by anti-Catholicism emerged in Northern states such as Ohio, the old politics of race continued to dominate in the South. Only weeks after Hayes's victory in Ohio signaled a successful new Republican strategy in the North, Mississippi was redeemed by the forces of white supremacy. The weight of heavy taxes to support public projects, such as public education for all, heightened the racial animus in that Southern state. "The Mississippi Plan," the approach used by redeemers there to carry the state election, mixed honeyed promises of racial equity and fairness with widespread intimidation and violent and bloody incidents. Once in power, Mississippi's white supremacists cut taxes and impeached Thomas W. Cardozo, the state's corrupt African-American superintendent of public education. Ultimately, Cardozo was allowed to resign rather than undergo a formal trial. Republican governor Adelbert Ames was also driven into a premature retirement by a newly elected hostile Democratic legislature.

In one of his last communications with the redeemer legislature, Ames pleaded that the public-school system erected by the Republicans be maintained. But Mississippi's tax revolters had had enough. Mississippi then had the third highest tax rate in the nation, even though the state was the seventh poorest from a standpoint of per-capita wealth. One-fifth of the state's land mass was in receivership due to non-payment of taxes. Economic hardship fed racial outbursts leading to the electoral victory by the Democrats. President Grant was aware of the downward spiral of Reconstruction in Mississippi but chose not to intervene with troops as he had earlier done in Louisiana lest the Northern Republican anti-Catholic strategy being tried in the Ohio election be undermined by a renewal of widespread white racial sympathy.[27] As a result, the Republicans carried Ohio and the Democrats swept Mississippi as a sectionalized drama of religion and race shaped the last years of Reconstruction.

Mississippi's redeemers made a pretense of continuing the funding of black schools at levels equivalent to the state's white schools. However, under the new regime, dissemination of the school funds was decentralized down to local school boards, which made it virtually impossible for federal authorities to monitor the actual unequal disbursement of funds.[28] Meanwhile, in Virginia, the opponents of black public education practiced no similar dissimulation. The ongoing problem of Virginia's state debt encouraged an open white-supremacist assault on public education as an unnecessary expense. One argument used was that religion, the basis of both public and private morality, could not be adequately taught in state schools. William Ruffner, Virginia's State Superintendent of Schools, countered by noting that in the relatively homogeneous Protestant environment of Virginia, there was no need to teach a faith-based morality in the public schools as the surrounding Protestant culture met that need. But religious concerns were not primary in Virginia's public-school debates of 1875 and 1876. Racial considerations were. White racists attacked, claiming that it was a waste of tax money to try to improve African Americans through education. God, they said, had made blacks inferior; and public-school reformers committed blasphemy in trying to be "wiser than God." Sensing that Reconstruction was in retreat following the defeat of the mixed-schools reform in 1874, these racist critics urged that Virginia both abolish public education and directly challenge the act of Congress in 1870 that had readmitted Virginia. That statute had required Virginia to maintain a public-school system forever, a requirement that Virginia's public-school opponents said compromised Virginia's sovereignty. Is Virginia "a real state" or not? they rhetorically asked. Unless Virginia directly confronted the issue by abolishing public education, the state would continue to live in a condition of "sham sovereignty." Ruffner succeeded in holding off these baying hounds, but their howls were heard in nearby Washington, D.C., and sent a clear message to the capital's Republicans that the South would never join the Republicans' anti-Catholic crusade to protect the public schools.[29]

And so, the Republican party concentrated on the North. As race was making a "solid South," Republicans hoped that religion could produce a "solid North" to counteract it. Republicans emphasized the close global correlation between Catholicism and poverty. In Europe, prosperity and material progress flourished in Protestant countries. In those dominated by the Roman Catholic church, backwardness and poverty abounded. Catholics countered by noting that Christ did not come into the world to transform men and women into skillful money-changers. Republicans also identified the Roman Catholic church with an authoritarianism hostile to democratic mores. Catholics replied that the worst tyrant in Europe was Otto von Bismarck, who was idealized by the Republicans. For their part, Catholic thinkers wondered out loud whether true liberty could survive any long experience with the kind of Germanic, homogeneous "liberty" envisioned by the Republican party.[30]

The arrival of this religious culture struggle on the stage of national politics in 1875–1876 encouraged a broader discussion of the state of the Union than had been seen in a decade. The Gilded Age caused many to reevaluate the rapid changes then transforming the American landscape. Much of their analysis was somewhat superficial, but some thought-provoking discussion was present as well. Republicans tended to blame all social problems on the twin fountains of ignorance—the continuing slave culture of the South and the anti-democratic Roman Catholic church in the North. This attack enabled them to avoid their own subterranean fears that the continuing Industrial Revolution encouraged increasing an undesirable class conflict and social stratification. Roman Catholic pundits had a perspective that more honestly acknowledged that the Industrial Revolution had an underside of increasing misery for the toiling masses. Catholic thinkers warned of a rising secular laissez-faire selfishness, contrary to Christian teaching and promoted by the Republican party. In response, Republicans employed Darwinian analogies to justify hardening attitudes toward the poor and destitute.

The essential Catholic position, however, did not anticipate Marx. Indeed, it was ironically similar to the Republican mentality. Both Republicans and Catholics focused on proper moral education as the best palliative for the nation's ills. Catholic critics of "Godless" public schools ignored their own role in driving the Bible and Protestant religious practices from public education. Their point was that only in schools firmly underwritten with religious authority could any form of meaningful moral education be conducted. Edmund F. Dunne, both a leading Catholic critic of the public schools and Chief Justice of the Supreme Court of Arizona Territory, noted that rising crime rates among the nation's youth were directly attributable to faulty moral education in the public schools. He emphasized that leaving moral education to Sunday schools was a foolish suggestion of secularists:

Is not that a very perfunctory manner of disposing of so important a subject? Has not the moral tone of our community, under the operation of this theory, already fallen below that standard at which a nation is safe even in the hands of its own people? Do we not need more morality in the community, more people who believe in God? Are not our public men too corrupt? . . . Is there not a screw loose somewhere in our social organization? And do you not think the system of ignoring religious instruction six-sevenths of the time in the life of our young people has something to do with it? Is not such a consequence the natural outcome of such a system?[31]

Dunne emphasized that while the state could not teach religion in a heterogeneous society, it was folly to allow a system of moral laissez-faire to be grafted on American life. He predicted that if current trends were allowed to continue, the public schools themselves would become fountainheads of immorality and the Republic would be destroyed in due course, not from any foreign enemy but from a rottenness within. He foretold a time when the only moral function left to the state would be to supply policemen and jailers to sweep up and store the human refuse spawned in the amoral American public school. His solution to prevent this was a division of the school fund, to create several types of publicly funded religious schools, suited to the diverse peoples making up the United States. In this way, morality could effectively be restored in public education. Protestants could have their own schools. They would no longer have to worry about watering down their program of moral instruction in a vain effort to accommodate Catholics, Jews, and others. And, of course, Roman Catholics could have their own schools, funded at public expense.[32]

Orestes Brownson was greatly impressed with Dunne's argument and repeated it virtually verbatim in the last issue of his *Brownson's Quarterly Review*, which was published in October 1875. In this last public statement before his death, Brownson warned of the long-term effects of rejecting the Roman Catholic plea to divide the public-school funds among the leading religious faiths and predicted that ultimately the public-school system would result in a society of amoral citizens disconnected from any spiritual grounding. A self-determining minority, he noted, might lead upright lives divorced from any religious faith, but the masses could never see right from wrong in the absence of religious authority. Thus, secular public schools of the future would produce "Frankensteins, . . . a creature formed like a man in all respects, except that the moral faculties are left out: an intellectual monster turned loose upon society, with no other motive in life than to gratify its desires and keep out of the penitentiary!" He grieved that only Roman Catholics seemed to see this national danger clearly and advised that Catholics needed to unite into "Catholic Unions," political action groups that were already being formed. Brownson noted the significant numbers of Catholics then in the Democratic party and urged all good Catholics to withhold their support from any politician that failed to take up the great cause of returning moral teaching to public education. "The great question for us Catholics, and the great question even for our country," he concluded, "is the school question."[33]

Catholic leaders rushed into the fray, armed with a conviction that they alone could save the Republic. The following month, a papal statement on the American public school arrived from the Vatican to instruct the faithful. This document damned the nation's public schools for having teachers "selected from every sect indiscriminately." These teachers, the report continued, infused "into the young minds the seeds of error and vice." The statement also damned public schools for mixing the sexes "in the same class and classroom," thus endangering the morals of both genders. The Pope called for every Catholic congregation to erect separate Catholic schools, so as to deny all Catholic parents any excuse for sending their children to the public schools. The report concluded by encouraging American bishops to excommunicate parents sending their children to public schools in districts where a Catholic alternative existed.[34] In late 1875, both Catholic leaders and Republicans appeared eager for a cultural confrontation centering on both the American public school and questions of morality in American public life.

That autumn, in Newtown, Connecticut, one Father McCartin visited the local public school in his parish. Bible reading was still conducted in that particular school, and the priest arrived just as the teacher began to read from the Bible. Arthur Day, the teacher in question, was the son of a Baptist minister and took his duties in this particular aspect of the curriculum quite seriously. Father McCartin interrupted the exercise and instructed the Catholic students in attendance to pay no attention to the heretic teacher. Outraged, Mr. Day complained to the school board of this invasion of his classroom. Several days later, his school Bible was stolen, but he brought another one to school the next day. With Bible reading renewed, his Catholic students walked out in the midst of the exercise. A little later that same day, Father McCartin led the delinquent students back into the classroom and in front of Mr. Day instructed them to ignore all Bible reading in the future. The shocked teacher then ordered the priest from his classroom, and when that command was ignored a scuffle ensued. Frightened children fled the classroom in the midst of their battling elders. The next day, a surly group of young men and boys blocked Day's entrance into the school and pelted him with rocks as he fled the vicinity. All of this occurred only weeks following Hayes' victory in Ohio. The incident was widely publicized in the Republican press.[35]

Catholic parents were in a quandary as their church seemingly declared war on the public school. Impoverished Catholics could not pay even the nominal sums required by parochial schools. Yet the threat of excommunication faced those who continued sending their children to public schools. As a result, increasing numbers of Catholic children stopped going to school at all. The Republican solution to this dilemma was compulsory education. State law could require the education of all children. Governmentally mandated education had virtually eliminated illiteracy in Germany. One Republican newspaper explained the matter for those interpreting such laws as an infringement upon individual liberty: "The idea that the parent can possess a right to keep children in ignorance belongs to an obsolete period. . . . The man who raises ignorant children is a public enemy, who propagates the seeds of crime and pauperism and disorder. He is an incendiary who applies the torch to his neighbor's house." Republicans then were fond of comparing the Catholic Irish to African Americans concerning the subjects of education and self-improvement. Typically, they cast the former as apathetic degenerates in contrast to blacks, whose postwar zeal to acquire education was fast becoming legendary.[36]

Early in the following year, news from New Mexico Territory arrived that fueled the growing controversy. W. G. Ritch, serving as that territory's superintendent of public instruction, reported that Jesuits were systematically taking over the public schools there. New Mexico already had a Roman Catholic majority, and this news was taken as an indicator of what Northern states could expect as soon as they also acquired Catholic majorities. The federally appointed upper house of the territorial legislature supported both Ritch's and the territorial governor's pleas to outlaw any sectarian influence in the public schools, but this action was blocked by a popularly elected Roman-Catholic lower house. Ritch reported to U.S. Commissioner of Education John Eaton, Jr., that Congress needed to take control of the situation. Whether in Ohio or faraway New Mexico, the American Union was seemingly threatened by an international Roman-Catholic conspiracy to undermine the public school.[37]

James G. Blaine hoped to be the Republican nominee in 1876. President Grant not so secretly desired that he himself would be

renominated for an unprecedented third term. Rutherford B. Hayes had
also acquired the presidential fever. There were other hopefuls as well;
but among all in the race, these three paid the most attention to the
school issue. Each hoped to acquire a reputation as the national leader
of a popular civil-religious crusade. Hayes had shown the way with his
successful gubernatorial campaign in Ohio. Early on, savvy politicians
had thought that the currency question was then far more pressing than
the school issue, but subsequently they realized that the voters held
different priorities. And so, adjustments were made to make public
education the premier question of the coming Presidential campaign.
Harper's Weekly put it this way: "Inflation may be a more imminent peril
than the subversion of the school system. But it is less vitally threatening, because it has not behind it that complete organization, that relent-
less purpose, that impersonal persistence, which belong to the Roman
hierarchy."[38] Translated, this meant that the school question was ideally
suited for demagogic exploitation by Republican fear-mongers.

The school issue allowed the Republicans to present themselves as
the champions of progress, fighting against medieval forces of ignorance and superstition directed from Rome. Anti-Catholicism allowed
the party to keep the Southern issue alive, despite the country's clear
rejection of racial educational equity in 1874. In the South, Republicans
said, Democrats fought progress by denying blacks educational opportunity: in the North, the Democratic party was the handmaiden of the
Roman Catholic church seeking to destroy the public school. "In one
corner of the Union," *Harper's Weekly* editorialized, "they whip teachers,
in another betray them into the power of the foreign priest."[39] The
party's anti-Catholic Northern strategy was inexorably tied to the ongoing Republican program of reconstructing Southern culture; for to
oppose Ultramontane Catholics was to oppose unreconstructed rebels,
and vice versa. And to oppose them both was to continue Reconstruction. "The church puts the Democratic party in office," a Pennsylvania
Republican newspaper editorialized, "and the Democratic party will
put the church of Rome in power."[40]

Democrats sensed that the Republican strategy could well revive
Reconstruction, which they initially thought had been permanently laid
to rest in the midterm elections of 1874. Immediately after the landslide
of 1874, a complete Democratic party victory in 1876 had commonly
been predicted. But one year later, it was too close to call. Nineteen
states then leaned toward the Democrats; an equal number tilted in the
Republican direction. "The states are about equally divided between the
two great parties," concluded one Democratic daily.[41] This situation
boded for a no-holds-barred political struggle in 1876. Republicans were

encouraged to become hysterical over the imagined Ultramontane threat to American public education, for only hyperbole could possibly break the deadlock.

However, on another level, the school issue was very real indeed. American public education was then in the process of changing its most fundamental assumptions, exposing a raw cultural nerve-ending that politicians irritated for their own purposes. In the original conception of the American public school, generalized Protestant religious authority had underwritten a strict program of moral education which was seen as the foundation of the entire curriculum. Over time, that foundation had eroded; and throughout the 1870s the gradual collapse of the *traditional* American public school was obvious to all. Americans of a conservative evangelical bent, the very voters sought in the Republicans' Northern strategy of 1875–1876, were especially concerned. As the Bible was deemphasized in the public schools to accommodate the sensibilities of a heterogeneous society, a troubled peace was all that was gained. Many Americans worried that the traditional moral underpinnings of public education were slipping away as a result. Given that the Roman Catholic church was the most powerful entity calling for the end of Protestant practices in the public schools, many held Catholics responsible for this fundamental change, which was unwanted by the majority.

Ironically, Roman Catholics felt a very similar malaise. Both Catholics and many Protestants held that meaningful moral education relied inevitably on religious authority. Without the latter, moral education could rest only on sweet reason, an insufficient resource for battling the mysterious, subterranean forces of a predominantly sinful human nature. The Protestant majority was at a crossroads. It could concede the logic of the Roman Catholic position and divide the school funds among a limited number of religious understandings, or it could demand that the non-Protestant minority conform to majoritarian views. Given their fears of a future Roman-Catholic majority, Protestants were in no mood to pick the first option, which in their minds would actually invite a Roman-Catholic takeover. Their hope lay in amending the federal constitution to protect that part of the American tradition in public education that could yet be salvaged. Accordingly, they fell into line behind the latter option of exploiting their current majoritarian strength.

An editorial in the *Atlantic Monthly* directly addressed the cultural issue of the gradual secularization of public education. As 1876 was the centennial celebration year, the journal reviewed for its readership a century of national experience. It emphasized that the original purpose of the public schools had been to provide primarily moral education, with intellectual instruction being a lesser priority. But, the *Atlantic Monthly* concluded, in the 1870s this historic relationship was being reversed. Slowly, subtly, the American public school was sacrificing "heart education" in favor of "head education." The editorial warned that this shift posed a long term threat to the very existence of a republican form of government in the United States. Referring to intellectual education without a moral foundation, the editorial quoted Indiana's current school superintendent: "Is it not giving teeth to the lion and fangs to the serpent?" Just as Orestes Brownson only months before had portrayed the graduates of secular schools as Frankenstein monsters, this journal of intellectual Protestant opinion portrayed them as carnivorous beasts and venomous serpents.[42]

Nostalgically, Republican politicians advocated preserving a form of public education that had already largely passed from the scene. The position taken was impractical but immensely popular. There was no political advantage in analyzing the situation dispassionately and concluding that both Protestants and Catholics held identical concerns. It was more politically profitable to blame the Roman Catholic church for the demise of traditional American public education than to cite the nation's increasing cultural diversity as the real cause of change. In any case, the Republican strategy achieved the desired short-term result. *Harper's Weekly* proclaimed that the party had discovered a winning issue and designated it "the most important element in the Ohio election." It also noted that the Hayes' victory in Ohio put "the Republican party in a stronger position" than it had held for a long time. Both Blaine and Grant concurred. Opportunistic politics demanded that a meaningful educational issue be confronted in a way guaranteed to win votes.[43]

The Blaine Amendment

President Grant himself unveiled the national party's new direction on September 29, 1875, even before the outcome in Ohio was known. The occasion was an address to Union veterans in Des Moines, Iowa. Grant told his audience that as the nation approached its first centennial, it was a good time to strengthen "the foundation" of the Republic—the American public school. He warned against the Catholic threat to divide the school funds and called for preservation of a public education "unmixed with sectarian, pagan or atheistical dogmas." In addition, he prophesied that in 1876 the dividing line of American politics would not be Mason and Dixon's, but between "patriotism and intelligence on the one side, and superstition, ambition, and ignorance

FIGURE 8.1

"The Pope's Big Toe."
"If we are to have another contest in the near future of our national existence,
I predict that the dividing line will not be Mason and Dixon's."
—Grant's Speech on Our Public School System.

Harper's Weekly, October 30, 1875.

on the other." After reviewing the speech, *The Nation* sarcastically noted: "General Grant's interest in the school question is apparently greater than most people supposed."[44] Tammany Hall was more direct in its criticism. New York City's Democratic party blasted the Des Moines speech as designed to resurrect Reconstructionist "Caesarism:" "Baffled and defeated in every previous scheme to strengthen his political fortunes," a Tammany pamphlet reported, "the President at last changes front in the face of his victorious opponents, discards the 'bloody shirt' as an obsolete rag, and, nailing to the mast the black flag of Know-Nothingism, unsheathes his sword for a 'religious war.'"[45] The Liberal-Republican *New York Tribune* made the same point more delicately: "Every politician knows that there is no subject on which the average well-to-do citizen in the country districts is so sensitive as upon the possibility of Roman Catholic aggression, particularly with reference to the schools."[46]

Three weeks after Grant spoke at Des Moines, Blaine also moved into the public-school arena. In a letter to a prominent Republican in Ohio, Blaine wrote that the leading political issue in the Ohio campaign was likely to be replicated elsewhere. In an effort to upstage all rivals, he hinted that soon he would propose a final settlement of the matter "in some definite and comprehensive way."[47] Early in December, he introduced a constitutional amendment designed to prohibit any use of official state school funds for parochial education. In this way, his name became tied to what then appeared as the leading issue in the upcoming campaign. The *Independent*, New York City's liberal Protestant newspaper, exulted that the proposed Blaine Amendment was guaranteed to restore the Republican party to complete control of the federal government:

> If [the] Democracy, with its large majority in the lower house, on account of its political affiliation with Roman Catholics and its dependence for support on Catholic votes, chooses to reject it, then let [the] Democracy take the responsibility of the choice. This quasi-secret game between a religious sect and a political party has been played long enough. Let it be played openly, if it must be played at all. The people will then see the game and vote accordingly.[48]

Grant was not prepared to surrender leadership on this issue to his primary Republican rival; and so in his annual message to Congress on December 7, 1875, he returned to the subject. He recommended a more comprehensive amending of the constitution that would not only ban a sectarian division of the states' school funds, but would also do the following: (1) Guarantee a public education to every American; (2) prevent the public schools from teaching "religious, atheistic, or pagan tenets;" (3) tax church properties at rates comparable to business corporations; and (4) bar from the right of suffrage any new voters unable to pass a literacy test by the year 1890.[49]

His proposal was rambling and in the end trampled on too many political toes to wrest control of the emerging issue away from Blaine. Nevertheless, his comments do warrant some discussion here. His first point was a bold move to take away control of public education from the states and make clear the federal government's dominant role. In 1870, Congress had used the Guarantee Clause to promote the same end, requiring Virginia, Mississippi, and Texas to maintain systems of public education in perpetuity. But with the passage of years, that federal command was relegated to memory more than reality. Texas had virtually dismantled its public schools, Virginia was actively discussing their abolition, and a politically divided Congress was incapable of action. Through 1873, Congress had considered federal aid to education, an idea that many believed would see federal controls follow in its wake. In 1874, Nevada's Republican Senator William M. Stewart had suggested a constitutional amendment on this matter alone.[50] Grant's first point called for reactivating Stewart's idea. Blaine's proposal was much more cautious. Blaine worded his own amendment in negative language, prohibiting the states from engaging in certain activities, rather than making an obvious grab for federal control of education. Before moving toward that larger goal, most Republican strategists preferred to focus on a more achievable prize, namely enactment of the Blaine Amendment. The rest could follow in due course.

Grant's second point mystified even the party faithful. Apparently, he himself knew what he intended to communicate regarding "religious, atheistic, or pagan tenets." In any case, this point also fell flat. His third suggestion that church properties bear greater tax burdens was popular with those who assumed that the Roman Catholic church would suffer the most under taxation. But, in fact, leading Protestant denominations would have felt even greater pain had that idea been implemented; and the matter was dropped. At that time, only Alabama, Mississippi, and Missouri taxed church property as all other properties. The overwhelming majority of states exempted church property from taxation. This particular point was not likely to win the applause of either local or national majorities.[51] Grant's fourth and final suggestion was ultimately the most important of them all, for this helped shape subsequent events. When 1890 finally arrived, the state of Mississippi constitutionally provided for a literacy test designed to disfranchise its African-American voters. Grant had made the suggestion with the assumption that federally guaranteed educational opportunity would precede any disfranchisement of those failing to take advantage of a free education. In any case, by that later date, Southerners remembered only that the idea of disfranchisement on educational grounds had been proposed by the titular head of Republican Reconstruction, President Ulysses S. Grant himself.

Smarting over the ominous anti-Catholicism sweeping through the Republican party, the Catholic press attempted to maintain composure. One Catholic commentary on Grant's earlier Des Moines address mockingly agreed with his every word. The President, the account noted, said that he wanted public education free from sectarian influence. Then, it continued, he had best join with the Catholic church in driving all Protestant practices from the public schools. "The reading of the scriptures as a public ceremony is as distinctive to them," *The Catholic World* wrote in describing Protestants, "as the celebration of mass would be to Catholics." Accordingly, the journal concluded, the public schools needed to be purged of this and other similar Protestant religious practices if they were to be truly non-sectarian.[52]

One Catholic observer, the Right Reverend James O'Connor, warned Catholics not to take the Republican religious crusade lightly. While suggesting that the Republicans had adopted the ploy to divert attention from more embarrassing issues, O'Connor noted that Bismarck had done the same thing in Germany with great political success. He advised Catholics to quiet their just plea for a division of public-school funds, as the Protestant majority was clearly deaf to hearing the logic of their position. Continuing Catholic agitation of the issue could only feed a stronger Republican backlash. Catholics generally heeded this advice, and in the end it enabled them to overcome the momentary threat posed by Republicans intent on resurrecting Reconstruction on a religious theme.[53]

O'Connor's recommendation was especially wise, because the Blaine Amendment was politically flawed from the outset. There was a good chance that the Republican position, now tied to Blaine's proposal, would eventually self-destruct. In crafting his amendment, Blaine had followed the advice of Elisha P. Hurlbut, a well-known constitutional expert on the issue of religion and public education. Early in the decade, Hurlbut had advocated removal of the Bible from the public schools as a way of ending the religious strife. Hurlbut's acceptance within the rising anti-Catholic movement had been earned by his strident nationalism and his desire to centralize governmental functions. But he was a secularist as well, and as such represented only a minority position within the anti-Catholic crusade. Most Republicans favored keeping the Bible in the public schools at all costs, even if that presence was more symbolic than real. Blaine's Amendment was silent on the specific matter of the Bible in the public schools, but it did seek to prevent "an establishment of religion" at the state level. The Blaine Amendment's exact wording was:

> No State shall make any law respecting an establishment of religion or prohibiting the free exercise thereof; and no money raised by taxation in any state for the support of public schools, or derived from any public fund therefor, nor any public lands devoted thereto, shall ever be under the control of any religious sect, nor shall any money so raised or lands so devoted be divided between religious sects or denominations.

One could interpret this language as requiring a removal of the Bible from the public schools.[54] With time, this proposal would be revealed as not truly reflecting Republican attitudes. Given this inherent weakness in the Republican proposal, Catholic passivity was thoroughly warranted.

At that time, most Protestants were generally oblivious to any logical contradiction between supporting God and the Bible in the public schools while at the same time opposing any sectarian influence there. In their minds, Roman Catholicism was a particular sect representing a distinctive theology, just as Arminian Protestants held sectarian views opposed to those represented by traditional Calvinists. From the beginning of public education in the United States, "religion" had been favored in the schools while "sectarianism" had not been. Horace Mann's program of religious instruction had been based on a generalized Protestant understanding, avoiding all sectarian doctrinal disputes. From the standpoint of this tradition, Bible reading, hymn singing, and recitation of the Lord's Prayer in public education constituted neither an establishment of religion nor sectarian education. The assumption of the majority was that the United States was a Christian nation. It was neither a Methodist nation, nor a Baptist nation, nor a Catholic nation. Within these assumptions, Republican allegiance to the Blaine Amendment made sense. However, when challenged and confronted with tightly reasoned arguments, this position became highly vulnerable.[55]

Pamphleteer William H. Van Nortwick wanted nothing left to chance. He wanted the Blaine Amendment altered to include a specific reference mandating Bible reading in the public schools. He quoted Joseph Story, the highly respected Harvard Law Professor who a generation earlier had simultaneously served on the United States Supreme Court. Story had once noted that as Christianity was the revealed truth, it was the "special duty of government to foster it among all the citizens and subjects."[56] Van Nortwick's suggestion was ignored until it was too late.

In the end, House Democrats outmaneuvered the Republicans by making a weakened version of the Blaine Amendment their own, which completely undermined the Republican strategy of demagogic electioneering. By August, their victory was apparent; but well into the centennial year, through both parties' national conventions and the selections of both candidates, the Republicans rested on the false hope that they were riding the crest of a powerful civil-religious issue that could restore Republican control to every branch of the federal government. Subsequently, they saw this expectation unravel.

Between December, 1875, when Blaine first introduced his proposed amendment, and August, 1876, when the Democrats defused the issue, both parties sparred over religion in American public education.[57] From the outset, it was clear that this injection of religion into the political arena had consequences for Reconstruction. This could be seen in the situation in Texas. In the fall of 1875, Texas had effectively discontinued public education, in contradiction to the congressional Reconstruction mandate of 1870. In January, 1876, African-American protesters met in Houston and framed a petition to Congress demanding a federal reversal of this state decision. As they lacked control of the House of Representatives, Republicans were in a weak position to push for enforcement of the special conditions regarding Texas' readmission to the Union in 1870. But if anti-Catholicism eventually enabled the party to regain control of the House, then Reconstruction could be reactivated in Texas and elsewhere.[58]

Daniel Ullmann, a leader in both the Know-Nothing movement of the 1850s and the anti-Catholic upsurge of the 1870s, masterfully wove together the themes of anti-Catholicism and racial equity. He told an audience in New York City on February 22, 1876, that the American Union was being assaulted simultaneously by an international Ultramontane conspiracy and by a Southern-based states-rights ideology, which had not been eradicated by the Civil War as it should have been. Catholic extremists and unreconstructed rebels, he said, both relied on the decentralization of American government to achieve their ends. Both were opposed to public education, supposedly because both needed mass ignorance to achieve their ends. Ullmann saw the need to move toward more centralized government so that public education could both be preserved from those who would destroy it and be promoted where the forces of ignorance tried to prevent it from taking root. He suggested that the American tradition of state-centered governance was no longer suitable to the modern age. Some states, such as Texas, had fallen prey to the old rebel spirit. Other states, such as his own New York, were threatened by Catholic dominance. Disease in any particular state affected the entire national body. Therefore, the nation itself needed to prescribe the most effective remedies. The Blaine Amendment needed to be adopted to counteract the Catholic menace, and the Constitution's Guarantee Clause needed to be reactivated to crush once and for all the rebel spirit dividing America. He concluded by calling upon the federal government to "guarantee to every state an unsectarian system of free and universal education."[59]

Bishop Bernard J. McQuaid of Rochester, New York, generally recognized the wisdom of the Roman Catholic strategy of staying quiet during the months before the matter would be actively debated in Congress. But, he was an educator by temperament; and when he perceived that the non-Catholic population did not understand a particular Roman-Catholic concept, he was compelled to make a valiant attempt to explain the matter in terms anyone could understand. On occasion he contributed essays to *The Independent*, a Protestant newspaper often hostile to Roman Catholicism. Early on, he had quietly opposed the Vatican Council's ruling in favor of Papal Infallibility in 1870, but supported the doctrine once the decision was made. He explained to Protestant critics that the doctrine did not claim that the Pope was God or that the Pope was not a sinner as all other men. It only meant, he emphasized, that the Pope was the head of the church in matters of faith and morals.[60] In February, with the Roman Catholic position on education causing a national uproar, Bishop McQuaid again stepped forward to explain the Catholic position to non-Catholics in terms that he hoped they could understand.

McQuaid's chosen forum was the city of Boston, a place of growing Roman Catholic influence and high intellectual Protestant tradition. His audience in Horticulture Hall was, as expected, primarily anti-Catholic but courteous nonetheless. In turn, the Catholic prelate was patient and congenial. He advanced that meaningful education, by its very nature, had to be sectarian. Children are inquisitive, and when they ask about the meaning of life and death and right and wrong, a neutral answer cannot satisfy. Nevertheless, he noted, the American public school was drifting toward secularism and a neutral stance on such fundamental questions. He feared what kind of citizens would be raised in the slowly emerging amoral educational environment. Attempts might still be made to teach the children principles of morality and simple decency. But, he warned, they would ultimately fail. Without the support of supernatural spiritual authority, the teaching of virtue could not effectively compete with the natural force of human selfishness.[61]

Mcquaid's address drew the wrath of *Harper's Weekly*. State-supported sectarian schools, the journal emphasized, would undermine the Reconstruction dream of one people harmoniously orchestrated from the political center. The journal's response in this particular instance revealed a deep-seated hostility to any religious loyalties that might threaten the primacy of nation worship. For some Republicans, "religion" was only valuable if it met the civil-religious needs of producing a desirable national consciousness. This was the essence of Bismarck's *Kulturkampf*. It was also present in its American imitation. It was a mind set encouraged by the philosophy of Georg Hegel and consumed with a worship of material progress, a suitable national religion for the Gilded Age. Mcquaid's words fell on infertile ground. Thereafter, until Congress debated the Blaine Amendment in August, Catholic leaders exercised a remarkable self-restraint on the school question.[62]

By contrast, Democratic politicians noisily skirmished with their Republican opponents during these months of waiting for the issue to come to a head. Ridicule was a favorite Democratic weapon. "Our President last Fall turned Vice-Regent," one Missouri Democrat told the House, "and like Paul, in addition to his multiform burdens, took upon himself the care of all the churches." Democrats attacked Blaine as well. Indeed, they focused most of their attention on the latter, as he appeared to be the one most likely to be nominated by the Republicans. Their attacks on Blaine focused on his supposed corruptibility. They claimed that in getting land grants for railroad corporations, he had sold his past influence as Speaker of the House. On May 31, they scored their most telling hit as one James Mulligan of Boston began his testimony of personal knowledge concerning Blaine's alleged corrupt dealings. The Republican front-runner's energies were consumed in a frenzied effort to defend himself; but ironically the Democratic attack may have strengthened his chances to secure the nomination, as most of the Republican-party faithful disbelieved the charges, which they saw motivated solely by partisanship.[63]

In the end, Blaine did not receive the nomination, largely due to the intraparty jealousy of Roscoe Conkling. Instead, Catholic-baiting Rutherford B. Hayes won the prize. His lack of any real national reputation together with his association with the most popular issue of the

FIGURE 8.2

"Goin' to St. Louis"
During the presidential campaign of 1876, Republicans attempted to portray
the campaign of Samuel J. Tilden as a fraud. They claimed that the Tilden
camp exemplified the worst in American life—Tammany Hall's political
corruption, Roman Catholic hostility to public education, Ku Klux Klan
violence and the "Rag Baby" of inflationary paper currency.

Harper's Weekly, July 8, 1876.

day ultimately secured his nomination. Hayes was nominated on June 16, in Cincinnati, where the decade's anti-Catholic movement had begun. In the early summer of 1876, Republicans were confident of riding the school question onto victory. "We were never so alive politically as now," a friend of John Eaton, Jr., wrote from Cincinnati. "The enthusiasm is remarkable, including all shades of Republicanism. We get the whole loaf this time." Emphasizing racial issues had left the Republicans divided. Emphasizing religion unified the party so that even recapturing the House seemed likely. On June 28, the Democratic national convention, meeting in St. Louis, nominated Samuel J. Tilden, Governor of New York. With the principal combatants finally identified, the campaign began in earnest.[64] The strength of the anti-Catholic antidote was about to be tested.

9

THE END OF RECONSTRUCTION

In 1876, political decorum dictated that presidential candidate Hayes not play a publicly active role in his own campaign. Nonetheless, he kept in close communication with party leaders in order to control the direction of the campaign. Hayes was concerned that the Democrats' nomination of New York Governor Samuel J. Tilden made his own chances in New York doubtful. He instructed James Garfield, his campaign's liaison in the House, to attack Tilden's failure to defend public education against Roman-Catholic encroachments in New York. He also communicated to Garfield that he hoped that the anti-Catholic campaign might yet awaken some latent support in the Protestant South. But most of his correspondence that summer concerned his fears that Republicans were being outfoxed by Democrats in the House's discussion of the Blaine Amendment. As a general in the Civil War, Hayes knew the fear of being flanked by the enemy. As a presidential candidate, he slowly realized that he had been cleverly outmaneuvered in what he had hoped would be the determining issue in the campaign.[1]

On August 4, the Democrat-controlled House Judiciary Committee reported a version of the Blaine Amendment with a unique proviso: unlike the other Reconstruction amendments, this one could never be interpreted to enlarge the powers of Congress. If enacted, this modification could only be used by the courts to void state actions violating the amendment's specific requirements. Under this Democratic party product, Congress could never take national action to insure that the Ultramontane "conspiracy" would be thwarted in the states as a whole or in any portion of them. This change guaranteed that the amendment could never be used as an excuse for the federal government to take over American public education.[2] Hayes rushed a telegram to Garfield:

> I have just read the amendment on the schools question reported by your House committee. Is it not an effort to get rid of our issue without accomplishing what the public sentiment demands? It seems to me you should amend it. Strike out the clause that gives

Congress no legislative power to enforce the provision and insert the usual clause giving Congress power to enforce it by appropriate legislation. Think of this. Would it not be best to vote against the amendment proposed if it is not perfected? It is an important thing to have this amendment one that will be effectual.[3]

House Republicans were trapped. If they opposed the revised Blaine Amendment on some subtle point not easily explained to the average voter, their contrariness would seem motivated by petty partisanship. Yet, if they voted for it, they would be collaborating in the Democrats' gutting of the amendment. Exhibiting skillful handling, the Democratic leadership forced the Republican choice by corralling an overwhelming Democratic majority in favor of the revised measure. With a solid Democratic phalanx supporting the measure, the Republican votes were rendered almost superfluous. House Republicans scrambled to rationalize a decision to vote for the weakened amendment rather than appear to be in favor of sectarian education by voting against it. For the record, George Frisbie Hoar noted that while he would vote in favor of the watered-down Democrat version, the Guarantee Clause could still be used by a future Republican Congress to take over public education in any state in which Roman Catholics attempted to control the schools. A disappointed Hayes correctly sensed that the apparent House interparty unity in the vote destroyed the issue for the upcoming campaign.[4]

The vote in the House was 180 to 7, well beyond the two-thirds majority required for passage. All seven of those voting in the negative were Democrats from former slave states, depriving the Republicans of any cause to claim that Ultramontanes controlled a significant number of Northern Democrats. The fact that twice as many Democrats as Republicans voted for the proposed amendment practically emasculated the issue for campaign purposes. One Nashville newspaper celebrated: "Its adoption in the House . . . is an effort, and a successful effort, to take it altogether out of the domain of politics." This Democratic party newspaper realized that the real purpose of the original Blaine Amendment had been "to divest the states of their authority or to confer it on the national government." It described the Republican design as a "stupendous stride toward centralization, toward complete change in our system of government." The original proposal, commented the daily, had been intended "to turn over the children to be educated by the federal government." Democrats crowed, knowing that henceforth they politically controlled what had once appeared as a dangerous Republican appeal to ugly religious prejudice.[5]

As the issue was taken up in the Republican Senate, news arrived of a statement addressed "To the People of the United States," made by Archbishop John Baptist Purcell of Cincinnati. Purcell had led the Catholic cause in the Cincinnati Bible War and thus had much experience in maneuvering effectively in this civil-religious culture struggle. Purcell's latest move complemented the House endorsement of the modified Blaine Amendment. His statement claimed that the Roman Catholic church was not opposed to American public education and that all that Catholics wanted was the freedom to educate their own children in parochial schools. He even claimed that the church was not insistent that public-school funds be used to support Catholic schools. The Republican press reacted in disbelief. Purcell's statement, timed to have momentary political effect, in no way represented the true position of the Roman Catholic church. It was propaganda, pure and simple, designed to sway the uninformed. Nonetheless, the statement further muddled what Republicans had hoped would be the clarifying issue in the campaign.[6]

The original Blaine Amendment had been flawed as it only barred designated state school funds from being used for sectarian purposes. If enacted, the original proposal would have allowed any state to aid parochial schools by means other than dividing the school fund—such as direct appropriations. Hayes advised that Senate Republicans take advantage of the Democrats' deliberate clouding of the issue to rewrite the amendment completely, expressing in nonambiguous language exactly all that the Republican party really wanted for the nation. Then, he predicted, the Democratic party would have to show its true colors; and Republicans again could "make an issue which will destroy all chance of Democratic success in the Fall."[7] Hayes's revived optimism was groundless. By this point, the damage could not be repaired. A complete Republican redrafting of the Blaine Amendment in August, after the party had supported the original language since the previous December, could only portray Republicans as confused and disorganized. The loophole in Blaine's original language that was identified by Hayes had been recognized as early as January.[8] Yet the problem had been allowed to drift by overconfident Republican managers. By August, whatever the Senate Republicans did with the matter could not undo the Democrats' superior position, won by skillful congressional leadership. Similar to the Confederates at Fredericksburg or Union forces at Gettysburg, Democrats held the advantageous high ground.

The weakness of the Republican position was reflected in a *Chicago Tribune* editorial urging the Senate to pass the House version of the amendment quickly before the session ended.[9] If the editorial staff of a major urban Republican daily could advise such a course, how could any Senate revision clarify the issue for the average voter? By itself, this editorial exemplified that the Democratic strategy had succeeded. By uniting behind a diluted Blaine Amendment in the House, the Democrats had avoided being tarred by the Republican anti-Catholic campaign. Having been smeared by the Democrats' racist attacks in 1874, Republicans had overconfidently assumed that their own appeal to popular prejudice in 1876 would be just as successful. They were wrong, not because the majority of the voting public disagreed with the campaign of innuendo and fear which they had waged, but because of Democratic party skillful maneuvering and Roman Catholic self-restraint in handling this volatile issue. Republicans had not exercised a similar self-restraint and caution in 1874 and had lost ground because of that.

In August, the Democrats showed that in American politics sometimes the most effective way to disarm one's opponents is to appear to agree with them. Meanwhile, Republicans further helped the Democrats' cause. In redrafting the amendment in the Senate in order to ensure clear Democratic party opposition, the Republicans had to reject the work of Blaine himself. The party appeared internally confused and ineffective in defining what was really at stake in the presumed Roman Catholic threat to the American public school. Democrat Henry Watterson's Louisville *Courier-Journal* crowed: "Blaine's school amendment was pronounced a most brilliant thing by the Republicans when he offered it. When the Democratic House passed it, the Republicans denounced it. They are very consistent."[10] To the average voter, it must have appeared that all the Republicans were interested in was an election-year quarrel over trifles. While the Republican objective in modifying the amendment in the Senate was to control the damage already done, the public's confusion over the bungled issue revealed that the matter had in fact already been damaged beyond all repair.

The *Atlanta Constitution* predicted that the House action "spoiled tons of Republican campaign literature which had been prepared to show an alliance between the Catholic church and the Democratic party."[11] Nevertheless, Senate Republicans remained unrealistically hopeful that the campaign literature might yet be made effective. They first restored Congress's authority to expand the constitutional mandate with enabling legislation. Up to this point, they were only undoing the damage done to the measure by the House. But then they went well beyond that in stipulating numerous specific ways in which states could not aid sectarian schools in addition to Blaine's original prohibition against dividing the school fund. In redesigning the amendment to cover multiple contingencies, Senate Republicans were embarrassing Blaine himself, who had recently been elected to the Senate. This gesture was meant not only to improve on his original language but to serve notice that the Senate gave no special deference to former House Speaker Blaine. Senator Roscoe Conkling, Blaine's intraparty rival, took especial glee in this. By the time that the Senate completed its rewriting, Blaine would not be able to tell any resemblance between the new result and his own original effort.

Throughout 1876, Blaine's intraparty enemies had circulated rumors of his supposed softness toward Roman Catholicism. Blaine's mother had been a Roman Catholic. She had raised him in that faith. He had only converted to his father's Presbyterianism upon reaching adulthood.[12] Innuendoes abounded that Blaine's original proposal had only specifically protected state school funds and had not outlawed special appropriations to Catholic schools due to an intentional oversight on his part. It was perhaps just as well that Blaine did not take his Senate seat immediately but stayed in Maine throughout the summer recuperating from an illness that he had contracted at the Cincinnati convention.

Senate Republicans justified making the amendment read like detailed legislation by noting that Tilden knew all the tricks of getting around the original Blaine amendment and needed to be thwarted by very specific language. Republicans broadcast the myriad ways in which Tilden's New York had allowed a subtle Roman Catholic takeover of public education there without explicitly dividing the school fund. For example, in 1873, the Poughkeepsie's Board of Education had absorbed two Catholic schools into its public school system. Theoretically, the local school board ran the two schools, but in reality the church ran the schools as before. The largely Catholic school board deferred to the local Catholic bishop on all educational questions. The Catholic teachers of these schools were paid with public funds. The Poughkeepsie arrangement made a mockery of an already existing state constitutional amendment forbidding a division of the school fund for the support of sectarian schools. Catholics called this arrangement "The Poughkeepsie Plan" and sought to replicate it elsewhere.[13] The Senate Republicans left no doubts that the Poughkeepsie Plan would be outlawed under their revision of the Blaine Amendment, whereas it would have passed muster under both the original version and the Democrats' revision.

Isaac P. Christiancy, a Republican from Michigan, convinced his Senate colleagues to enlarge the scope of the proposal not only to outlaw all forms of state aid to parochial schools but possible future federal aid as well. He feared that without this expansion, a future Roman Catholic national majority might spur Congress to aid Catholic education with land grants or other forms of federal largess. In his mind, the vague language of the First Amendment prohibiting Congress from making "an establishment of religion" was not sufficient. He suggested an elaborate and specific constitutional statement that left no doubt so that the threat would be eliminated once and for all. Senate Democrats observed all of this Republican bluster with amused contempt. Democrat Eli Saulsbury of Delaware taunted these anti-Catholic warriors. He asked why the Senate Republicans did not support the original Blaine Amendment, even if they could not support the House revision. A confident Democratic editor of the Nashville *Daily American* assured his readers that nothing that the Republicans did in the Senate could make any difference. "One thing is certain," he wrote, "the passage of the resolution by the House has already taken the subject out of the political field of discussion."[14]

In this last attempt to revive the lost momentum of Reconstruction, Republican Senator George F. Edmunds of Vermont blended the themes of an impending Roman-Catholic danger and the obliteration of African-American opportunity evidenced in Texas's dismantling of its public school system. Before the Senate, he spoke bravely of resurrecting the Guarantee Clause in order to thwart the enemies of Reconstruction— Catholics and former Confederates alike. Yet all present knew that as long as Democrats controlled the House, Texas could do as it pleased. However, said Edmunds, if the voters would awaken to the coordinated Democratic-party threats to the public school in both North and South, Republicans might still regain control of the government and again move forward with their nationalizing agenda.[15]

On August 11, the Republican-controlled Senate Judiciary Committee submitted its revision of the Blaine Amendment. Unlike Blaine's brief original effort, this new statement was complicated, convoluted, and difficult to read. If Hayes and the Senate Republicans hoped to educate the public by this alternate draft, they were sorely mistaken. The revision read:

> *Section 1.* No State shall make any law respecting an establishment of religion, or prohibiting the free exercise thereof; and no religious test shall ever be required as a qualification to any office or public trust under any state. No public property and no public revenue of, nor any loan of credit by or under the authority of, the United States, or any state, territory, district, or municipal corporation, shall be appropriated to or made or used for the support

of any school, educational or other institution under the control of any religious or anti-religious sect, organization, or denomination, or wherein the particular creed or tenets of any organization, or denomination shall be taught. And no such particular creed or tenets shall be read or taught in any school or institution supported in whole or in part by such revenue or loan of credit; and no such appropriation or loan of credit shall be made to any religious or anti-religious sect, organization, or denomination, or to promote its interests or tenets. This article shall not be construed to prohibit the reading of the Bible in any school or institution; and it shall not have the effect to impair the rights of property already vested.

Section 2. Congress shall have power, by appropriate legislation, to provide for the prevention and punishment of violation of this article.[16]

This revision sought to ensure that the amendment could never be interpreted to mandate a removal of Bible reading from the public schools. It also sought to meet every possible specific contingency that might arise, not trusting courts to interpret the framers' original intent. Most important, it directly empowered Congress to determine how best to *prevent* violations of the article from occurring in the first place. From the perspective of Senate Republicans, the United States Supreme Court was then twisting the original intent of the last sections of each of the other Reconstruction amendments. In March 1876, in both *United States v. Reese* and *United States v. Cruikshank*, the Court held that the word "appropriate" in the final section of each of these amendments could be used against Congressional control over individual civil rights.[17] To show their disapproval with this reasoning, the Senate Republicans crafted the last section of the school amendment to emphasize that determining the full meaning of the amendment would rest primarily with Congress, not the courts. Under the Senate revision, Congress could use the new amendment to centralize American public education in order *to prevent* a sectarian takeover at the state or local level.

A specific enforcement clause had not been included in Blaine's original draft. Blaine himself had intended that the Constitution's elastic or "necessary and proper" clause could be used for that purpose. As House Democrats had explicitly prohibited that interpretation in their own revision of Blaine's handiwork, Senate Republicans argued that it was necessary to spell out Blaine's presumed original intent in no uncertain terms.[18]

Hayes was pleased with the Senate's delineation of the differences between the two major parties in this matter. "The Senate committee has reported *our* amendment," he wrote, "and the House gave the Democratic amendment. Let the people choose. It is not important to pass it through the Senate at this session. Let it be debated and considered by the country."[19] Unfortunately, all of this educating effort was lost on the voters. It was too difficult to understand. It was impossible to explain to persons not versed in the fine points of Constitutional theory. Ultimately, the Democratic smoke screen proved far more effective among the electorate than the Republican effort at reclarification.

Senate Democrats clearly understood the long-term stakes involved. Theodore Fitz Randolph, a Democrat from New Jersey, discerned the Republican intention to take over the American system of public education and rule it from the center of national government. He saw in this Republican vision of America's future the strangulation of American liberty. His fellow Senate Democrats felt likewise. On August 14, the final vote occurred, with twenty-eight Senators (all Republicans) in favor of the revision and sixteen Senators (all Democrats) against. This was short of the two-thirds majority required for ratification. The unanimity on both sides of the aisle revealed the intent of the Reconstruction spirit in the proposal and the nature of its opposition. Republicans who could not abide centralization on issues of race readily cooperated in supporting the nation-centered ethos associated with protecting and promoting the traditional (Protestant) American public school against Roman Catholic interlopers.[20]

Religion was the unifying factor in this centralizing vision. In a major address preceding the final vote, Republican Senator Frederick T. Frelinghusen of New Jersey spoke to this issue: "That pure and undefiled religion which appertains to the relationship and responsibility of man to God, is readily distinguishable from the creeds of sects." The national celebration of Thanksgiving, institutionalized by a Republican administration during the Civil War, was in the realm of religion, as was Bible reading in the public schools. Senator Lewis V. Bogy, a Roman-Catholic Democrat from Missouri, attacked Frelinghuysen's assumption that religion and sectarianism could be separated in any meaningful way. He emphasized that he himself did not oppose religion or sectarianism in public education; rather, he opposed exclusivist Protestant sectarianism masquerading as something other than what it really was. He noted that while he shared Frelinghusen's fear of the steady growth of secularism in public education and American life in general, he feared a tyranny of the majority in the name of Frelinghusen's national "religion" even more. In Bogy's opinion, the nation stood at an educational crossroads that either led "back to the days of pure paganism" and the ultimate degradation of the Republic or forward toward a division of the school funds among the variety of sects making up American religious culture. He feared the first alternative might emerge, not because of the Protestant majority's preference for paganism but because of its unreasoning anti-Catholicism.[21]

Francis Kernan, a Democrat from New York and also a Roman Catholic, took another tack. He urged that public education be left to local control, as that was traditional in American life. Religion, he urged, should be left out of congressional discussions. At the local level, majorities could choose the style of religion or irreligion that they found most harmonious with public education. Republican war horse Oliver Morton reared at Kernan's remarks, which he said might not only allow abominations such as the Roman Catholic "Poughkeepsie Plan" but also eventually an establishment of the Roman Catholic church in Kernan's own New York. John W. Stevenson, a Kentucky Democrat, responded that while he was "a Protestant from head to foot," he feared Republican centralization far more than the logical implication of Kernan's remarks. For Stevenson, racial considerations were uppermost. All participants in this discussion knew that religion and race were at issue simultaneously. "The bloody shirt," said Bogy in this regard, "can no longer call out the mad bull. . . . Another animal has to be brought forth by these matadors to engage the attention of the people in this great arena in which we are soon all to be combatants. The Pope, the old Pope of Rome, is to be the great bull we are all to attack."[22]

The contest between centralization and states rights divided the parties during the nation's centennial year. Fully revealing this, House Republican William H. Baker of New York introduced a symbolic resolution stating that the federal government is supreme in American government. This was quickly countered by a Democratic party alternative reaffirming Madisonian states rights.[23] House Democrat William B. Spencer of Louisiana portrayed his party's position as the middle way between two extremes. He confessed that in his youth he had supported the secession movement, which had pushed states rights to an improper extreme. He compared that mistaken position with the Republican stance in 1876 that sought and demanded "the consolidation of all governmental powers in the hands of the federal government." Both extremes, he noted, were wrong. "Either extreme leads to the destruction of the Union," he told the House, "and the one no more than the other. The middle ground between these two extremes is in this, as in all things else, the only true one." In 1876, the Democratic party stood for Madisonian dual-federalism, the middle ground between the extremes of Calhounian states rights and Republican centralism. While the Civil War had killed the former, noted Spencer, Republican support for the latter was leading America toward a Bismarckian consolidation of government. Spencer hoped that in 1876 this Bismarckian influence, tending "to the subversion of free government," might finally be buried at the polls.[24]

William Lawrence, a Republican colleague of Spencer in the House, readily agreed that Republicans wanted to centralize American government and predicted that a complete Republican victory in the fall would lead to an active and aggressive use of the Guarantee Clause in public education. Texas was especially put on notice. He also predicted that as soon as his party regained control of the House, the equal protection clause of the Fourteenth Amendment would be used by Congress more aggressively to transform the Southern states. Even without the Blaine Amendment, Lawrence was confident that the Constitution possessed the sufficient language needed to nationalize public education. The crucial element that was lacking was Republican control of the House.[25]

While generally confident that the Republican school issue had been successfully derailed, Democrats still cautiously warned of the dangers implicit in the Senate version of the Blaine Amendment. In the words of the *Atlanta Constitution*, the Republican revision proposed giving "Congress new and extraordinary powers to interfere in the local affairs of the states." The New Orleans *Daily Picayune* called it "another step . . . in the direction of centralization." The New Orleans daily ominously described three different kinds of campaign postcards which the Republicans had prepared. "Old Guard Cards" were being sent to Union war veterans. "Young Guard Cards" were being sent "to young men about to cast their first vote." The third version was the "School Guard Card." It was being mailed to all voters thought "to be opposed to the Catholic religion, or their interference with the common school funds of the country, or who are sensitive upon this subject." The numbers of each kind of card revealed the Republican campaign strategy: Republicans intended to distribute the cards "in about the ratio of one of the Young Guard to two of the Old Guard and seven of the School Guard." This information, reported the newspaper, indicated that the Republicans intended to "erect anew the gallows of Salem" as soon as they regained complete control of the federal government. But Democrats were confident that they could prevent that from occurring.[26]

Congress recessed with irreconcilable versions of the Blaine Amendment favored by the two parties. The National Anti-Papal League, favoring the Republican version, provided its post-session assessment of the anti-Catholic issue. It praised the Senate Republicans for challenging the House Democrats' effort to obscure the ideological difference between the two parties. But at the same time, it feared that the Democrats had succeeded in confusing the matter for the average voter. Because of this, it went so far as to concede defeat. "This first national victory over Protestantism and Republicanism," the League's official statement mourned, "has filled every Roman Catholic heart with rejoicing."[27]

In desperation, Republicans attempted to personalize the school issue around the figure of Samuel Tilden. They closely examined his career as the supposed "reform" governor of New York in an effort to demonstrate that he was originally a pro-Catholic Tammany-Hall "subchief." They portrayed his supposed bringing of "Boss" William Marcy Tweed to justice as a political sham. During the years when Tweed had aided Roman Catholic education and simultaneously robbed New York of millions, Tilden had served as the chairman of the Central Committee of the New York Democratic Party and had refused to acknowledge or support a popular citizens' protest against Tweed. Angry anti-Tweed organizers had sought Tilden's assistance and participation in a campaign protesting New York City's funneling of public funds to Roman-Catholic schools, and Tilden had refused. "The man who would refuse to preside at, or allow his name to be used in connection with a public meeting to preserve the integrity of our common schools," concluded one anti-Catholic pamphlet, "is not a safe man to place at the head of the nation." The influential *Chicago Daily Tribune* recounted this same history and concluded: "No man who is unwilling to pay taxes for the support of Catholic schools, churches, and convents, no man who believes in our free schools as the basis of our prosperity as a country, can for one moment support Tilden."[28]

James Garfield had been severely embarrassed by his House opponents' skillful handling of the school issue. But he hoped that personalizing the issue might yet turn the tide. Democrats were then claiming that their passage of the amendment in the House proved that they were not tools of the Roman Catholic hierarchy and no threat to the Republic. But what if it could be proven that their titular leader was demonstrably untrustworthy on the school question? Then voters might awaken to the dangers posed by the Tilden candidacy. Garfield spent much time that fall both recounting and denouncing the history of Tilden's behavior concerning Tweed and the school issue in New York.[29]

Democrats fought back, claiming that Tilden had "attacked Tweed from the start, when he was at the height of his power." Yet historian Keith Ian Polakoff supports the Republican charge that Tilden was largely a phony reformer. He portrays Tilden as ignoring the Tweed scandal until a partisan cover-up was no longer possible. "When Tilden finally acted," Polakoff concludes, "it was to make certain that Tweed was overthrown by Democrats rather than Republicans, lest the party itself be smashed in the process."[30]

Republicans made a great deal of Tilden's gubernatorial approval of the "Gray-Nuns Act," that had first passed the New York state legislature in 1871 and was renewed in 1875, when Tilden signed a measure that gave automatic state teacher credentials to an order of nuns in the Roman Catholic church. Originally, the act had seemed a practical expedient for authorizing acceptable teachers for public schools in heavily Roman-Catholic districts. But in 1875 and 1876, the Republicans used this event to demonstrate the practical workings of the Ultramontane conspiracy to take over America's public schools. *Harper's Weekly* reported the measure as "another illustration of the constant and insidious effort of the Roman Catholic hierarchy to obtain control of the schools which it wishes to destroy." Sensing the measure's potential countereffectiveness as a weapon for anti-Catholic Republicans, the New York Democratic state legislature and Governor Tilden had repealed the act in February 1876. Nevertheless, Republicans continued telling the story of Tilden's involvement in this supposed Jesuitical conspiracy to undermine American public education.[31]

Thomas Nast contributed to the Republican anti-Catholic campaign as it peaked in the fall of 1876. One Nast cartoon of this time portrays a wolf pushing its snarling head in through the door of a public school. A variety of school children, including one African American boy, are pushing the door from the inside with all of their might to keep the wolf out, while a little girl alerts Uncle Sam who is reaching for his rifle on a mantle adorned with two plaques reading "The Union Forever" and "No Sectarianism." The collar around the wolf's neck reads "Democracy" and its dog tag is labeled "The Foreign Roman Church."[32] In this propaganda campaign, Republican literature especially reminded the voters that Senators Bogy and Kernan, both Roman Catholics, voted against the Senate version of the Blaine Amendment. Tilden's own silence on the school question in his letter of acceptance following his presidential nomination was noted in Republican tracts as revealing his effort to avoid discussing the very question that Americans found most pressing. Voters were incessantly reminded of the Geghan Act in Ohio and the Gray-Nuns Act in New York. "These possibilities," concluded one Republican campaign pamphlet, "should arouse intelligent citizens of all creeds, whether of native or foreign birth, to the danger that threatens our country if the Roman Catholic element, through the success of [the] Democracy, should obtain control of our national affairs. If knowledge of what has been done in Germany through priestism will awaken our people to the designs of the same power in the United States, the firm stand of Bismarck was not taken an hour too soon."[33]

As the American version of the *Kulturkampf* reached its crescendo, the Republicans glorified all things Germanic. Republican party campaign literature reminded German-Americans that the party of Hayes followed Bismarck and cultivated knowledge, repelled sectarianism, demanded general education, and valued social order. Democrats were portrayed as having backed Napoleon III in the Franco-Prussian War. Americans of English and German heritage were exalted as "two progressive elements of a single race that traces its source to the forests of Saxony and Bavaria." *Harper's Weekly* concluded: "In the Republican party alone can Germans find a safe refuge." Republicans employed Carl Schurz, the nation's leading German-born politician, who went on the stump for Hayes blasting "Roman-Catholic Democrats."[34]

Democrats waged a counterattack focusing upon those Germans who wished to be left alone by Republican religious fanatics. Republicans, charged Democratic campaign literature, both called for German beer halls to be closed on the Sabbath and at times tried to prohibit alcoholic beverages altogether. Democrats circulated a false story that Hayes himself, as a supposed member of the Centennial Commission, had "voted against opening the Philadelphia Exposition on Sundays." They also described the Republican nominee as devoted to the "Puritan and 'mucker' Sabbath" and his wife Lucy's adherence to the temperance cause "and all other hideous things the Germans hate so profoundly." At times, Republicans themselves provided grist for the Democrats by railing against the "Saloon Democracy;" each instance of this threatened to lose a German vote gained by the school question.[35]

The Republican campaign was admittedly anti-Catholic but Hayes differentiated this from being antiforeign. By contrast, Democrats sought to portray Hayes as hostile to Americans who were foreign-born, whatever their religious orientation. When Hayes's personal secretary carelessly sent a note of appreciation to an organization favoring restricting the right of suffrage to native-born Americans alone, Democrats attacked Hayes as both a religious bigot and a nativist. Schurz was called in to control any damage created by this side issue. After reviewing the results in Ohio's October elections, Hayes concluded that the Democratic attempt to link him with Know-Nothingism had failed. "It is perfectly well known," wrote Hayes, "that I do not favor the exclusion of foreigners from the ballot or from office, and that I do oppose Catholic interference and all sectarian interference with political affairs— and especially with the schools." He saw the last point as crucial, "particularly with non-Catholic foreigners."[36]

Speaking to a Hayes Club in the district where he would soon be elected to Congress for the first time, thirty-three-year-old William McKinley used the school issue in his own appeal for votes. Robert G. Ingersoll, perhaps the Republicans' most effective campaigner, also repeatedly turned to the issue throughout the fall of 1876. "I want free schools, and I want them divorced from sectarian influence," he screamed at a huge Republican rally in New York City. At times, Republican speakers used the issue to bash the Roman Catholic church. At times, they turned the issue southward to blast unreconstructed rebels. Democrats, whether North or South, were portrayed as hostile to public education and against the American national vision that had emerged from the Civil War. By contrast, Republicans presented their own party as the protector of both the public school and, indeed, the Union itself. "Let me say, Mr. Democrat," Ingersoll told his New York audience, the largest to hear a political speech there during the 1870s, "we are keeping the country for your children. We are keeping education for your children. We are keeping the old flag for your children."

Despite the fact that Democratic gubernatorial candidate Wade Hampton was then waging a redeemer pro-public-education political campaign in South Carolina, Republicans portrayed all Democratic politicians as enemies of the public schools. Later, during the interparty negotiations following the disputed Presidential election of 1876, Republicans would come to appreciate Hampton's seemingly sincere support for public education; but during the campaign itself no such concession was given. Typical of campaign rhetoric was a *Harper's Weekly* statement of October 14: "The worst enemies of the children— our Northern Democrats—look on approvingly while their savage [Southern] associates whip the school-master and shut the public schools." In a close election, no quarter could be given; regarding Hampton's South Carolina campaign, it truly seemed as if the candidate's violent supporters wearing red shirts characterized the Democratic party attitude there far more accurately than did their patrician leader.[37]

Wanting effective campaign material, Republican Congressman William Lawrence requested assistance from U.S. Commissioner of

FIGURE 9.1

"The Solid South."
In the campaign of 1876, Republicans portrayed the
"Solid South" as adamantly opposed to public education
despite some evidence to the contrary.

Harper's Weekly, November 11, 1876.

Education John Eaton, Jr., to supply horrific examples of Southern violations of the Republican public-school ideal. He went so far as to suggest that Eaton write an information-packed polemical statement for Lawrence's later political use. The Republican campaign spirit was best evidenced by Emery A. Storrs, a Republican leader in Freeport, Illinois, who told a rally there: "We erect schoolhouses, the rebels tear them down. We send teachers; they slaughter them." Recovered from his summer illness, Blaine used a different but no less effective campaign rhetoric to blast the Democratic Party's attitude toward public education. In a speech in Chicago late in October, Blaine described the South as a place "where you find three gallons of whisky to one spelling-book, and the Democrats are in an immense majority."[38]

Despite this Republican lambasting, the public-education movement appeared to be making genuine progress in the Democratic South. In fact, in 1876, the most outspoken advocate in the nation for federal aid to public education was Democrat Gilbert C. Walker of Virginia. In 1870, Walker had been the newly elected governor whom Charles Sumner had demonized as a secret enemy of the public school. Sumner successfully had parlayed that portrayal into a Congressional mandate that Virginia never abandon public education. Under that warning, Walker had obediently worked with William Ruffner to establish a working public-school system in the state. By 1876, Walker represented Virginia in the House of Representatives and called for federal aid to education. The continuing depression had virtually silenced Republicans on that specific means for centralizing public education. Nevertheless, Walker pressed to keep the idea alive in hopes that an economic recovery might soon restore the federal funds needed to inaugurate such a program. In 1876, Walker was attacked by other Democrats who portrayed him as a fool willing to fall into the Republicans' centralizing gambit. Nonetheless, his witness suggested that Southern attitudes toward public education were changing.[39] Had this evidence not existed, Republican efforts to persuade Northern voters that Democrats were sinking public education's expansion in the South might have been more effective.

During the Presidential campaign, Republicans tried to explain away the Walker phenomenon as not typical of Southern Democrats, who were characterized as "the enemies of popular education and the destroyers of free schools." Walker himself was dismissed as a mere "hopeful sign." In addition, it was noted that Walker was not typical because he was a Northerner by birth and had come to Virginia after the war originally as a conservative Republican. Henry W. Blair, who in the next decade would work closely with Southern politicians to further the cause of federal aid to education, in 1876 disregarded any and all hope for future intersectional educational cooperation. Blair cast Democratic party redeemers as the enemies of knowledge in their supposed purpose to maintain "Bourbon" control over the South. Likewise, he cast Northern Democrats as "Romish propagandists" and enemies of public education. Focused for the campaign that would determine whether or not Reconstruction could be revived, Blair portrayed the goal of the Democratic party, North and South, as "the insidious destruction or emasculation of the free schools."[40]

Finally, the election came. The initial results showed Tilden the victor. Republican House leader James Garfield blamed the apparent defeat on "the combined power of rebellion, Catholicism and whiskey— a trinity very hard to conquer." Hayes also brooded at this time and worried about the fate of the freedmen of the South. Given that Hayes is today commonly thought of as having had no real thought for African Americans at the close of Reconstruction, the focus of his recorded concern at the time when he thought he had lost is most interesting.[41] Within days, Republicans realized that the extremely close election returns still gave Hayes a chance. Over the next five months, the party mobilized to win the presidency by parliamentary maneuvers. Fraud was present on both sides in the contest, but ultimately Republican deceit carried the day. The result was achieved by means that strained the democratic process. It is inconceivable that Reconstruction could have survived this most wrenching experience in American political history. In any case, Hayes presided over a process that conceded that he would not attempt the impossible. And Reconstruction came to an end.

In the confusion over the close tally of the electoral votes, it was clear that the Republicans were weaker than they had been even after the disastrous elections of 1874. As in 1874, they failed to win the House. Worse than 1874, they no longer enjoyed a clear title to the Presidency. Reconstruction had been in retreat for many years due to declining public support. Nonetheless, up until the election of 1876, brave talk of using the Guarantee Clause against recalcitrant states continued. In the months immediately afterward, some Republicans thought in revolutionary terms, of retaining President Grant in power by totally extra-constitutional means in order to prevent a Tilden victory. But, by and large, the Reconstruction spirit was completely spent following the election. Although Hayes eventually was declared the winner in the most disputed presidential election in all of American history, Reconstruction effectively ended with his Pyrrhic victory.

The anti-Catholic issue did not disappear entirely. It remained in the political wings for years. Early in 1877, New Hampshire's voters rejected a proposed state constitutional amendment to allow Roman Catholics to become public-school teachers. This ban remained there until the end of the century. The Republican national platform of 1880 again called for a revival of the Blaine Amendment. In 1884, Blaine himself was the party's nominee. At that time, ironically, he tried to play down his role in the anti-Catholic campaign of 1876 and resurrected memories of his own Catholic upbringing and his pro-Irish policies during his brief stint as Secretary of State during Garfield's Presidency, all in a vain effort to win at least a few Catholic votes in a likely close election. But in the end, a comment by an overzealous Protestant supporter that the Democracy was the party of "rum, Romanism and rebellion" negated his efforts at bridge-building and effectively killed his chances. Virulent anti-Catholicism erupted again in 1887 with the creation of the American Protective Association. That organization made Roman-Catholic designs on public education a point of high political agitation once more. Anti-Catholicism lived on. But for the moment, the confused outcome of the Presidential contest of 1876 greatly deflated the vision of fashioning a national unity on an anti-Catholic theme.[42]

In 1876, with the admission of Colorado to statehood, Congress had insisted that that new state bar any aid to sectarian education in its proposed constitution. Thereafter, an antisectarian boilerplate appeared in the educational section of the constitution of every state seeking admission to the Union.[43] For their part, Roman Catholics maintained their insistence that public education be purged of Protestant religious practices. Caught between these two millstones, religion was steadily squeezed out of public education throughout most of the nation. Julius H. Seelye, a national spokesman for all of those Protestants who mourned this development, had been an ideologue of the civil-religious culture struggle throughout the seventies. Thereafter, as president of Amherst College, he continued to decry both the ongoing Roman Catholic push to divide the school funds and the growing secularization of American public education. "The first," he noted, "means delivering posterity, body and soul, into the hands of the Romists; the second means destruction to our system of education." He credited the mounting social problems of growing industrialization and urbanization to the removal of the Bible from the public schools and predicted that a nation based upon secular public education would ultimately disintegrate into anarchy and violence. Into the eighties, he wrote bitter essays for leading journals citing the loss to the nation of what he saw as the guiding spirit of Reconstruction, the creation of a uniform national culture founded on true religion.[44]

Reflections on the Era

Eric Foner has termed Reconstruction "America's unfinished revolution."[45] This language obviously refers solely to the racial aspects of Reconstruction. Reconstruction was indeed the beginning of an ongoing sporadic civil-rights movement, spanning more than a century, and continuing to this day. But it was both the beginning and the end of an American experiment with a quasi-Hegelian vision of a perfected nation, directed from the center of American government.[46] Although fragments of this perspective have lingered on in American life, the United States has never seen its likes again, at least as it appeared in its totality in the 1870s. In the twentieth century, American government has centralized, but not on the model of Reconstruction's visionaries. This latter-day centralization has been carried out in a pragmatic, non-ideological spirit by the likes of Franklin Delano Roosevelt and Lyndon Johnson. The closest that modern centralizers have come to promoting a guiding principle is to celebrate "pluralism," which is anti-ideological by its very nature. Contrast this modern reality with Reconstruction's dreamers who wanted a nation not merely united but unified, under the authority of a national "religion," which they strained to distinguish from what they regarded as inappropriate sectarian (Roman Catholic) linkages with government.

In 1875, when the Reconstruction spirit was still strong, James Freeman Clarke, a member of the New England intellectual/religious elite, had commented that only in a formal sense was there no established church in the United States. He saw the historic relationship between Christianity and the American public school as in effect creating an established religion. With public education expanding, he then saw this "religion" as on its way to becoming truly a national establishment, as contrasted to a local preference.[47] However, the effective termination of Reconstruction in 1876 ended this vision.

Julius Seelye grieved the passing of "moral earnestness" in politics following the election of 1876. He saw what he regarded as an unhealthy opportunistic spirit among politicians, who had come to support only that which was momentarily popular. Before 1876, he wrote, the Republican party had generally stood for the position "that what is right the people ought to will, and that nothing is lawful or should be chosen unless it has an authority with which men's reason and choice have nothing other to do than to discover and obey." In a brief golden age of Reconstruction, Seelye recalled, idealists had set up a standard that voters initially "were sure to reject, but to which they were nevertheless uncompromisingly summoned, and which at length compelled the choices which were at first refused." Reconstruction, he wrote, had recognized "man's organic relationship with his fellow man." It had acknowledged that the nation "represents the highest moral will." In days past, the Republican party had boldly stated that moral will, but by the 1880s, those days were gone.[48]

The religious side to Reconstruction ebbed and ceased to direct the nation's course. Fortuitously, its quasi-Hegelian overtones died out. Its bigoted and arrogant tones of exclusivity were slower to depart, but ceased to shape public policy to the degree that was attempted during Reconstruction. And yet, not all of the religious discourse in American politics during the 1870s was self serving. Citizens then actively discussed fundamental issues concerning the nature of education and the role of religious sensibilities in affairs of state. Not always recognized, religious issues, race, and national reconstruction continue necessarily in an ongoing dance in American life. National cohesion in a multicultural polity such as ours cannot exist without some sense of the whole, some purpose and meaning to our collective life. We need not necessarily agree on any national mission statement, but we should be engaged in a meaningful dialog concerning our national vision. And this search for national purpose must inevitably incorporate a spiritual dimension. In this limited sense, even the religious aspects of Reconstruction remain an unfinished revolution for our own time to rediscover and advance.

NOTES

Introduction

1. Eric Foner, *Free Soil, Free Labor, Free Men: The Ideology of the Republican Party Before the Civil War* (New York: Oxford University Press, 1970), 15–20.

1. Prologue to the Seventies

1. David Nasaw, *Schooled to Order: A Social History of Public Schooling in the United States* (New York: Oxford University Press, 1979), 36; Stephen B. Oates, ed., *Portrait of America*, 5th ed., 2 vols. (Boston: Houghton Mifflin Co., 1991), I: 178–96.

2. Herbert M. Kliebard, ed., *Religion and Education in America: A Documentary History* (Scranton, Penn.: International Textbook Co., 1969), 5–7; Carl F. Kaestle, *Pillars of the Republic, Common Schools and American Society, 1780–1860* (New York: Hill and Wang, 1983), 88–89.

3. Kaestle, *Pillars of the Republic*, 148, 152–53, 166–67, 192; Robert B. Downs, *Horace Mann, Champion of the Public Schools*, 2nd ed. (New York: Twayne Publishers, Inc., 1974), 28–32: Burke A. Hinsdale, *Horace Mann and the Common School Revival in the United States* (New York: Charles Scribner's Sons, 1898), 105–8.

4. Ronald E. Butchart, *Northern Schools, Southern Blacks, and Reconstruction, Freedmen's Education, 1862–1875* (Westport, Conn.: Greenwood Press, 1980), 9, 17, 74, 155, 202, 209; Kenneth Stampp and Leon F. Litwack, comps., *Reconstruction, An Anthology of Revisionist Writings* (Baton Rouge: Louisiana State University Press, 1969), 435–38; George M. Fredrickson, *The Black Image in the White Mind, The Debate on Afro-American Character and Destiny, 1817–1914* (New York: Harper and Row, 1971), 194–97.

5. William Gillette, *Retreat from Reconstruction, 1869–1879* (Baton Rouge: Louisiana State University Press, 1979), xiv; also see Lawanda and John H. Cox, eds., *Reconstruction, the Negro, and the New South* (New York: Harper and Row, 1973), xxviii.

6. Michael Perman, ed., *Major Problems in the Civil War and Reconstruction* (Lexington, Mass.: D.C. Heath and Co., 1991), 404; Eric Foner,

"Thaddeus Stevens, Confiscation, and Reconstruction," in *The Hofstadter Aegis, A Memorial,* eds. Stanley Elkins and Eric McKitrick (New York: Alfred A. Knopf, 1974), 160, 179, 182; Michael Perman, *Emancipation and Reconstruction, 1862–1879* (Arlington Heights, Ill.: Harlan Davidson, 1987), 36: Eric Foner, *Reconstruction, America's Unfinished Revolution, 1863–1877* (New York: Harper and Row, 1988), 134; *House Report No. 30,* 40th Cong., 2nd Sess., pp. 13–14.

7. "Reformed Text Books," *De Bow's Review,* 5 (Dec. 1868): 1107–8.

8. Edgar Wallace Knight, *The Influence of Reconstruction on Education in the South,* 2nd ed. (New York: Arno Press, 1969), 100; Marcus C. S. Noble, *A History of the Public Schools of North Carolina* (Chapel Hill: University of North Carolina Press, 1930), 219–32; J. Mills Thornton III, "Fiscal Policy and the Failure of Radical Reconstruction in the Lower South," in *Region, Race, and Reconstruction: Essays in Honor of C. Vann Woodward,* eds. J. Morgan Kousser and James M. McPherson (New York: Oxford University Press, 1982), 378–81.

9. William Channing Gannett and Edward Everett Hale, "The Education of the Freedmen," *North American Review* 101 (Oct. 1865): 530; John W. Blassingame, "The Union Army as an Educational Institution for Negroes, 1862–1865 " *Journal of Negro Education* 34, (Spring 1965): 152–59; Delo E. Washington, "Education of Freedmen and the Role of Self-Help in a Sea Island Setting, 1862–1982," *Agricultural History* 58 (July 1984): 442–45; *House Report No. 30,* 40th Cong., 2nd Sess., pp. 20–25.

10. Marjorie H. Parker, "Some Educational Activities of the Freedmen's Bureau," *Journal of Negro History* 23 (Winter 1954): 9–10., House Exec. Doc. No. 1, 39th Cong., 2nd Sess., pp. 716–17.

11. James D. Anderson, *The Education of Blacks in the South, 1860–1935* (Chapel Hill: University of North Carolina Press, 1988), 1–15; Luther Porter Jackson, "The Educational Efforts of the Freedmen's Bureau and Freedmen's Aid Societies in South Carolina, 1862–1872," *Journal of Negro History* 8 (Jan. 1923): 28; Jacqueline Jones, *Soldiers of Light and Love, Northern Teachers and Georgia Blacks, 1865–1873* (Chapel Hill: University of North Carolina Press, 1980), 9–26.

12. Jones, *Soldiers of Light,* 67, 139, 145; Parker, "Some Educational Activities," 19; Leon Litwack, *Been in the Storm So Long, The Aftermath of Slavery* (New York: Vantage Books, 1979), 453, 478; James M. McPherson, "The New Puritanism: Values and Goals of Freedmen's Education in America," in *The University in Society,* ed. Lawrence Stone, 2 vols. (Princeton: Princeton University Press, 1974), 2: 611–39; James M. McPherson, "White Liberals and Black Power in Negro Education, 1865–1915," *American Historical Review* 75 (June 1970): 1357–86.

13. William T. Alderson, Jr., "The Freedmen's Bureau and Negro Education in Virginia," *North Carolina Historical Review* 29 (Jan. 1952): 72; Elizabeth

Bethel, "The Freedmen's Bureau in Alabama," *The Journal of Southern History* 14 (Feb. 1948): 61–62: Walter L. Fleming, comp., *Documentary History of Reconstruction, Political, Military, Social, Religious, Educational and Industrial, 1865 to 1906*, 2 vols. (New York: McGraw-Hill, 1966: 1906–1907 reprint), 2: 167, 175.

14. Lawanda and John Cox, eds., *Reconstruction*, 38; *Cong. Globe*, 39th Cong., 1st Sess., pp. 321–22, 915–17, 3838, 3842; *Ibid.*, 40th Cong., 2nd Sess., p. 1996: Alton Hornsby, Jr., "The Freedmen's Bureau Schools in Texas, 1865–1870," *Southwestern Historical Quarterly* 76 (April 1973): 414.

15. John Eaton, Jr., *Report of the Commissioner of Education Made to the Secretary of the Interior for the Year 1870, With Accompanying Papers* (Washington: Government Printing Office, 1870), 286–87; *New York Times*, February 10, 1906, p.9, col. 5.

16. Foner, *Reconstruction*, 39–42. An attempt to mandate that the Southern states would create public school systems failed in Congress, but the expectation remained nonetheless. See Michael Les Benedict, *A Compromise of Principle, Congressional Republicans and Reconstruction, 1863–1869* (New York: W.W. Norton and Co., 1974), 242–43; David Tyack, Thomas James, Aaron Benavot, *Law and the Shaping of Public Education* (Madison: University of Wisconsin Press, 1987), 134.

17. Gannett and Hale, "Education of the Freedmen," p. 538; William P. Vaughn, "Partners in Segregation: Barnas Sears and the Peabody Fund," *Civil War History* 10 (Sept. 1964): 260.

18. Earle H. West, "The Peabody Fund and Negro Education, 1867–1880," *History of Education Quarterly* 6 (Summer 1966): 4–8: Vaughn, "Partners in Segregation," 260–74; *Cong. Globe*, 40th Cong., 1st Sess., pp. 28–30; R. W. D. Connor, "The Peabody Fund," *South Atlantic Quarterly* 4 (April 1905): 169–81; Jabez L.M. Curry, *A Brief Sketch of George Peabody and a History of the Peabody Fund Through Thirty Years* (Cambridge: University Press, 1898), 23–24.

19. William F. Messner, "Black Education in Louisiana, 1863–1865," *Civil War History* 22 (March 1976): 53; Daniel C. Gilman, "Thirty Years of the Peabody Education Fund," *Atlantic Monthly* 79 (Feb. 1897): 161–66.

20. Henry Allen Bullock, *A History of Negro Education in the South, From 1619 to the Present* (Cambridge: Harvard University Press, 1967), 49; Litwack, *Storm*, 490; Foner, *Reconstruction*, 321–22.

21. Edgar W. Knight, "Reconstruction and Education in South Carolina," *South Atlantic Quarterly* 18 (Oct. 1919): 357, 361; Edgar W Knight, "Reconstruction and Education in Virginia, " *South Atlantic Quarterly* 15 (Jan./April 1936): 29–34, 158; David Tyack and Robert Lowe, "The Constitutional Moment: Reconstruction and Black Education in the South," *American Journal of Education* 94 (Feb. 1986): 247.

22. William Preston Vaughn, *Schools for All, the Blacks and Public Education in the South, 1865–1877* (Lexington: University of Kentucky Press, 1974), 78, 84; Roger A. Fischer, *The Segregation Struggle in Louisiana, 1862–1877* (Urbana: University of Illinois Press, 1974), 93–102, 110–32; Fredrickson, *The Black Image in the White Mind*, 188–190; Fleming, comp., *Documentary History of Reconstruction*, 2: 187–90; "The Respectful Remonstrance, On Behalf of the White People of South Carolina, Against the Constitution of the Late Convention of that State, Now Submitted to Congress for Ratification, 1868" (pamphlet in Huntington Library manuscripts, San Marino, CA), 7–8; Knight, "South Carolina," 353; Alderson, "Freedmen's Bureau," 77; Henry Lee Swint, *The Northern Teacher in the South, 1862–1870*, 2nd ed. (New York: Octagon Books, 1967), 129.

23. J. L. Diman, "Religion in America, 1776–1876," *North American Review* 122 (Jan. 1876): 38–40; Kliebard, ed., "Religion and Education," 90.

24. Senate Mis. Doc. No. 5, 39th Cong., 1st Sess., p. 1 (emphasis is theirs); also see Andrew Jackson Rickoff, "A National Bureau of Education," *American Journal of Education* 16 (March 1866): 299–310: Emerson E. White, "National Bureau of Education," *American Journal of Education* 16 (March 1866): 177–86; *House Mis. Doc. No. 41*, 39th Cong. 1st Sess., pp. 1–3; *Cong. Globe*, 39th Cong., 1st Sess., p. 2967.

25. *Cong. Globe*, 39th Cong., 1st Sess., pp. 2969, 3044–48, 3270; *Cong. Globe*, Appendix, 39th Cong., 2nd Sess., pp. 197–99; "Department of Education Report," *House Report, No. 25*, 40th Cong., 3rd Sess., p. 1; Gordon Canfield Lee, *The Struggle for Federal Aid, First Phase: A History of the Attempts to Obtain Federal Aid for the Common Schools, 1870–1890* (New York: Bureau of Publications, Teachers College, Columbia University, 1949), 26; *House Exec. Doc. No. 315*, 41 Cong., 2nd Sess., pp. 3, 64, 71–72, 133, 137, 140, 195–217, 223–31, 254.

26. S. N. Clark to John Eaton, Jr., Chicago, February 10, 1870; J. B. Merwin to John Eaton, Jr., St. Louis, March 7, 1870; D. B. Hager to John Eaton, Jr., n.p., March 14, 1870; C. Warren to John Eaton, Jr., Washington, D.C., Dec. 2, 1870; John Eaton, Jr., to Barnas Sears, Washington, D.C., no month, no day, 1870 (Eaton Collection, Special Collections, Hoskins Library, University of Tennessee, Knoxville); *House Exec. Doc. No. 299*, 40th Cong., 2nd Sess., pp. 1–17; Edith Nye MacMullen, *In the Cause of True Education: Henry Barnard and Nineteenth Century School Reform* (New Haven: Yale University Press, 1991), 269–78: Robert Bingham Downs, *Henry Barnard* (Boston: Twayne Publishers, 1977), 45–46; Donald R. Warren, *To Enforce Education, A History of the Founding Years of the United States Office of Education* (Detroit: Wayne State University Press, 1974), 96, 104–5, 110–21.

27. "Education as an Element in the Reconstruction of the Union, a Lecture by J. P. Wickersham, Principal of the Pennsylvania State Normal School, Millersville, Pennsylvania, Delivered before the National Teachers'

Association, at Harrisburg, Pennsylvania, August 18, 1865" (pamphlet in Huntington Library manuscripts), 8–11; Fleming, comp. *Documentary History of Reconstruction*, 2: 171–74.

28. Garfield. "The Future of the Republic, Its Dangers and Its Hopes, An Address Delivered Before the Literary Socieities of Hudson College, July 2, 1873" (Cleveland: Nevins Bros., 1873) (pamphlet at Huntington Library), pp. 9–15; Burke A. Hinsdale, ed., *President Garfield and Education, Hiram College Memorial* (Boston: James R. Osgood and Co., 1882), 233–44.

29. John Eaton, Jr., "Report of the Commissioner of Education, 1871," *House Executive Document* 1, 42nd Cong., 2nd Sess., pp. 62, 67.

30. William Hepworth Dixon, *White Conquest*, 2 vols. (London: Chatto and Windus, 1876), 1: 233; Ibid., 2: 166, 345; "A National Education," *Harper's Weekly* 17 (September 6, 1875): 770; Ibid. 18 (December 5, 1874): 991; John Eaton, Jr., *Report of the Commissioner of Education for the Year 1874* (Washington, D.C.: GPO, 1875), 19; *New York Times*, March 7, 1871, p. 4, col. 3; Ibid., September 14, 1874, p. 4, col. 4; John Eaton, Jr., *Report of the Commissioner of Education for the Year 1873* (Washington, D.C.: GPO, 1874), 39; Eaton, "Report . . . , 1871," *House Executive Document* 1, 41st Cong., 3rd Sess., pp. 273, 347; William Hepworth Dixon, *New America*, 2 vols. (London: Hurst and Blackett, 1867), 2: 272; John Eaton, Jr., *Report of the Commissioner of Education for the Year 1872* (Washington, D.C.: GPO, 1873), 169.

31. *Chicago Tribune*, March 22, 1871, p. 2, col. 1; *New York Times*, March 24, 1871, p. 4, col. 4; *The Daily Picayune* [New Orleans], May 24, 1871, p. 4, col. 2; Rev. Isaac T. Hecker, "The Recent Events in France," *The Catholic World* 14 (Dec. 1871): 303.

32. n.a., "A National Education Fund," *The Republic: A Monthly Magazine Devoted to the Dissemination of Political Information* 1 (March 1873): 36–37.

33. Henry Wilson, "New Departure of the Republican Party," *The Atlantic Monthly* 27 (Jan. 1871): 114, 118–19.

34. Ibid., 119–20.

35. Victor Howard has written a book showing that religion played an important role in *informing* Radical Republican politics prior to 1870. See his *Religion and the Radical Republican Movement, 1860–1870* (Lexington: The University Press of Kentucky, 1990).

2. Church, State, and School

1. Henry A. Ford and Kate B. Ford, comps., *History of Cincinnati, Ohio, With Illustrations and Biographical Sketches* (Cleveland: L. A. Williams & Co., 1881), 168.

2. n.a., *The Bible in the Public Schools, Opinions of Individuals and of the Press* (New York: J. W. Schermerhorn & Co., 1870), 62–71; Amory Dwight Mayo, ed., *The Bible in the Public Schools, Addresses of Rev. A. D. Mayo and Rev. Thos. Vickers, of Cincinnati* (New York: J. W. Schermerhorn & Co., 1870), 61–63.

3. Mayo, ed., *Bible in the Public Schools*, 33, 61–63.

4. *Harper's Weekly* 19 (May 8, 1875): 384; Harold M. Helfman, "The Cincinnati 'Bible War,' 1869–1870," *The Ohio State Archaelogical and Historical Quarterly* 60 (Oct. 1951): 369–86.

5. *Superior Court of Cincinnati, the Bible in the Public Schools, Arguments in the Case of John D. Minor et al. versus the Board of Education of the City of Cincinnati* (Cincinnati: Robert Clarke & Co., 1870), 8–9, 13–14, 18–19.

6. Ibid., 390–91, 395, 405–6, 410–11, 414–15.

7. Herbert S. Duffy, *William Howard Taft* (New York: Minton, Balch & Co., 1930), 7–8, 25, 30, 51, 59, 65. Happily for the family name, Alphonso Taft's political proscription was not passed on to his progeny. His son William became President of the United States and his grandson Robert, a powerful United States Senator.

8. *The Bible in the Public Schools, Arguments Before the Superior Court of Cincinnati in the Case of Minor v. Board of Education of Cincinnati* (1870) *with the Opinions of the Court and the Opinion on Appeal of the Supreme Court of Ohio* (*New Introduction by Robert G. McCloskey*) (New York: Da Capo Press, 1969), 228; Charles Richard Williams, comp. *Diary and Letters of Rutherford Birchard Hayes, Nineteenth President of the United States*, 5 vols. (New York: Kraus Reprint Co., 1971), 3: 82.

9. George Hoadly, a Unitarian and a great-grandson of Jonathan Edwards, served with Matthews on the school board's legal staff in this case. Unlike Matthews, he was a Democrat and later served as Presidential candidate Samuel Tilden's lawyer in the disputed election of 1876. Whereas Republicans associated with the anti-Bible stance were virtually blackballed in electoral politics, Hoadly was elected Democratic governor of Ohio in 1883. Democrats placed far less emphasis on this issue, which they saw as demogogic fodder for Republicans, than did the party of Taft, Matthews, and Hayes. See *Bible in the Public Schools . . . (Introduction by Robert G. McCloskey)*, xii; Philip D. Jordan, *Ohio Comes of Age, 1873–1900* (Columbus: State Archaeological and Historical Society, 1943), 50.

10. *Superior Court of Cincinnati*, 355, 357, 360, 375, 376, 384; *The Independent*, Feb. 24, 1870, p. 4, col. 1.

11. Loyd D. Easton, *Hegel's First American Followers, The Ohio Hegelians: John B. Stallo, Peter Kaufmann, Moncure Conway, and August Willich, with Key Writings* (Athens: Ohio University Press, 1966), 59–71: n. a., "The Bible and

School Question," *The Christian World* 21 (April 1870): 113–17; *Bible in the Public Schools . . . (Introduction by Robert G. McCloskey)*, 64, 67, 80-83, 85, 93.

12. Damon Y. Kilgore, "The Bible in Public Schools, Address Upon a Resolution to Petition the Board of Education to Exclude the Bible from the Public Schools. Delivered Before the Liberal League of Philadelphia, October 17, 1875" (Philadelphia: Liberal League, 1875) (pamphlet at Huntington Library), 19–20; Robert Green Ingersoll, *The Gods and Other Lectures* (Peoria, Ill.: n.p., 1874), 14, 22.

13. *Bible in the Public Schools . . . (Introduction by Robert G. McCloskey)*, 284–85.

14. *Bible in the Public Schools, Opinions of Individuals and of the Press*, 8–9, 12–13; Rev. Samuel T. Spear, D. D., "Secular Education in Public Schools," *The Independent*, Feb. 10, 1876, p. 4, cols. 1–4.

15. *The Christian Union*, April 12, 1871, p. 232, col. 4.

16. Ibid., July 23, 1870, p. 38, col. 3; Ibid., August 20, 1870, p. 97, cols. 1–2; Ibid., August 27, 1870, p. 120, col. 4; Ibid., Sept. 24, 1870, p. 178, col. 4; Ibid., Oct. 1, 1870, p. 200, cols. 3–4, and p. 201, col. 1; Ibid., Oct. 15, 1870, p. 226, cols. 2–3; Henry Ward Beecher, *Patriotic Addresses* (New York: Fords, Howard & Hulbert, 1887), 764.

17. *Bible in the Public Schools, Opinions of Individuals and of the Press*, 41–51.

18. John Eaton, Jr., "Report of the Commissioner of Education, 1870," *House Executive Document 1*, 41st Cong., 3rd Sess., pp. 409–12; *The Christian Union*, June 12, 1872, p.2, col. 3; no author, "The Bible and School Question," *The Christian World* 21 (April 1870): 114.

19. n.a., "The School Question," *The Christian World* 21 (Feb. 1870): 40; *Bible in the Public Schools, Opinions of Individuals and of the Press*, 78–83, 92–98; Amory Dwight Mayo, ed., *The Bible in the Public Schools, Addresses of Rev. A. D. Mayo and Rev. Thomas Vickers, of Cincinnati* (New York: J. W. Schermerhorn & Co., 1870), 12–3.

20. Rev. Mark J. Hurley, *Church-State Relationships in Education in California* (Washington, D.C.: The Catholic University of America, 1948), 53; Mr. (illegible) Porter to John Eaton, Jr., Chicago, March 3, 1881 (Eaton Papers, Special Collections, Hoskins Library, University of Tennessee, Knoxville): James W. Sanders, *The Education of an Urban Minority: Catholics in Chicago, 1833–1965* (New York: Oxford University Press, 1977), 24–25, 33; *The Independent*, Jan. 6, 1876, p. 6, col. 4; *The Chicago Daily Tribune*, Oct. 5, 1875, p. 1, cols. 5–7; John Eaton, Jr., *Report of the Commissioner of Education for the Year 1873* (Washington, D.C.: GPO, 1874), 224–25; John Eaton, Jr., *Report of the Commissioner of Education for the Year 1876* (Washington, D.C.: GPO, 1878), 250.

21. John H. Westerhoff III, *McGuffey and His Readers, Peity, Morality, and Education in Nineteenth-Century America* (Nashville: Abington, 1978), 17, 75, 87–90, 100–3, 107; Richard D. Mosier, *Making the American Mind, Social and Moral Ideas in the McGuffey Readers* (New York: Russell and Russell, 1965), 89, 114, 122; Edward Eggleston, *The Schoolmaster's Stories for Boys and Girls* (Boston: Henry L. Shepard & Co., 1874), 130, 231–32.

22. Obadiah Bruen Brown, *The Song Reader, A Public School Singing Book* (Boston: Ditson & Co., 1870), 247–57; Cornelius C. Baldwin, "Moral Maxims, For Schools and Families" (Petersburg, VA: D'Arcy Paul and Co., 1876) (pamphlet at Huntington Library), 5–16; Professor Hayman, ed., *Acme Songs for Families and Schools. This Edition of 8,000 Copies Is Presented to the Pupils in the Public Schools of Poughkeepsie, and Dutchess County, New York* (New York: Acme Publishing Bureau, 1882), 1, 3, 5, 7, 9, 13, 15, 33, 48, 50; Andre Vessiot, "Instruction in Morals and Civil Government" (Washington, D.C.: Department of the Interior, Bureau of Education, GPO, 1882), 1–4; Mrs. Julia McNair Wright, *Practical Life; or, Ways and Means for Developing Character and Resources* (Philadelphia: J. C. McCurdy & Co., 1882), 191–92; Leslie Stephen, *The Science of Ethics* (New York: G. P. Putnam's Sons, 1882), 172–263; Michael Kammen, *Mystic Chords of Memory, The Transformation of Tradition in American Culture* (New York: Alfred A. Knopf, 1991), 194; for a state-by-state review of the extent of religious education in American public schools in the midseventies, see Francis Adams, *The Free School System of the United States* (London: Chapman and Hall, 1875), 146–59.

23. n.a., "The School Question," *The Christian World*, 21 (Feb. 1870): 55–60.

24. Orestes A. Brownson, "Valedictory," *Brownson's Quarterly Review*, Last Series 3 (Oct. 1875): 523–27.

25. Robert Michaelson, *Piety in the Public School, Trends and Issues in the Relationship between Religion and the Public School in the United States* (London: The McMillan Co., 1970), 119.

26. Rev. Samuel T. Spear, D.D., "The Methodist Convention at Syracuse," *The Independent*, March 10, 1870, p. 2, col. 2; Paul Kleppner, *The Third Electoral System, 1853–1892* (Chapel Hill: University of North Carolina Press, 1979), 222, 224.

27. Evangelical Protestants regularly used terms such as "Jesuitical conspiracy" or "ultramontane conspiracy" rather than "Roman Catholic conspiracy." Their inference was that if only the Roman Catholic church could be rid of its extremist leadership, it could be harmonious with American patriotism. Henry Wilson was a political spokesman for this view. Henry Wilson, "New Departure of the Republican Party," *The Atlantic Monthly* 27 (Jan. 1871): 114–20; Joseph F. Gower and Richard M. Leliaert, eds., *The Brownson-Hecker Correspondence* (South Bend: University of Notre Dame Press, 1979), 299–300.

28. n.a., "Church and State," *The Catholic World* 11 (May 1870): 145–60.

29. Mayo, *The Bible in the Public Schools*, 94, 97; *The Christian World* 21 (April 1870): 119; Ibid. 21 (July 1870): 200.

30. Rev. Julius H. Seelye, "The Christian Element in the State, A Sermon Delivered Before the Executive and Legislative Departments of the Government of Massachusetts, at the Annual Election, Wednesday, Jan. 5, 1870" (Boston: Wright and Potter, State Printers, 1870) (pamphlet at Huntington Library), 5–6, 10–11, 17–18, 20–26.

31. Rev. Richard Gleason Greene, "Christianity a National Law. An Election Sermon Preached Before the Executive and Legislative Departments of the Government of Massachusetts, in Hollis Street Church, Boston, Wednesday, January 7, 1874" (Boston: Wright and Potter, State Printers, 1874) (pamphlet at Huntington Library), 11, 18, 23, 28, 41, 44–45; in 1877, another Massachusetts state sermon was given on the same theme of Christianity as the national religion: see Rev. B. F. Hamilton, "'God in Government,' A Sermon Delivered Before the Executive and Legislative Departments of the Government of Massachusetts at the Annual Election, Wednesday January 3, 1877" (Boston: Albert J. Wright, State Printer, 1877) (pamphlet at Huntington Library).

32. Rev. Henry Martin Scudder, D.D., "The Catholics and the Public Schools" (New York: Mason, Baker & Pratt, 1873) (pamphlet at Huntington Library), 11–17.

33. John Eaton, Jr., "Report of the Commissioner of Education, 1870," 29; *The Bible in the Public Schools, Opinions of Individuals and of the Press*, 62–71: Michaelson, *Piety in the Public School, Trends and Issues*, 103; Ellen Lovell Evans, *The German Center Party, 1870–1933, A Study in Political Catholicism* (Carbondale: Southern Illinois University Press, 1981), 68–69.

34. Prof. Tayler Lewis, "Church and State," *The Independent*, 22 (April 28, 1870), p. 1, cols. 3–4.

35. Elisha Mulford, *The Nation: The Foundations of Civil Order and Political Life in the United States* (New York: Hurd and Houghton, 1870), 358, 364–65, 368, 371–72, 381–84, 398, 400, 416.

36. Rev. Rufus W. Clark, D.D., *The Question of the Hour: The Bible and the School Fund* (Boston: Lee and Shepard, 1870), 11, 29, 40–41, 56, 78–79, 83, 86, 102, Appendix (p. 2).

37. "The School Question," *The Christian World*, 21 (Feb. 1870): 44–46; Eric L. McKitrick, ed., *Slavery Defended: The Views of the Old South* (Englewood Cliffs, N.J.: Prentice-Hall, 1963), 11.

38. Alexis de Tocqueville, *Democracy in America*, edited by Richard D. Heffner (New York: New American Library, 1956), 117, 255.

39. Rev. Edwin T. Winkler, "Rome: Past, Present and Future, An Address Delivered Before the Southern Baptist Convention, In New Orleans, On Saturday, May 12, 1877" (Atlanta: James P. Harrison & Co., 1877) (pamphlet at Huntington Library), 3, 17–18, 20.

40. Mayo, *The Bible in the Public Schools*, 217; Rev. William Aikman, D.D., "Romanism at the South," *The Independent*, August 24, 1871, p. 2, cols. 3–4. Religious considerations then enabled white Republicans to mute their racial and class prejudices, so far as African Americans were concerned. Similarly, racial prejudice enabled Protestant Democrats to mute their religious and class prejudices, so far as Irish-American Catholics were concerned. Barbara J. Fields has argued that class is a more meaningful concept than race in discerning the dynamics of Reconstruction, yet at no time during Reconstruction did class solidarity enable significant numbers of Americans to mute either religious or racial antipathies although Frederick Douglass hoped for such a result. The only other possibility for class to emerge as a dominant consideration is to argue that both religious and racial sensibilities were simply symptoms of a false consciousness serving to divide the working class. Rather than pursuing this type of analysis, I have sought instead to portray the racial and religious belief systems of that era as they were presented at that time. See Barbara J. Fields, "Ideology and Race in American History," in *Region, Race and Reconstruction, Essays in Honor of C. Vann Woodward*, eds. J. Morgan Kousser and James M. McPherson York: Oxford University Press, 1982), 143–77.

41. Morton Borden, "The Christian Amendment," *Civil War History* 25 (June 1979): 156–67; John Bernard Stallo, "State Creeds and Their Modern Apostles. A Lecture Delivered in Rev. Mr. Vickers' Church, Cincinnati, on the Evening of April 3, 1870" (Cincinnati: R. Clarke, 1872), iii–viii: *The Independent*, May 12, 1870, p.2, cols. 3–5.

42. Jon C. Teaford, "Toward a Christian Nation: Religion, Law and Justice Strong," *Journal of Presbyterian History* 54 (Winter 1976): 422–37; *The Independent*, Feb. 19, 1874, p. 4, cols. 1–4; Philip Schaff, "Church and State in the United States," *Papers of the American Historical Association* 2 (1888): 420–21.

43. *The Christian Union*, Jan. 4, 1871, p. 3, col. 4.

44. Joseph P. Thompson, *Church and State in the United States, With An Appendix on the German Population* (Boston: James R. Osgood, and Co., 1873), 18–9, 25–26, 28, 113, 139; for a similar opinion, see John M. Leavitt, "Rome and Her Council," *The American Quarterly Church Review*, 22 (April 1870): 121.

45. Thompson, *Church and State*, 140–45, 152–53.

46. John Eaton, Jr., "Report of the Commissioner of Education, 1870," 254–55; *The Board of Education of the City of Cincinnati v. John D. Minor et al.*, 23; *Ohio State Reports, Granger*, 211; *The Christian Union*, July 2, 1873, p. 10, col. 1; Burton Confrey, *Secularism in American Education, Its History* (Washington,

D.C.: The Catholic University of America, 1931), 101; Bernard Mandel, "Religion and the Public Schools of Ohio," *The Ohio State Archaelogical and Historical Quarterly* 58 (April 1949): 195; John Lurie, "The Fourteenth Amendment: Use and Application in Selected State Court Civil Liberties Cases, 1870–1890—A Preliminary Assessment," *American Journal of Legal History* 28 (Oct. 1984): 303; Samuel Windsor Brown, *The Secularization of American Education, As Shown by State Legislation, State Constitutional Provisions and State Supreme Court Decisions*, 2nd ed. (New York: Russell & Russell. 1967), 144–45.

47. *The Independent*, August 12, 1875, p. 1, col. 4; John Eaton, Jr., *Report of the Commissioner of Education for the Year 1874* (Washington, D.C.: GPO, 1875), 328.

3. Dividing the School Funds

1. Diane Ravitch, *The Great School Wars: New York City, 1805–1973, A History of the Public Schools as Battlefield of Social Change* (New York: Basic Books, 1974), 93n; Rufus W. Clark, D.D., *The Question of the Hour, The Bible and the School Fund* (Boston: Lee and Shepard, 1870), 6; Eugene Lawrence, "The Democracy and Its Papal Guides," *Harper's Weekly* 19 (Oct. 9, 1875): 823.

2. Eugene Lawrence. "The Legislature and the Public Schools," *Harper's Weekly* 18 (Nov. 7, 1874): 918; Rev. Samuel T. Spear, D.D., "Roman Catholicism and the Public Schools," *The Independent*, Jan. 13, 1870, p. 1, cols. 7–8; Jesse T. Peck, D.D., "The Catholic School Question," *The Christian World* 20 (July 1869): 206–8.

3. Clark, *The Question of the Hour*, 29, 95; George P. Edgar, comp., "Both Sides of School Question, Attitude of the Democratic and Republican Parties" (New York: Holt Brothers, 1880) (pamphlet at Huntington Library), 3, 10; S.N. Clark to John Eaton, Jr., Chicago, April 7, 1870 (Eaton Papers, Special Collections, Hoskins Library, University of Tennessee, Knoxville).

4. Samuel Windsor Brown. *The Secularization of American Education, as Shown by State Legislation, State Constitutional Provisions and State Supreme Court Decisions* (New York: Russell and Russell, 1912), 95; *The Independent*, Feb. 22, 1872, p. 4, cols. 4–5; *Harper's Weekly* 18 (October 24, 1874): 870; Paul Kleppner, *The Third Electoral System, 1853–1892: Parties, Voters, and Political Cultures* (Chapel Hill: University of North Carolina Press, 1979), 146, 231–34; Richard J. Jensen, *The Winning of the Midwest: Social and Political Conflict, 1888–1896* (Chicago: University of Chicago Press, 1971), 59–61.

5. New York City Council of Political Reform, "Five Reports: 1) Surface Street Railroads; Value of their Franchises; Profits; Taxation; 2) A Tammany Permit Bureau; 3) Sectarian Appropriations of Public Money; 4) The Exposure of the Tammany Frauds; and 5) Duty of the State to Protect the Free Common Schools by Amendments to the Constitution, January 23, 1873" (New York:

Evening Post Steam Presses, 1873) (pamphlet at Huntington Library), Report #3, pp. 3, 10–6; Rev. Edward M. Connors, *Church-State Relationships in Education in the State of New York* (Washington, D.C.: The Catholic University of America Press, 1951), 94–96.

6. n.a., "Church and State," *Harper's Weekly* 17 (March 1, 1873): 170; George R. Crooks, "The Catholics and the Free Schools," Ibid. 20 (January 1, 1876): 10–11.

7. Ibid. 17 (Dec. 27, 1873): 1154–55; Ibid. 17 (Nov. 8, 1873): 986–87; *The Independent*, Oct. 30, 1873, p. 1362, col. 1; Zachary Montgomery, *The Poison Fountain or, Anti-Parental Education. Essays and Discussions on the School Question from a Parental and Non-Sectarian Standpoint, Wherein the Decline of Parental Authority, the Downfall of Family Government, and the Terrible Growth of Crime, Pauperism, Insanity and Suicides, in America, Are Traced Directly and Unmistakably to Our Anti-Parental Public School System* (San Francisco: Published by the Author, 1878), 1, 184–85. Although in this work, Montgomery pitched his opposition to the public schools in "non-sectarian" terms, he was, in fact, a long-time Catholic spokesman against public education.

8. John Eaton, Jr. , *Report of the Commissioner of Education for the Year 1875* (Washington, D.C.: GPO, 1876), xxxv.

9. *The Independent*, March 13, 1873, p. 339, cols. 1–2: *Harper's Weekly* 17 (Sept. 27, 1873): 854.

10. Rev. Samuel T. Spear, D.D., "Religion and the Constitution," *The Independent*, July 14, 1870, p. 2, cols. 1–2: Ibid., Feb.22, 1872, p. 4, cols. 4–5.

11. Elisha P. Hurlbut, *A Secular View of Religion in the State, and The Bible in the Public Schools* (Albany, New York: Joel Munsell, 1870), 5.

12. Ibid., 13–14, 17–18, 20–21, 24, 37–40.

13. *The Independent*, Jan. 11, 1872, p. 4, col. 3; *Harper's Weekly* 17 (Aug. 30, 1873): 756; Rev. Calvin A. Poage, "Lecture on 'Our Public Schools,' August 31st, 1873" (San Francisco: G. W. Hagans, 1873) (pamphlet at Bancroft Library, U.C., Berkeley), 14; n.a., "The School Question," *The Catholic World* 11 (April 1870): 100–1; *The Christian Union*, Oct. 11, 1871, p. 228, cols. 1–4; n.a., "Education," *The Atlantic Monthly* 35 (Feb. 1875): 254.

14. In Arthur M. Schlesinger, Jr.'s judgment, Brownson was not only the leading American *Catholic* intellectual of his age, but the leading American intellectual of any persuasion. See Arthur M. Schlesinger, Jr., *Orestes A. Brownson, A Pilgrim's Progress* (Boston: Little, Brown and Co., 1939), 294; Rev. Joseph Emerson, "O. A. Brownson on Catholic Schools," *The Christian World* 21 (May 1870): 135–37; Neil G. McCluskey, ed., *Catholic Education in America: A Documentary History* (New York: Teachers College, Columbia University, 1964), 102–20; James M., McDonnell, Orestes A. *Brownson and Nineteenth-Century*

Catholic Education (New York: Garland Publishing, 1988), 156–59, 162, 166., Orestes A. Brownson, "Whose Is the Child?" *Brownson's Quarterly Review (Last Series)* 3 (July 1873): 289–92; Rev. Samuel T. Spear, D.D., "The Solution of the School Question," *The Independent*, Jan. 20, 1870, p. 1, cols. 4–6; n.a., "Who Is to Educate Our Children?" *The Catholic World* 14 (January 1872): 433–47; Rev. P. Bayma, S.J., "The Liberalistic View of the Public School Question," *American Catholic Quarterly Review* 2 (Jan.–Oct. 1877): 1, 11–12.

15. Bayma, "The Liberalistic View," 5, 10–2, 14, 16, 26; W. M. Marshall, LL.D., "Secular Education in England and the United States," *American Catholic Quarterly Review* 1 (Jan.–Oct. 1876): 278–312; Joseph F. Gower and Richard M. Leliaert, eds., *The Brownson-Hecker Correspondence* (South Bend: University of Notre Dame Press, 1979), 312–13.

16. *The Chicago Tribune*, Feb. 4, 1875, p. 4, col. 7; Ibid., Feb. 14, 1875, p. 8, col. 7; *The Independent*, May 27, 1875, p. 5, cols. 1–3.

17. *The Independent*, Dec. 31, 1874, p. 15, cols. 1–2: Rev. James A. Burns, *The Growth and Development of the Catholic School System in the United States* (New York: Benziger Bros., 1912), 189–91, 253–58: W. F. Jamieson, *The Clergy, A Source of Danger to the American Republic* (Chicago: Published by W. F. Jamieson, 1872), 186.

18. n.a., "The Educational Question," *The Catholic World* 9 (April 1869): 122; Right Rev. Richard Gilmour, D.D., *Bible History Containing the Most Remarkable Events of the Old and New Testaments, To Which Is Added a Compendium of Church History. For the use of the Catholic Schools in the United States*, 2nd ed. (New York: Benziger Bros., 1881), 103–4; n.a., "The School Question," *The Christian World* 21 (Feb. 1870): 35.

19. n.a., "The School Question," *The Christian World* 21 (Feb. 1879): 58: Henry Ward Beecher, *Patriotic Addresses* (New York: Fords, Howard, & Hulbert, 1887), 756; *The Independent*, July 30, 1874, p. 18, col. 2; Ibid., Aug.20, 1874, p. 16, col. 3; Ibid., July 8, 1875, p. 14, col. 1; Ibid., Feb. 10, 1876, p. 1, col. 1; John E. Doyle, *Plymouth Church and Its Pastor, or Henry Ward Beecher and His Accusers* (Hartford, CN: The Park Publishing Co., 1874), 263; Altina L. Waller, *Reverend Beecher and Mrs. Tilton, Sex and Class in Victorian America* (Amherst: University of Massachusetts Press, 1982), 1, 4, 6–14, 16, 52–53, 99–100, 109–10, 115–16, 126, 137; Clifford E. Clark, Jr., *Henry Ward Beecher, Spokesman for a Middle-Class America* (Urbana: University of Illinois Press, 1978), 182, 187–94, 222–24; Charles F. Marshall, *The True History of the Brooklyn Scandal, Being a Complete Account of the Trial of the Rev. Henry Ward Beecher, of Plymouth Church, Brooklyn, Upon Charges Preferred by Theodore Tilton* (Philadelphia: National Publishing Co., 1875), 600–1, 609.

20. Orestes A. Brownson, "Bismarck and the Church," *Brownson's Quarterly Review (Last Series)* 2 (April 1873): 268, 271; *The Christian Union*, Sept. 6, 1871, 152: 1–2; Ibid., Sept. 13, 1871, 165: 3.

21. Orestes A. Brownson, "Democracy Favors Inequality, and Is a Heavy Burden to the People," *Brownson's Quarterly Review (Last Series)* 2 (April 1873): 235–59.

22. Orestes A. Brownson, "The Papacy and the Republic," Ibid. 1 (Jan. 1873): 21–33; Orestes A. Brownson, "Education and the Republic," Ibid. 2 (Jan. 1874): 37–54.

23. Orestes A. Brownson, "The Public School System," Ibid. 3 (Oct. 1875): 536: Gower and Leliaert, eds, *The Brownson-Hecker Correspondence*, 291–93.

24. Gower and Leliaert, eds., Ibid., 278–83; Rev. Aug. J. Thebaud, S.J., "The Church and the State," *American Catholic Quarterly Review* 2 (Jan.–Oct. 1877): 449–50; n.a., "The Secular Not Supreme," The Catholic World 13 (Aug. 1871): 688; David J. O'Brien, *Isaac Hecker, An American Catholic* (New York: Paulist Press, 1992), 242–58.

25. W. M. Marshall, LL.D., "Secular Education in England and the United States," *American Catholic Quarterly Review* 1 (Jan.–Oct. 1876): 278–312; Rev. John M. Leavitt, "Rome and Her Council," *American Catholic Quarterly Review* 22 (April 1870): 122; William Lloyd Garrison, "Papal Infallibility," *The Independent*, June 9, 1870, 1: 5–6; no author, "The Catholic of the Nineteenth Century," *The Catholic World* 11 (July 1870): 436, 440; Rev. Isaac T. Hecker, "Unification and Education," *The Catholic World* 13 (April 1871): 5–10.

26. Orestes A. Brownson, "The Church Above the State," *Brownson's Quarterly Review (Last Series)* 3 (July 1873): 352–67: no author, "The New Board of Education," *Harper's Weekly* 17 (April 12, 1873): 290; Charles Richard Williams, comp., *Diary and Letters of Rutherford Birchard Hayes, Nineteenth President of the United States*, 5 vols. (New York: Kraus Reprint Co., 1971) 3: 248; Right Rev. Ingraham Kip, D.D., "Characteristics of the Age: A Charge to the Clergy of the Diocese of California" (San Francisco: Cubery Sr Co., 1876) (pamphlet at Huntington Library), 13; *New York Times*, Oct. 1, 1871, p. 4, cols. 4–5; *Harper's Weekly* 17 (May 3, 1873): 362; Ibid, 17 (July 5, 1873): 570; Ibid. 18 (Dec. 19, 1874): front cover and 1046; Ibid. 18 (Feb. 7, 1874): 136; Ibid. 18 (Feb. 28, 1874): 204; Henry Ward Beecher, *Patriotic Addresses* (New York: Fords, Howard, & Hulbert, 1887), 756.

27. *The Christian Union*, July 12, 1871, p. 24, col. 4; Ibid., July 19, 1871, p. 40, cols. 1–2, and p. 445, col. 1; Ibid., Aug. 16, 1871, p. 102, col. 3.

28. *The Independent*, July 20, 1871, p. 4, cols. 1–2: *The Christian Union*, Nov. 8, 1871, p. 296, cols. 1–3.

29. *The Christian Union*, March 8, 1871, p. 153, col. 1; Ibid., April 12, 1871, p. 233, col. 3; "American Irish and American Germans," *Scribner's Monthly* 6 (June 1873): 172–79.

30. Arthur M. Schlesinger, Jr., *The Disuniting of America* (New York: W. W. Norton and Co., 1991), 29.

31. *The Independent*, Jan. 12, 1871, p. 2, cols. 4–5.

32. John Eaton, Jr., *Report of the Commissioner of Education for the Year 1875* (Washington, D.C.: GPO, 1876), 140; *The Christian Union*, Feb. 1, 1871, p. 73, col. 1; Ibid., April 5, 1871, p. 215, col. 1; Henry Ward Beecher, "Compulsory Education" [Speech of Jan. 9, 1873, in *New York Tribune*, lectures and letters— Extra Sheet, no date] (Newspaper fragment in Huntington Library manuscripts); New York City Council of Political Reform, "Report on Compulsory Education, Dec. 30, 1873" (New York: Evening Post Steam Presses, 1874) (pamphlet at Huntington Library), 1–12; John Eaton, Jr., "Report of the Commissioner of Education, 1870," *House Executive Document 1*, 41st Cong., 3rd Sess., p. 273; *Harper's Weekly* 17 (Feb.8, 1873): 114; Ibid. 18 (Jan. 17, 1874): 50–1; Ibid. 18 (Dec. 5, 1874): 991; *The Chicago Daily Tribune*, Feb. 4, 1875, p. 4, col. 7; David Tyack, Thomas James, Aaron Benavot, *Law and the Shaping of Public Education, 1785–1954* (Madison: University of Wisconsin Press, 1987), 96–98.

33. n.a., "The School Question," *The Catholic World* 11 (April 1870): 95–104; n.a., "A Word to the *Independent*," *The Catholic World* 13 (April 1871): 252.

34. *Harper's Weekly* 17 (Nov. 8, 1873): 1000; Ibid. 17 (Nov. 15, 1873): 1010; Ibid. 18 (Nov. 7, 1874): 918; Felice A. Bonadio, *North of Reconstruction, Ohio Politics, 1865–1870* (New York: New York University Press, 1970), 1, 23, 194; Philip D. Jordan, *Ohio Comes of Age, 1873-1900* (Columbus: Ohio State Archaelogical and Historical Society, 1943), 32–36, 40–41, 44–49; *The Independent*, Sept. 10, 1874, p. 17, col. 4; Rufus King, *Ohio, First Fruits of the Ordinance of 1787*, 2nd ed. (Boston: Houghton, Mifflin and Co., 1903), 416; George W. Knepper, *Ohio and Its People* (Kent, Ohio: Kent State University Press, 1989), 277; George P. Edgar (Secretary of National School League), comp., "Both Sides of School Question, Attitude of the Democratic and Republican Parties" (New York: Holt Brothers, 1880) (pamphlet at Huntington Library), 12–13.

35. Eugene Holloway Roseboom and Francis Phelps Weisenburger, *A History of Ohio* (New York: Prentice-Hall, 1934), 339–41.

36. (Charles Henry Pullen), *Miss Columbia's Public School; or, Will It Blow Over? By a Cosmopolitan. With 72 Illustrations by Thomas Nast* (New York: Frances B. Felt & Co., 1871), 33, 36, 37, 39–40.

37. Ibid., 41, 55, 81.

38. For a representative sample of Eugene Lawrence's articles glorifying Bismarck's *Kulturkampf*, see his "German Americans," *Harper's Weekly* 17

(March 15, 1873): 203; "Lawless Bishops," Ibid. 17 (March 29, 1873): 246; "A Divided Allegiance," Ibid. 19 (March 13, 1875): 218; "Master and Slaves," Ibid. 19 (May 1, 1875): 357; "The Public Schools and Their Foes," Ibid. 19 (May 8, 1875): 386; "Political Priests," Ibid. 19 (September 25, 1875): 782; "Germany and the School Question," Ibid. 19 (October 2, 1875): 805–6.

4. Educating the Freedmen

1. G. S. Ghurye, *Caste and Race in India* (Bombay: Popular Prakashan, 1969), 172–73; R. C. Zaehner, *Hinduism* (London: Oxford University Press, 1962), 142; Carl Degler, *Neither Black Nor White, Slavery and Race Relations in Brazil and the United States* (Madison: University of Wisconsin Press, 1971), 287–92. Barbara J. Fields has emphasized that white racism is a concept having no real meaning outside of specific ideological contexts necessarily defined by class and economic considerations. See Barbara J. Fields, "Ideology and Race in American History," *Region, Race and Reconstruction, Essays in Honor of C. Vann Woodward*, edited by J. Morgan Kousser and James M. McPherson (New York: Oxford University Press, 1882), 143–77. An elaboration of her thesis can be seen in Noel Ignatiev, *How the Irish Became White* (New York: Routledge, 1995), 178–88. From this neo-Marxist perspective, African American and Irish members of the working class were artificially divided by a false racial fetish. While not ignoring class issues in this history, I do not emphasize them to the point of reducing the dramatic political interplay between racial and religious prejudices that dominated the political discourse of Reconstruction during the 1870s. For additional commentary concerning Barbara J. Field's essay, see endnote #40 in Chapter 2.

2. Albion W. Tourgee, *An Appeal to Caesar* (New York: Fords, Howard, and Hulbert, 1884), 269, 283–85.

3. Ibid., 390–91; John S. Hager, *The Louisiana Case. Equality of Man and Social Equality of Race. Speech of Hon. John S. Hager, of California, in the Senate of the United States, Wednesday, February 17, 1875* (Washington, D.C.: GPO, 1875), 30–31.

4. Leon Litwack, *North of Slavery, The Negro in the Free States, 1790–1860* (Chicago: University of Chicago Press, 1961), 113–52.

5. Hager, *The Louisiana Case*, 35; Thomas Francis Bayard, *White and Black Children in Public Schools. Speech of Hon. Thomas F. Bayard . . . Delivered in the Senate of the United States, May 4, 1872* (Washington, D.C.: F. & J. Rives and G.A. Bailey, 1872), 9.

6. George Weston, *The Progress of Slavery in the United States* (Washington, D.C.: Published by the Author, 1857), 122–26; *New York Times*, March 7, 1871, p. 4, col. 3; *Cong. Globe, Appendix*, 42nd Cong., 2nd Sess., pp.

15–17. In 1889, Virginian Lewis H. Blair attempted to persuade his fellow whites that "mixed schools" would not lead to cultural decay among whites. "The higher are rarely, if ever," he wrote, "demoralized by the lower. Influence descends, and if we mingle in the same schools the whites will not be demoralized, because they are the higher, the nobler, the richer; but the blacks through the influence of the whites will be elevated. The danger of contamination will not be from black but from bad white children." Segregated schooling, he argued, alone kept blacks in a degraded condition, and, he proposed, it was up to superior whites to "rescue" them. Blair attempted to force whites to confront the logic of their own racism, which he obviously shared. It did not work. As G. Vann Woodward notes, Blair's argument "had little influence" in changing any minds. In truth, whites believed their culture to be more refined and delicate than that of African Americans, but they also believed that their culture was weaker in an environment of free and open competition and could not survive racial integration. See Lewis H. Blair, *A Southern Prophecy: The Prosperity of the South Dependent Upon the Elevation of the Negro*, ed. C. Vann Woodward (Boston: Little, Brown and Co., 1964), xi, 145, 149, 182.

7. "Message of the President of the United States, Communicating in Compliance with a Resolution of the Senate of the 12th Instant, Information in Relation to the States of the Union Lately in Rebellion, Accompanied by a Report of Carl Schurz," *Senate Executive Documents*, 39th Cong., 1st Sess., #2, pp. 15–16, 27–32.

8. John Eaton, Jr., "Report of the Commissioner of Education, 1871," *House Executive Document I*, 42nd Cong., 2nd Sess., pp. 22–23, 388–89; "Letter of the Secretary of the Interior Communicating in Compliance with the Resolution of the Senate of the 8th of December, 1870, the Reports of the Board of Trustees of Colored Schools of Washington and Georgetown," *Senate Executive Documents*, 41st Cong., 3rd Sess., #20, pp. 8–9, 11–14.

9. Charles Stearns, *The Black Man of the South and the Rebels; or, the Characteristics of the Former, and the Recent Outrages of the Latter* (New York: American News Company, 1872), 218, 331–38; Job E. Stevenson, Ku-Klux Conspiracy. *Speech of Hon. Job E. Stevenson, of Ohio, Delivered in the House of Representatives, May 30, 1872* (Washington, D.C.: n.p., 1872), 5; Charles Nordhoff, *The Cotton States in the Spring and Summer of 1875* (New York: Burt Franklin, 1965: 1876 reprint), 22.

10. Nordhoff, *Cotton States*, 49.

11. Edward King, *The Southern States of North America: A Record of Journeys in Louisiana, Texas, the Indian Territory, Missouri, Arkansas, Mississippi. Alabama, Georgia, Florida, South Carolina, North Carolina, Kentucky, Tennessee, Virginia, West Virginia and Maryland* (London: Blackie & Son, 1875), 316, 779.

12. Stearns, *Black Man of the South*, 388–89, 479, 482.

13. Mark Twain and Charles Dudley Warner, *The Gilded Age, A Tale of Today*, 2 vols. (New York: F. F. Collier and Son Co., 1873), 1: 200; Steams, *Black Man of the South*, 517–19.

14. Sir George Campbell, *White and Black, The Outcome of a Visit to the United States* (New York: Negro Universities Press, 1969: 1879), 133–34.

15. *Harper's Weekly* 17 (June 14, 1873): 499.

16. Charles Sumner, *Equality Before the Law; Unconstitutionality of Separate Colored Schools in Massachusetts, Argument of Charles Sumner, Esq., Before the Supreme Court of Massachusetts, in the Case of Sarah C. Roberts vs. the City of Boston, Dec. 4, 1849* (Washington, D.C.: F. & J. Rives and George A. Bailey, 1870), 9, 14–15 (emphases are Sumner's); Carl F. Kaestle, *Pillars of the Republic, Common Schools and American Society, 1780–1860* (New York: Hill and Wang, 1983), 178–79.

17. L. B. Eaton to John Eaton, Jr., Memphis, March 15, 1871 (Eaton Papers, Special Collections, Hoskins Library University of Tennessee, Knoxville); Beverly Wilson Palmer, ed., *The Selected Letters of Charles Sumner*, 2 vols. (Boston: Northeastern University Press, 1990), 2: 289–91, 553; David Donald, *Charles Sumner and the Rights of Man* (New York: Alfred A. Knopf, 1970), 251–52.

18. Edgar W. Knight, "Reconstruction and Education in Virginia," *South Atlantic Quarterly* 15 (Jan./April 1916): 29–35.

19. Richard Lowe, "Another Look at Reconstruction in Virginia," *Civil War History* 32 (March 1986): 72–75.

20. *Cong. Globe, Appendix*, 41st Cong., 2nd Sess., p. 45; R. W. Hughes to William G. Brownlow, Richmond, Virginia, Jan. 16, 1870 (Brownlow Papers, Special Collections, Hoskins Library, University of Tennessee, Knoxville); Congress had just reinstated military rule for Georgia, because of its legislature's refusal to seat elected African-American representatives. Due to Georgia's obstinacy, Congress required it to ratify the Fifteenth Amendment, a requirement beyond what it had initially needed to do to be first readmitted in 1868. The concept of states rights was not high on the Republican agenda in 1870. See Kenneth Coleman, et al., *A History of Georgia* (Athens: University of Georgia, 1991: 2nd ed.), 214–15.

21. *Cong. Globe*, 41st Cong., 2nd Sess., pp. 598–99, 602, 605.

22. Ibid., pp. 442–43; Charles T. Adams to John Eaton, Jr., Chicago, Jan. 28, 1870; A. L. Snow to John Eaton, Jr., Tazwell, Tenn., Feb. 10, 1870; John C. Nelson to John Eaton, Jr., Kingston, Tenn., March 3, 1870; Charles D. McGuffey to John Eaton, Jr., Cincinnati, Oct. 24, 1870 (Eaton Papers); Stephen V. Ash, *Middle Tennessee Society Transformed, 1860–1870: War and Peace in the Upper South* (Baton Rouge: Louisiana State University Press, 1988), 179n;

Charles William Dabney, *Universal Education in the South*, 2nd ed., 2 vols. (New York: Arno Press & The New York Times, 1969), 1: 297–301.

23. *Journal of the Proceedings of the Convention of Delegates Elected by the People of Tennessee, to Amend, Reverse, or Form and Make a New Constitution for the State. Assembled in the City of Nashville, Jan. 10, 1870* (Nashville: Jones, Purvis & Co., 1870), 436–38: *Cong. Globe, Appendix*, 41st Cong., 2nd Sess, p. 60.

24. *Cong Globe*, 41st Cong., 2nd Sess, pp. 71–72, 469–71, 492–95.

25. Ibid., pp. 546, 566.

26. Ibid., pp. 569, 644, 725.

27. Ibid., pp. 1254, 1255, 1259.

28. Ibid., pp. 1323–24, 1327–28.

29. Ibid., pp. 1366, 1970, 2271.

30. Dabney, *Universal Education In the South*, 1: 143.

31. Ibid., 144–48; Eaton, "Report . . . 1871," 10; Walter J. Fraser, "William Henry Ruffner and the Establishment of Virginia's Public School System, 1870–1874," *Virginia Magazine of History and Biography* 79 (July 1971): 265–69; William Henry Ruffner, *The Public Free School System. Dr. Dabney Answered by Mr. Ruffner* (Richmond: *Richmond Dispatch* and *Richmond Enquirer*, 1876), 9–10, 41; *Virginia School Report, 1871. First Annual Report of the Superintendent of Public Instruction, For the Year Ending August 31, 1871* (Richmond: C.A. Schaffter, Superintendent Public Printing, 1871), 109; William A. Link, *A Hard Country and a Lonely Place: Schooling, Society and Reform in Rural Virginia, 1870–1920* (Chapel Hill: University of North Carolina Press, 1986), 17.

32. Gilbert Carlton Walker, "Letter of Governor Walker on the Public School System, September 28, 1870," *The Educational Journal of Virginia* 1 (Oct. 1870): 394–96; William H. Ruffner, "Letter to County Superintendents of Schools, Oct. 1, 1870," Ibid., 397–400.

33. Knight, "Education in Virginia," 159, 162–67; Cornelius J. Heatwole, *A History of Education in Virginia* (New York: The Macmillan Co., 1916), 220–27, 243; n.a., "Thoughts on Repudiation of the Debt of Virginia" (Charlottesville, VA: Jefferson Book and Job Print Rooms, 1875?) (pamphlet at Huntington Library), 4–7, 9: "Clergyman," "Repudiation Is Theft—Forcible Adjustment Highway Robbery" (Richmond: n.p., 1876) (pamphlet at Huntington Library), 2, 4, 5, 12–13, 15–16; Republican Party, Virginia State Central Committee, "An Address to the People of Virginia" (Richmond: n.p., 1876) (pamphlet at Huntington Library), 3.

34. A. S. Rankin to John Eaton, Jr., Mhoons Landing, Mississippi, Nov. 14, 1871 (Eaton Papers). Rankin's "actual" salary of $45 per month in 1871 was

higher than the average reported for Mississippi in 1877. In that latter year, both male and female teachers in Mississippi were averaging $29 per month. Of course, Rankin's $45 in state script could only be redeemed for $2.25. John Eaton, Jr., *Report of the Commissioner of Education for the Year 1877* (Washington, D.C.: Government Printing Office, 1879), xix; Richard Nelson Current, *Those Terrible Carpetbaggers, A Reinterpretation* (New York: Oxford University Press, 1988), 317; Kenneth M. Stampp and Leon F. Litwack, comps, *Reconstruction, An Anthology of Revisionist Writings* (Baton Rouge: Louisiana State University Press, 1969), 338–69; Allen W. Trelease, *White Terror, The Ku Klux Klan Conspiracy and Southern Reconstruction* (New York: Harper & Row, 1971), 294; Eric Foner, *Reconstruction, America's Unfinished Revolution, 1863–1877* (New York: Harper and Row, 1988), 367, 375–76.

35. H. R. Pease to John Eaton, Jr., Jackson, Mississippi, August 5, 1871 (Eaton Papers); Foner, *Reconstruction,* 376; William C. Harris, *The Day of the Carpetbagger, Republican Reconstruction in Mississippi* (Baton Rouge: LSU Press, 1979), 311–36, 619; Richard Aubrey McLemore, ed., *A History of Mississippi,* 2 vols. (Hattiesburg: University and College Press of Mississippi, 1973), 1: 623–34; Stuart Grayson Noble, *Forty Years of the Public Schools in Mississippi, With Special Reference to the Education of the Negro* (New York: Press of Teachers' College, Columbia University, 1918), 10, 14, 33, 36, 38–41, 45; James Wilford Garner, *Reconstruction in Mississippi* (New York: The MacMillan Co., 1901), 356–66, 370–71, 404–5; Nordhoff, *The Cotton States . . . 1875,* 74; Walter L. Fleming, comp., *Documentary History of Reconstruction, Political, Military, Social, Religious, Educational & Industrial, 1865 to the Present Time,* 2 vols. (Cleveland, Ohio: The Arthur H. Clark Co., 1907), 2: 398.

36. *The Christian Union,* November 15, 1871, p. 310, col. 4; Carl H. Moneyhon, "Public Education and Texas Reconstruction Politics, 1871–1874," *Southwestern Historical Quarterly* 92 (Jan. 1989): 393–416; Frederick Eby, *The Development of Education in Texas* (New York: The MacMillan Co., 1925), 158–69; Samuel Windsor Brown, *The Secularization of American Education, As Shown by State Legislation, State Constitutional Provisions and State Supreme Court Decisions,* 2nd ed. (New York: Russell and Russell, 1967), 50; John J. Lane, *History of Education in Texas* (Washington, D.C.: GPO, 1903), 32; *Journal of the Constitutional Convention of the State of Texas, Begun and Held at the City of Austin, September 6th, 1875* (Galveston: The "News" Office, 1875), 45, 55, 79, 80, 119, 123, 136, 142, 395, 510, 511, 516, 523, 608; William Riley Davis, *The Development and Present Status of Negro Education in East Texas* (New York: Columbia University, 1934), 14–16.

37. John Eaton, Jr., *Report of the Commissioner of Education for the Year 1873* (Washington: GPO, 1874), 384–85; Eby, *Education in Texas,* 159.

38. Clara Mildred Thompson, *Reconstruction in Georgia, Economic, Social, Political, 1865–1872,* 2nd ed. (Gloucester, Mass.: Peter Smith, 1964), 229, 271, 275, 336–38; Dorothy Orr, *A History of Education in Georgia* (Chapel Hill:

University of North Carolina Press, 1950) 207; Alan Conway, *The Reconstruction of Georgia* (Minneapolis: University of Minnesota Press, 1966), 86, 92–95, 99; Stearns, *The Black Man of the South*, 482; Robert Somers, *The Southern States Since the War, 1870–1875* (London and New York: MacMillan and Co., 1871), 98–99.

39. Eaton, *Report . . . 1873*, p. xiv; Eaton, *Report . . . 1874*, 71–72.

40. J. H. Glendening to John Eaton, Jr., Fort Smith, Arkansas, August 14, 1871 (Eaton Papers); Nordhoff, *The Cotton States*, 39; Dabney, *Universal Education in the South*, 1: 390–91.

41. John Eaton, Jr. *Report of the Commissioner of Education for the Year 1872* (Washington, D.C.: GPO, 1873), xviiin.

42. Nordhoff, *The Cotton States*, 45, 52, 67, 72.

43. Betty Porter, "The History of Negro Education in Louisiana," *Louisiana Historical Quarterly* 25 (July 1942): 758; Joe Gray Taylor, *Louisiana Reconstructed, 1863–1877* (Baton Rouge: LSU Press, 1974), 465; Eaton, *Report . . . 1872*, 134; Eaton, *Report . . . 1874*, 148; Fleming, comp., *Documentary History of Reconstruction*, 2: 198–99.

44. John Wallace, *Carpet-bag Rule in Florida; The Inside Workings of the Reconstruction of Civil Government in Florida After the Close of the Civil War*, 2nd ed. (Gainsville: University of Florida Press, 1964), 325–26; Edward King, *The Southern States of North America, A Record of Journeys In Louisiana, Texas, The Indian Territory, Missouri, Arkansas, Mississippi, Alabama, Georgia, Florida, South Carolina, North Carolina, Kentucky, Tennessee, Virginia, West Virginia and Maryland* (London: Blackie & Son, 1875), 421.

45. Dabney, *Universal Education in the South*, 1: 332–34; Fleming, comp., *Documentary History of Reconstruction*, 2: 205–6.

46. Eaton, *Report . . . 1874*, 65.

47. Somers, *Southern States Since the War*, 169–71; King, *Southern States of North America*, 343; Fleming, comp., *Documentary History of Reconstruction*, 2: 198.

48. Daniel Jay Whitener, "Public Education in North Carolina During Reconstruction, 1865–1876," *Essays in Southern History*, ed. Fletcher Melvin Green (Chapel Hill: University of North Carolina Press, 1949), 67–71, 75–77, 88–90; Dabney, *Universal Education in the South*, 1: 174–176; M. C. S. Noble, *A History of the Public Schools of North Carolina* (Chapel Hill: University of North Carolina, 1930), 354.

49. Edgar W. Knight, "Reconstruction and Education in South Carolina," *South Atlantic Quarterly* 18 (1919): 56–58, 61, 368; King, *Southern States of North America*, 463.

50. "Proceedings of the Tax-Payers' Convention of South Carolina. Held at Columbia, Beginning May 9th, and Ending May 12, 1871" (Charleston: Edward Perry, Printer, 1871) (pamphlet at Huntington Library), 17, 22, 45, 59, 61, 117; Dabney, *Universal Education in the South*, 234.

51. Hon. Daniel Wolsey Voorhees, "The Plunder of Eleven States by the Republican Party. Speech of Hon. Daniel W. Voorhees, of Indiana. Delivered in the House of Representatives, March 23, 1872" (Washington, D.C.: F. & J. Rives & G. A. Bailey, 1872) (pamphlet at Huntington Library), 13, 14.

52. *The Enterprise and Mountaineer* (Greenville, South Carolina), Sept. 11, 1872, p. 4, cols. 1–4; Alrutheus Ambush Taylor, *The Negro in South Carolina During Reconstruction*, 2nd ed. (New York: Russell and Russell, 1969), 196–97; for a thesis stressing the significance of the white complaint about high taxes in Southern states during Reconstruction, see J. Mills Thornton III, "Fiscal Policy and the Failure of Radical Reconstruction in the Lower South." *Region, Race, and Reconstruction: Essays in Honor of C. Vann Woodward*, eds. J. Morgan Kousser and James M. McPherson (New York: Oxford University Press, 1982), 351–52, 354–55.

53. Eaton, *Report . . . 1872*, 313; Eaton, *Report . . . 1873*, 363; Eaton, *Report . . . 1874*, 388; Francis Butler Simkins and Robert Hilliard Woody, *South Carolina During Reconstruction* (Chapel Hill: Univ. of North Carolina Press, 1932), 437–39.

54. *The Christian Union*, Dec. 31, 1873, p. 540, col. 3; Ibid., March 4, 1874, p. 170, col. 1.

55. Richard Lathers, "South Carolina. Her Wrongs and the Remedy. Remarks of Col. Richard Lathers, Delivered at the Opening of the Taxpayers' Convention, in Columbia, S.C., Tuesday, Feb. 17, 1874" (n.p., n.p., 1874) (pamphlet at Huntington Library), 3, 6–7, 9.

56. Republican Party. South Carolina. State Central Committee, Samuel J. Lee, Chairman, Protem., "Reply to the Memorial of the Taxpayers' Convention, Addressed to the Honorable the [*sic*] Senate and House of Representatives of the United States" (Columbia: Republican Printing Co., 1874) (pamphlet at Huntington Library), 2–5, 7–8; John S. Reynolds, *Reconstruction in South Carolina, 1865–1877* (Columbia, S.C.: The State Co., Publishers, 1905), 245–65; for a modern account of thievery in Southern Republican regimes during Reconstruction, see Mark Wahlgren Summers, *The Era of Good Stealings* (New York: Oxford University Press, 1993), 153–65.

57. *New York Times*, May 20, 1871, p.8, col. 1; Eaton, "Report . . . 1870," 147; Eaton, *Report . . . 1871*, 185; Eaton, *Report . . . 1872*, 126–27; Eaton, *Report . . . 1873*, 125, 127, 131; Dabney, *Universal Education in the South*, 2: 278–79,

58. John C. Harkness to John Eaton, Jr., Wilmington, Delaware, Feb. 13, 1871 and May 9 and 22, 1871 (Eaton Papers); Eaton, "Report . . . 1870," 157; Eaton, *Report for 1873*, xv, 63, 154; Eaton, *Report . . . 1874*, 55, 133–34.

5. Federal Aid to Education

1. James Pyle Wickersham, "Education as an Element in the Reconstruction of the Union, A Lecture by J. P. Wickersham, Principal of the Pennsylvania State Normal School, Millersville, PA, Delivered Before the National Teachers' Association, at Harrisburg, PA, Aug. 18, 1865" (Boston: Press of Geo. C. Rand & Avery, 1865) (pamphlet at Huntington Library), (emphasis is his); *Cong. Globe*, 39th Cong., 1st Sess., p. 3044.

2. A. S. Barnes to John Eaton, Jr., New York City, Feb. 3, 1870; S. N. Clark to John Eaton, Jr., Chicago, Feb. 17, 1870; D. B. Hagar to John Eaton, Jr., Salem, Mass., Feb. 28, 1870; Barbour Lewis to John Eaton, Jr., Memphis, March 18, 1870; H. Pomeroy to John Eaton, Jr., Chattanooga, March 25, 1870; Barnas Sears to John Eaton, Jr., Staunton, Virginia, April 2, 1870; W. F. Prosser to John Eaton, Nashville, Nov. 11, 1870 (Eaton Papers, Special Collections, Hoskins Library, University of Tennessee, Knoxville); *Senate Executive Document No. 74*, 41st *Cong.*, 2nd *Sess.*, pp. 1–2; *Cong. Globe*, 41st Cong., 2nd Sess., pp. 759–66, 2317; Albion Tourgee, *An Appeal to Caesar* (New York: Fords, Howard, and Hulbert, 1884), 409–10; Gordon Canfield Lee, *The Struggle for Federal Aid, First Phase: A History of the Attempts to Obtain Federal Aid for the Common Schools, 1870–1890* (New York: Bureau of Publications, Teachers College, Columbia University, 1949), 42.

3. *Cong. Globe*, 41st Cong., 2nd Sess., pp. 2318–19.

4. Ibid., pp. 2320–21.

5. Ibid., p. 2322.

6. Richard E. Welch, Jr., *George Fisbie Hoar and the Half-Breed Republicans* (Cambridge, Mass.: Harvard University Press, 1971), 23–25.

7. Walter J. Fraser, "William Henry Ruffner and the Establishment of Virginia's Public School System, 1870–1874," *Virginia Magazine of History and Biography* 79 (July 1971): 272; William Henry Ruffner, "The Public Free School System. Dr. Dabney Answered by Mr. Ruffner" (Richmond: *Richmond Dispatch* and *Richmond Enquirer*, 1876) (pamphlet at Huntington Library), 8; William Henry Ruffner, "The National Bureau of Education," *The Educational Journal of Virginia* 2 (January 1871): 119.

8. *Cong. Globe*, Appendix, 41st Cong., 2nd Sess., pp. 478–85; *Cong. Globe*, 41st Cong., 3rd Sess., pp. 808–9.

9. "Biography of George F. Hoar," p. 2, in William Horatio Barnes, *History of the Congress of the United States [The 41st Congress, 1869–1871]* (New York: W. H. Barnes & Co., 1871); *The Christian Union*, Dec. 10, 1870, p. 360, cols. 3–4.

10. *Cong. Globe*, Appendix, 41st Cong., 3rd Sess., pp. 77–81.

11. Ibid., Appendix. pp. 95–98: George F. Hoar, *Autobiography of Seventy Years*, 2 Vols. (New York: Charles Scribner, 1903), 1: 264.

12. Rev. Isaac T. Hecker, "Unification and Education," *The Catholic World* 13 (April 1871): 3–4.

13. *Cong. Globe*, 41st Cong., 3rd Sess., pp. 1054–57, 1060; Robert G. Newby and David B. Tyack, "Victims Without Crimes: Some Historical Perspectives on Black Education," *Journal of Negro Education* 40 (Summer 1971): 193; W. H. Stilwell to John Eaton, Jr., Dec. 22, 1870 (Eaton Papers).

14. *Cong. Globe*, 41st Cong., 3rd Sess., pp. 1060–61.

15. Ibid., p. 1061. Within several years, the judicial burden of backlogged indictments in the South resulting from this legislation persuaded the Attorney General to back off from enforcing the acts. Interestingly, the Grant administration pursued a much more active use of this legislation to prevent Democratic Party intimidation and Irish-Catholic violence at the polls in New York City rather than Ku Klux Klan terrorism in the South. This is a good example of how anti-Catholicism and Reconstruction often dovetailed. See C. Vann Woodward, *American Counterpoint, Slavery and Racism in the North-South Dialogue* (Boston: Little, Brown & Co., 1971: 1964 reprint), 182–83; Robert A. Horn, "National Control of Congressional Elections" (Ph.D. Dissertation, Princeton, 1942), 143, 154–55, 183–87.

16. Gordon Canfield Lee, *The Struggle for Federal Aid, First Phase: A History of the Attempts to Obtain Federal Aid for the Common Schools, 1870–1890* (New York: Bureau of Publications, Teachers College, Columbia University, 1949), 46–47; *Cong. Globe*, Appendix, 42nd Cong., 2nd Sess., pp. 17–19.

17. Kenneth R. Johnson, "Legrand Winfield Perce: A Mississippi Carpetbagger and the Fight for Federal Aid to Education," *Journal of Mississippi History* 34 (Nov. 1972): 331–51; Eaton, "Report . . . 1870," 10–1.

18. National Democratic Executive Resident Committee, "The Robbery of the Public Lands! The Public Lands for the People!" (n.p.: n.p., n.d.) (pamphlet at Huntington Library), 1–8; n.a., "The Republican Party, The Standard-Bearer Of Civilization and National Progress" (n.p.: n.p., n.d.) (pamphlet at Huntington Library), 3; *Cong. Globe*, 42nd Conf., 2nd Sess., pp. 535–36, 564–70.

19. n.a., "A National Education Fund," *The Republic: A Monthly Magazine Devoted to the Dissemination of Political Information* 1 (March 1873): 36.

20. *Cong. Globe*, 42nd Cong., 2nd Sess., pp. 568–70; J. Edwards Clarke to John Eaton, Jr., New York City, Jan. 25, 1872 (Eaton Papers).

21. *Cong. Globe*, 42nd Cong., 2nd Sess., pp. 791, 855–56; Ibid., Appendix, pp. 17, 20, 38–41.

22. *Cong. Globe*, 42nd Cong., 2nd Sess., pp. 592, 792; n.a., "A National Education Fund," *The Republic* 1 (March 1873): 37.

23. *Cong. Globe, Appendix*, 42nd Cong., 2nd Sess., pp. 15–17.

24. Jonathan Lurie, "The Fourteenth Amendment: Use and Application in Selected State Court Civil Liberties Cases, 1870–1890—A Preliminary Assessment," *American Journal of Legal History* 28 (Oct. 1984): 305–6; Rev. Otis Gibson, "'Chinaman or White Man, Which?' Reply to Father Buchard, Delivered in Platt's Hall, San Francisco, Friday Evening, March 14, 1873" (San Francisco: *Alta California* Printing House, 1873) (pamphlet at Huntington Library), 23, 26, 29; William Lucas Steele, *Galesburg Public Schools, Their History and Work, 1861–1911* (Galesburg: Board of Education, 1911), 43–46; Eaton, "Report . . . 1870," 61, 112; Eaton, "Report . . . 1871," 17–18; Eaton, *Report . . . 1872*, 78, 216, 272; Eaton, *Report . . . 1873*, 80.

25. *Cong. Globe*, 42nd Cong., 2nd Sess., pp. 795, 800, 851.

26. Ibid., pp. 862–63, 882, 1043; G. H. Atkinson to John Eaton, Jr., Moline, Illinois, Feb. 12, 1872 (Eaton Papers).

27. n.a., "The Republican Party, The Friend of Education at the South, The Educational Fund Bill" (Washington, D.C., n.p., n.d.) (pamphlet at Huntington Library), 4; W. F. Prosser to John Eaton, Jr., Nashville, January 30, 1872 and February 3, 1872 (Eaton Papers).

28. (Unknown) to John Eaton, Jr., Knoxville, Tennessee, January 5, 1871 (Eaton Papers).

29. n.a., "Our Educational Outlook," *Scribner's Monthly* 4 (May 1872): 97–103.

30. A. S. Fiske to John Eaton, Jr., Rochester, New York, May 9 1872; J. M. Gregory to John Eaton, Jr., Champaign, Illinois, Dec. 7, 1872 (Eaton Papers); George F. Hoar, "Education in Congress," *Old and New* 5 (May 1872): 599–600.

31. William Henry Ruffner, *Virginia School Report, 1873, Third Annual Report of the Superintendent of Public Instruction, For the Year Ending August 31, 1873* (Richmond: R. F. Walker, Superintendent [of] Public Printing, 1873), 196, 198, 200, 203, 206; Booker T. Washington, *Up from Slavery* (New York: Viking Penguin, 1986: 1901 reprint), 83.

32. John Hope Franklin, ed., *Reminiscences of an Active Life: The Autobiography of John Roy Lynch* (Chicago: University of Chicago Press, 1970), xiv, xv; Vernon Lane Wharton, *The Negro in Mississippi, 1865–1890*, 2nd ed. (New York: Harper and Row, 1965), 162; Kenneth R. Johnson, "Legrand Winfield Perce: A Mississippi Carpetbagger and the Fight for Federal Aid to Education," *Journal of Mississippi History* 34 (Nov. 1972): 356.

33. Fred L. Israel, ed., *The State of the Union Messages of the Presidents, 1790–1966*, 3 Vols. (New York: Chelsea House, Robert Hector Publishers, 1966), 2: 1252; *Cong. Globe*, 42nd Cong., 3rd Sess., pp. 1250–51; George F. Hoar, *Autobiography of Seventy Years*, 2 vols. (New York: Charles Scribner, 1903), 1: 264–65; Walter J. Fraser, "William Henry Ruffner and the Establishment of Virginia's Public School System, 1870–1874," *Virginia Magazine of History and Biography* 79 (July 1971): 273.

34. *Cong. Record*, 43rd Cong., 1st Sess., Vol. 2, Part 1, pp. 104, 149–50, 463–66, 489–91.

35. Ibid., pp. 612–13; *The Christian Union*, Nov. 12, 1873, p. 386, col. 3.

36. James A. Garfield to George Hamilton, January 6, 1874, Washington, D.C. (Garfield Papers, Huntington Library); n.a. "What to do with the Surplus," *The Atlantic Monthly* 25 (Jan. 1870): 72–77; Robert V. Remini, *Andrew Jackson* (Boston: Twayne Publishers, 1966), 126–27, 130–40; David Tyack, Thomas James, Aaron Benavot, *Law and the Shaping of Public Education, 1785–1954* (Madison: University of Wisconsin Press, 1987), 36; n.a., "The Financial Record of President Grant's Administration" (n.p.: n.p., 1872) (pamphlet at Huntington Library), 1–8; James A. Garfield, "Revenues and Expenditures, Speech of Hon. James A. Garfield, of Ohio, in the House of Representatives, Thursday, March 5, 1874" (Washington, D.C.: J. H. Cunningham, 1874) (pamphlet at Huntington Library), 5, 7.

37. Henry George, "Our Land and Land Policy, National and State" (San Francisco: White & Bauer, 1871) (pamphlet at Huntington Library), 3; also see E. T. Peters, "The Policy of Railroad Land Grants Before the Pre-emptor's Union in Metzerot Hall, Washington, D.C., on Wednesday Evening, April 27, 1870" (n.p.: n.p., n.d.) (pamphlet at Huntington Library), 14.

38. *Daily Dispatch* (Richmond, Virginia), Feb. 9, 1872, p. 2, col. 2; Samuel Sullivan Cox, "Economy-Education-Mixed Schools. Speech of Hon. S. S. Cox, Member of Congress from New York City, on the Education and Civil Rights Bills, Delivered January 13, 1874" (Washington, D.C.: GPO, 1874), 3–4, 8–10, 17; *Cong. Record*, 43rd Cong., 1 Sess., pp. 614, 619; Ibid., Appendix, p. 71.

6. Reconstruction's Racial Dissolution

1. David Donald, *Charles Sumner and the Rights of Man* (New York: Alfred A. Knopf, 1970), 152, 251–52, 282, 317, 351.

2. Beverly Wilson Palmer, ed., *The Selected Letters of Charles Sumner*, 2 vols. (Boston: Northeastern University Press, 1990), 2: 306, 424.

3. Lawanda and John H. Cox, eds., *Reconstruction, The Negro and the New South* (New York: Harper & Row, 1973), 123; Richard Nelson Current, *Those Terrible Carpetbaggers* (New York: Oxford University Press, 1988), 285–86.

4. W. E. Burghardt DuBois, "Does the Negro Need Separate Schools?" *Journal of Negro Education* 4 (July 1935): 328–29, 335; Carter Godwin Woodson, *The Mis-education of the Negro*, 2nd ed. (Washington, D.C.: The Associated Publishers, 1969), 28–29.

5. Barnas Sears, "Objections to Public Schools Considered: Remarks at the Annual Meeting of the Trustees of the Peabody Education Fund, New York, October 7, 1875" (Boston: Press of John Wilson and Son, 1875) (pamphlet at Huntington Library), 3; Alvah Hovey, *Barnas Sears: A Christian Educator, His Making and Work* (New York: Silver, Burdett & Co., 1902), 126–28; Earle H. West, "The Peabody Fund and Negro Education, 1867–1880," *History of Education Quarterly* 6 (Summer 1966): 6–8, 13, 15; Walter L. Fleming, comp., *Documentary History of Reconstruction, Political, Military, Social, Religious, Educational and Industrial, 1865 to 1906*, 2 vols. (New York: McGraw-Hill, 1966: 1906–1907 reprint), 2: 194–95; Robert G. Newby and David B. Tyack, "Victims Without Crimes: Some Historical Perspectives on Black Education," *Journal of Negro Education* 40 (Summer 1971): 192–206.

6. Lyman Tremain to John Eaton, Jr., Washington, D.C., June 1, 1874 (Eaton Papers, Special Collections, Hoskins Library, University of Tennessee, Knoxville); William P. Vaughn, "Partners in Segregation: Barnas Sears and the Peabody Fund," *Civil War History* 10 (Sept. 1964): 274; John Hope Franklin, "Jim Crow Goes to School: The Genesis of Legal Segregation in Southern Schools," *South Atlantic Quarterly* 58 (Spring 1959): 231–32; John Eaton, Jr., *Grant, Lincoln and the Freedmen* (New York: Longmans, Green, & Co., 1907), 263–64; John Eaton, Jr., "Report of the Commissioner of Education," *House Executive Document #1*, 42nd Cong., 2nd Sess., pp. 6, 10; *Savannah Morning News*, May 23, 1874, p. 1, col. 6; *Memphis Daily Appeal*, May 27, 1874, p. 2, col. 3.

7. Horace Mann Bond, *The Education of the Negro in the American Social Order*, 2nd ed. (New York: Octagon Books, 1966), 53–54; Leslie H. Fishel, Jr., "Repercussions of Reconstruction, The Northern Negro, 1870–1883," *Civil War History* 14 (Dec. 1968): 328–29, 331, 340–42; Leon Litwack, *Been in the Storm So Long, The Aftermath of Slavery* (New York: Vintage Books, 1979), 488–94; James M. McPherson, "White Liberals and Black Power in Negro Education, 1865–1915," *American Historical Review* 75 (June 1970): 1360–62.

8. *Senate Executive Document #20*, 41st Cong., 3rd Sess., pp. 5, 7, 10, 34–35; *Cong. Globe*, 42nd Cong., 2nd Sess., p.433.

9. James M. McPherson, "Abolitionists and the Civil Rights Act of 1875," *Journal of American History* 52 (Dec. 1965): 507–8; *Cong. Globe*, 42nd Cong., 2nd Sess., pp. 384, 3259–60.

10. *Cong. Globe*, 42nd Cong., 2nd Sess., pp. 384–85; Appendix, Ibid., p. 27.

11. *Cong. Globe*, 42nd Cong., 2nd Sess., p. 3193.

12. *Garnes v. McCann and Others*, 21 Ohio Reports, 198; J. Morgan Kousser, *Dead End: The Development of Nineteenth-Century Litigation on Racial Discrimination in Schools* (Oxford: Oxford University Press, 1986), 10.

13. *Cong. Globe*, 42nd Cong., 2nd Sess., pp. 3257–58; Leonard Ernest Erickson, "The Color Line in Ohio Public Schools, 1829–1890" (Ph.D. dissertation: The Ohio State University, 1959), 241–42; John Eaton, Jr., *Report of the Commissioner of Education for the Year 1872* (Washington, D.C.: GPO, 1873), 273.

14. *Cong. Globe*, 42nd Cong., 2nd Sess., pp. 524–25, 843–44.

15. Ibid., pp. 728, 763.

16. Appendix, Ibid., p. 13.

17. John Eaton, Jr. *Report of the Commissioner of Education for the Year 1873* (Washington, D.C.: GPO, 1874), xiii, xv, 79–80, 125, 154.

18. Erickson, "The Color Line in Ohio Public Schools," 246, 249, 251–52, 254.

19. William Lucas Steele, *Galesburg Public Schools, Their History and Work, 1861–1911* (Galesburg, Ill.: Board of Education, 1911), 43–46; *New York Times*, Oct. 9, 1873, p. 4, col. 2.

20. Donald, *Sumner and the Rights of Man*, 580.

21. *House Misc. Doc.*, *No. 58*, 42nd Cong, 3rd Sess., pp. 1–3; *House Misc. Doc.*, *No. 25*, 43rd Cong., 1st Sess., p. 1; *Cong. Record*, 43rd Cong., 1st Sess., pp. 101, 325, 1135.

22. Richard H. Cain, "Civil Rights Bill, Speech of Hon. Richard H. Cain, of South Carolina, Delivered in the House of Representatives, Saturday, January 24, 1874" (n.p.: n.p., 1874) (pamphlet at Huntington Library), 3–4; Alonzo J. Ransier, *Civil Rights, Speech of Hon. Alonzo J. Ransier, of South Carolina, in the House of Representatives, February 7, 1874* (Washington, D.C.: GPO, 1874), 4, 8, 12–4.

23. Henry Sullivan Williams, "The Development of the Negro Public School System in Missouri," *The Journal of Negro History* 5 (April 1920): 145.

24. Michael Perman, *The Road to Redemption: Southern Politics, 1869–1879* (Chapel Hill: University of North Carolina Press, 1984), 135–39; Michael Perman, ed., *Major Problems in the Civil War and Reconstruction* (Lexington, Mass.: D. C. Heath and Co., 1991), 541–46; William Hepworth Dixon, *White Conquest*, 2 vols. (London: Chatto and Windus, 1876), 2: 148–49.

25. Peter D. Klingman, *Josiah Walls, Florida's Black Congressman of Reconstruction* (Gainsville: The University Presses of Florida, 1976), 102, 104–5.

26. Erickson, "The Color Line in Ohio Public Schools," 333–36, 339–40, 345; Frank V. Quillan, *The Color Line in Ohio, A History of Race Prejudice in a Typical Northern State*, 2nd ed. (New York: Negro Universities Press, 1969), 107–8; Michael Perman, *Emancipation and Reconstruction, 1862–1879* (Arlington Heights, Ill.: Harlan Davidson, 1987), 80–81.

27. *House Misc. Doc., No. 44*, 43rd Cong., 1st Sess., pp. 1–4; *House Misc. Doc., No. 25*, 43rd Cong., 1st Sess., p. 1; Ransier, "Civil Rights, Speech . . . , Feb. 7, 1874," p. 12.

28. *House Misc. Doc., No. 58*, 42nd Cong, 3rd Sess., pp. 1–3.

29. William C. Harris, *The Day of the Carpetbagger, Republican Reconstruction in Mississippi* (Baton Rouge: LSU Press, 1979), 313–16, 336, 351, 603; Warren A. Ellem, "Who Were the Mississippi Scalawags?" *Journal of Southern History* 38 (May 1972): 234–35, 239–40; David H. Donald, "The Scalawag in Mississippi Reconstruction," *Journal of Southern History* 10 (Nov. 1944): 450–55; Otto H. Olsen, ed., *Reconstruction and Redemption in the South* (Baton Rouge: LSU Press, 1980), 86–87, 93, 95, 96; Kenneth M. Stampp and Leon F. Litwack, comps., *Reconstruction, An Anthology of Revisionist Writings* (Baton Rouge: LSU Press, 1969), 338–69; William S. McFeely, *Grant, A Biography* (New York: W. W. Norton & Co., 1981), 418–25.

30. Richard H. Abbott, *The Republican Party and the South, 1855–1877, The First Southern Strategy* (Chapel Hill: University of North Carolina Press, 1986), 229.

31. *House Misc. Doc., No. 60*, 43rd Cong., 1st Sess., pp. 1–2; Charles William Dabney, *Universal Education in the South*, 2 vols. (New York: Arno Press and the *New York Times*, 1969), 1: 153–61.

32. Williams, "Negro Public School System in Missouri," 153–59.

33. Samuel Sullivan Cox, *Economy-Education-Mixed Schools. Speech of Hon. S. S. Cox, Member of Congress From New York City, on the Education and Civil Rights Bills, Delivered January 13, 1874* (Washington, D.C.: GPO, 1874), 10.

34. Elias Nason, *The Life and Times of Charles Sumner, His Boyhood, Education, and Public Career* (Boston: B.B. Russell, 1874), 336; *Memorial Addresses on the Life and Character of Charles Sumner, A Senator of Massachusetts, Delivered in the Senate and House of Representatives, 43rd Congress, 1st Session, April 27, 1874, With Other Tributes of Respect* (Washington, D.C.: GPO, 1874), 44.

35. Nason, *Life and Times of Charles Sumner*, 340–41; John Greenleaf Whittier, "Sumner" (Boston: n.p., 1874) (pamphlet at Huntington Library), 3.

36. Samuel Johnson, "A Memorial of Charles Sumner. A Discourse Delivered at the Parker Memorial Meeting-House, To the Twenty-Eighth Congregational Society, of Boston, on Sunday, March 15, 1874" (Boston: A. Williams & Co., 1874) (pamphlet at Huntington Library), 8–9 ,11, 13–14; Whittier, "Sumner," 5; Henry Ward Beecher, *Plymouth Pulpit, Sermons Preached In Plymouth Church, Brooklyn, By Henry Ward Beecher, March–September, 1874* (New York: Fords, Howard, & Hulbert, 1892), 7, 17–18; Charles Edwards Lester, *Life and Public Services of Charles Sumner* (New York: U.S. Publishing Co., 1874), 532–33; Jeremiah Chaplin and J. D Chaplin, *Life of Charles Sumner, With an Introduction by Hon. William Claflin* (Boston: D. Lothrop & Co., 1874), 497–98.

37. William M. Cornell, ed., *Charles Sumner: Memoir and Eulogies, A Sketch of His Life by the Editor, An Original Article by Bishop Gilbert Haven, and the Eulogies Pronounced by Eminent Men* (Boston: James M. Earle, 1874), 335–36; *Memorial Addresses on the Life*, 32, 60–61, 83, 87–88, 101,103.

38. Carl Schurz to Samuel C. Cobb, Washington, D.C., March 21, 1874 (Schurz Papers, Huntington Library); Carl Schurz, *Eulogy on Charles Sumner by Carl Schurz* (Boston: Lee and Shepard, 1874), 4, 13–14, 30, 36, 43–44, 46, 75–76; James Freeman Clarke, "Oration Delivered Before the City Government and Citizens of Boston, in Music Hall, July 5, 1875" (Boston: Rockwell and Churchill, City Printers, 1875) (pamphlet at Huntington Library), 42.

39. *Harper's Weekly*, 18 (April 11, 1874): 311.

40. *Cong. Record*, 43rd Cong., 1st Sess., pp. 3452, 4081–82; historian Ena Farley provides information that suggests that Pratt's assumption that the bill would not result in Northern urban blacks attending white schools was faulty. In many Northern urban centers, blacks were not congregated in any particular section, but rather distributed over an entire city. As a result, a black school was often located too far from African-American homes to make school attendance practical. Consequently, many Northern urban blacks could acquire real educational opportunity only as soon as mixed schools were mandated, either by state or nation. For a description of the even distribution of black population over the cities of New York, see Ena Farley, *The Underside of Reconstruction in New York: The Struggle Over the Issue of Black Equality* (New York: Garland Publishing, 1993), 124–34.

41. Ibid., p. 4116; Walter J. Fraser, Jr., "Black Reconstructionists in Tennessee," *Tennessee Historical Quarterly* 34 (Winter 1975): 378–79; *Republican Banner* (Nashville, Tenn.), April 29, 1874, p. 4. cols. 3–4; Ibid., April 30, 1874, p. 4, cols. 2–3; for background on Shaw in Tennessee politics, see Barbour Lewis to John Eaton, Jr., Memphis, Oct. 14, 1870 (Eaton Papers).

42. *Cong. Record*, 43rd Cong., 1st Sess., pp. 4117, 4154.

43. Fraser, "Black Reconstructionists in Tennessee," 379; *Nashville Union and American*, May 3, 1874, p. 2, col. 3; *Memphis Daily Appeal*, May 31, 1874, p.

1, cols. 2–4; *Cong. Record*, 43rd Cong., 1st Sess., pp. 4143–44; Lewis V. Bogy, *Civil Rights and Uncivil Wrong, Speech of Hon. Lewis V. Bogy, of Missouri, in the United States Senate, May 22, 1874* (Washington, D.C.: GPO, 1874), 13.

44. *Harper's Weekly* 18 (May 9, 1874): 391; Thomas M. Norwood, *Civil Rights, Speech of Hon. Thomas M. Norwood, of Georgia, Delivered in the United States Senate, April 30 and May 4, 1874* (Washington, D.C.: GPO, 1874), 19.

45. *Cong. Record.* 43rd Cong., 1st Sess., p. 4089.

46. Ibid., pp. 4115, 4151; Appendix, *Cong. Record*, 43rd Cong., 1st Sess., p. 359; Augustus S. Merrimon, *Civil Rights. Speech of Hon. A. S. Merrimon, of North Carolina, in the United States Senate, May 22, 1874* (Washington, D.C.: GPO, 1874), 37.

47. *Cong. Record*, 43rd Cong., 1st Sess., pp. 4162, 4164; Appendix, *Cong. Record*, 43rd Cong., 1st Sess., p. 322; Bogy, *Speech of . . . May 22, 1874*, pp. 4, 13.

48. *Cong. Record*, 43rd Cong., 1st Sess., pp. 4146, 4160; Appendix, *Cong. Record*, 43rd Cong., 1st Sess., p. 233; Neill S. Brown to William Gannaway Brownlow, Nashville, June 30, 1874 (Brownlow Collection, Special Collections, Hoskins Library, University of Tennessee, Knoxville); William S. Speer, comp., *Sketches of Prominent Tennesseans, Containing Biographies and Records of the Families Who Have Attained Prominence in Tennessee* (Nashville: Albert B. Tavel, 1888), 7–10; *Winchester Journal* (Winchester, Indiana), June 3, 1874, p. 2, col. 1.

49. *Cong. Record*, 43rd Cong., 1st Sess., p. 4083; Appendix, *Cong. Record*, 43rd Cong., 1st Sess., p. 342; *Republican Banner* (Nashville, Tenn.), April 29, 1874, p. 4, cols. 3–4; Ibid., April 30, 1874, p. 2, col. 2; p. 4, cols. 2–3.

50. Rev. Otis Gibson, "'Chinaman or White Man, Which?' Reply to Father Buchard, Delivered in Platt's Hall, San Francisco, Friday Evening, March 14, 1873" (San Francisco: *Alta California* Printing House, 1873) (pamphlet at Huntington Library), 23; Appendix, *Cong. Record*, 43rd Cong., 1st Sess., p. 359.

51. *Cong. Record*, 43rd Cong., 1st Sess., p. 4116; Appendix, *Cong. Record*, 43rd Cong., 1st Sess., p. 307; Lillian A. Pereyra, *James Lusk Alcorn, Persistent Whig* (Baton Rouge: LSU Press, 1966), 147, 160.

52. Norwood, *Speech of . . . April 30 and May 4, 1874*, 32; Appendix, *Cong. Record*, 43rd Cong., 1st Sess., pp. 311–12, 315; Merrimon, *Speech on . . . May 22, 1874*, 15, 23, 26.

53. *Harper's Weekly* 18 (Oct. 10, 1874): 830–31.

54. Ibid. 18 (May 23, 1874): 430–31; Appendix, *Cong. Record*, 43rd Cong., 1st Sess., p. 358; *Cong. Record.* 43rd Cong., 1st Sess., pp. 3453, 4150.

55. *Cong. Record*, 43rd Cong., 1st Sess., p. 4164; Everette Swinney, "Enforcing the Fifteenth Amendment, 1870–1877," *Journal of Southern History* 28 (May 1962): 205–8; while I basically agree with the interpretation presented in Robert J. Kaczorowski's "Revolutionary Constitutionalism in the Era of the Civil War and Reconstruction," *New York University Law Review* 61 (November 1986): 863–940, his thesis places too much emphasis upon the Supreme Court's *Slaughterhouse* decision in shutting down Radical Reconstruction. (See p. 938.) Popular reaction to the Senate's passage of Sumner's Supplementary Civil Rights bill, far more than any supposed deference to the federal courts, was the determining factor in what Kaczorowski terms "the reduction of Southern blacks to peonage, the creation of Jim Crow, and the demise of the Republican Party in the South." (See p. 938.)

56. *Cong. Record*, 43rd Cong., 1st Sess., p. 4176; *The Christian Union* (New York City), May 27, 1874, p. 423, col. 1; *The Cincinnati Daily Enquirer*, May 24, 1874, p. 4, col. 2; *The Independent* (New York City), June 4, 1874, p. 16, cols. 3–4; *Republican Banner* (Nashville, Tenn.), May 24, 1874, p. 2, col. 3; *The Daily Journal* (Wilmington, N.C.), May 28, 1874, p. 2, col. 2; *Courier Journal* (Louisville, Kentucky), May 25, 1874, p. 2, col. 4.

57. *Savannah Morning News*, May 27, 1874, p. 2, col. 1: *Daily Dispatch* (Richmond, Virginia), May 27, 1874, p. 2, col. 1; Alexander Shiras to John Eaton, Jr., Washington, D.C., May 9, 1874; John D. Philbrick to John Eaton, Jr., Boston, May 13, 1874; Thomas W. Harvey to John Eaton, Jr., Columbus, Ohio, May 13, 1874; William H. Ruffner to John Eaton, Jr., Richmond, May 16, 1874; Lyman Tremain to John Eaton, Jr., Washington, D.C., June 1, 1874 (Eaton Papers).

58. Appendix, *Cong. Record*, 43rd Cong., 1st Sess., p. 477; *Harper's Weekly*, 18 (June 27, 1874): 534; *Daily Dispatch* (Richmond), May 26, 1874, p. 2. col. 1; *Savannah Morning News*, May 25, 1874. p. 2, col. 2.

59. *Washington National Monument. Shall the Unfinished Obelisk Stand [as] a Monument of National Disgrace and National Dishonor? Speeches of Hon. Norton P. Chipman, of the District of Columbia, Hon. R.C. McCormick, of Arizona, Hon. Jasper D. Ward, of Illinois, Hon. John B. Storm, of Pennsylvania, Hon. J. B. Sener, of Virginia, Hon. S. S. Cox, of New York, in the House of Representatives, June 4, 1874* (Washington, D.C.: GPO, 1874), 18–19, 22–23.

7. Backlash: 1874

1. Charles Nordhoff, *The Cotton States In the Spring and Summer of 1875* (New York: Burt Franklin, 1965: 1876 reprint), 95–96; *New York Times*, Sept. 15, 1874, p. 3, cols. 3–4.

2. J. G. de Roulhac Hamilton, *Reconstruction in North Carolina*, 2nd ed. (Gloucester, Mass.: Peter Smith, 1964), 616–18.

3. Otto H. Olsen, *Carpetbagger's Crusade: The Life of Albion Winegar Tourgee* (Baltimore: The Johns Hopkins Press, 1965), 203.

4. Sarah Woolfolk Wiggins, *The Scalawag in Alabama Politics, 1865–1881* (University, Ala.: University of Alabama Press, 1977), 92–94, 98, 101; Edward C. Williamson, "The Alabama Election of 1874," *Alabama Review* 17 (July 1964): 215–16; Nordhoff, *The Cotton States*, 22, 91–93; Otto H. Olsen, ed., *Reconstruction and Redemption in the South* (Baton Rouge: LSU Press, 1980), 59–63; Howard N. Rabinowitz, "From Exclusion to Segregation: Southern Race Relations, 1865–1890," *Journal of American History* 63 (Sept. 1976): 333; Ellis Paxson Oberholtzer, *A History of the United States Since the Civil War*, 5 vols., (New York: The MacMillan Co., 1917–1937), 3: 199.

5. Horace Andrews to John Eaton, Jr., Memphis, June 6, 1874 (Eaton Papers, Special Collections, Hoskins Library, University of Tennessee, Knoxville); Minutes of the Fentress County [Tennessee] Democratic and Conservative Meeting, Jamestown, Tenn., Sept. 7, 1874 (Special Collections, Hoskins Library, University of Tennessee, Knoxville); *Harper's Weekly* 18 (Sept. 19, 1874): 769–70; Ibid. 18 (Oct. 3, 1874): 813; John Eaton, Jr., *Report of the Commissioner of Education for the Year 1874* (Washington, D.C.: GPO, 1875), 397.

6. *New York Times*, June 5, 1874, p. 5, col. 5; *The Daily Journal* (Wilmington, N.C.), Aug. 8, 1874, p. 1, col. 2; *Harper's Weekly* 18 (Sept. 26, 1874): 790.

7. Ross A. Webb, *Kentucky in the Reconstruction Era* (Lexington: University Press of Kentucky, 1979), 85; *Harper's Weekly* 18 (Aug. 29, 1874): 710.

8. J. Morgan Kousser, "Separate but *not* Equal: The Supreme Court's First Decision on Racial Discrimination in Schools," *Journal of Southern History* 46 (Feb. 1980): 38; John Eaton, Jr., *Report of the Commissioner of Education for the Year 1875* (Washington, D.C.: GPO, 1876), 137; Webb, *Kentucky in the Reconstruction Era*, 86.

9. Conservative Party [Virginia], "The Congressional Canvass. Ninth Virginia District. Nominee of the Conservative Party" (Wytheville, VA: n.p. 1874) (pamphlet at Huntington Library), 14–15

10. *St. Louis Dispatch*, Nov. 9, 1874, p. 4, col. 4.

11. James T. White & Co., comp., *Notable Names in American History, A Tabulated Register, Third Edition of Whites Conspectus of American Biography* (Clifton, N.J.: James T. White & Co., 1973), 118–20.

12. Leon F. Litwack, *North of Slavery; The Negro in the Free States, 1790–1860* (Chicago: University of Chicago Press, 1961).

13. Eaton, *Report of the Commissioner . . .* , *1874*, 81–82; Roger D. Bridges, "Equality Deferred: Civil Rights for Illinois Blacks, 1865–1885," *Journal of the*

Illinois State Historical Society 74 (Summer 1981): 96–97, 100, 108; Robert L. McCaul, *The Black Struggle for Public Schooling in Nineteenth Century Illinois* (Carbondale: Southern Illinois University Press, 1987), 118, 121, 137.

14. Eaton, *Report of the Commissioner* . . . , *1874*, 102; *The Independent* (New York City), Jan. 7, 1875, p. 17, col. 3; Emma Lou Thornbrough, *Indiana in the Civil War Era, 1850–1880* (Indianapolis: Indiana Historical Bureau, 1965), 483.

15. *Harper's Weekly* 18 (Aug. 8, 1874): 650; Ibid. 18 (Aug. 22, 1874): 690; *New Orleans Times Picayune*, Dec. 18, 1874, p. 4, col. 2.

16. A. P. Marble to John Eaton, Jr., Worcester, Mass., Oct. 13, 1874 (Eaton Papers); *Harper's Weekly* 18 (Oct. 3, 1874): 810; Ira V. Brown, "Pennsylvania and the Rights of the Negro, 1865–1887," *Pennsylvania History* 28 (Jan. 1961): 46, 54–55; *The Daily Journal* (Wilmington, N.C.), Aug. 29, 1874, p. 1, col. 1; Harrisburg newspaper quoted in Frank B. Evans, *Pennsylvania Politics, 1872–1877: A Study in Political Leadership* (Harrisburg: The Pennsylvania Historical and Museum Commission, 1966), 125–26; Lancaster newspaper quoted in *The York Gazette* (York, Pennsylvania), May 11, 1874, p. 2, col. 1; Ibid., Sept. 22, 1874, p. 2, col. 3; Ibid., Sept. 29, 1874, p. 2, col. 1.

17. *Harper's Weekly* 18 (Aug. 1, 1874): 630; Ibid., 18 (Sept. 26, 1874): 790; Truman Smith's comments are quoted in C. Edward Lester, *Life and Public Services of Charles Sumner* (New York: United States Publishing Co., 1874), 678–81; *Savannah Morning News*, June 8, 1874, p. 1, col. 3.

18. Quoted in *Harper's Weekly* 18 (Sept. 19, 1874): 770.

19. Eaton, *Report of the Commissioner* . . . , *1874*, 328; Erikson, "The Color Line in Ohio Public Schools," 346.

20. *New York Times*, Sept. 3, 1874, p. 2, col. 3; Ibid., Sept. 5, 1874, p. 5, col. 1.

21. *Cleveland Daily Plain Dealer*, Aug. 27, 1874, p. 2, col. 5; Ibid., Sept. 3, 1874, p. 2, col. 2; Ibid., Oct. 9, 1874, p. 3, col. 5; Ibid., Oct. 16, 1874, p. 2, col. 2.

22. Ibid., Nov. 4, 1874, p. 2, col. 2 (emphasis made by editorial).

23. *The Independent* (New York City), Sept. 10, 1874, p. 17. col. 4; *New York Times*, Sept. 1, 1874, p. 4, col. 5.

24. James A. Garfield to Edmund Burritt Wakefield, Hiram, Ohio, October 19, 1874 (Garfield Papers, Huntington Library); Eaton, *Report of the Commissioner* . . . , *1874*, p. v; *Winchester Journal* (Winchester, Indiana), Nov. 11, 1874, p. 2, col. 1.

25. *Evening Bulletin* (Philadelphia, PA), Nov. 9, 1874, p. 4, col. 1; *The York Gazette* (York, Pennsylvania), Nov. 17, 1874, p. 2, col. 2; *New York Times*, Nov. 4, 1874, p. 4, col. 4; Ibid., Feb. 4, 1875, p. 1. cols. 1–2; Eaton, *Report of the Commissioner* . . . , *1875*, 292.

26. *New Orleans Times Picayune*, Dec. 18, 1874, p. 4, col. 2; "Education," *Atlantic Monthly* 34 (Sept. 1874): 379–82.

27. *Cincinnati Daily Enquirer*, Nov. 4, 1874, p. 4. col. 2; Ibid., Nov. 6 1874, p. 4, col. 1; *Sedalia Democrat* quoted in *St. Louis Dispatch*, Nov. 7, 1874, p. 2, col. 4; *Daily Dispatch* (Richmond), Nov. 6, 1874, p. 2, cols. 2–3; Ibid., Nov. 11, 1874, p. 2, col. 2.

28. Henry Ward Beecher, *Plymouth Pulpit, Sermons Preached in Plymouth Church, Brooklyn, By Henry Ward Beecher, Sept. 1874–March 1875* (New York: Fords, Howard & Hulbert, 1890), 14.

29. *Atlanta Constitution*, Nov. 6, 1874, p. 3, col. 5; Ibid., Nov. 11, 1874, p. 2, col. 2; Gordon's nationalistic victory speech in Atlanta is quoted in *The York Gazette* (York, Pennsylvania), Nov. 10, 1874, p. 2, col. 2, demonstrating the effectiveness of this Southern spokesman with Northern audiences.

30. *New York Herald*, Nov. 4, 1874, p. 3, col. 1.

31. *Ohio State Journal* (Columbus), Feb. 23, 1875, p. 2, cols. 1–2; *Illinois Journal* (Springfield), Nov. 7, 1874, p. 2, cols. 1–2; *Atchison Daily Champion* (Atchison, Kansas), Nov. 8, 1874, p. 2, col. 2.

32. *Boston Evening Transcript*, Nov. 4, 1874, p. 3, cols. 1–2; Benjamin F. Butler, Speech of *Hon. Benjamin F. Butler on Civil Rights, Delivered in the House of Representatives, February 4, 1875* (Washington, D.C.: GPO, 1875), 8; *Cong. Record*, 43rd Cong., 2nd Sess., pp. 1005–6.

33. *Erie Gazette* (Erie, Penn.), Oct. 20, 1874, p. 2, col, 1; *Frank Leslie's Illustrated Newspaper* (New York City), Nov. 21, 1874, p. 2, col. 2; *St. Louis Dispatch*, Nov. 6, 1874, p. 1. col. 3; *Republican Banner* (Nashville, Tenn.), April 29, 1874, p. 2, col. 2; Ibid., Nov. 5, 1874, p. 2, col. 2; *Burlington Free Press and Times* (Burlington, Vt.), Nov. 11, 1874, p. 2, cols. 1–3; *Boston Evening Transcript, Nov. 11,* 1874, p. 6. cols. 2–3.

34. James M. McPherson, "Abolitionists and the Civil Rights Act of 1875." *Journal of American History* 52 (Dec. 1965): 507; William P. Vaughn, "Separate and Unequal: The Civil Rights Act of 1875 and Defeat of the School Integration Clause," *Southwestern Social Science Quarterly* 48 (Sept. 1967): 149; William B. Hesseltine, "Economic Factors in the Abandonment of Reconstruction," *Mississippi Valley Historical Review* 22 (Sept. 1935): 204–9.

35. Eric Foner, *Reconstruction, America's Unfinished Revolution, 1863–1877* (New York: Harper & Row, 1988), 512, 524; see transcripts of both Robert Ingersoll's September 11, 1876, campaign speech in New York City (the best attended political event in that city during the 1870s) in *Chicago Tribune*, September 14, 1876, p. 1. cols. 2–7, and his October 21, 1876, campaign speech in Chicago in Ibid., Oct. 23, 1876, p. 2, cols. 1–6.

36. William Gillette, *Retreat from Reconstruction, 1869–1879* (Baton Rouge: LSU Press, 1979), 198–99, 218, 220, 223, 238–58; historians Michael Perman and Richard H. Abbott also emphasize the impact of the Civil Rights bill on the elections of 1874. See Michael Perman, *The Road to Redemption: Southern Politics, 1869–1879* (Chapel Hill: University of North Carolina Press, 1984), 140–41; Richard H. Abbott, *The Republican Party and the South, 1855–1877, The First Southern Strategy* (Chapel Hill: University of North Carolina Press, 1986), 230–31; Mark Wahlgren Summers' *The Era of Good Stealings* (New York: Oxford University Press, 1993), 255, while emphasizing popular backlash against political corruption in the elections of 1874, concedes: "The civil rights issue played a big role, and south of the Ohio River a commanding one."

37. Kenneth M. Stampp and Leon F. Litwack, comps., *Reconstruction, An Anthology of Revisionist Writings* (Baton Rouge, LSU Press, 1969), 264–75, 299–322; Hon. Matt. W. Ransom, *The South Faithful to Her Duties, Speech on Hon. Matt. W. Ransom, of North Carolina, in the United States Senate, February 17, 1875* (Washington, D.C.: GPO, 1875), 17–18, 20, 30.

38. Michael Perman, ed., *Major Problems in the Civil War and Reconstruction, Documents and Essays* (Lexington, Mass.: D.C. Heath and Co., 1991), 563; *The Daily Journal* (Wilmington, N.C.), June 8, 1876, p. 2, col. 2.

39. J. Morgan Kousser, *Dead End: The Development of Nineteenth-Century Litigation on Racial Discrimination in Schools* (New York: Oxford University Press, 1986), 10; Thomas M. Cooley, "The Guarantee of Order and Republican Government in the States," *The International Review* 2 (1875): 61–62, 68–69, 77–79, 82; [anonymous], "The Guarantee of Order and Republican Governments in the States," *Central Law Journal* 2 (1875): 18–20; William M. Wiecek, *The Guarantee Clause of the U.S. Constitution* (Ithaca: Cornell University Press, 1972), 231–32.

40. *New Orleans Times Picayune*, Dec. 11, 1874, p. 8, col. 5.

41. George W. Cable, *The Negro Question*, ed. Arlin Turner (Garden City, N.Y.: Doubleday & Co., 1958), 8–9, 26; Joe Gray Taylor, *Louisiana Reconstructed, 1863–1877* (Baton Rouge: LSU Press, 1974), 471–72; *New Orleans Times Picayune*, Dec. 15, 1874, p. l, cols. 4–5; Ibid., Dec. 16, 1874, p. 1, col. 7.

42. *New Orleans Times Picayune*, Dec. 16, 1874, p. 4, cols. 2–3.

43. Ibid., Dec. 16, 1874, p. 4, cols. 2–3.

44. Ibid., Dec. 17, 1874, p. 2, col. 3.

45. Ibid., Dec. 18, 1874, p. 1, col. 3.

46. John W. Blassingame, *Black New Orleans, 1860–1880* (Chicago: University of Chicago Press, 1973), 117–19; Louis R. Harlan, "Desegregation in New Orleans Public Schools During Reconstruction," *American Historical*

Review 67 (April 1962): 663–75; Roger A. Fischer, *The Segregation Struggle in Louisiana, 1862–1877* (Urbana: University of Illinois Press, 1974), 127–32.

47. *New Orleans Times Picayune*, Dec. 5, 1874, p. 7, col. 12; Ibid., Dec. 17, 1874, p. 8, col. 1; *Republican Banner* (Nashville, Tenn.), Nov. 6, 1874, p.1, col. 5; *Nashville Union and American*, Feb. 7, 1875, p. 2, col. 2; Matthew H. Carpenter, *Civil Rights. Speech of Hon. Matt. H. Carpenter, of Wisconsin, in the United States Senate, February 27, 1875* (Washington, D.C.: GPO, 1875), 6–7; Gillette, *Retreat From Reconstruction*, 279.

48. J. Ambler Smith, *Civil Rights. Speech of Hon. J. Ambler Smith, of Virginia, in the House of Representatives, February 3, 1875* (Washington, D.C.: GPO, 1875), 9; Appendix, *Cong. Record*, 43rd Cong., 2nd Sess., pp. 15–24; *Cong. Record*, 43rd Cong., 2nd Sess., pp. 945, 947, 981–82, 998–1000, 1010–11; Kenneth Eugene Mann, "Richard Harvey Cain, Congressman, Minister and Champion for Civil Rights," *Negro History Bulletin* 35 (March 1972): 64–66; Hon. Thomas F. Bayard, *Civil Rights, Speech of Hon. Thomas F. Bayard, of Delaware, in the United States Senate, February 26, 1875* (Washington, D.C.: GPO, 1875), 11; McPherson, "Abolitionists and the Civil Rights Act of 1875," 509; Charles, R. Lofgren, *The Plessy Case, A Legal-Historical Interpretation* (New York: Oxford University Press, 1987), 71.

49. William P. Vaughn, "Separate and Unequal: The Civil Rights Act of 1875 and Defeat of the School Integration Clause," *Southwestern Social Science Quarterly* 48 (Sept. 1967): 154.

50. Perman, *Road to Redemption*, 139. Taking accounts, following the election of 1876, Henry Ward Beecher's *Christian Union* ultimately blamed blacks for the demise of Reconstruction: "The claim which they set up in 1873 for admission upon equal terms to all the white schools of the South was utterly destructive to the whole educational scheme. And when they not only made this demand, but enforced it by proscribing all Republicans who would not assent to it, and actually voted for Democrats in order to defeat such Republicans, they destroyed the Republican organization at the South, and with it sacrificed their own power to control permanently any Southern state." This editorial blamed blacks for failing to push realistically for the best education that they could receive in a racially segregated setting and concluded: "Men who do not know how to take half a loaf, will always succeed in getting no bread." (See *Christian Union* (New York City), Nov. 22, 1876, p. 110, cols. 1–3.) Interestingly, this editorial made no mention of Charles Sumner's critical role in mentoring the African-American leadership to take such a self-destructive course. The disinclination to blame Charles Sumner for the demise of Reconstruction has an old and distinguished pedigree.

51. Sumner's contemporaries frequently criticized his course and accurately predicted its ultimate result. Only when his efforts succeeded in partially shaping the course pursued by the masses of African-American

voters were Republican leaders forced to suspend their well-reasoned judgment. The sentiment at the time of Sumner's death likewise lubricated the slippery slope toward political disaster. In other words, the evaluation of Sumner provided here does not constitute hindsight as it was contemporaneous with the man himself. For a philosophical argument equating avoidance of judging historical figures with a belief in historical inevitability, see Hans Meyerhoff, ed., *The Philosophy of History in Our Time* (Garden City, N.Y.: Doubleday & Co., 1959), 249–69.

52. *Memphis Daily Appeal*, May 24, 1874, p. 1, col. 1.

8. The Anti-Catholic Antidote

1. *Harper's Weekly* 19 (Oct. 16, 1875): 842.

2. John Eaton, Jr., *Report of the Commissioner of Education for the Year 1875* (Washington, D.C.: GPO, 1876), 27, 61,72–73, 137, 139.

3. Barnas Sears, "Objections to Public Schools Considered: Remarks at the Annual Meeting of the Trustees of the Peabody Education Fund, New York, Oct. 7, 1875" (Boston: Press of John Wilson and Son, 1875) (pamphlet at Huntington Library), 3.

4. *The Daily Picayune* (New Orleans), Jan. 10, 1875, p. 6, col. 5.

5. Dorothy Orr, *A History of Education in Georgia* (Chapel Hill: University of North Carolina Press, 1950), 207, 213, 219.

6. n.a., "Education," *The Atlantic Monthly* 35 (June 1875): 760.

7. *The Independent* (New York City). Sept. 10, 1874, p. 17, col. 4

8. *Cincinnati Daily Enquirer*, April 3, 1875, p. 4, col. 1; *Harper's Weekly* 19 (May 8, 1875): 374–75; Harry Barnard, *Rutherford B. Hayes and His America*, 2nd ed. (New York: Russell & Russell, 1967), 272–73.

9. *Harper's Weekly* 19 (May 1, 1875): 357.

10. Eugene H. Roseboom and Francis P. Weisenberger, *A History of Ohio* (Columbus: The Ohio State Archaeological and Historical Society, 1961), 233.

11. Charles Richard Williams, ed., *Diary and Letters of Rutherford Birchard Hayes, Nineteenth President of the United States*, 5 vols. (New York: The Ohio State Archaelogical and Historical Society/Krause Reprint Co., 1971: 1924 reprint), 3: 273–74.

12. Charles Richard Williams, *The Life of Rutherford Birchard Hayes*, 2 vols. (Boston: Houghton Mifflin Co., 1914), 1: 397–400; Lewis Alexander

Leonard, *Life of Alphonso Taft* (New York: Hawke Publishing Co., 1920), 146–48; Rutherford B. Hayes to James G. Blaine, Fremont, Ohio, June 16, 1875, reproduced in Gail Hamilton, *Biography of James G. Blaine* (Norwich, Conn.: The Henry Bill Publishing Co., 1895), 375.

13. Williams, *Life of Hayes*, 1: 390–91, 397–400; Henry James Brown and Frederick D. Williams, eds., *The Diary of James A. Garfield*, 4 vols. (n.p.: Michigan State University Press, 1967–1981), 3: 118, 120.

14. Thurman speech reprinted in *Republican Banner* (Nashville, Tenn.), Aug. 1, 1875, p. 1, col. 2; Ibid., Aug. 29, 1875, p. 2, col. 2; for evidence that Democrats were fully aware that Republicans were shifting from racial to religious topics, see *The York Gazette* (York, Pennsylvania), July 13, 1875, p. 2, col. 1.

15. The National Anti-Papal League (New York City), "Politics and the School Question" (New York: The National Anti-Papal League, 1876) (pamphlet at Huntington Library), 4.

16. Rutherford B. Hayes to Col. A.T. Witkoff, Athens, Ohio, August 8, 1875, in Williams, ed., *Diary and Letters*, 3: 290; Brown and Williams, eds., *Diary of Garfield*, 3: 143; James Quay Howard, *The Life, Public Services and Select Speeches of Rutherford B. Hayes* (Cincinnati: Robert Clarke & Co., 1876), 252.

17. "Politics and the School Question," p. 12; Williams, *Life of Hayes*, 1: 405–6, 410; Barnard, *Rutherford B. Hayes*, 275; Forrest W. Clouts, "The Political Campaign of 1875," *Ohio Archaelogical and Historical Publications* 31 (1922): 40.

18. *Harper's Weekly* 19 (July 10, 1875): 558–59; Ibid. 19 (June 12, 1875): 474; Ibid. 19 (June 19, 1875): 494–95; Ibid, 19 (Sept. 18, 1875): 762: Ibid, 19 (Sept. 25, 1875): 782; D.C. Gilman, "Education in America, 1776–1876," *North American Review* 122 (Jan. 1876): 207; gradually, American nationalism worked its way into the Roman Catholic church and at the end of the century surfaced in the so-called "Americanist controversy" within that church. In this later internal debate, Bishop John Ireland of St. Paul, Minnesota, represented the most modern position possible with Roman Catholicism, halfway between the poles occupied by Gilmour and Taft in 1875. Ireland "argued for the unique compatibility between Catholicism and Americanism for as he put it, 'between Church and Country . . . one is not to be put before the other.'" See Glen Janus, "Bishop Bernard McQuaid: On 'True' and 'False' Americanism." *U.S. Catholic Historian* 2 (Summer 1993): 59.

19. John Leng, *America in 1876. Penciling During a Tour in the Centennial Year: With a Chapter on the Aspects of American Life* (Dundee: Dundee Advertiser Office, 1877), 274; James P. Wickersham, "Pennsylvania at the Centennial Exposition of 1876. Circular of Information to Those Desiring to Prepare Educational Material for Exhibition" (Harrisburg: B. F. Meyers, State Printer, 1876) (pamphlet at Huntington Library), 5.

20. William Dean Howells, *Sketch of the Life and Character of Rutherford B. Hayes, Also a Biographical Sketch of William A. Wheeler* (New York: Hurd and Houghton, 1876), 109–10.

21. Samuel Windsor Brown, *The Secularization of American Education, As Shown by State Legislation, State Constitutional Provisions and State Supreme Court Decisions*, 2nd ed. (New York: Russell and Russell, 1967), 104, 111–12, 117; Elwood P. Cubberly, *Public Education in the United States, A Study and Interpretation of American Educational History* (Boston: Houghton Mifflin Co., 1919), 180.

22. *The Daily Journal* (Wilmington, North Carolina), January 24, 1875, p. 1, col. 2; Ibid., Feb. 23, 1875, p. 4, cols. 4–5; Ibid., Feb. 25, 1875, p. 4, col. 4; Ibid., Feb. 28, 1875, p. 4, col. 4.

23. Ibid., Feb. 25, 1875, p. 4, col. 5; Louis R. Harlan, ed., *The Booker T. Washington Papers*, 14 vols. (Urbana: University of Illinois Press, 1972–1989), 2: 57–58; *The Independent* (New York City), Nov. 27, 1873, p. 8, cols, 1–4.

24. *The Enterprise and Mountaineer* (Greenville, South Carolina), May 26, 1875, p. 2, cols. 1–2; Ibid., Aug. 11, 1875, p. 3, col. 3; Ibid., Oct. 6, 1875, p. 1, cols. 4–6; Jeremiah 13: 23; *The Daily Journal* (Wilmington, N.C.), May 1, 1875, p. 2, col. 3.

25. Charles Reagan Wilson, "The Religion of the Lost Cause: Ritual and Organization of the Southern Civil Religion, 1865–1920," *Journal of Southern History* 46 (May 1980), 219–38.

26. Frederick Eby, *The Development of Education in Texas* (New York: The Macmillan Co., 1925), 173.

27. Euline W. Brock, "Thomas W. Cardozo: Fallible Black Reconstruction Leader," *Journal of Southern History* 47 (May 1981): 200–1; Blanche Ames, *Adelbert Ames, 1835–1933: General, Senator, Governor* (New York: Argosy-Antiquarian Limited, 1964), 462; Otto H. Olsen, ed., *Reconstruction and Redemption in the South* (Baton Rouge: LSU Press, 1980), 93–108.

28. William C. Harris, *The Day of the Carpetbagger, Republican Reconstruction in Mississippi* (Baton Rouge: LSU Press, 1979), 703–4; Vernon Lane Wharton, *The Negro in Mississippi, 1865–1890*, 2nd ed. (New York: Harper & Row, 1965), 244–55; Stuart Grayson Noble, *Forty Years of the Public Schools in Mississippi, With Special Reference to the Education of the Negro* (New York: Press of Teacher's College, Columbia University, 1918), 48–52; Henry Allen Bullock, *A History of Negro Education in the South, From 1619 to the Present* (Cambridge: Harvard University Press, 1967), 86–87; Edward Mayers, *Lucius Q. C. Lamar: His Life, Times, and Speeches* (Nashville: Publishing House of the Methodist Episcopal Church, South, 1896), 255.

29. William H. Ruffner, "The Public Free School System, Dr. Dabney Answered by Mr. Ruffner" (n.p.: n.p., 1876) (pamphlet at Huntington Library),

2–4, 6, 9–10, 28, 30–32, 39; "Civis" [Bennett Puryear, et al.), "The Public School in its Relations to the Negro" (Richmond: Clemmitt & Jones, 1877) (pamphlet at Huntington Library), 6–9, 11–14, 16–17, 19, 21, 30, 32.

30. Rev. Hugh Miller Thompson, ed., "Is Romanism the Best Religion for the Republic?" (New York: Church Journal Office, 1874) (pamphlet at Huntington Library), 10; F. X. Weninger, D. D. of the Society of Jesus, 'Reply to Hon. R. W. Thompson, Secretary of the Navy, Addressed to the American People" (New York: P. O'Shea, 1877) (pamphlet at Huntington Library), 16, 27–28, 31, 68, 76–77.

31. Hon. Edmund F. Dunne, "Our Public Schools: Are They Free for All, Or Are They Not?" (San Francisco: Cosmopolitan Printing Co., 1875) (pamphlet at Huntington Library), 16.

32. Ibid., 3, 8, 25, 29, 32–33, 42.

33. Orestes Brownson, "The Public School System," *Brownson's Quarterly Review, Last Series* 3 (Oct. 1875): 517, 519, 523–25, 528, 532, 535–38.

34. Neil G. McCluskey, ed., *Catholic Education in America: A Documentary History* (New York: Teachers College, Columbia University, 1964), 122–26; John Tracy Ellis, ed., *Documents of American Catholic History* (Milwaukee: The Bruce Publishing Co., 1962), 401–4

35. *Harper's Weekly* 19 (Dec. 11, 1875): 1003

36. n.a., "Education," *The Atlantic Monthly* 35 (March 1875): 381–84; John Eaton, Jr., *Report of the Commissioner of Education for the Year 1875* (Washington, D.C.: GPO, 1876), 330; *Sacramento Union*, Feb. 14, 1876, p. 2, col. 2; *Harper's Weekly* 19 (Jan. 9, 1875): 40; Ibid. 19 (May 15, 1875): 412.

37. John Eaton, Jr., *Report . . . for the Year 1875*, 500–5; Hon. W. G. Ritch, "1875. Education in New Mexico. Third Annual Report to the National Bureau of Education, With Statistical Tables" (Santa Fe: Northwestern Steam Printing House, 1876) (pamphlet at Huntington Library), 3, 6.

38. *Harper's Weekly* 19 (Oct. 23, 1875): 854.

39. Ibid. 19 (May 8, 1875): 386.

40. Quoted in Frank B. Evans, *Pennsylvania Politics, 1872–1877: A Study in Political Leadership* (Harrisburg: The Pennsylvania Historical and Museum Commission, 1966), 195–96.

41. *Enterprise and Mountaineer* (Greenville, South Carolina), Nov. 10,. 1875, p. 2, col. 1.

42. n.a., "Education," *Atlantic Monthly* 37 (Feb. 1876): 252.

43. *Harper's Weekly* 19 (Nov. 6, 1875): 894, 902.

44. John Tracy Ellis, ed., *Documents of American Catholic History* (Milwaukee: The Bruce Publishing Co., 1962), 392; *The Nation* 21 (Oct. 7, 1875): 22:1; Grant attended Metropolitan Church (Methodist) in Washington, D.C. For the three Sundays preceding his Des Moines address, the minister of that congregation, who was also a close confidant of the President, preached on the threat of the Roman Catholic church to American public education. Grant, who supposedly was in attendance at these services, took this ministerial message to heart. See Ralph E. Morrow, *Northern Methodism and Reconstruction* (East Lansing: Michigan State University Press, 1956), 217–18.

45. Democratic Party (New York City). "Address of Tammany Hall to the Electors of the County" (New York: n.p., 1875) (pamphlet at Huntington Library), 6–7.

46. Quoted in Vincent P. DeSantis, "Catholicism and Presidential Elections, 1865–1900," *Mid-America* 42 (April 1960): 70.

47. Blaine's letter of Oct. 20, 1875, reproduced in Appendix, *Cong. Record*, 44th Cong., 1st Sess., p. 277.

48. *The Independent* (New York City). Dec. 9, 1875, p. 14, cols. 2–3.

49. Fred L. Israel, ed., *The State of the Union Messages of the Presidents, 1790–1966*, 3 vols. (New York: Chelsea House, Robert Hector Publishers, 1966), 2: 1295–96, 1317–18; *The Independent* (New York City), Jan. 13, 1876, p. 3, cols. 2–4; see Thomas Nast cartoons in *Harper's Weekly* 19 (Oct. 23, 1875): 860–61; Ibid. 19 (Oct. 30, 1875): 873.

50. Eugene Lawrence, "The First Century of the Republic: Educational Progress," *Harper's New Monthly Magazine* 51 (Nov. 1875): 856; *Harper's Weekly* 19 (Dec. 25, 1875): 1042.

51. Eugene Lawrence, "Lawless Bishops," *Harper's Weekly* 17 (March 29, 1873): 246; Ibid. 17 (May 17, 1873): 410–11; Ibid. 19 (Dec. 25, 1875): 1038; Rev. Father Stack, "Mitred Tyrants," Ibid. 19 (July 10, 1875): 558–59; Ibid. 20 (July 29, 1876): 615; n.a., "Education," *Atlantic Monthly* 35 (April 1875): 510–12; [Joseph Warren Alden], "The Political Trinity of Despotism. A Chapter from Romanism in the United States. By a Puritan of the Nineteenth Century" (Cambridge, Mass.: The Principia Club, 1876) (pamphlet at Huntington Library), 6; James Parton, "Taxation of Church Property" (Boston: Free Religious Association, 1873) (pamphlet at Huntington Library), 17; Rev. E. M'Chesney, "Taxation of Church Property," *Methodist Quarterly* (4th Series) 58 (April 1876): 243–56, 256n; also see n.a., "Taxation of Church Property," *The Nation* 22 (Jan. 13, 1876): 23; *The Independent* (New York City), March 25, 1875, p. 16, cols. 3–4; n.a., "The President's Message," *The Catholic World, A Monthly Magazine of General Literature and Science* 22 (Oct. 1875–March 1876): 707–9

52. n.a., "The President's Speech at Des Moines," *The Catholic World, A Monthly Magazine of General Literature and Science* 22 (Oct. 1875–March 1876), 434–38, 442; Tyler Anbinder, "Ulysses S. Grant, Nativist," *Civil War History* 43 (June 1997): 130–38.

53. Right Rev. James O'Connor, D.D., "Anti-Catholic Prejudice," *American Catholic Quarterly Review* 1 (Jan. 1876): 17–18, 20–21.

54. See *Cong. Record*, 44th Cong., 1st Sess., p. 205, for the Blaine Amendment. For commentary, see *The Independent* (New York City), Jan. 13, 1876, p. 3, cols. 2–4; Elisha P. Hurlbut, *A Secular View of Religion in the State, and The Bible in the Public Schools* (Albany, New York: Joel Munsel, 1870), 39–40; Samuel T. Spear, D. D., *Religion in the State, and The Bible in the Public Schools* (New York: Dodd, Mead & Co., Publishers, 1876), 39–41.

55. *Harper's Weekly* 19 (Dec. 11, 1875): 1003; "Rules, Regulations, and Course of Study for the Public Schools of the Town of Brockton, Adopted by the School Committee, December, 1875" (Brockton, Mass.: Brockton Gazette Office, 1876) (pamphlet at Huntington Library), 4; "Course of Instruction, and Rules and Regulations, for the Public Schools, of the Borough of Hazleton, PA, Adopted by the Board of Directors, August 26, 1875" (Hazleton, PA: Published by the Board of Directors, 1875) (pamphlet at Huntington Library), 12; John Leng, *America in 1876, Pencilings During a Tour in the Centennial Year: With a Chapter on the Aspects of American Life* (Dundee: Dundee Advertiser Office, 1877), 330–31; *The Independent* (New York City), Feb. 10, 1876, p. 4, cols. 1–4.

56. William H. Van Nortwick, *The Anti-Papal Manual: A Book of Ready Reference for American Protestants* (New York: Holt Bros., 1876), 31.

57. *Cong. Record*, 44th Cong., 1st Sess., p. 205.

58. *Cong. Record*, 44th Cong., 1st Sess., p. 5213; *Harper's Weekly* 20 (Jan. 15, 1876): 46–47; Ibid. 20 (Jan. 29, 1876): 91.

59. Daniel Ullmann, "Amendments to the Constitution of the United States. Non-Sectarian and Universal Education. Veteran Association, Order of United Americans, Annual Dinner, New York, Feb. 22, 1876. Remarks of Daniel Ullmann, LL.D." (New York: Baker and Godwin, 1876) (Pamphlet at Huntington Library), 4, 6–12; for a rich account of Ullmann's involvements in the Know-Nothing movement of the 1850s, see Tyler Anbinder, *Nativism and Slavery, The Northern Know Nothings and the Politics of the 1850s* (New York: Oxford University Press, 1992), 77–87.

60. *The Independent* (New York City), Jan. 20, 1876, p. 81, cols. 1–4; Frederick J. Zwierlein, *The Life and Letters of Bishop McQuaid, Prefaced With the History of Catholic Rochester Before His Episcopate*, 3 vols. (Rochester: The Art Print Shop, 1925–1928), 2: 54–55, 57, 60, 62.

61. Rev. P. Bayma, S. J., "The Liberalistic View of the Public School Question," The *American Catholic Quarterly Review* 2 (Jan. 1877): 1; McQuaid's line of reasoning can be found in Bishop Bernard John McQuaid, "Christian Free Schools" (Rochester: n.p., 1871?) (available in microfiche through "Pamphlets in American History"), 18–21, 30; David J. O'Brien, *Isaac Hecker, An American Catholic* (New York: Paulist Press, 1992), 309; while exhibiting certain liberal tendencies throughout his tenure as Bishop of Rochester, McQuaid became imbroiled in the Roman Catholic "Americanist" controversy during the 1880s and 1890s that effectively labeled him a "conservative" thereafter. This later controversy, concerning the proper role of American nationalism within Roman Catholicism, was virtually unknown in the 1870s, when all Catholic bishops, whether exhibiting liberal tendencies or not, acknowledged the indisputable supremacy of the church over their lives. The relatively liberal McQuaid of the 1870s refused to move with the nationalistic spirit of the late nineteenth century but sought to find a position that at least accommodated love of country to some degree. See Glen Janus, "Bishop Bernard McQuaid: On 'True' and 'False' Americanism," *U.S. Catholic Historian* 2 (Summer 1993): 54, 57, 60–61.

62. *Harper's Weekly* 20 (March 11, 1876): 203.

63. Appendix, *Cong. Record*, 44th Cong., 1st Sess., pp. 29–31; Norman E. Tutorow, *James Gillespie Blaine and the Presidency, A Documentary Study and Source Book* (New York: Peter Lang, 1989), 8, 35–37.

64. W. R. Thrall to John Eaton, Jr., Cincinnati, June 19, 1876 (Eaton Papers); Keith Ian Polakoff, *The Politics of Inertia, The Election of 1876 and the End of Reconstruction* (Baton Rouge: LSU Press, 1973), 58–67; Gail Hamilton, *Biography of James G. Blaine* (Norwich, Conn.: The Henry Bell Publishing Co., 1895), 375, 396–97, 399, 402.

9. The End of Reconstruction

1. Hayes's diary entry, July 8, 1876; Hayes to Garfield, July 8, 1876; Hayes to Garfield, August 4, 1876; Hayes to Garfield, August 5, 1876, in Charles Richard Williams, ed., *Diary and Letters of Rutherford B. Hayes, Nineteenth President of the United States*, 2nd ed., 5 vols. (New York: Krause Reprint Co., 1971), 3: 333, 338–39; William Dean Howells, *Sketch of the Life and Character of Rutherford B. Hayes, Also a Sketch of William A. Wheeler* (New York: Hurd and Houghton, 1876), 124.

2. *Cong. Record*, 44th Cong., 1st Sess., p. 5186.

3. Hayes to Garfield, Aug. 5, 1876, in Williams, ed., *Diary and Letters of Hayes*, 3: 338–39.

4. Hayes to Sherman, Aug. 7, 1876, Ibid., 3: 339–40; also see Republican William Lawrence's speech on the Guarantee Clause, given after Hoar's remarks, in *Cong. Record*, 44th Cong., 1st Sess., pp. 5190–91.

5. Appendix, *Cong. Record*. 44th Cong., 1st Sess., pp. 265–66; Ibid., p. 278; *Daily American* (Nashville), Aug. 5, 1876, p. 2, cols. 2–3; *Courier-Journal* (Louisville), Aug. 10, 1876, p. 2, col. 5.

6. Purcell's statement reprinted in the *Chicago Daily Tribune*, Aug. 20, 1876, p.13, col. 1; *Harper's Weekly* 20 (Sept. 2, 1876): 715; n.a., "Politics and the School Question. Attitude of the Republican and Democratic Parties in 1876" (n.p.: n.p., 1876) (pamphlet at Huntington Library), 14.

7. Hayes to Sherman, Aug. 7, 1876 in Williams, ed., *Diary and Letters of Hayes*, 3: 339–40.

8. *The Independent* (New York City), Jan. 13, 1876 p. 3, cols. 2–4.

9. *Chicago Daily Tribune*, Aug. 7, 1876, p. 4, cols. 3–4. Modern historians have also been confused about the Blaine Amendment. A fairly good account is Steven K. Green's "The Blaine Amendment Reconsidered," *American Journal of Legal History*, 36 (Jan. 1992), 38–69. But his narrative also encourages confusion by claiming that the proposal "fell four votes short in the Senate of being submitted to the states" (p. 38). The Senate (Republican) version was diametrically opposed to the House (Democratic) version. Neither house was prepared to support the measure of the other.

10. *Courier-Journal* (Louisville), Aug. 13, 1876, p. 2, col. 2.

11. *Atlanta Constitution*, Aug. 9, 1876, p. 2, col. 3.

12. Vincent P. DeSantis, "Catholicism and Presidential Elections, 1865–1900," *Mid-America* 42 (April 1960): 74.

13. Rev. James A. Burns, *The Growth and Development of the Catholic School System in the United States* (New York: Benziger Bros., 1912), 253–58; John Webb Pratt, *Religion, Politics, and Diversity: The Church-State Theme in New York History* (Ithaca: Cornell University Press, 1967), 199–200.

14. *Cong. Record*, 44th Cong., 1st Sess., pp. 5245–46. *Daily American*, (Nashville), Aug. 13, 1876, p. 2, col. 2.

15. *Cong. Record*, 44th Cong., 1st Sess., pp. 5246–47.

16. Ibid., pp. 5453.

17. *United States v. Reese*, 92 U.S. 218, 220 (1876).

18. Frederick T. Frelinghusen, *Educational Amendment to the Constitution. Speech of Hon. F. T. Frelinghusen, of New Jersey, in the U.S. Senate, August 14, 1876* (Washington, D.C.: GPO 1876), 3.

19. Hayes to Garfield, Aug. 12, 1876 (emphasis is Hayes's), in Williams, ed., *Diary and Letters of Hayes*, 3: 343.

20. *Cong. Record*, 44th Cong., 1st Sess., pp. 5454–56, 5595.

21. Frelinghusen, *Education Amendment*, pp. 3–4.

22. *Cong. Record*, 44th Cong., 1st Sess., pp. 5580–91.

23. *Harper's Weekly* 20 (Oct. 7, 1878): 814; Appendix, *Cong. Record*, 44th Cong. 1st Sess., pp. 201–2.

24. Appendix, *Cong. Record*, 44th Cong., 1st Sess., pp. 304–306.

25. Ibid., pp. 318–21; William Lawrence to John Eaton, Jr., Washington, D.C., July 25, 1876 (Eaton Papers, Special Collections, Hoskins Library, University of Tennessee, Knoxville).

26. *The Daily Picayune* (New Orleans), Aug. 12, 1876, p. 4, col. 2; Ibid., Aug. 13, 1876, p. 2, col. 2; *Atlanta Constitution*, Aug. 17, 1876, p. 2, col. 2.

27. The National Anti-Papal League, "Politics and the School Question" (New York: National Anti-Papal League, 1876) (pamphlet at Huntington Library), 11.

28. John Franklin Miller, "The Issues. A Logical Argumentative Speech. The History of the Republican and Democratic Parties Contrasted. Tilden Shown Up in His True Colors" (San Francisco: n.p., 1876) (pamphlet at Huntington Library), 5–6; The National Anti-Papal League, "The Democratic Party and the Public Schools. Gov. Tilden Favors Appropriations for the Support of Roman Catholic Parochial Schools" (New York: The National Anti-Papal League, 1876) (pamphlet at Huntington Library), 2, 8; *Chicago Daily Tribune*, Sept. 30, 1876, p. 4, cols. 2–3.

29. Harry James Brown and Frederick D. Williams, eds., *The Diary of James A. Garfield*, 4 vols. (n.p.: Michigan State University Press, 1967–1981), 3: 328.

30. National Democratic Committee, "Reform. For President, Samuel J. Tilden. For Vice President, Thomas A. Hendricks. What Tilden Has Done. In Breaking Rings. The Tweed Ring." (New York: National Democratic Committee, 1876) (pamphlet at Huntington Library), 1–20; Keith Ian Polakoff, *The Politics of Inertia, The Election of 1876 and the End of Reconstruction* (Baton Rouge: LSU Press, 1973), 72–73.

31. *Harper's Weekly* 20 (Jan. 15, 1876): 43, 47; Ibid. 20 (Feb. 12, 1876): 136; Benjamin E. Buckman, *Samuel J. Tilden Unmasked!* (New York: Published for the Author, 1876) (book at Huntington Library), 88, 90, 108–9.

32. *Harper's Weekly* 20 (Sept. 26, 1876): 755–56.

33. n.a., "Politics and the School Question. Attitude of the Republican and Democratic Parties in 1876" (n.p.: n.p., 1876) (pamphlet at Huntington Library), 8–10, 15.

34. *Harper's Weekly* 20 (Oct. 21, 1876): 854: *Chicago Tribune*, Sept. 1, 1876, p. 1, cols. 2–7.

35. *Chicago Tribune*, Sept. 5, 1876, p. 4, col. 3. Ibid., Sept. 10, 1876, p. 4, col. 1; Ibid., Sept. 11, 1876, p. 8, col. 5; John E. Baur, "A President Visits Los Angeles: Rutherford B. Hayes' Tour of 1880," *Historical Society of Southern California* 37 (March 1955): 42; J. W. Fuller to John Eaton, Jr., Toledo, Ohio, April 30, 1872 (Eaton Papers).

36. Charles Richard Williams, *The Life of Rutherford Birchard Hayes, Nineteenth President of the United States*, 2 vols. (Boston: Houghton Mifflin Co., 1914), 1:477; *Chicago Daily Tribune*, Oct. 7, 1876, p. 1, col. 5; Hayes to R. C. McCormick, Oct. 14, 1876, in Williams, ed., *Diary and Letters of Hayes*, 3: 366–67.

37. William McKinley, "William McKinley to 'The Hayes Club': Speech on Rutherford B. Hayes, October 2, 1876, Ohio" (typescript at Huntington Library); *Chicago Daily Tribune*, Sept. 14, 1876, p. 1, cols. 2–7; John Eaton, Jr., *Report of the Commissioner of Education for the Year 1875* (Washington, D.C.: GPO, 1876), 388–89: *The Enterprise and Mountaineer* (Greenville, S.C.), Sept. 6, 1876, p. 2, col. 1; Ibid., Oct. 18, 1876, p. 2, col. 2; *Daily American* (Nashville), Aug. 15, 1876, p. 2, col. 2; *Harper's Weekly* 90 (Oct. 14, 1876): 830–1.

38. William Lawrence to John Eaton, Jr., Washington, D.C., July 25, 1876; Charles Eaton to John Eaton, Jr., Toledo, Ohio, July 25, 1876 (Eaton Papers); *Chicago Daily Tribune*, Sept. 18, 1876, p. 1, cols. 2–6; Ibid., Oct. 29, 1876, p. 2, cols. 1–7.

39. Gilbert Carlton Walker, "Public Lands for Educational Purposes. Speech of Hon. Gilbert C. Walker of Virginia in House on May 29, 1876" (Washington, D.C.: n.p., 1876) (pamphlet at Huntington Library), 3, 6–7, 9, 11–2.

40. Hon. Henry W. Blair, "'Free Schools—Are They in Danger? If So, From What Sources?' Speech of Hon. Henry W. Blair of New Hampshire, in the House of Representatives, Saturday, July 29, 1876" (n.p.: n.p., 1876) (pamphlet at Huntington Library), 1–8, 10, 15–8.

41. Garfield quoted in Theodore Clarke Smith, *The Life and Letters of James Abram Garfield*, 2 vols. (New Haven: Yale University Press, 1925), 1: 613; Williams, *Life of Hayes*, 1: 496–97.

42. "The Constitutional Convention. The Constitution of New Hampshire As Amended by the Constitutional Convention Held at Concord, On the First Wednesday of December, A.D., 1876: With the Several Questions

Involving the Amendments Proposed, As Submitted by the Convention to the Vote of the People" (Concord: Edward A. Jenks, 1877) (pamphlet at Huntington Library), 2; Mary P. Thompson, "Anti-Catholic Laws in New Hampshire," *The Catholic World* 51 (May 1890): 196–97; George P. Edgar, comp., "Both Sides of School Question, Attitude of the Democratic and Republican Parties" (New York: Holt Bros., 1880) (pamphlet at Huntington Library), 3–4.

43. "The Constitution of the State of Colorado, Adopted in Convention, March 14, 1876; also the Address of the Convention to the People of Colorado, Election, Saturday, July 1, 1876" (Denver: Tribune Book and Job Printing House, 1876) (pamphlet at Huntington Library), 15–16, 27–28; Harold A. Buetow, *Of Singular Benefit, The Story of Catholic Education in the United States* (London: The Macmillan Co., 1970), 154–63; V. T. Thayer, *The Attack Upon the American Secular School* (Boston: The Beacon Press, 1951), 18.

44. [Joseph Warren Alden], "Despotism vs. Republicanism, Fourth Chapter from Vaticanism Unmasked; or Romanism in the United States. By A Puritan in the Nineteenth Century" (Cambridge, Mass.: The Principia Club, 1877) (pamphlet at Huntington Library), 8; Julius H. Seelye, "Should the State Teach Religion?" *The Forum* I (June 1886): 427–33.

45. Eric Foner, *Reconstruction: America's Unfinished Revolution, 1863–1877* (New York: Harper & Row, 1988).

46. While many modern historians have itemized various ways in which Reconstruction evidenced a centralizing spirit, this understanding has not gone unchallenged. The most notable dissenter is Michael Les Benedict, who argues that Reconstruction was essentially "state-based" in its nationalism, that is, Reconstruction was not oriented toward creating a federal administrative structure to guide American life from the political center. See his "Preserving the Constitution: The Conservative Basis of Radical Reconstruction," *Journal of American History* 61 (June 1974): 65–90, and "Preserving Federalism: Reconstruction and the Waite Court," *The Supreme Court Review* (Chicago: University of Chicago Press, 1978): 39–79. For an example of historical literature identifying centralizing legislation during Reconstruction, see William M. Wiecek, "The Reconstruction of Federal Judicial Power, 1863–1875," *American Journal of Legal History* 13 (Oct. 1969): 333–59.

47. James Freeman Clarke, "Oration Delivered Before the City Government and Citizens of Boston, In Music Hall, July 5, 1875" (Boston: Rockwell and Churchill, City Printers, 1875) (pamphlet at Huntington Library), 15, 46.

48. Julius H. Seelye, "The Moral Character in Politics," *North American Review* 139 (Oct. 1884): 301–9; for additional commentary on the "moral decline" of the Republican party after 1876, see Ralph Waldo Emerson, "Fortune of the Republic. Lecture Delivered at the Old South Church, March

30, 1878" (Boston: Houghton, Osgood & Co., 1878) (pamphlet at Huntington Library), 8, 12–13, 22.

BIBLIOGRAPHY

Manuscripts

Brownlow, William G. (Parson), Papers. Special Collections, Hoskins Library, University of Tennessee, Knoxville.

Eaton, John, Jr., Papers. Special Collections, Hoskins Library, University of Tennessee, Knoxville.

Garfield, James, Papers. Huntington Library.

McKinley, William. "William McKinley to 'The Hayes Club': Speech on Rutherford B. Hayes, October 2, 1876, Ohio." Typescript at Huntington Library.

Newman, Francis William. "What is Germany?" 1872 poem in manuscript collections, Huntington Library, #HM 7138.

Schurz, Carl, Papers. Huntington Library.

Newspapers and Periodicals

American Catholic Quarterly Review

American Journal of Education

The American Quarterly Church Review

Atchison Daily Champion (Atchison, KS)

Atlanta Constitution

Atlantic Monthly

Boston Evening Transcript

Brownson's Quarterly Review (Last Series).

Burlington Free Press and Times (Burlington, VT)

The Catholic World, A Monthly Magazine of General Literature and Science

Chicago Daily Tribune

The Christian Union (New York)

The Christian World

The Cincinnati Daily Enquirer

Cleveland Daily Plain Dealer

Courier Journal (Louisville, KY)

Daily American (Nashville)

Daily Dispatch (Richmond, VA)

The Daily Journal (Wilmington, NC)

The Daily Picayune (NO)

De Bow's Review

The Educational Journal of Virginia

The Enterprise and Mountaineer (Greenville, SC)

Erie Gazette (Erie, PA)

Evening Bulletin (Philadelphia, PA)

Frank Leslie's Illustrated Newspaper (New York)

Harper's Weekly

Illinois Journal (Springfield)

The Independent (New York)

Memphis Daily Appeal

Methodist Quarterly

Nashville Union and American

The Nation

New York Herald

New York Times

New York Tribune

North American Review

Ohio State Journal (Columbus)

Old and New

The Republic: A Monthly Magazine Devoted to the Dissemination of Political Information

Republican Banner (Nashville, TN)

Sacramento Union

Saint Louis Dispatch

Savannah Morning News

Scribner's Monthly

Winchester Journal (Winchester, IN)

The Woman's Journal: Boston and Chicago

The York Gazette (York, PA)

Published Letters and Private Documents

Beecher, Henry Ward. *The Original Plymouth Pulpit, Sermons of Henry Ward Beecher, in Plymouth Church, Brooklyn, September 1869 to March 1870*. New York, 1898.

———. *Plymouth Pulpit, Sermons Preached in Plymouth Church, Brooklyn, By Henry Ward Beecher, March-September, 1874*. New York, 1892.

———. *Plymouth Pulpit, Sermons Preached in Plymouth Church, Brooklyn, By Henry Ward Beecher, Sept. 1874–March 1875*. New York, 1890.

———. *Patriotic Addresses*. New York, 1887.

Brown, Henry James, and Frederick D. Williams, eds. *The Diary of James A. Garfield*. 4 vols. East Lansing, Mich., 1967–1981.

Evarts, Sherman, ed. *Arguments and Speeches of William Maxwell Evarts*, 3 vols. New York, 1919.

Gower, Joseph F., and Richard M. Leliaert, eds. *The Brownson-Hecker Correspondence*. South Bend, IN, 1979.

Harlan, Louis R., ed. *The Booker T. Washington Papers*. 14 vols. Urbana, IL, 1972–1989.

Williams, Charles Richard, comp. *Diary and Letters of Rutherford Birchard Hayes, Nineteenth President of the United States*. 5 vols. New York, 1971.

Government Documents

A. United States Documents and Reports

Congressional Globe

Congressional Record

Eaton, John, Jr. *Report of the Commissioner of Education Made to the Secretary of the Interior for the Year 1870, With Accompanying Papers*. Washington, DC, 1870.

——. *Report of the Commissioner of Education for the Year 1872*. Washington, DC, 1873.

——. *Report of the Commissioner of Education for the Year 1873*. Washington, DC, 1874.

——. *Report of the Commissioner of Education for the Year 1874*. Washington, DC, 1875.

——. *Report of the Commissioner of Education for the Year 1875*. Washington, DC, 1876.

——. *Report of the Commissioner of Education for the Year 1876*. Washington, DC, 1878.

——. *Report of the Commissioner of Education for the Year 1877*. Washington, DC, 1879.

Israel, Fred L., ed. The State of the Union Messages of the President, 1790–1966, 3 vols. New York, 1966.

39th Cong., 1st Sess. (1865–1866). *House Misc. Doc. No. 41:* "Memorial of the National Association of State and City School Superintendents, Asking for the Establishment of a National Bureau of Education."

39th Cong., 1st Sess. (1865–1866). Senate Executive Documents, No. 2: " . . . Report of Carl Schurz."

39th Cong., 1st Sess. (1865–1866). *Senate Misc. Doc. No. 5:* "Petition of the Town of Medford, Middlesex County, Mass., For Governmental Aid in Securing Free Education to All Children in the United States."

39th Cong., 2nd Sess. (1866–1867). *House Exec. Doc. No. 5:* "Message of the President of the United States."

40th Cong., 2nd Sess. (1867–1868). *House Exec. Doc. No. 299:* "Report of Commissioner of Education, June 2, 1868."

40th Cong., 2nd Sess. (1867–1868). *House Report No. 30:* "Report, Bureau of Freedmen and Refugees."

40th Cong., 3rd Sess. (1868–1869). *House Report. No. 25:* "Department of Education Report."

41st Cong., 2nd Sess. (1869–1871). *House Exec. Doc. No. 355:* "Report of Professor H. Bernard on Schools in District of Columbia, With General Educational Matter."

41st Cong., 2nd Sess. (1869–1870). *Senate Executive Document No. 74:* "Message of the President of the United States Recommending the Adoption of Means to Promote Education Throughout the Country, March 30, 1870."

41st Cong., 3rd Sess. (1870–1871). *House Executive Document, No. 1:* "Report of the Commissioner of Education, 1870."

41st Cong., 3rd Sess. (1870–1871). *Senate Executive Documents, No. 20:* "Reports of the Board of Trustees of Colored Schools of Washington and Georgetown."

42nd Cong., 2nd Sess. (1871–1872). *House Executive Document, No. 1:* "Report of the Commissioner of Education, 1871."

42nd Cong., 3rd Sess. (1872–1873). *House Executive Doc., No. 58:* "Memorial of Colored Citizens Praying for Civil Rights."

43rd Cong., 1st Sess. (1873–1874). *House Executive Doc., No. 25:* "Resolutions of the Legislature of South Carolina Relative to the Civil Rights Bill."

43rd Cong., 1st Sess. (1873–1874). *House Executive Doc., No. 44:* "National Convention of Colored Persons Praying to be Protected in Their Civil Rights."

43rd Cong., 1st Sess. (1873–1874). *House Executive Doc., No. 60:* "Resolutions of the Legislature of Virginia Against the Passage of the Civil Rights Bill."

Reynolds v. Sims, 377 U.S. 533 (1964).

United States v. Reese, 92 U.S. 218, 220 (1876).

Wesbury v. Sanders, 376 U.S. 1 (1964).

B. State and Local Documents

Brockton City Schools. "Rules, Regulations, and Course of Study for the Public Schools of the Town of Brockton, Adopted by the School Committee, December, 1875." Brockton, MA, 1876 (pamphlet at Huntington Library).

California Assembly. "The Chinese Question. Report of the Special Committee on Assembly Bill No. 13," Appendix, Journal of the Senate and Assembly. 2 vols. Sacramento, 1870. 2: Document 26.

Cincinnati Superior Court. The Bible in the Public Schools, Arguments in the Case of John D. Minor et al. v. the Board of Education of the City of Cincinnati. Cincinnati, 1870.

Cincinnati Superior Court. *The Board of Education of the City of Cincinnati v. John D. Minor et al.* 23 *Ohio State Reports, Granger*, 211.

Colorado Constitutional Convention. "The Constitution of the State of Colorado, Adopted in Convention, March 14, 1876; Also the Address of the Convention to the People of Colorado, Election, Saturday, July 1, 1876." Denver, 1876 (pamphlet at Huntington Library).

Hazleton City Schools. "Course of Instruction, and Rules and Regulations, for the Public Schools, of the Borough of Hazleton, PA, Adopted by the Board of Directors, August 26, 1875." Hazleton, PA, 1875.

New Hampshire Constitutional Convention. "The Constitutional Convention. The Constitution of New Hampshire as Amended by the Constitutional Convention Held at Concord, On the First Wednesday of December, A.D., 1876: With the Several Questions Involving the Amendments Proposed, As Submitted by the Convention to the Vote of the People." Concord, 1877 (pamphlet at Huntington Library).

Ohio Supreme Court. *Garnes v. McCann and Others*, Ohio Reports, 198.

Tennessee Constitutional Convention. *Journal of the Proceedings of the Convention of Delegates Elected by the People of Tennessee, to Amend, Reverse, or Form and Make a New Constitution for the State. Assembled in the City of Nashville, Jan. 10, 1870.* Nashville, 1870.

Texas Constitutional Convention. *Journal of the Constitutional Convention of the State of Texas, Begun and Held at the City of Austin, September 6th, 1875.* Galveston, 1875.

Virginia Superintendent of Public Instruction, *Virginia School Report, 1871. First Annual Report of the Superintendent of Public Instruction, For the Year Ending August 31, 1871.* Richmond, 1871.

———. *Virginia School Report, 1873. Third Annual Report of the Superintendent of Public Instruction, For the Year Ending August 31, 1873.* Richmond, 1873.

Nineteenth-Century Monographs and Special Studies

A. Books

Adams, Francis. *The Free School System of the United States.* London, 1875.

Barnard, Henry, et al. ["An Eminent Corps of Scientific and Literary Men"], *First Century of National Existence: The United States As They Were and Are.* Baltimore, 1875.

Barnes, William Horatio. *History of the Congress of the United States [The 41st Congress, 1869–1871].* New York, 1871.

Blair, Lewis H. *A Southern Prophecy: The Prosperity of the South Dependent Upon the Elevation of the Negro.* Ed. C. Vann Woodward. Boston, 1889/1964 reprint.

Brace, Charles Loring. *The Dangerous Classes of New York, and Twenty Years' Work Among Them.* New York, 1872.

Brookes, James H., *Is the Bible True? Seven Addresses,* 3rd ed. St. Louis, c. 1877.

Brown, Obadiah Bruen, *The Song Reader, A Public School Singing Book.* Boston, 1870.

Buckman, Benjamin E. *Samuel J. Tilden Unmasked!* New York, 1876.

Cable, George W. *The Negro Question: A Selection of Writings on Civil Rights in the South.* Ed. Arlin Turner. Garden City, NY, 1958.

Campbell, Sir George. *White and Black, The Outcome of a Visit to the United States.* New York, 1879/1969 reprint.

Chaplin, Jeremiah, and J.D. Chaplin. *Life of Charles Sumner, With an Introduction by Hon. William Claflin.* Boston, 1874.

Clark, Rev. Rufus W., D.D. *The Question of the Hour: The Bible and the School Fund.* Boston, 1870.

[Cooke, Nicholas Francis]. *Satan in Society. By a Physician.* New York, 1870.

Cornell, William M., ed. *Charles Sumner: Memoir and Eulogies, A Sketch of His Life by the Editor, An Original Article by Bishop Gilbert Haven, and the Eulogies Pronounced by Eminent Men.* Boston, 1874.

Curry, Jabez L. M. *A Brief Sketch of George Peabody and a History of the Peabody Fund Through Thirty Years.* Cambridge, 1898.

Dixon, William Hepworth. *New America,* 2 vols. London, 1867.

———. *White Conquest,* 2 vols. London, 1876.

Doty, Duane. *A Statement of the Theory of Education in the United States of America as Approved by Many Leading Educators.* Washington, D.C., 1874.

Doyle, John E. *Plymouth Church and Its Pastor, or Henry Ward Beecher and His Accusers.* Hartford, Conn., 1874.

Eggleston, Edward. *The Schoolmaster's Stories for Boys and Girls.* Boston, 1874.

Ellis, Dr. John B. *Free Love and Its Votaries, or American Socialism Unmasked. Being an Historical and Descriptive Account of the Rise and Progress of the Various Free Love Associations in the United States.* New York, 1870.

Ford, Henry, and Kate B. Ford, comps. *History of Cincinnati, Ohio, With Illustrations and Biographical Sketches*. Cleveland, 1881.

Gilmour, Right Rev. Richard, D.D. *Bible History, Containing the Most Remarkable Events of the Old and New Testaments, To Which Is Added a Compendium of Church History. For the Use of the Catholic Schools in the United States*. New York, 1869/1881 reprint.

Hamilton, Gail. *Biography of James G. Blaine*. Norwich, CN, 1895.

Hayman, Professor, ed., *Acme Songs for Families and Schools. This Edition of 8,000 Copies Is Presented to the Pupils in the Public Schools of Poughkeepsie, and Dutchess County, New York*. New York, 1882.

Hinsdale, Burke A. *Horace Mann and the Common School Revival in the United States*. New York, 1898.

————. ed. *President Garfield and Education, Hiram College Memorial*. Boston, 1882.

Howard, James Quay. *The Life, Public Services and Select Speeches of Rutherford B. Hayes*. Cincinnati, 1876.

Howells, William Dean. *Sketch of the Life and Character of Rutherford B. Hayes, Also a Biographical Sketch of William A. Wheeler*. New York, 1876.

Hurlbut, Elisha P. *A Secular View of Religion in the State, and the Bible in the Public Schools*. Albany, NY, 1870.

Ingersoll, Robert Green. *The Gods and Other Lectures*. Peoria, IL, 1874.

Jamieson, W. F. *The Clergy, A Source of Danger to the American Republic*. Chicago, 1872.

King, Edward. *The Southern States of North America: A Record of Journeys in Louisiana, Texas, the Indian Territory, Missouri, Arkansas, Mississippi, Alabama, Georgia, Florida, South Carolina, North Carolina, Kentucky, Tennessee, Virginia, West Virginia and Maryland*. London, 1875.

King, Rufus. *Ohio, First Fruits of the Ordinance of 1787*. Boston, 1888/1903 reprint.

Leng, John. *America In 1876. Pencillings During a Tour in the Centennial Year: With a Chapter on the Aspects of American Life*. Dundee, Scotland, 1877.

Lester, Charles Edwards. *Life and Public Services of Charles Sumner*. New York, 1874.

Linton, Elizabeth Lynn, ed., *Modern Women and What Is Said About Them, A Reprint of a Series of Articles in the Saturday Review, Second Series*. New York, 1870.

————, *Ourselves, A Series of Essays on Women*. London, 1870.

McCloskey, Robert, comp. *The Bible in the Public Schools, Arguments Before the Superior Court of Cincinnati in the Case of Minor v. Board of Education of Cincinnati (1870) with the Opinions of the Court and the Opinion on Appeal of the Supreme Court of Ohio (New Introduction by Robert G. McCloskey)*. New York, 1870/1969 reprint.

Marshall, Charles F. *The True History of the Brooklyn Scandal, Being a Complete Account of the Trial of the Rev. Henry Ward Beecher, of Plymouth Church, Brooklyn, Upon Charges Preferred by Theodore Tilton*. Philadelphia, 1875.

Mayers, Edward. *Lucius Q. C. Lamar: His Life, Times, and Speeches*. Nashville, 1896.

Mayo, Amory Dwight, ed. *The Bible in the Public Schools, Addresses of Rev. A. D. Mayo and Rev. Thos. Vickers, of Cincinnati*. New York, 1870.

Montgomery, Zachary. *The Poison Fountain or, Anti-Parental Education. Essays and Discussions on the School Question from a Parental and Non-Sectarian Standpoint, Wherein the Decline of Parental Authority, the Downfall of Family Government, and the Terrible Growth of Crime, Pauperism, Insanity and Suicides, in America, are Traced Directly and Unmistakably to our Anti-Parental Public School System*. San Francisco, 1878.

Mulford, Elisha. *The Nation: The Foundations of Civil Order and Political Life in the United States*. New York, 1870.

Nason, Elias. *The Life and Times of Charles Sumner, His Boyhood, Education, and Public Career*. Boston, 1874.

National Educational Association. *The Addresses and Journal of Proceedings of the National Educational Association, Session of the Year 1876, in Baltimore, Maryland*. Salem, OH, 1876.

No author. *The Bible in the Public Schools, Opinions of Individuals and of the Press*. New York, 1870.

No author. *Questions Upon Books of the New Testament, With Sundry References to Different Parts of the Bible: Designed for the Use of Schools and Families, Compiles by a Teacher*. Baltimore, 1872.

Nordhoff, Charles. *The Cotton States in the Spring and Summer of 1875*. New York, 1876/1965 reprint.

Northrop, Birdsey G. *Schools and Communism, National Schools, and Other Papers*. New Haven, CN, 1879.

Randall, S. S. *First Principles of Popular Education and Public Instruction*. New York, 1868.

Schaff, Philip, D. D. *The Person of Christ: The Miracle of History, With a Reply to Strauss and Renan, and a Collection of Testimonies of Unbelievers.* Boston, 1865.

Schurz, Carl. *Eulogy on Charles Sumner by Carl Schurz.* Boston, 1874.

Smalley, Eugene Virgil, *A Brief History of the Republican Party From Its Organization to the Presidential Campaign of 1884.* New York, 1884.

Somers, Robert. *The Southern States Since the War, 1870–1871.* London, 1871.

Spear, Samuel T., D.D. *Religion and the State, or, the Bible and the Public Schools.* New York, 1876.

Speer, William S., comp. *Sketches of Prominent Tennesseans, Containing Biographies and Records of the Families Who Have Attained Prominence in Tennessee.* Nashville, 1888.

Stearns, Charles. *The Black Man of the South and the Rebels; or, the Characteristics of the Former, and the Recent Outrages of the Latter.* New York, 1872.

Stephen, Leslie. *The Science of Ethics.* New York, 1882.

Thompson, Joseph P., *Church and State in the United States, With an Appendix on the German Population.* Boston, 1873.

Tocqueville, Alexis de. *Democracy in America.* Ed. Richard D. Heffner. New York, 1956.

Todd, Rev. John, D.D. *The Sunset Land; or, The Great Pacific Slope.* Boston, 1870.

Tourgee, Albion W. *An Appeal to Caesar.* New York, 1884.

Twain, Mark. *The Adventures of Tom Sawyer.* New York, 1875/1920 reprint.

———. and Charles Dudley Warner. *The Gilded Age, A Tale of Today.* 2 vols. New York, 1873.

Ulrici, Hermann. *Strauss as a Philosophical Thinker. A Review of his Book "The Faith and the New Faith," and a Confutation of Its Materialistic Views.* Trans. Charles P. Krauth, D.D. Philadelphia, 1874.

Van Nortwick, William H., *The Anti-Papal Manual: A Book of Ready Reference for American Protestants.* New York, 1876.

Wallace, John. *Carpet-bag Rule in Florida; The Inside Workings of the Reconstruction of Civil Government in Florida After the Close of the Civil War.* Gainsville, Florida, 1888/1964 reprint.

Weston, George. *The Progress of Slavery in the United States.* Washington, D.C., 1857.

White, Carlos, *Ecce Femina: An Attempt to Solve the Woman Question, Being an Examination of the Arguments in Favor of Female Suffrage by John Stuart Mill and Others, and a Presentation of Arguments Against the Proposed Change In the Constitution of Society.* Boston, 1870.

Wright, Mrs. Julia McNair. *Practical Life; or, Ways and Means for Developing Character and Resources.* Philadelphia, 1882.

Zeller, Eduard. *David Friedrich Strauss In His Life and Writings.* London, 1874.

B. Articles, Essays, Pamphlets, Sermons, Speeches, and Memorials

Abbot, Francis E. "Christian Propagandism." Toledo, 1871 (pamphlet at Huntington Library).

———. "The Political Trinity of Despotism. A Chapter from Romanism in the United States. By a Puritan of the Nineteenth Century." Cambridge, MA, 1876 (pamphlet at Huntington Library).

Baldwin, Cornelius C. "Moral Maxims, For Schools and Families." Petersburg, VA, 1876 (pamphlet at Huntington Library).

Barnard, Henry. "The System of Public Instruction in Prussia." *The American Journal of Education* 19 (1870): 609–81.

Bayard, Thomas Francis. *White and Black Children in Public Schools. Speech of Hon. Thomas F. Bayard . . . Delivered in the Senate of the United States, May 4, 1872.* Washington, D.C., 1872.

———. *Civil Rights, Speech of Hon. Thomas F. Bayard, of Delaware, in the United States Senate, February 26, 1875.* Washington, D.C., 1875.

Becker, George Ferdinand. "Education: Its Relations to the State and to the Individual, and Its Methods: A Series of Lectures," *Bulletin of the University of California* 28 (Dec. 1877): 49–50.

Billings, Edward Coke. "The Struggle Between the Civilization of Slavery and That of Freedom, Recently and Now Going on in Louisiana. An Address Delivered by Edward C. Billings, Esq., of New Orleans, at Hatfield, Mass., Oct. 20, 1873." Northhampton, MA, 1873 (pamphlet at Huntington Library).

Blair, Hon. Henry W. "'Free Schools—Are They in Danger? If So, From What Sources?' Speech of Hon. Henry W. Blair of New Hampshire, in the House of Representatives, Saturday, July 29, 1876." No Place, 1876 (pamphlet at Huntington Library).

Bogy, Lewis V. *Civil Rights and Uncivil Wrong, Speech of Hon. Lewis V. Bogy, of Missouri, in the United States Senate, May 22, 1874.* Washington, DC, 1874.

Burgess, John W. "The 'Culturconflict' in Prussia." *Political Science Quarterly* 2 (June 1887): 313–40.

Butler, Benjamin F. *Speech of Hon. Benjamin F. Butler on Civil Rights, Delivered in the House of Representatives, February 4, 1875.* Washington, DC, 1875.

Cain, Richard H. "Civil Rights Bill, Speech of Hon. Richard H. Cain, of South Carolina, Delivered in the House of Representatives, Saturday, January 24 1874." No Place, 1874 (pamphlet at Huntington Library).

Carpenter, Matthew H. *Civil Rights. Speech of Hon. Matt. H. Carpenter, of Wisconsin, in the United States Senate, February 27, 1875.* Washington, DC, 1875.

Chipman, Hon. Norton P., et al. *Washington National Monument. Shall the Unfinished Obelisk Stand [as] a Monument of National Disgrace and National Dishonor? Speeches of Hon. Norton P. Chipman, of the District of Columbia, Hon. R. C. McCormick, of Arizona, Hon. Jasper D. Ward, of Illinois, Hon. John B. Storm, of Pennsylvania, Hon. J. B. Sener, of Virginia, Hon. S. S. Cox, of New York, in the House of Representatives, June 4, 1874.* Washington, DC, 1874.

Church of Jesus Christ of Latter Day Saints. "Proceedings in Mass Meeting of the Ladies of Salt Lake City, to Protest Against the Passage of Cullom's Bill, January 14. 1870." Salt Lake City, 1870 (pamphlet in Huntington Library).

Claflin, Tennessee (Tennie) Celeste. "The Ethics of Sexual Equality. A Lecture Delivered by Tennie C. Claflin, at the Academy of Music, New York. March 29, 1872." New York, 1873 (pamphlet at Huntington Library).

Clark, Thomas March. "Our National Crises. An Oration Delivered Before the City Authorities and Citizens of Providence, July 4th, 1871." Providence, RI, 1871 (pamphlet at Huntington Library).

Clarke, James Freeman. "Oration Delivered Before the City Government and Citizens of Boston, in Music Hall, July 5, 1875." Boston, 1875 (pamphlet at Huntington Library).

"Clergyman." "Repudiation Is Theft—Forcible Adjustment Highway Robbery." Richmond, VA, 1876 (pamphlet at Huntington Library).

Collins, Charles Terry. "The Modern Migration of Nations, or, the Danger and Duty of the Hour." New York, 187? (pamphlet at Huntington Library).

Conservative Party [Virginia]. "The Congressional Canvass. Ninth Virginia District. Nominee of the Conservative Party." Wytheville, VA, 1874 (pamphlet at Huntington Library).

Cooley, Thomas M. "The Guarantee of Order and Republican Government in the States," *The International Review* 2 (1975): 57-87.

Cox, Samuel Sullivan. *Economy-Education-Mixed Schools. Speech on Hon. S. S. Cox, Member of Congress from New York City, on the Education and Civil Rights Bills, Delivered January 13, 1874.* Washington, DC, 1874.

Democratic Party (New York City). "Address of Tammany Hall to the Electors of the County." New York, 1875 (pamphlet at Huntington Library).

Dunne, Hon. Edmund F. "Our Public Schools: Are They Free for All, Or Are They Not?" San Francisco, 1875 (pamphlet at Huntington Library).

Edgar, George P., comp. "Both Sides of School Question, Attitude of the Democratic and Republican Parties." New York, 1880 (pamphlet at Huntington Library).

Emerson, Ralph Waldo. "Fortune of the Republic. Lecture Delivered at the Old South Church, March 30, 1878." Boston, 1878 (pamphlet at Huntington Library).

Evarts, William M. "Eulogy of Chief-Justice Chase, Delivered by William M. Evarts, Before the Alumni of Dartmouth College, at Hanover, June 24, 1874." Hanover, NH, 1874 (pamphlet at Huntington Library).

Frelinghusen, Frederick T. *Educational Amendment to the Constitution. Speech of Hon. F. T. Frelinghusen, of New Jersey, in the U.S. Senate, August 14, 1876.* Washington, DC, 1876.

Furber, Rev. Daniel L., D.D. "Religion and Education in a Republic. A Sermon Delivered Before His Excellency John D. Long, His Honor Byron Weston, the Honorable Council, and the Legislature of Massachusetts, At the Annual Election, Wednesday, January 5, 1881." Boston, 1881 (pamphlet located at Huntington Library).

Garfield, James A. "The Future of the Republic, Its Dangers and Its Hopes, An Address Delivered Before the Literary Societies of Hudson College, July 2, 1873." Cleveland, 1873 (pamphlet at Huntington Library).

———. "Revenues and Expenditures, Speech of Hon. James A. Garfield, of Ohio, in the House of Representatives, Thursday, March 5, 1874." Washington, DC, 1874 (pamphlet at Huntington Library).

George, Henry. "Our Land and Land Policy, National and State." San Francisco, 1871 (pamphlet at Huntington Library).

("A Georgia Republican"). "The Southern Question. The Bourbon Conspiracy to Rule or Destroy the Nation." Washington, DC, 1876 (pamphlet at Huntington Library).

Gilman, Daniel C. "Thirty Years of the Peabody Education Fund," *Atlantic Monthly* 79 (Feb. 1897): 161–66.

Gibson, Rev. Otis. "'Chinaman or White Man, Which?' Reply to Father Buchard, Delivered in Platt's Hall, San Francisco, Friday Evening, March 14, 1873." San Francisco, 1873 (pamphlet at Huntington Library).

Gladstone, Hon. W. E., M.P. "The Vatican Decrees in Their Bearing on Civil Allegiance: A Political Expostulation, With the Replies of Archbishop Manning and Lord Acton." New York, 1874 (pamphlet at Huntington Library).

————. "Vaticanism: An Answer to Reproofs and Replies." New York, 1875 (pamphlet at Huntington Library).

Greene, Rev. Richard Gleason. "Christianity a National Law. An Election Sermon Preached Before the Executive and Legislative Departments of the Government of Massachusetts, in Hollis Street Church, Boston, Wednesday, January 7, 1874." Boston, 1874 (pamphlet at Huntington Library).

Hager, John S. "The Louisiana Case. Equality of Man and Social Equality of Race. Speech of Hon. John S. Hager, of California, in the Senate of the United States, Wednesday, February 17, 1875." Washington, DC, 1875 (pamphlet at Huntington Library).

Hamilton, Rev. B. F. "'God in Government,' A Sermon Delivered Before the Executive and Legislative Departments of the Government of Massachusetts at the Annual Election, Wednesday, January 3, 1877." Boston, 1877 (pamphlet at Huntington Library).

Ingersoll, Robert G. "The Meaning of the Declaration. A Centennial Oration: Delivered by Robert G. Ingersoll, Peoria, Illinois, July 4, 1876. Also, Speech at Cincinnati Convention, Nominating James G. Blaine." Peoria, IL, 1876 (pamphlet at Huntington Library).

Johnson, Samuel. "A Memorial of Charles Sumner. A Discourse Delivered at the Parker Memorial Meeting-House, To the Twenty-Eighth Congregational Society, of Boston, on Sunday, March 15, 1874." Boston, 1874 (pamphlet at Huntington Library).

Kilgore, Damon Y. "The Bible in Public Schools, Address Upon a Resolution to Petition the Board of Education to Exclude the Bible from the Public Schools. Delivered Before the Liberal League of Philadelphia, October 17, 1875." Philadelphia, 1875 (pamphlet at Huntington Library).

Kip, Right Rev. Ingraham, D.D. "Characteristics of the Age: A Charge to the Clergy of the Diocese of California." San Francisco, 1876 (pamphlet at Huntington Library).

Lathers, Richard. "South Carolina. Her Wrongs and the Remedy. Remarks of Col. Richard Lathers, Delivered at the Opening of the Taxpayers' Convention, in Columbia, S.C., Tuesday, Feb. 17, 1874." No Place, 1874 (pamphlet at Huntington Library).

McQuaid, Bishop Bernard John. *Christian Free Schools*. Rochester, NY, 1871.

Magill, Edward H. "An Address Upon the Co-Education of the Sexes." Philadelphia, 1873 (pamphlet at Huntington Library).

Merrimon, Augustus S. *Civil Rights. Speech of Hon. A. S. Merrimon, of North Carolina, in the United States Senate, May 22, 1874.* Washington, DC, 1874.

Miller, John Franklin. "The Issues. A Logical Argumentative Speech. The History of the Republican and Democratic Parties Contrasted. Tilden Shown Up in His True Colors." San Francisco, 1876 (pamphlet at Huntington Library).

Mungen, William. *The Heathen Chinese. Speech of Hon. William Mungen, of Ohio, Delivered in the House of Representatives, January 7, 1871.* Washington, DC, 1871.

National Anti-Papal League (New York City). "The Democratic Party and the Public Schools. Gov. Tilden Favors Appropriations for the Support of Roman Catholic Parochial Schools." New York, 1876 (pamphlet at Huntington Library).

————. "Politics and the School Question." New York, 1876 (pamphlet at Huntington Library).

National Democratic Committee. "Reform. For President, Samuel J. Tilden. For Vice President, Thomas A. Hendricks. What Tilden Has Done. In Breaking Rings. The Tweed Ring." New York, 1876 (pamphlet at Huntington Library).

National Democratic Executive Resident Committee. "The Robbery of the Public Lands! The Public Lands for the People!!" No Place, No Date (pamphlet at Huntington Library).

National Labor Union. "Address of the National Labor Union, to the People of the United States, on Money, Land, and other Subjects of National Importance." Washington, DC, 1870 (pamphlet at Huntington Library).

Newman, Rev. John P., D.D. "Religious Liberty. A Free Church in a Free Country, Non-Religious, But Not Irreligious. Europe and America Contrasted and Compared. Power and Glory of a Free Christianity. Our Perils and Our Hopes. A Thanksgiving Discourse, Delivered in the Metropolitan Memorial Methodist Episcopal Church, Washington, D.C., November 25, 1875, By Rev. John P. Newman, D.D., Pastor." Washington, DC, 1875 (pamphlet at Huntington Library).

New York City Council of Political Reform. "Five Reports. 1) Surface Street Railroads; Value of Their Franchises; Profits; Taxation. 2) A Tammany Permit Bureau. 3) Sectarian Appropriations of Public Money. 4) The Exposure of the Tammany Frauds; and 5) Duty of the State to Protect the Free Common Schools by Amendments to the Constitution, January 23, 1873." New York, 1873 (pamphlet at Huntington Library).

————. "Report on Compulsory Education, Dec. 30, 1873." New York, 1874 (pamphlet at Huntington Library).

No Author. "Crippling the National Government." Washington, DC, 1876 (pamphlet at Huntington Library).

No Author. "The Financial Record of President Grant's Administration," No Place, 1872 (pamphlet at Huntington Library).

No Author. "The Guarantee of Order and Republican Governments in the States," *Central Law Journal* 2 (1875): 18–20.

No Author. "Politics and the School Question. Attitude of the Republican and Democratic Parties in 1876." No Place, 1876 (pamphlet at Huntington Library).

No Author. "The Respectful Remonstrance, On Behalf of the White People of South Carolina, Against the Constitution of the Late Convention of that State, Now Submitted to Congress for Ratification, 1868." No Place, 1868 (pamphlet in Huntington Library).

No Author. "Thoughts on Repudiation of the Debt of Virginia" Charlottesville, VA, 1875? (pamphlet at Huntington Library).

No Author. "Politics and the School Question. Attitude of the Republican and Democratic Parties in 1876." No Place, 1876 (pamphlet at Huntington Library).

No Author. "Visitors' Guide to the Centennial Exhibition and Philadelphia, 1876." Toronto, Ont. 1876 (pamphlet at Huntington Library).

Norwood, Thomas M. *Civil Rights, Speech of Hon. Thomas M. Norwood, of Georgia, Delivered in the United States Senate, April 30 and May 4, 1874.* Washington, DC, 1874.

Parton, James. "Taxation of Church Property." Boston, 1873 (pamphlet at Huntington Library).

Peters, E. T. "The Policy of Railroad Land Grants Before the Pre-emptor's Union in Metzerot Hall, Washington, D.C., on Wednesday Evening, April 27, 1870." No Place, No Date (pamphlet at Huntington Library).

Poage, Calvin A. "Lecture on 'Our Public Schools,' August 31st, 1873." San Francisco, 1873 (Pamphlet at Bancroft Library, U.C., Berkeley).

Pryor, Hon. Roger Atkinson. "The Religious and the Secular Culture. An Address Before the Alumni of Hampden Sydney College, Virginia, 12th June, 1873." New York, 1873 (pamphlet at Huntington Library).

(Pullen, Charles Henry). *Miss Columbia's Public School; or, Will It Blow Over? By a Cosmopolitan. With 72 Illustrations by Thomas Nast.* New York, 1871.

(Puryear, Bennett, et al.). "Civis" "The Public School in its Relations to the Negro." Richmond, VA, 1877 (pamphlet at Huntington Library).

Ransier, Hon. Alonzo J. "Civil Rights, Speech of Hon. Alonzo J. Ransier of South Carolina, in the House of Representatives, February 7, 1874." Washington, DC, 1874.

Ransom, Hon. Matt. W. "The South Faithful to Her Duties, Speech of Hon. Matt. W. Ransom, of North Carolina, in the United States Senate, February 17, 1875." Washington, DC, 1875.

Republican Party. "The Republican Party, The Friend of Education at the South, The Educational Fund Bill." Washington, DC, No Date (pamphlet at Huntington Library).

———. "The Republican Party, The Standard-Bearer Of Civilization And National Progress." No Place, No Date (pamphlet at Huntington Library).

Republican Party, Virginia State Central Committee. "An Address to the People of Virginia." Richmond, VA, 1876 (pamphlet at Huntington Library).

Republican Party. South Carolina. State Central Committee, Samuel J. Lee, Chairman, Protem. "Reply to the Memorial of the Tax-payers' Convention, Addressed to the Honorable the [*sic*] Senate and House of Representatives of the United States." Columbia, SC, 1874 (pamphlet at Huntington Library).

Rickoff, Andrew Jackson. "A National Bureau of Education," *American Journal of Education* 16 (March 1866): 299–310.

Ritch, Hon. W. G. "1875. Education in New Mexico. Third Annual Report to the National Bureau of Education, With Statistical Tables." Santa Fe, NM, 1876 (pamphlet at Huntington Library).

Ruffner, William Henry. "The Public Free School System. Dr. Dabney Answered by Mr. Ruffner." Richmond, 1876 (Pamphlet at Huntington Library).

Schaff, Philip. "Church and State in the United States," Papers of the American Historical Association 2 (1888): 473–86.

Scudder, Rev. Henry Martin, D.D. "The Catholics and the Public Schools." New York, 1873 (pamphlet at Huntington Library).

Sears, Barnas. "Objections to Public Schools Considered: Remarks at the Annual Meeting of the Trustees of the Peabody Education Fund, New York, October 7, 1875." Boston, 1875 (pamphlet at Huntington Library).

Seelye, Rev. Julius H. "The Christian Element in the State, A Sermon Delivered Before the Executive and Legislative Departments of the Government of Massachusetts, at the Annual Election, Wednesday, Jan. 5, 1870." Boston, 1870 (pamphlet at Huntington Library).

———. "The Moral Character in Politics," *North American Review* 139 (Oct. 1884): 301–9.

———. "Should the State Teach Religion?" *The Forum* I (June 1886): 427–33.

Smith, J. Ambler. *Civil Rights. Speech of Hon. J. Ambler Smith, of Virginia, in the House of Representatives, February 3, 1875.* Washington, DC, 1875.

Stallo, John Bernard. "State Creeds and Their Modern Apostles. A Lecture Delivered in Rev. Mr. Vickers' Church, Cincinnati, on the Evening of April 3, 1870." Cincinnati, 1872.

Stevenson, Job E. *Ku-Klux Conspiracy. Speech of Hon. Job E. Stevenson, of Ohio, Delivered in the House of Representatives, May 30, 1872.* Washington, DC, 1872 (pamphlet at Huntington Library).

Straton, H. D. D. "A Nation's Perils, and the Grounds of Its Exaltation: A Sermon Preached in Evansville, Indiana, on Thanksgiving Day, November 26, 1874, by Rev. H. D. D. Straton, Pastor of the First Baptist Church." Evansville, Indiana, 1874 (pamphlet at Huntington Library).

Sumner, Charles. "Equality Before the Law; Unconstitutionality of Separate Colored Schools in Massachusetts, Argument of Charles Sumner, Esq., Before the Supreme Court of Massachusetts, in the Case of Sarah C. Roberts vs. the City of Boston, Dec. 4, 1849." Washington, DC, 1870 (pamphlet at Huntington Library).

Tax-Payers' Convention of South Carolina. "Proceedings of the Tax-Payers' Convention of South Carolina, Held at Columbia, Beginning May 9th, and Ending May 12, 1871." Charleston, 1871 (pamphlet at Huntington Library).

Thompson, Rev. Hugh Miller, ed. "Is Romanism the Best Religion for the Republic?" New York, 1874 (pamphlet at Huntington Library).

Ullmann, Daniel. "Amendments to the Constitution of the United States. Non-Sectarian and Universal Education. Veteran Association, Order of United Americans, Annual Dinner, New York, Feb. 22, 1876. Remarks of Daniel Ullmann, LL.D." New York, 1876 (pamphlet at Huntington Library).

U.S. Congress. "Memorial Addresses on the Life and Character of Charles Sumner, A Senator of Massachusetts, Delivered in the Senate and House of Representatives, 43rd Congress, 1st Session, April 27, 1874, With Other Tributes of Respect." Washington, DC, 1874.

Vessiot, Andre. "Instruction in Morals and Civil Government." Washington, DC, 1882.

Voorhees, Hon. Daniel Wolsey. *The Plunder of Eleven States by the Republican Party. Speech of Hon. Daniel W. Voorhees, of Indiana. Delivered in the House of Representatives, March 23, 1872.* Washington, DC, 1872.

Walker, Gilbert Carlton. "Public Lands for Educational Purposes. Speech of Hon. Gilbert C. Walker of Virginia in House on May 29, 1876." Washington, 1876.

Washburn, Emory. "Limitations of Judicial Power," *Journal of Social Science* 8 (May 1876), 140–46.

Weninger, F. X., D.D. of the Society of Jesus. "Reply to Hon. R. W. Thompson, Secretary of the Navy, Addressed to the American People." New York, 1877 (pamphlet at Huntington Library).

West., Henry J., comp. *The Chinese Invasion; Revealing the Habits, Manners and Customs of the Chinese, Political, Social and Religious, on the Pacific Coast.* San Francisco, 1873 (pamphlet at Huntington Library).

White, Emerson E. "National Bureau of Education," *American Journal of Education* 16 (March 1866): 177–86.

———. "The Relation of Education to Industry and Technical Training in American Schools" (Circulars of Information of the Bureau of Education, No. 2). Washington, DC, 1881.

Whittier, John Greenleaf. "Sumner." Boston, 1874 (pamphlet at Huntington Library).

Wickersham, James P. "Education as an Element in the Reconstruction of the Union, a Lecture by J. P. Wickersham, Principal of the Pennsylvania State Normal School, Millersville, Pennsylvania, Delivered before the National Teachers' Association, at Harrisburg, Pennsylvania, August 18, 1865." No Place, 1865 (pamphlet in Huntington Library).

———. "Pennsylvania at the Centennial Exposition of 1876. Circular of Information to Those Desiring to Prepare Educational Material for Exhibition." Harrisburg, PA, 1876 (pamphlet at Huntington Library).

Winkler, Rev. Edwin T. "Rome: Past, Present and Future, An Address Delivered Before the Southern Baptist Convention, In New Orleans, On Saturday, May 12, 1877." Atlanta, 1877 (pamphlet at Huntington Library).

Woodhull, Victoria C. "The Scare-crows of Sexual Slavery, An Oration, Delivered Before Fifteen Thousand People, at Silver Lake, Mass., Camp Meeting, on Sunday, August 17, 1873." New York, 1874 (pamphlet at Huntington Library).

Twentieth-Century Monographs and Special Studies

A. Books and Dissertations

Abbott, Richard H. *The Republican Party and the South, 1855–1877, The First Southern Strategy.* Chapel Hill, NC, 1986.

Ames, Blanche. *Adelbert Ames, 1835–1933: General, Senator, Governor.* New York, 1964.

Anbinder, Tyler. *Nativism and Slavery, The Northern Know Nothings and the Politics of the 1850s.* New York, 1992.

Ash, Stephen V. *Middle Tennessee Society Transformed, 1860–1870: War and Peace in the Upper South.* Baton Rouge, LA, 1988.

Barnard, Harry. *Rutherford B. Hayes and His America.* New York, 1954.

Benedict, Michael Les. *A Compromise of Principle, Congressional Republicans and Reconstruction, 1863–1869.* New York, 1974.

Blassingame, John W. *Black New Orleans, 1860–1880.* Chicago, 1973.

Brown, Samuel Windsor. *The Secularization of American Education, As Shown by State Legislation, State Constitutional Provisions and State Supreme Court Decisions.* New York, 1967.

Bonadio, Felice A. *North of Reconstruction, Ohio Politics, 1865–1870.* New York, 1970.

Bond, Horace Mann. *The Education of the Negro in the American Social Order.* New York, 1934/1966 reprint.

Buetow, Harold A. *Of Singular Benefit, The Story of Catholic Education in the United States.* London, 1970.

Bullock, Henry Allen. *A History of Negro Education in the South, From 1619 to the Present.* Cambridge, MA, 1967.

Burns, Rev. James A. *The Growth and Development of the Catholic School System In the United States.* New York, 1912.

Butchart, Ronald E. *Northern Schools, Southern Blacks, and Reconstruction, Freedmen's Education, 1862–1875.* Westport, CN, 1980.

Clark, Clifford E., Jr. *Henry Ward Beecher, Spokesman for a Middle-Class America.* Urbana, IL, 1978.

Coleman, Kenneth, et al. *A History of Georgia.* 2nd ed. Athens, Georgia, 1991.

Confrey, Burton. *Secularism in American Education, Its History.* Washington, DC, 1931.

Connors, Rev. Edward M. *Church-State Relationships in Education in the State of New York.* Washington, DC, 1951.

Conway, Alan. *The Reconstruction of Georgia.* Minneapolis, 1966.

Coulter, E. Merton. *The South During Reconstruction, 1865–1877.* Baton Rouge, 1947.

Cox, Lawanda and John H., eds. *Reconstruction, the Negro, and the New South.* New York, 1973.

Craig, Gordon A. *Germany, 1866–1945.* New York, 1978.

Curran, Francis X. *The Churches and the Schools, American Protestantism and Popular Elementary Education.* Chicago, 1954.

Current, Richard Nelson. *Those Terrible Carpetbaggers, A Reinterpretation.* New York, 1988.

Dabney, Charles William. *Universal Education in the South,* 2 vols. New York, 1936/1969 reprint.

Davis, William Riley. *The Development and Present Status of Negro Education in South Texas.* New York, 1934.

Degler, Carl. *Neither Black Nor White, Slavery and Race Relations in Brazil and the United States.* Madison, Wisconsin, 1971.

DeSantis, Vincent P. *Republicans Face the Southern Question.* Baltimore, 1959.

Donald, David. *Charles Sumner and the Rights of Man.* New York, 1970.

Downs, Robert Bingham. *Henry Barnard.* Boston, 1977.

———. *Horace Mann, Champion of the Public Schools.* New York, 1903/1974 reprint.

Duffy, Herbert S. *William Howard Taft.* New York, 1930.

Easton, Loyd D. *Hegel's First American Followers, The Ohio Hegelians: John B. Stallo, Peter Kaufmann, Moncure Conway, and August Willich, with Key Writings.* Athens, OH, 1966.

Eaton, John, Jr. *Grant, Lincoln and the Freedmen.* New York, 1907.

Eby, Frederick. *The Development of Education In Texas.* New York, 1925.

Elkins, Stanley, and Eric McKitrick, eds. *The Hofstadter Aegis, A Memorial.* New York, 1974.

Ellis, John Tracy, ed. *Documents of American Catholic History.* Milwaukee, 1962.

Erickson, Leonard Ernest. "The Color Line in Ohio Public Schools, 1829–1890." Doctoral dissertation: The Ohio State University, 1959.

Evans, Ellen Lovell. *The German Center Party, 1870–1933, A Study in Political Catholicism.* Carbondale, IL, 1981.

Evans, Frank B. *Pennsylvania Politics, 1872–1877: A Study in Political Leadership.* Harrisburg, PN, 1966.

Farley, Ena. *The Underside of Reconstruction New York: The Struggle Over the Issue of Black Equality.* New York, 1993.

Fischer, Roger A. *The Segregation Struggle in Louisiana, 1862–1877.* Urbana, IL, 1974.

Fleming, Walter L., comp. *Documentary History of Reconstruction, Political, Military, Social, Religious, Educational and Industrial, 1865 to 1906.* 2 vols. New York, 1906–1907/1966 reprint.

Foner, Eric. *Free Soil, Free Labor, Free Men: The Ideology of the Republican Party Before the Civil War.* New York, 1970.

———. *Reconstruction, America's Unfinished Revolution, 1863–1877.* New York, 1988.

Franklin, John Hope, ed. *Reminiscences of an Active Life: The Autobiography of John Roy Lynch.* Chicago, 1970.

Fredrickson, George M. *The Black Image in the White Mind, The Debate on Afro-American Character and Destiny, 1817–1914.* New York, 1971.

Garner, James Wilford. *Reconstruction in Mississippi.* New York, 1901.

Ghurye, G. S. *Caste and Race in India.* Bombay 1969.

Gillette, William. *Retreat from Reconstruction, 1869–1879.* Baton Rouge, 1979.

Glenn, Charles Leslie, Jr. *The Myth of the Common School.* Amherst, Mass., 1988.

Green, Fletcher Melvin, ed. *Essays in Southern History.* Chapel Hill, NC, 1949.

Hamilton, J. G. de Roulhac. *Reconstruction in North Carolina.* Gloucester, MA, 1914/1964 reprint.

Harris, William C. *The Day of the Carpetbagger, Republican Reconstruction in Mississippi.* Baton Rouge, 1979.

Hyman, Harold M. *A More Perfect Union. The Impact of the Civil War and Reconstruction on the Constitution.* New York, 1973.

——— and William M. Wiecek, *Equal Justice Under Law: Constitutional Development, 1835–1875.* New York, 1982.

Heatwole, Cornelius J. *A History of Education in Virginia.* New York, 1916.

Herreshoff, David. *American Disciples of Marx: From the Age of Jackson to the Progressive Era.* Detroit, 1967.

Hoar, George F. *Autobiography of Seventy Years.* 2 vols. New York, 1903.

Hoogenboom, Ari. *Rutherford B. Hayes: Warrior and President.* Lawrence, KS, 1995.

———. *The Presidency of Rutherford B. Hayes.* Lawrence, KS, 1988.

Hovey, Alvah. *Barnas Sears: A Christian Educator, His Making and Work.* New York, 1902.

Howard, Victor. *Religion and the Radical Republican Movement, 1860–1870.* Lexington, KY, 1990.

Horn, Robert A. "National Control of Congressional Elections." Ph.D. Dissertation, Princeton, 1942.

Hurley, Rev. Mark J. *Church-State Relationships in Education in California.* Washington, DC, 1948.

Ignatiev, Noel. *How the Irish Became White.* New York, 1995.

Jensen, Richard J. *The Winning of the Midwest: Social and Political Conflict, 1888–1896.* Chicago, 1971.

Jones, Jacqueline. *Soldiers of Light and Love, Northern Teachers and Georgia Blacks, 1865–1873.* Chapel Hill, NC, 1980.

Jordan, Philip D. *Ohio Comes of Age, 1873–1900.* Columbus, 1943.

Kaestle, Carl F. *Pillars of the Republic, Common Schools and American Society, 1780–1860.* New York, 1983.

Kleppner, Paul, *The Third Electoral System, 1853–1892.* Chapel Hill, NC, 1979.

Klingman, Peter D. *Josiah Walls, Florida's Black Congressman of Reconstruction.* Gainsville, FL, 1976.

Keller, Morton. *Affairs of State: Public Life in Late Nineteenth-Century America.* Cambridge, MA, 1977.

Knepper, George W. *Ohio and Its People.* Kent, OH, 1989.

Knight, Edgar Wallace. *The Influence of Reconstruction on Education in the South.* New York, 1913/1969 reprint.

Kohn, Hans. *American Nationalism, An Interpretive Essay.* New York, 1957/1961 reprint.

———. *Prophets and Peoples, Studies in Nineteenth Century Nationalism.* New York, 1946.

Kousser, J. Morgan. *Dead End: The Development of Nineteenth-Century Litigation on Racial Discrimination in Schools*. Oxford, England, 1986.

————, and James M. McPherson. *Region, Race, and Reconstruction: Essays in Honor of C. Vann Woodward*. New York, 1982.

Kutler, Stanley I. *Judicial Power and Reconstruction Politics*. Chicago, 1968.

Lane, John J. *History of Education in Texas*. Washington, DC, 1903.

Lee, Gordon Canfield. *The Struggle for Federal Aid, First Phase: A History of the Attempts to Obtain Federal Aid for the Common Schools, 1870–1890*. New York, 1949.

Leonard, Lewis Alexander. *Life of Alphonso Taft*. New York, 1920.

Link, William A. *A Hard Country and a Lonely Place: Schooling, Society and Reform in Rural Virginia, 1870–1920*. Chapel Hill, NC, 1986.

Litwack, Leon. *Been in the Storm So Long, The Aftermath of Slavery*. New York, 1979.

————. *North of Slavery, The Negro in the Free States, 1790–1860*. Chicago, 1961.

Livingstone, David N. *Darwin's Forgotten Defenders, The Encounter Between Evangelical Theology and Evolutionary Thought*. Grand Rapids, MI, 1987.

Lofgren, Charles R. *The Plessy Case, A Legal-Historical Interpretation*. New York, 1987.

McCaul, Robert L. *The Black Struggle for Public Schooling in Nineteenth- Century Illinois*. Carbondale, IL, 1987.

McCluskey, Neil G., ed. *Catholic Education in America. A Documentary History*. New York, 1964.

McDonnell, James M. *Orestes A. Brownson and Nineteenth-Century Catholic Education*. New York, 1988.

McFeely, William S. *Grant, A Biography*. New York, 1981.

McKitrick, Eric L., ed. *Slavery Defended: The Views of the Old South*. Englewood Cliffs, NJ, 1963.

McLemore, Richard Aubrey, ed. *A History of Mississippi*, 2 vols. Hattiesburg, MS, 1973.

MacMullen, Edith Nye. *In the Cause of True Education: Henry Barnard and Nineteenth-Century School Reform*. New Haven, CN, 1991.

Michaelson, Robert. *Piety in the Public School, Trends and Issues in the Relationship Between Religion and the Public School in the United States*. London, 1970.

Mohr, James, ed. *Radical Republicans in the North: State Politics During Recon-struction*. Baltimore, 1976.

Morgan, H. Wayne, ed. *The Gilded Age, A Reappraisal*. Syracuse, NY, 1963.

Morrow, Ralph E. *Northern Methodism and Reconstruction*. East Lansing, MI, 1956.

Mosler, Richard D. *Making the American Mind, Social and Moral Ideas in the McGuffey Readers*. New York, 1965.

Murphy, James B. *L. Q. C. Lamar, Pragmatic Patriot*. Baton Rouge, LA, 1973.

Nasaw, David. *Schooled to Order: A Social History of Public Schooling in the United States*. New York, 1979.

Noble, Marcus C. S. *A History of the Public Schools of North Carolina*. Chapel Hill, NC, 1930.

Noble, Stuart Grayson. *Forty Years of the Public Schools in Mississippi, With Special Reference to the Education of the Negro*. New York, 1918.

O'Brien, David J. *Isaac Hecker, An American Catholic*. New York, 1992.

Olsen, Otto H. *Carpetbagger's Crusade: The Life of Albion Winegar Tourgee*. Baltimore, 1965.

———. ed. *Reconstruction and Redemption in the South*. Baton Rouge, LA, 1980.

Orr, Dorothy. *A History of Education in Georgia*. Chapel Hill, NC, 1950.

Palmer, Beverly Wilson, ed. *The Selected Letters of Charles Sumner*, 2 vols. Boston, 1990.

Pereyra, Lillian A. *James Lusk Alcorn, Persistent Whig*. Baton Rouge, LA, 1966.

Perman, Michael. *Emancipation and Reconstruction, 1862–1879*. Arlington Heights, IL, 1987.

———. ed. *Major Problems in the Civil War and Reconstruction*. Lexington, MA, 1991.

———. *The Road to Redemption: Southern Politics, 1869–1879*. Chapel Hill, NC, 1984.

Polakoff, Keith Ian. *The Politics of Inertia, The Election of 1876 and the End of Reconstruction*. Baton Rouge, LA, 1973.

Pratt, John Webb. *Religion, Politics, and Diversity: The Church-State Theme in New York History*. Ithaca, NY, 1967.

Quillan, Frank V. *The Color Line in Ohio, A History of Race Prejudice in a Typical Northern State*. New York, 1913/1969 reprint.

Ravitch, Diane. *The Great School Wars: New York City, 1805–1973, A History of the Public Schools as Battlefield of Social Change.* New York, 1974.

Remini, Robert V. *Andrew Jackson.* Boston, 1966.

Reynolds, John S. *Reconstruction in South Carolina, 1865–1877.* Columbia, SC, 1905.

Rist, Ray C., ed. *Restructuring American Education, Innovations and Alternatives.* New Brunswick, NJ, 1972.

Roberts, Jon H. *Darwinism and the Divine in America, Protestant Intellectuals and Organic Evolution, 1859–1900.* Madison, Wisconsin, 1988.

Roseboom, Eugene Holloway, and Francis Phelps Weisenburger. *A History of Ohio.* New York, 1934.

Sanders, James W. *The Education of an Urban Minority: Catholics in Chicago, 1833–1965.* New York, 1977.

Schlesinger, Arthur M., Jr. *Orestes A Brownson, A Pilgrim's Progress.* Boston, 1939.

Simkins, Francis Butler, and Robert Hilliard Woody. *South Carolina During Reconstruction.* Chapel Hill, NC, 1932.

Smith, Theodore Clarke. *The Life and Letters of James Abram Garfield,* 2 vols. New Haven, CN, 1925.

Stampp, Kenneth, and Leon F. Litwack, comps. *Reconstruction, An Anthology of Revisionist Writings.* Baton Rouge, 1969.

Steele, William Lucas. *Galesburg Public Schools, Their History and Work, 1861–1911.* Galesburg, IL, 1911.

Stone, Lawrence, ed. *The University in Society,* 2 vols. Princeton, NJ, 1974.

Summers, Mark Wahlgren. *The Era of Good Stealings.* New York, 1993.

Swett, John. *Public Education in California, Its Origin and Development, with Personal Reminiscences of Half a Century.* New York, 1911.

Swint, Henry Lee. *The Northern Teacher in the South, 1862–1870.* New York, 1941/1967 reprint.

Taylor, Alrutheus Ambush. *The Negro in South Carolina During Reconstruction,* New York, 1924/1969 reprint.

Taylor, Joe Gray. *Louisiana Reconstructed, 1863–1877.* Baton Rouge, 1974.

Thayer, V. T. *The Attack Upon the American Secular School.* Boston, 1951.

Thompson, Clara Mildred. *Reconstruction in Georgia, Economic, Social, Political, 1865–1872.* Gloucester, MA, 1915/1964 reprint.

Thornbrough, Emma Lou. *Indiana in the Civil War Era, 1850–1880.* Indianapolis, 1965.

Trelease, Allen W. *White Terror, The Ku Klux Klan Conspiracy and Southern Reconstruction.* New York, 1971.

Tutorow, Norman E. *James Gillespie Blaine and the Presidency, A Documentary Study and Source Book.* New York, 1989.

Tyack, David, and Elisabeth Honsot. *Learning Together, A History of Coeducation in American Schools.* New Haven, 1990.

———. *Managers of Virtue, Public School Leadership in America, 1820–1980.* New York, 1982.

Tyack, David, and Thomas James, Aaron Benavot. *Law and the Shaping of Public Education, 1785–1954.* Madison, 1987.

Vaughn, William Preston. *Schools for All, the Blacks and Public Education in the South, 1865–1877.* Lexington, Kentucky, 1974.

Waller, Altina L. *Reverend Beecher and Mrs. Tilton, Sex and Class in Victorian America.* Amherst, MA, 1982.

Warren, Donald R. *To Enforce Education, A History of the Founding Years of the United States Office of Education.* Detroit, 1974.

Washington, Booker T. *Up From Slavery.* New York, 1901/1986 reprint.

Webb, Ross A. *Kentucky in the Reconstruction Era.* Lexington, 1979.

Welch, Richard E., Jr. *George Frisbie Hoar and the Half-Breed Republicans.* Cambridge, MA, 1971.

Westerhoff, John H., III. *McGuffey and His Readers, Peity, Morality, and Education in Nineteenth-Century America.* Nashville, 1978.

Wharton, Vernon Lane. *The Negro in Mississippi, 1865–1890.* New York, 1947/1965 reprint.

White, James T., & Co., comp. *Notable Names in American History, A Tabulated Register, Third Edition of White's Conspectus of American Biography.* Clifton, NJ, 1973.

Wiebe, Robert H. *The Search for Order, 1877–1920.* New York, 1967.

Wiecek, William M. *The Guarantee Clause of the U.S. Constitution.* Ithaca, NY, 1972.

Wiggins, Sarah Woolfolk. *The Scalawag In Alabama Politics, 1865–1881.* University, AL, 1977.

Williams, Charles Richard. *The Life of Rutherford Birchard Hayes,* 2 vols. Boston, 1914.

Wills, Garry. *Lincoln at Gettysburg, The Words That Remade America.* New York, 1992.

Woodson, Carter Godwin. *The Mis-education of the Negro.* Washington, DC, 1933/1969 reprint.

Woodward, C. Vann. *American Counterpoint, Slavery and Racism in the North-South Dialogue.* Boston, 1964/1971 reprint.

Zaehner, R. C. *Hinduism.* London, 1962.

Zwierlein, Frederick J. *The Life and Letters of Bishop McQuaid, Prefaced with the History of Catholic Rochester Before His Episcopate,* 3 vols. Rochester, NY, 1925–1928.

B. Articles and Essays

— Alderson, William T., Jr. "The Freedmen's Bureau and Negro Education in Virginia," *North Carolina Historical Review* 29 (Jan. 1952): 64–90.

Anbinder, Tyler. "Ulysses S. Grant, Nativist," *Civil War History* 43 (June 1997): 119–41.

Baur, John E. "A President Visits Los Angeles: Rutherford B. Hayes' Tour of 1880," *Historical Society of Southern California* 37 (March 1955): 33–47.

Benedict, Michael Les. "Federalism and the Limits of Civil Rights," *Major Problems In American Constitutional History.* ed. Kermit L. Hall. 2 vols. Lexington, MA, (1992) 1: 592–93.

———. "Preserving the Constitution: The Conservative Basis of Radical Reconstruction," *Journal of American History* 61 (June 1974): 65–90.

———. "Preserving Federalism: Reconstruction and the Waite Court," *The Supreme Court Review* (Chicago: University of Chicago Press, 1978): 39–79.

Bethel, Elizabeth. "The Freedmen's Bureau in Alabama," *The Journal of History* 14 (Feb. 1948): 49–92.

Blassingame, John W. "The Union Army as an Educational Institution for Negroes, 1862–1865," *Journal of Negro Education* 34 (Spring 1965): 152–59.

Borden, Morton. "The Christian Amendment," *Civil War History* 25 (June 1979): 156–67.

Bridges, Roger D. "Equality Deferred: Civil Rights for Illinois Blacks, 1865–1885," *Journal of Southern History Society* 74 (Summer 1981): 82–108.

Brock, Euline W. "Thomas W. Cardozo: Fallible Black Reconstruction Leader," *Journal of Southern History* 47 (May 1981): 183–206.

Brown, Ira V. "Pennsylvania and the Rights of the Negro, 1865–1887," *Pennsylvania History* 28 (Jan. 1961): 45–57.

Clouts, Forrest W. "The Political Campaign of 1875," *Ohio Archaelogical and Historical Publications* 31 (1922): 38–97.

Connor, R. W. D. "The Peabody Fund," *South Atlantic Quarterly* 4 (April 1905): 169–81.

DeSantis, Vincent P. "Catholicism and Presidential Elections, 1865–1900," *Mid-America* 42 (April 1960): 67–79.

Donald, David H. "The Scalawag in Mississippi Reconstruction," *Journal of Southern History* 10 (Nov. 1944): 447–60.

DuBois, W. E. Burghardt. "Does the Negro Need Separate Schools?" *Journal of Negro Education* 4 (July 1935), 328–35.

Ellem, Warren A. "Who Were the Mississippi Scalawags?" *Journal of Southern History* 38 (May 1972): 217–40.

Fishel, Leslie H., Jr. "Repercussions of Reconstruction, The Northern Negro, 1870–1883," *Civil War History* 14 (Dec. 1968): 325–45.

———. "Jim Crow Goes to School: The Genesis of Legal Segregation in Southern Schools," *South Atlantic Quarterly* 58 (Spring 1959): 225–35.

Fraser, Walter J. "Black Reconstructionists in Tennessee," *Tennessee Historical Quarterly* 34 (Winter 1975), 362–82.

———. "William Henry Ruffner and the Establishment of Virginia's Public School System, 1870–1874," *Virginia Magazine of History and Biography* 79 (July 1971): 259–79.

Green, Steven K. "The Blaine Amendment Reconsidered," *American Journal of Legal History* 36 (Jan. 1992): 38–69.

Harlan, Louis R. "Desegregation in New Orleans Public Schools During Reconstruction," *American Historical Review* 67 (April 1962), 663–75.

Helfman, Harold M. "The Cincinnati 'Bible War,' 1869–1870," *The Ohio State Archaelogical and Historical Quarterly* 60 (Oct. 1951): 369–86.

Hesseltine, William B. "Economic Factors in the Abandonment of Reconstruction," *Mississippi Valley Historical Review* 22 (Sept. 1935): 191–200.

Hornsby, Alton, Jr. "The Freedmen's Bureau Schools in Texas, 1865–1870," *Southwestern Historical Quarterly* 76 (April 1973): 397–417.

Jackson, Luther Porter. "The Educational Efforts of the Freedmen's Bureau and Freedmen's Aid Societies in South Carolina, 1862–1872," *Journal of Negro History* 8 (Jan. 1923): 1–40.

Janus, Glen. "Bishop Bernard McQuaid: On 'True' and 'False' Americanism." *U.S. Catholic Historian* 2 (Summer 1993): 53–76.

Johnson, Kenneth R. "Legrand Winfield Perce: A Mississippi Carpetbagger and the Fight for Federal Aid to Education," *Journal of Mississippi History* 34 (Nov. 1972): 331–56.

Jordan, Winthrop D. "Modern Tensions and the Origins of American Slavery," *Journal of Southern History* 27 (Feb. 1962): 18–30.

Kaczorowski, Robert J. "Revolutionary Constitutionalism in the Era of the Civil War and Reconstruction," *New York University Law Review* 61 (November 1986): 863–940.

Kelly, Alfred H. "The Congressional Controversy Over School Segregation, 1867–1875," *American Historical Review* 64 (April 1959): 537–63.

Knight, Edgar W. "Reconstruction and Education in South Carolina," *South Atlantic Quarterly* 18 (Oct. 1919): 350–64.

———. "Reconstruction and Education in Virginia, " *South Atlantic Quarterly* 15 (Jan./April 1916): 25–40, 157–74.

Kousser, J. Morgan. "Separate but not Equal: The Supreme Court's First Decision on Racial Discrimination in Schools," *Journal of Southern History* 46 (Feb. 1980): 17–44.

Lowe, Richard. "Another Look at Reconstruction in Virginia," *Civil War History* 32 (March 1986): 56–76.

Lurie, John. "The Fourteenth Amendment: Use and Application in Selected State Court Civil Liberties Cases, 1870–1890—A Preliminary Assessment," *American Journal of Legal History* 28 (Oct. 1984): 304–13.

McPherson, James M. "Abolitionists and the Civil Rights Act of 1875," *Journal of American History* 52 (Dec. 1965): 493–510.

———. "White Liberals and Black Power in Negro Education, 1865–1915," *American Historical Review* 75 (June 1970): 1357–86.

Mandel, Bernard. "Religion and the Public Schools of Ohio," *The Ohio State Archaelogical and Historical Quarterly* 58 (April 1949): 185–206.

Mann, Kenneth Eugene. "Richard Harvey Cain, Congressman, Minister and Champion for Civil Rights," *Negro History Bulletin* 35 (March 1972): 64–66.

Messner, William F. "Black Education in Louisiana, 1863–1865," *Civil War History*, 22 (March 1976): 41–59.

Moneyhon, Carl H. "Public Education and Texas Reconstruction Politics, 1871–1874," *Southwestern Historical Quarterly* 92 (Jan. 1989): 393–416.

Morain, Thomas. "The Departure of Males from the Teaching Profession in Nineteenth-Century Iowa," *Civil War History* 26 (June 1980): 160–70.

Newby, Robert G., and David B. Tyack. "Victims Without Crimes: Some Historical Perspectives on Black Education," *Journal of Negro Education* 40 (Summer 1971): 192–206.

Parker, Marjorie H. "Some Educational Activities of the Freedmen's Bureau," *Journal of Negro History* 23 (Winter 1954): 9–21.

Porter, Betty. "The History of Negro Education in Louisiana," *Louisiana Historical Quarterly* 25 (July 1942): 728–821.

Rabinowitz, Howard N. "From Exclusion to Segregation: Southern Race Relations, 1865–1890," *Journal of American History* 63 (Sept. 1976): 325–50.

Swinney, Everette. "Enforcing the Fifteenth Amendment, 1870–1877," *Journal of Southern History* 28 (May 1962): 202–18.

Teaford, Jon C. "Toward a Christian Nation: Religion, Law and Justice Strong," *Journal of Presbyterian History* 54 (Winter 1976): 422–37.

Tyack, David, and Robert Lowe. "The Constitutional Moment: Reconstruction and Black Education in the South," *American Journal of Education* 94 (Feb. 1986): 236–56.

Vaughn, William P. "Partners in Segregation: Barnas Sears and the Peabody Fund," *Civil War History* 10 (Sept. 1964): 260–74.

———. "Separate and Unequal: The Civil Rights Act of 1875 and Defeat of the School Integration Clause," *Southwestern Social Science Quarterly* 48 (Sept. 1967): 146–54.

Washington, Delo E. "Education of Freedmen and the Role of Self-Help in a Sea Island Setting, 1862–1982," *Agricultural History* 58 (July 1984): 442–55.

West, Earle H. "The Peabody Fund and Negro Education, 1867–1880," *History of Education Quarterly* 6 (Summer 1966): 3–21.

Wiecek, William M. "The Reconstruction of Federal Judicial Power, 1863–1875," *American Journal of Legal History* 13 (Oct. 1969): 333–59.

Williams, Henry Sullivan. "The Development of the Negro Public School System in Missouri," *The Journal of Negro History* 5 (April 1920): 137–65.

Williamson, Edward C. "The Alabama Election of 1874," *Alabama Review* 17 (July 1964): 210–18.

Wilson, Charles Reagan. "The Religion of the Lost Cause: Ritual and Organization of the Southern Civil Religion, 1865–1920," *Journal of Southern History* 46 (May 1980), 219–38.

General Works

Cubberly, Elwood P. *Public Education in the United States, A Study and Interpretation of American Educational History*. Boston, 1919.

Kammen, Michael. *Mystic Chords of Memory, The Transformation of Tradition in American Culture*. New York, 1991.

Kliebard, Herbert M., ed. *Religion and Education in America: A Documentary History*. Scranton, PN, 1969.

Meyerhoff, Hans, ed. *The Philosophy of History in Our Time*. Garden City, NY, 1959.

Oates, Stephen B., ed. *Portrait of America* 5th ed. 2 vols. Boston, 1991.

Oberholtzer, Ellis Paxson. *A History of the United States Since the Civil War*, 5 vols. New York, 1917–1937.

Schlesinger, Arthur M., Jr. *The Disuniting of America, Reflections on a Multicultural Society*. New York, 1992.

INDEX